FOUNTAINDALE PUBLIC LIBRARY DISTRICT
300 West Briarcliff Road
Bolingbrook, IL 60440-2894
(630) 759-2102

Shojo Beat

VAMPIRE KNIGHT
MEMORIES

VOLUME
4

STORY & ART BY
Matsuri Hino

The Story of VAMPIRE KNIGHT

Previously...

Vampire Knight is the story of Yuki Kuran, a pureblood vampire princess, who was brought up as a human.

A moment of peace has arrived after a fierce battle between humans and vampires. But Kaname Kuran, whose heart became the Ancestor Metal for weapons capable of killing vampires, continues to sleep within the coffin of ice. A thousand years later, Yuki gives Kaname her heart, and he is revived as a human. Yuki and Kaname's daughter, Ai, begins to tell him about the days that have passed...

Bombing incidents caused by the "Vampire King" begin to occur around the time headmaster Cross starts doubting his health. Once again a shadow is cast just when the gap between humans and vampires is starting to close. Aristocrats Ruka Souen and Akatsuki Kain hold their wedding during the troubled times. Upon seeing the happy couple, Yuki cannot help but wish for Zero to live a long life.

CHARACTERS

YUKI KURAN (CROSS)

The adopted daughter of the headmaster of Cross Academy. She is a pureblood vampire and the princess of the noble Kuran family. She has always adored Kaname, even when she did not have her memory.

KANAME KURAN

A pureblood vampire and the progenitor of the Kurans. He is Yuki's fiancé and was raised as her sibling. He knows Yuki's true identity and cares for her...

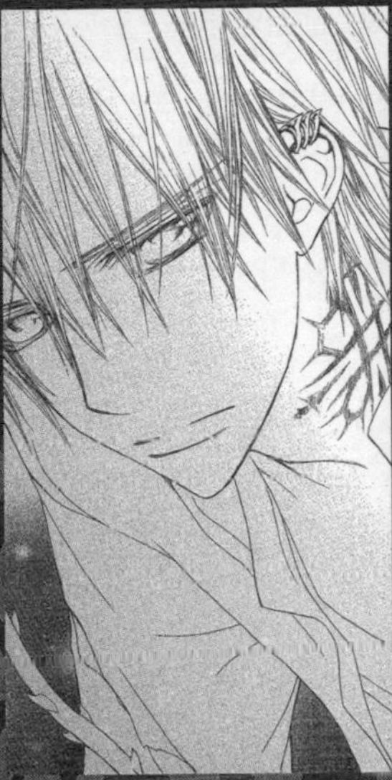

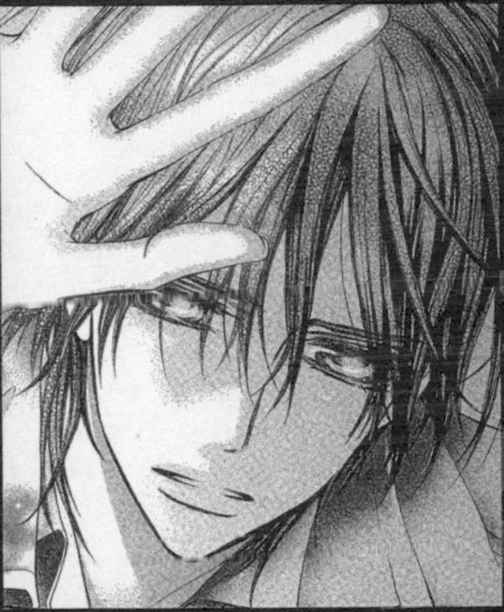

ZERO KIRYU

He was born into a family of vampire hunters and later was turned into a vampire. His parents were killed by a pureblood. He has agonized over his feelings for Yuki and his role as a vampire hunter.

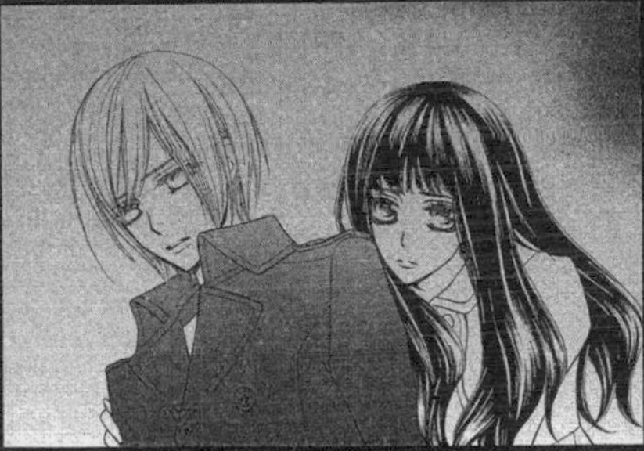

REN AND AI

Yuki's children

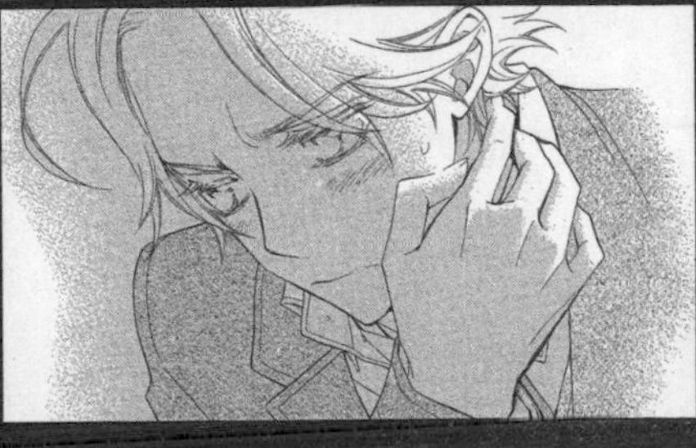

HANABUSA AIDO

He was an upperclassman in the Night Class. He is working to create a medicine that will turn vampires into humans...

VAMPIRE KNIGHT

MEMORIES

CONTENTS

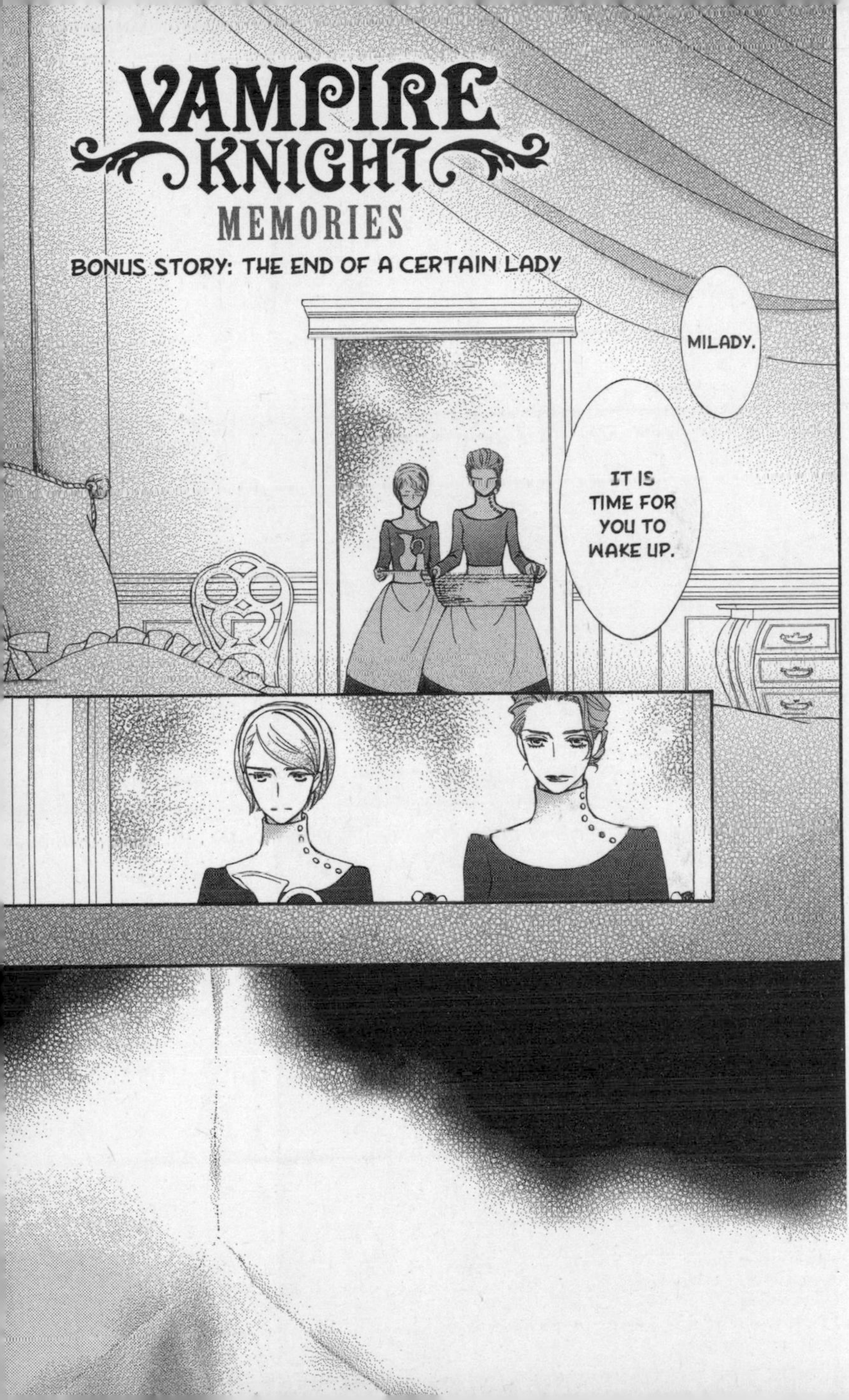
VAMPIRE KNIGHT
MEMORIES
BONUS STORY: THE END OF A CERTAIN LADY
MILADY.
IT IS TIME FOR YOU TO WAKE UP.

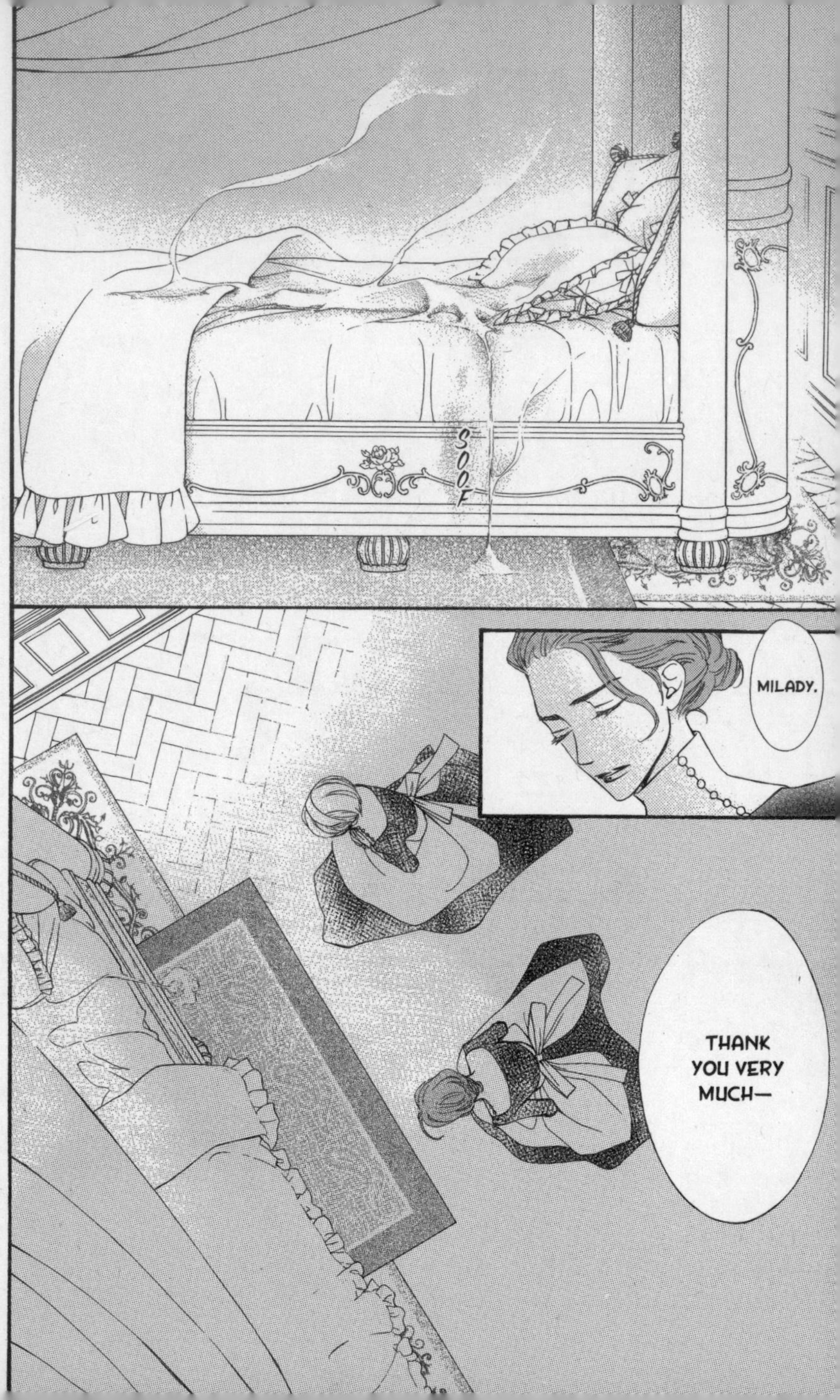
SOOF
MILADY.
THANK YOU VERY MUCH—

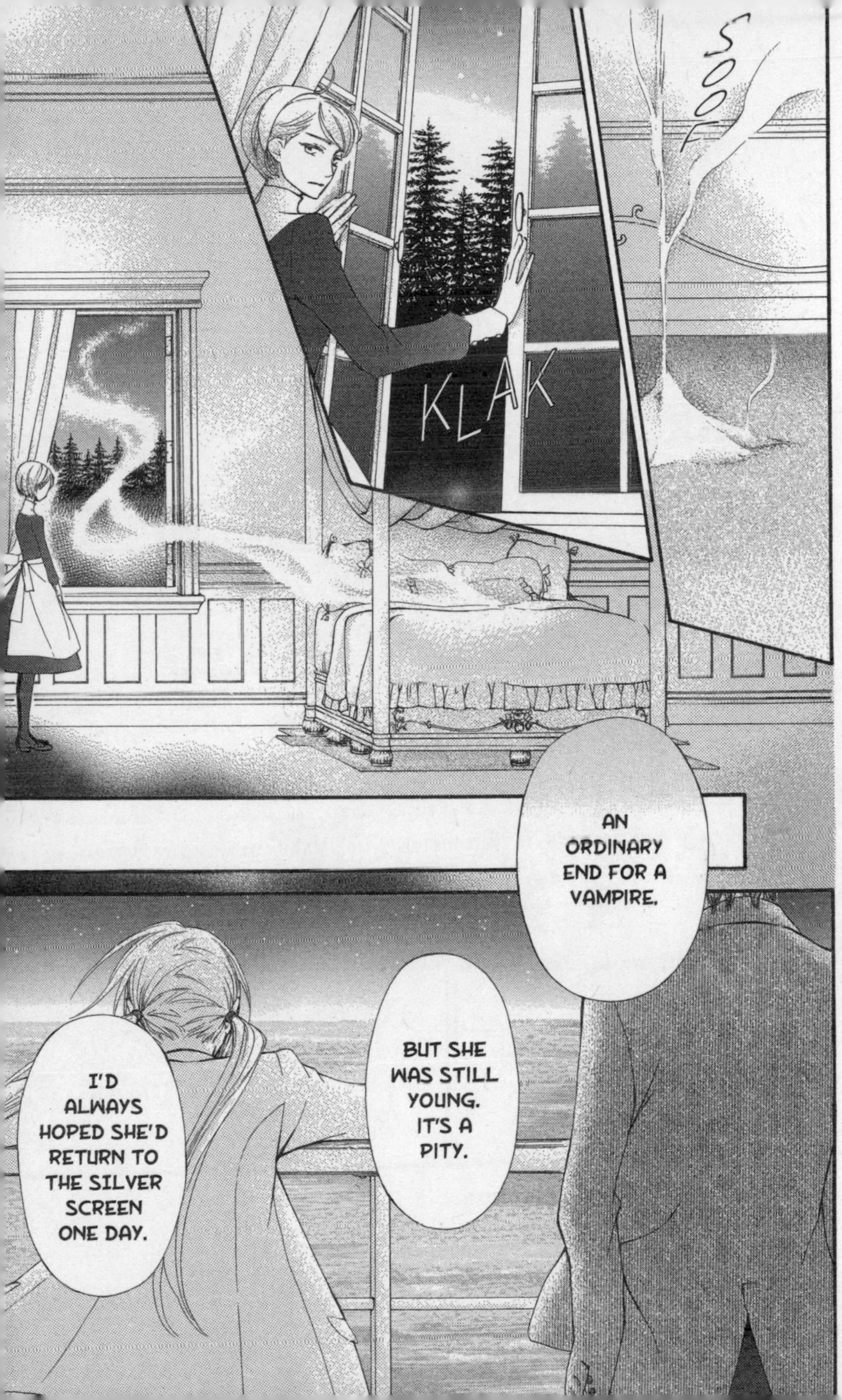
SOOF
KLAK
AN ORDINARY END FOR A VAMPIRE.
BUT SHE WAS STILL YOUNG. IT'S A PITY.
I'D ALWAYS HOPED SHE'D RETURN TO THE SILVER SCREEN ONE DAY.

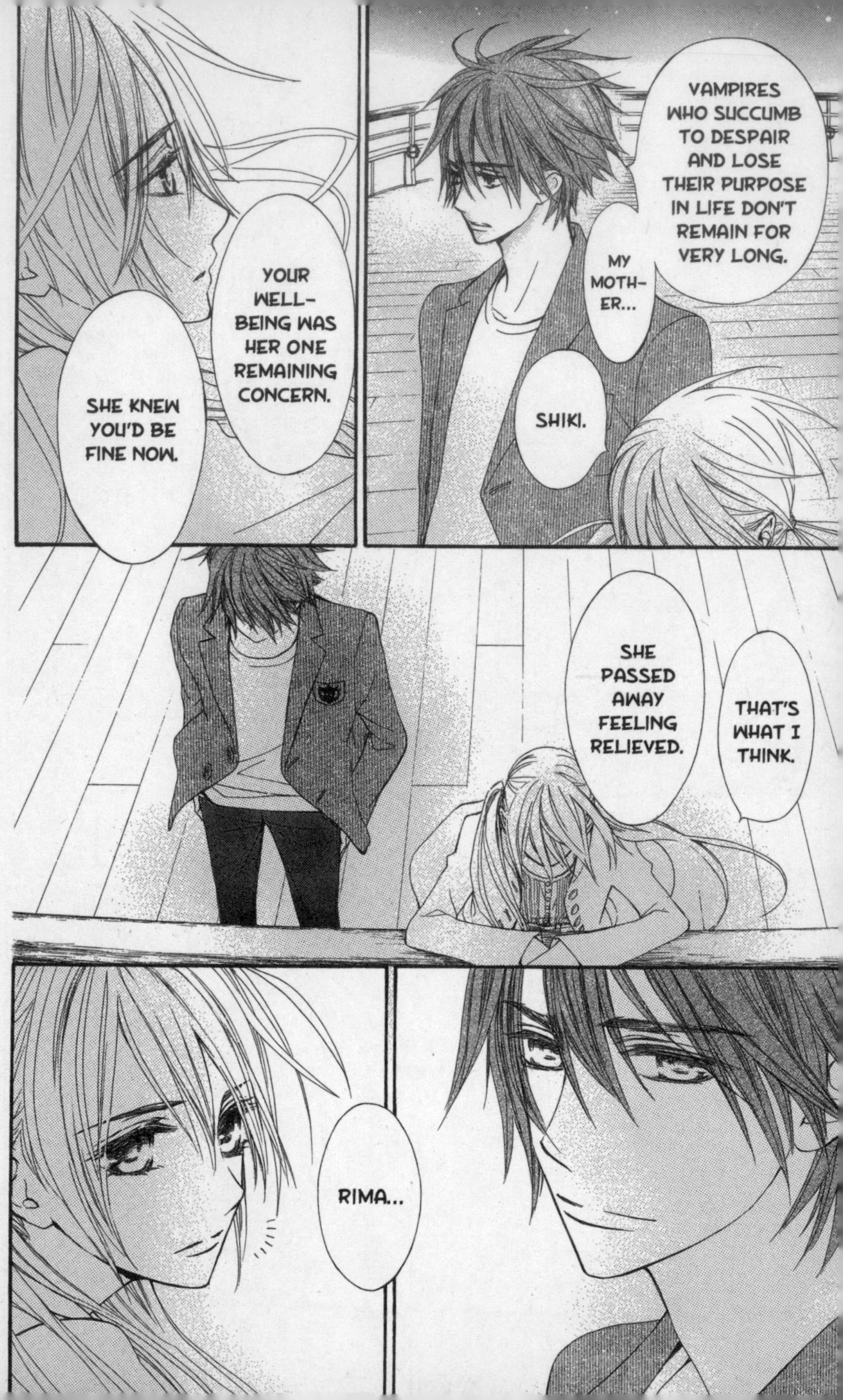
VAMPIRES WHO SUCCUMB TO DESPAIR AND LOSE THEIR PURPOSE IN LIFE DON'T REMAIN FOR VERY LONG.
MY MOTHER...
SHIKI.
YOUR WELL-BEING WAS HER ONE REMAINING CONCERN.
SHE KNEW YOU'D BE FINE NOW.
SHE PASSED AWAY FEELING RELIEVED.
THAT'S WHAT I THINK.
RIMA...

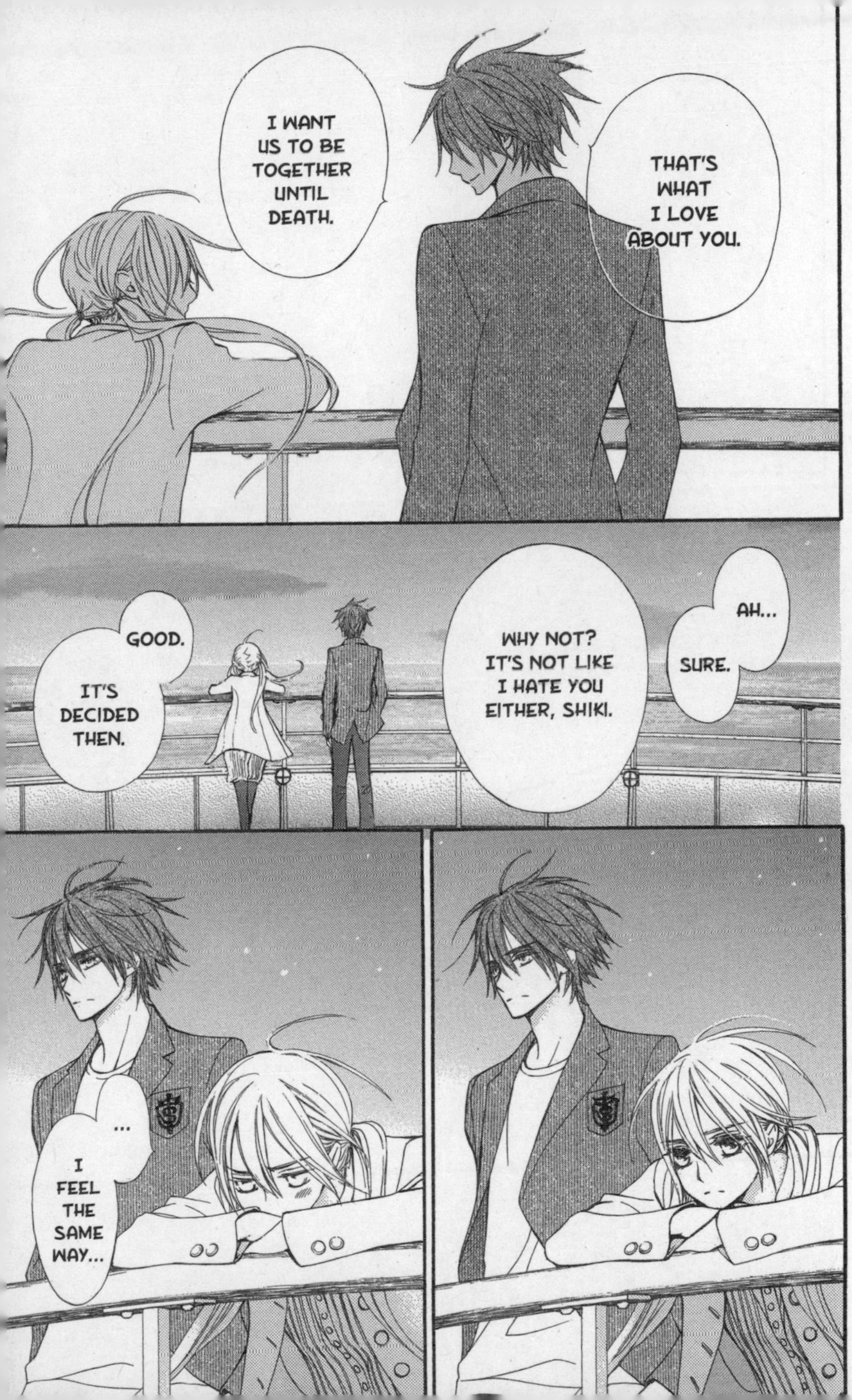
THAT'S WHAT I LOVE ABOUT YOU.
I WANT US TO BE TOGETHER UNTIL DEATH.
AH... SURE.
WHY NOT? IT'S NOT LIKE I HATE YOU EITHER, SHIKI.
GOOD. IT'S DECIDED THEN.
... I FEEL THE SAME WAY...

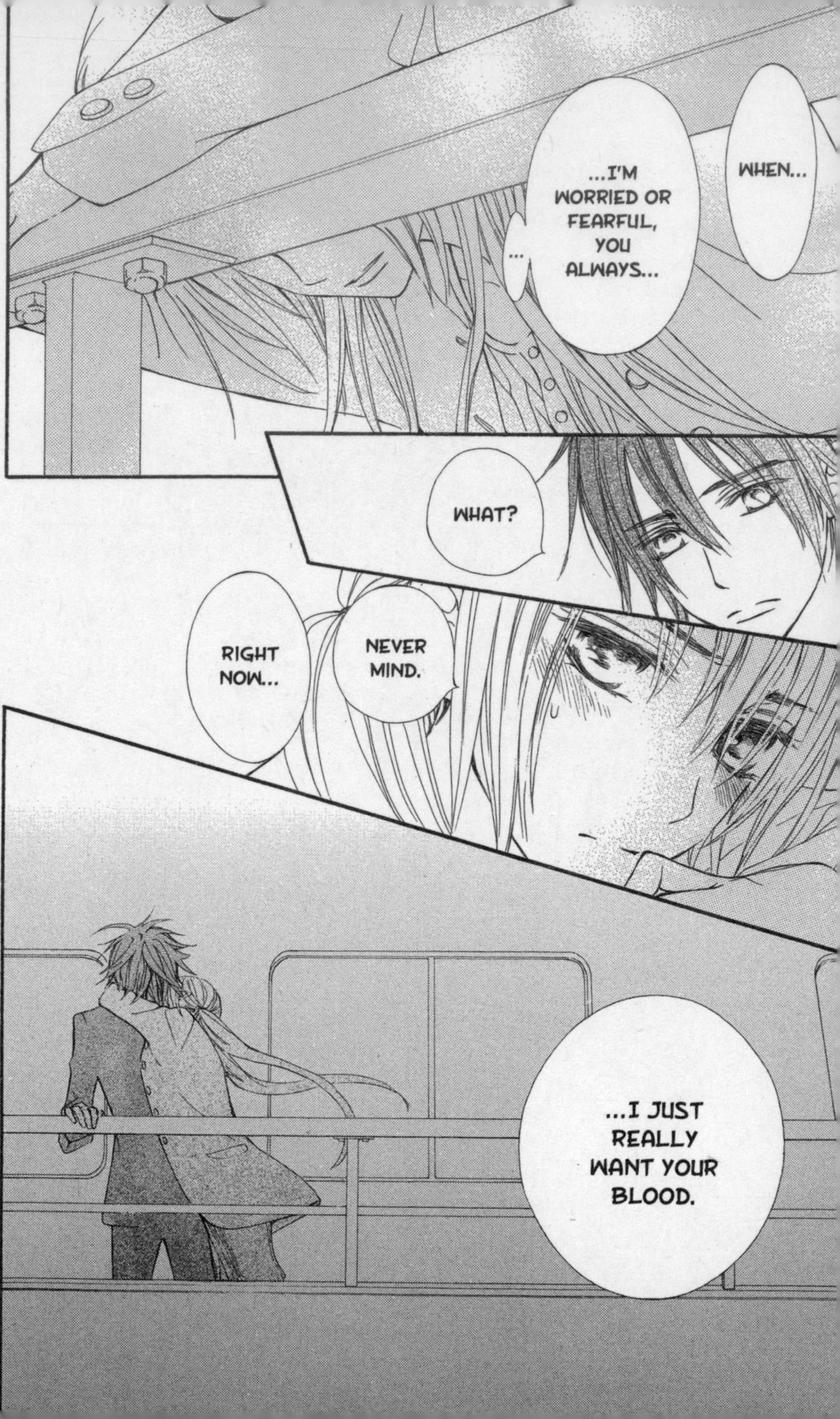
WHEN...
...I'M WORRIED OR FEARFUL, YOU ALWAYS...
...
WHAT?
NEVER MIND.
RIGHT NOW...
...I JUST REALLY WANT YOUR BLOOD.

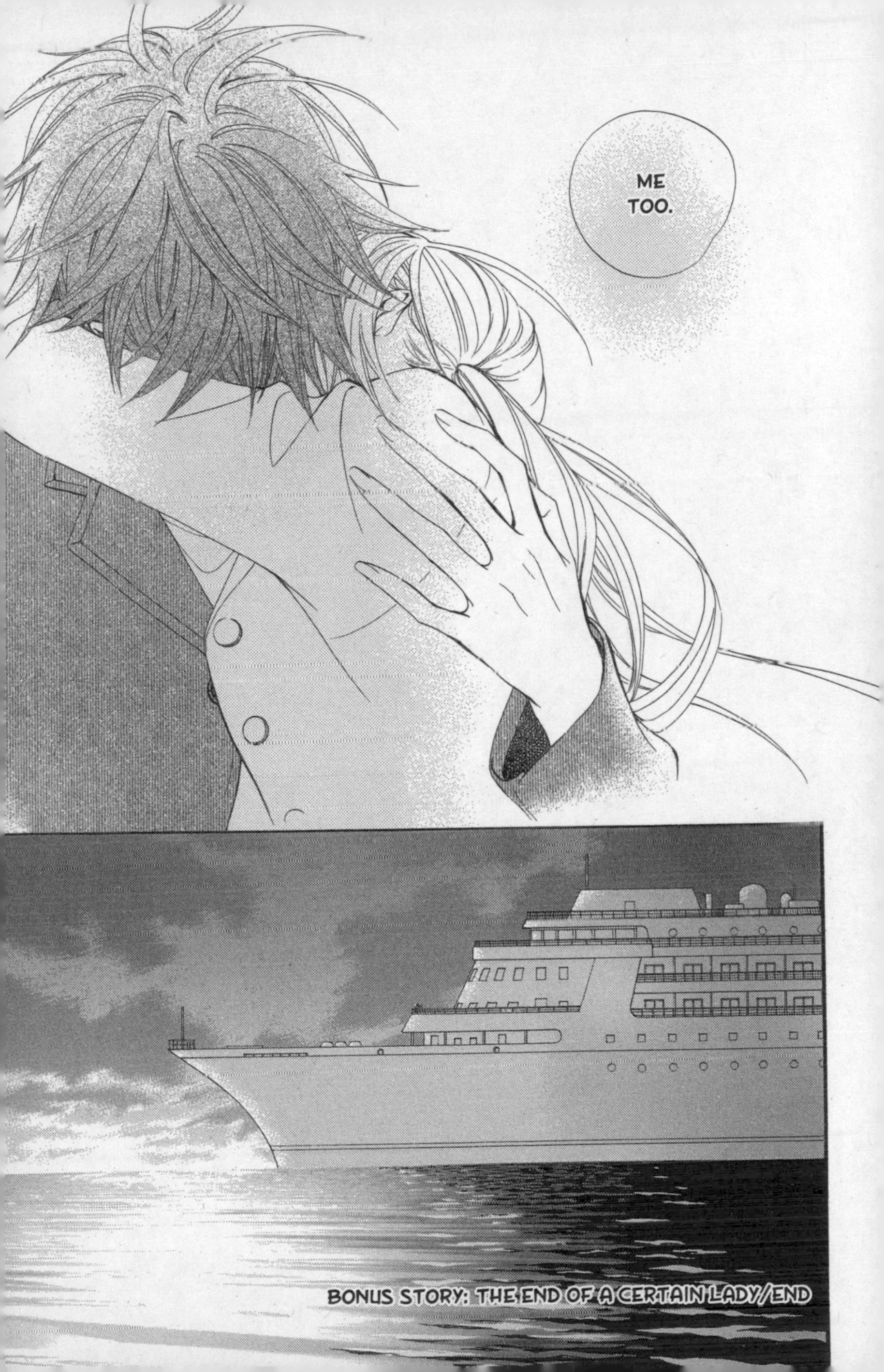
ME TOO.
BONUS STORY: THE END OF A CERTAIN LADY/END

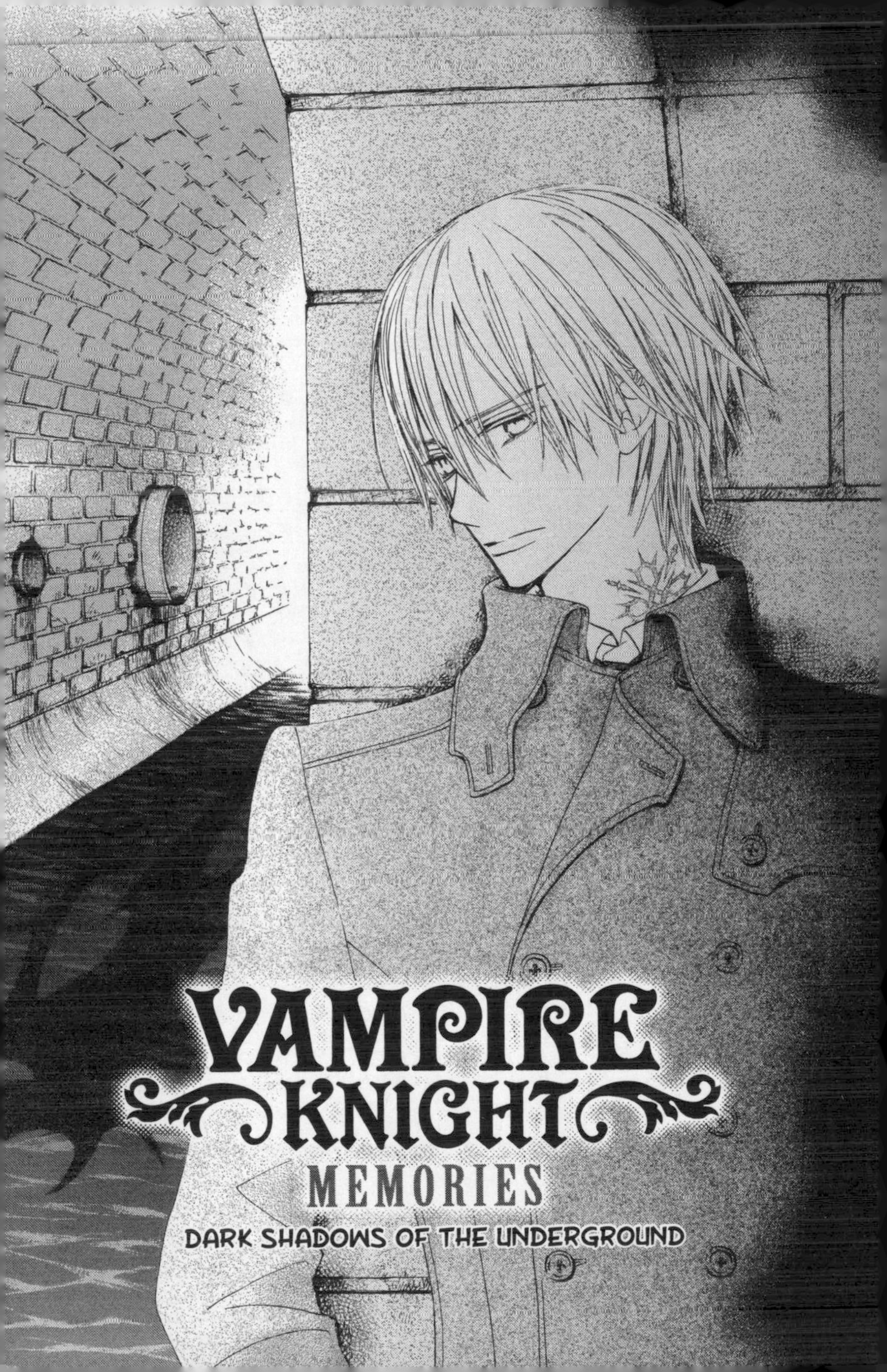
VAMPIRE KNIGHT
MEMORIES
DARK SHADOWS OF THE UNDERGROUND

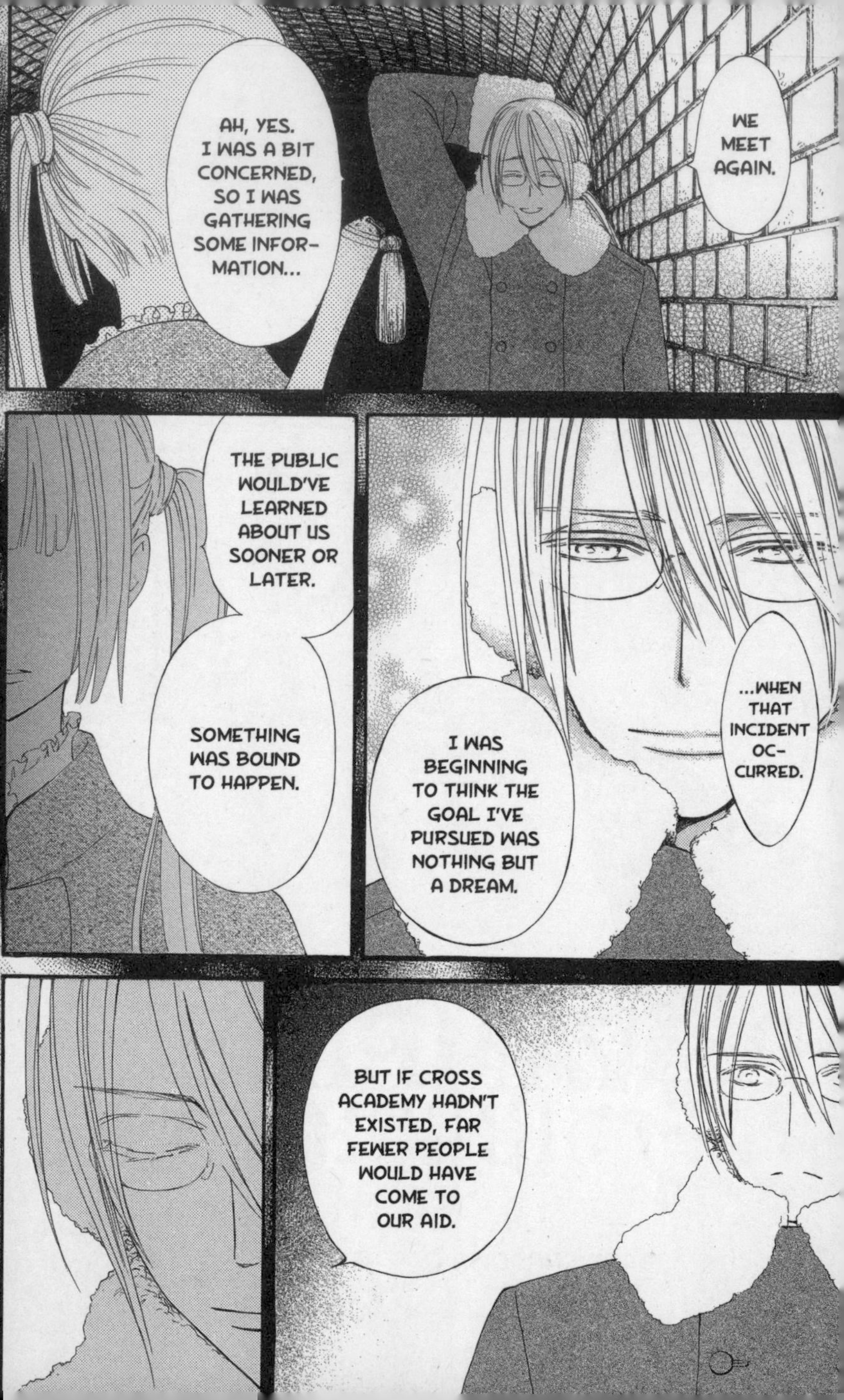
WE MEET AGAIN.
AH, YES. I WAS A BIT CONCERNED, SO I WAS GATHERING SOME INFOR-MATION...
I WAS BEGINNING TO THINK THE GOAL I'VE PURSUED WAS NOTHING BUT A DREAM.
...WHEN THAT INCIDENT OC-CURRED.
THE PUBLIC WOULD'VE LEARNED ABOUT US SOONER OR LATER.
SOMETHING WAS BOUND TO HAPPEN.
BUT IF CROSS ACADEMY HADN'T EXISTED, FAR FEWER PEOPLE WOULD HAVE COME TO OUR AID.

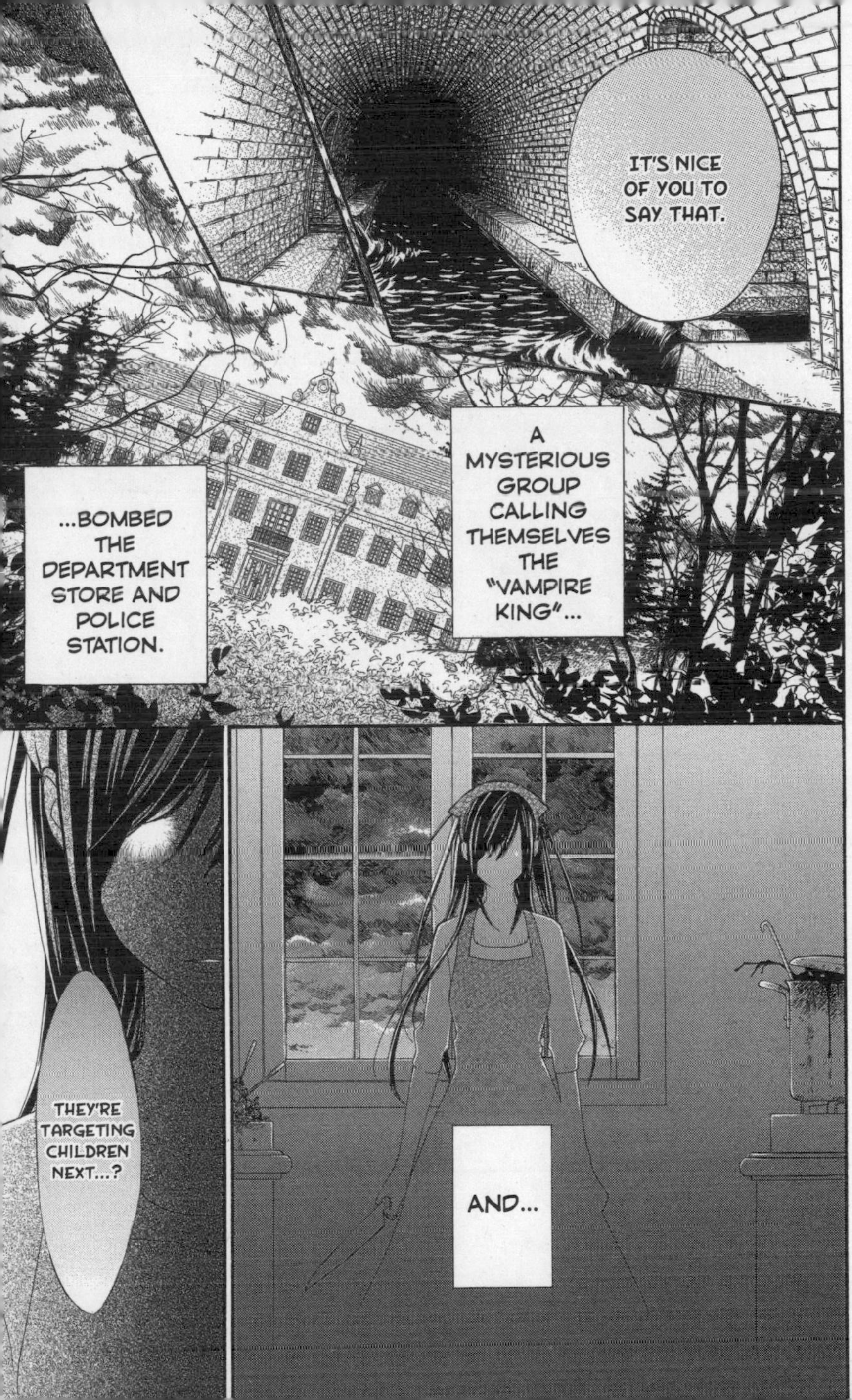
IT'S NICE OF YOU TO SAY THAT.
A MYSTERIOUS GROUP CALLING THEMSELVES THE "VAMPIRE KING"...
...BOMBED THE DEPARTMENT STORE AND POLICE STATION.
AND...
THEY'RE TARGETING CHILDREN NEXT...?

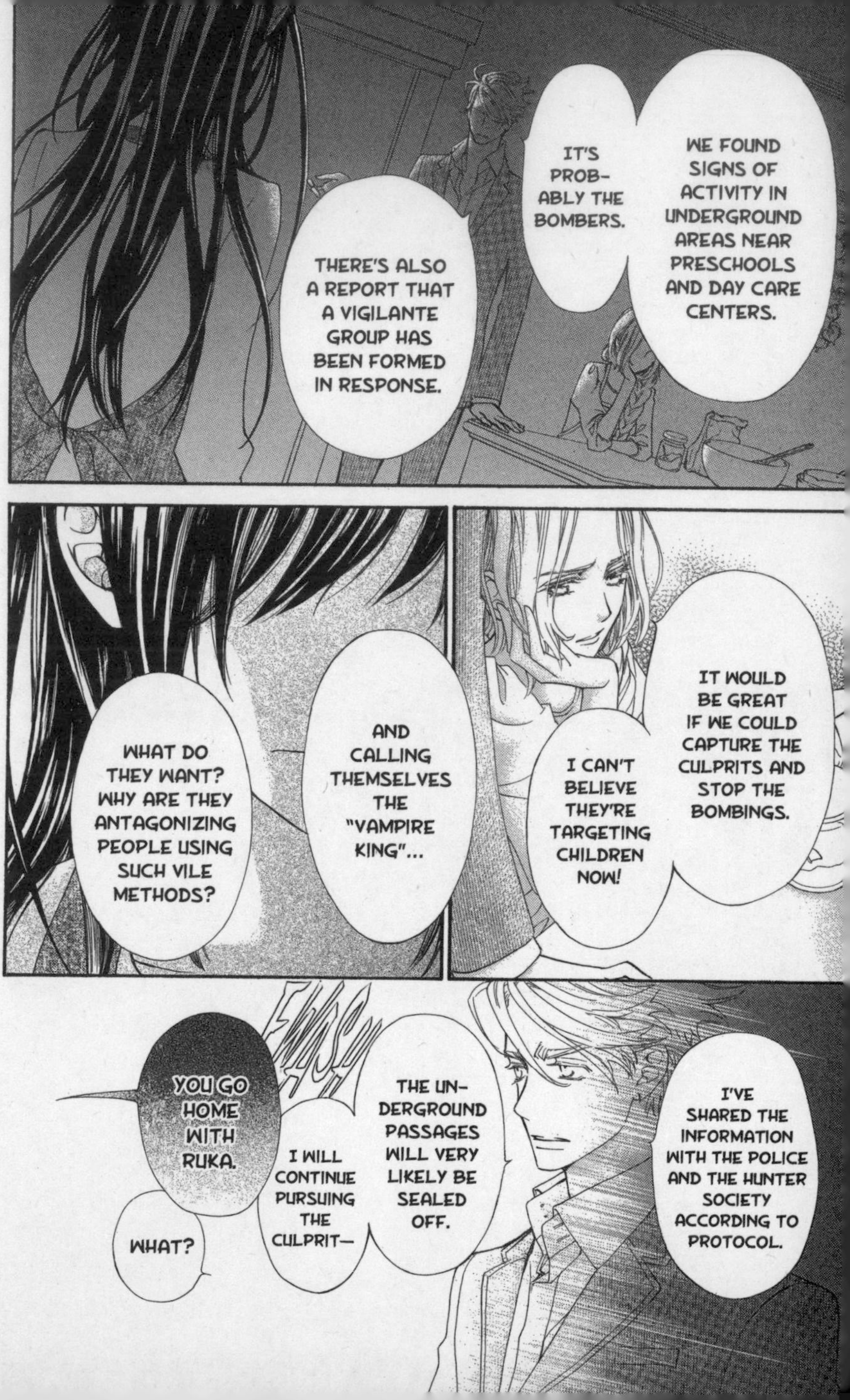
WE FOUND SIGNS OF ACTIVITY IN UNDERGROUND AREAS NEAR PRESCHOOLS AND DAY CARE CENTERS.
IT'S PROB-ABLY THE BOMBERS.
THERE'S ALSO A REPORT THAT A VIGILANTE GROUP HAS BEEN FORMED IN RESPONSE.
IT WOULD BE GREAT IF WE COULD CAPTURE THE CULPRITS AND STOP THE BOMBINGS.
I CAN'T BELIEVE THEY'RE TARGETING CHILDREN NOW!
AND CALLING THEMSELVES THE "VAMPIRE KING"...
WHAT DO THEY WANT? WHY ARE THEY ANTAGONIZING PEOPLE USING SUCH VILE METHODS?
I'VE SHARED THE INFORMATION WITH THE POLICE AND THE HUNTER SOCIETY ACCORDING TO PROTOCOL.
THE UN-DERGROUND PASSAGES WILL VERY LIKELY BE SEALED OFF.
I WILL CONTINUE PURSUING THE CULPRIT—
YOU GO HOME WITH RUKA.
WHAT?

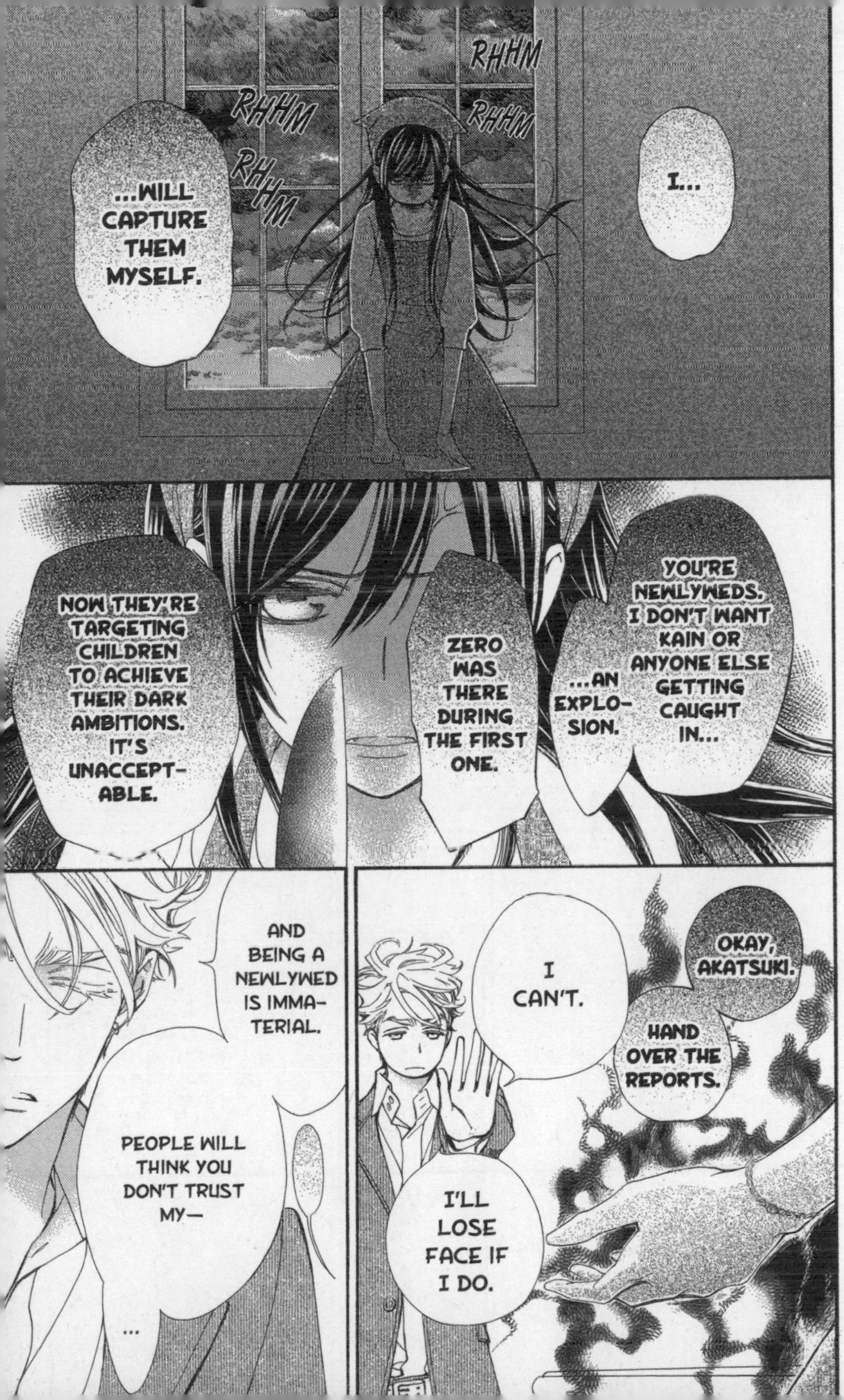
RHHM
RHHM
I...
RHHM
RHHM
...WILL CAPTURE THEM MYSELF.
YOU'RE NEWLYWEDS. I DON'T WANT KAIN OR ANYONE ELSE GETTING CAUGHT IN...
...AN EXPLOSION.
ZERO WAS THERE DURING THE FIRST ONE.
NOW THEY'RE TARGETING CHILDREN TO ACHIEVE THEIR DARK AMBITIONS. IT'S UNACCEPTABLE.
OKAY, AKATSUKI.
HAND OVER THE REPORTS.
I CAN'T.
I'LL LOSE FACE IF I DO.
AND BEING A NEWLYWED IS IMMATERIAL.
PEOPLE WILL THINK YOU DON'T TRUST MY—
...

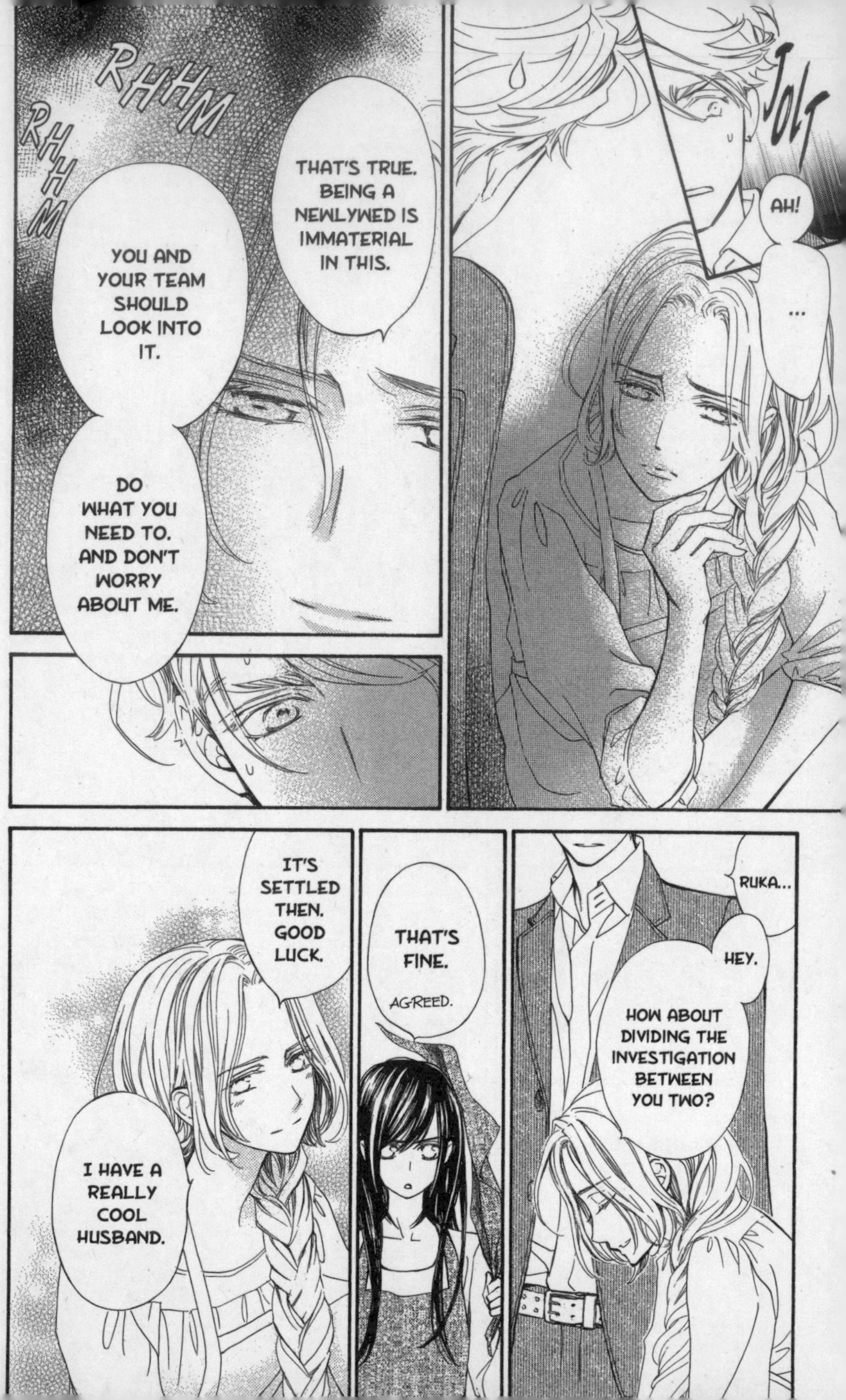
JOLT
AH!
...
RHHM
RHHM
THAT'S TRUE. BEING A NEWLYWED IS IMMATERIAL IN THIS.
YOU AND YOUR TEAM SHOULD LOOK INTO IT.
DO WHAT YOU NEED TO. AND DON'T WORRY ABOUT ME.
RUKA...
HEY.
HOW ABOUT DIVIDING THE INVESTIGATION BETWEEN YOU TWO?
THAT'S FINE.
AGREED.
IT'S SETTLED THEN. GOOD LUCK.
I HAVE A REALLY COOL HUSBAND.

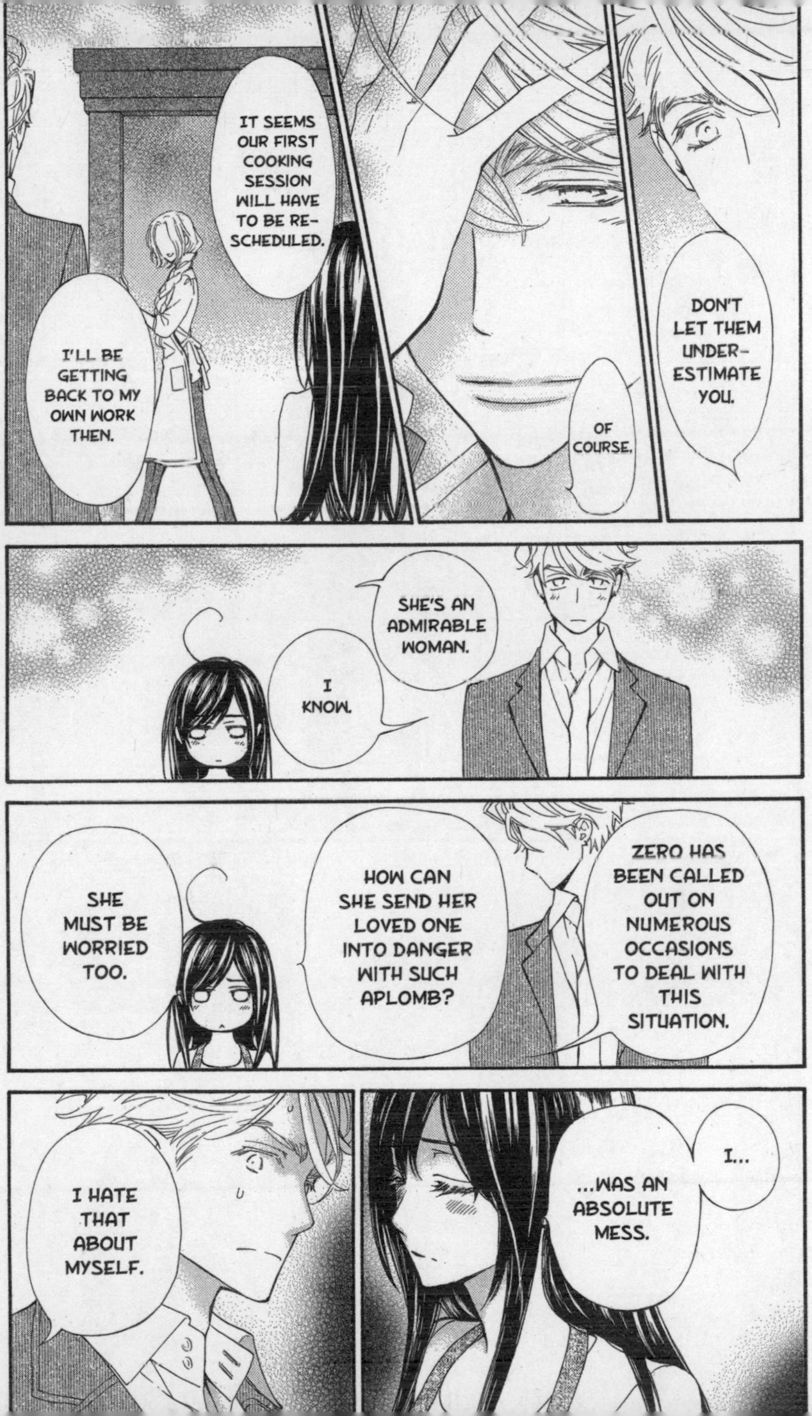
DON'T LET THEM UNDER-ESTIMATE YOU.
OF COURSE.
IT SEEMS OUR FIRST COOKING SESSION WILL HAVE TO BE RE-SCHEDULED.
I'LL BE GETTING BACK TO MY OWN WORK THEN.
SHE'S AN ADMIRABLE WOMAN.
I KNOW.
ZERO HAS BEEN CALLED OUT ON NUMEROUS OCCASIONS TO DEAL WITH THIS SITUATION.
HOW CAN SHE SEND HER LOVED ONE INTO DANGER WITH SUCH APLOMB?
SHE MUST BE WORRIED TOO.
I...
...WAS AN ABSOLUTE MESS.
I HATE THAT ABOUT MYSELF.

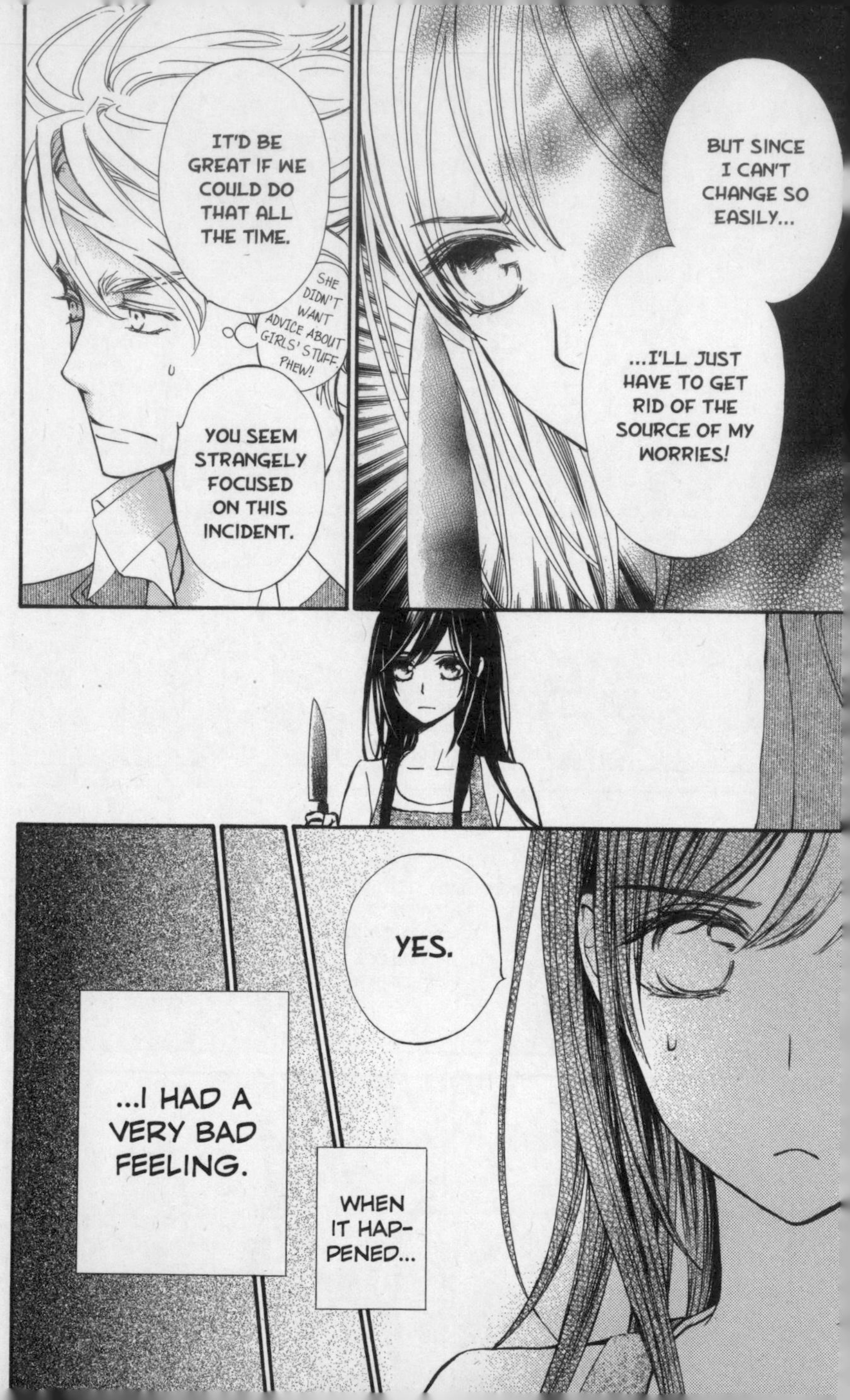
BUT SINCE I CAN'T CHANGE SO EASILY...
...I'LL JUST HAVE TO GET RID OF THE SOURCE OF MY WORRIES!
IT'D BE GREAT IF WE COULD DO THAT ALL THE TIME.
SHE DIDN'T WANT ADVICE ABOUT GIRLS' STUFF. PHEW!
YOU SEEM STRANGELY FOCUSED ON THIS INCIDENT.
YES.
WHEN IT HAP-PENED...
...I HAD A VERY BAD FEELING.

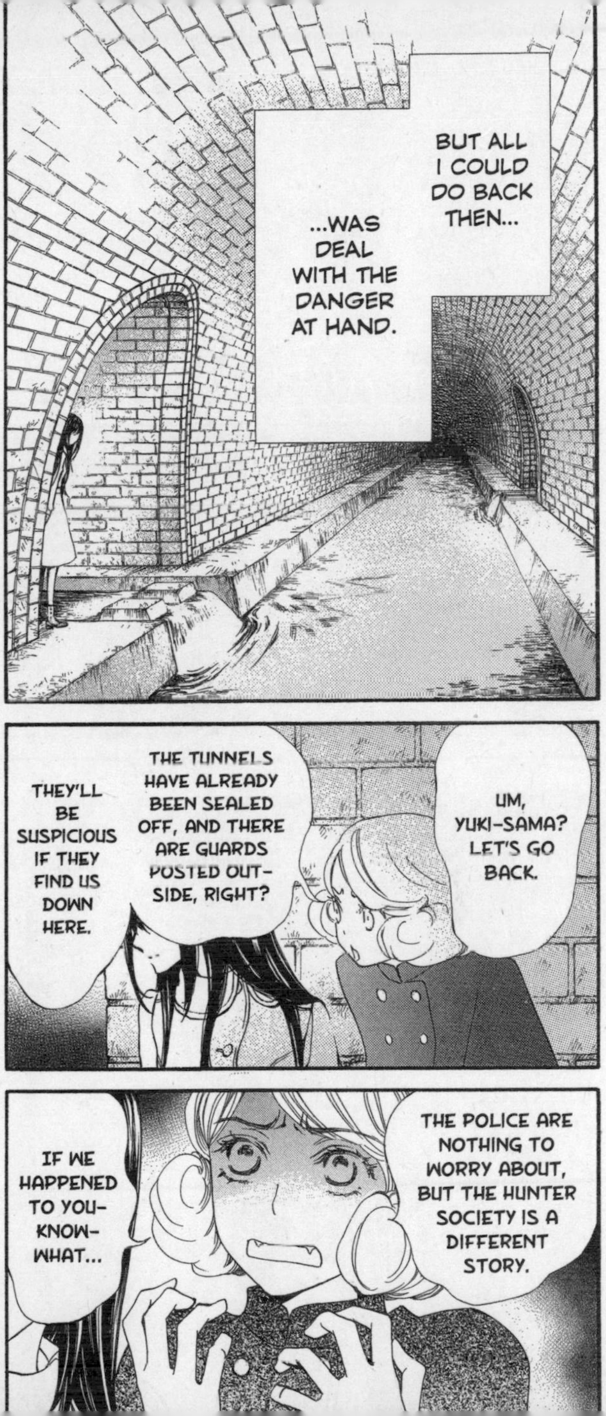
BUT ALL I COULD DO BACK THEN...
...WAS DEAL WITH THE DANGER AT HAND.
UM, YUKI-SAMA? LET'S GO BACK.
THE TUNNELS HAVE ALREADY BEEN SEALED OFF, AND THERE ARE GUARDS POSTED OUT-SIDE, RIGHT?
THEY'LL BE SUSPICIOUS IF THEY FIND US DOWN HERE.
THE POLICE ARE NOTHING TO WORRY ABOUT, BUT THE HUNTER SOCIETY IS A DIFFERENT STORY.
IF WE HAPPENED TO YOU-KNOW-WHAT...

I

Thank you very much for picking up volume 4 of *Vampire Knight Memories*. I will be entering my 25th year as a mangaka this autumn. I was able to continue working on *Memories* thanks to everyone who has been reading my work. Thank you very much.

There is a special edition for volume 4 in Japan that comes with a drama CD. I squeezed the three main characters on the covers for both editions. Did you notice that the theme I used in the past for drawing these three has changed...?

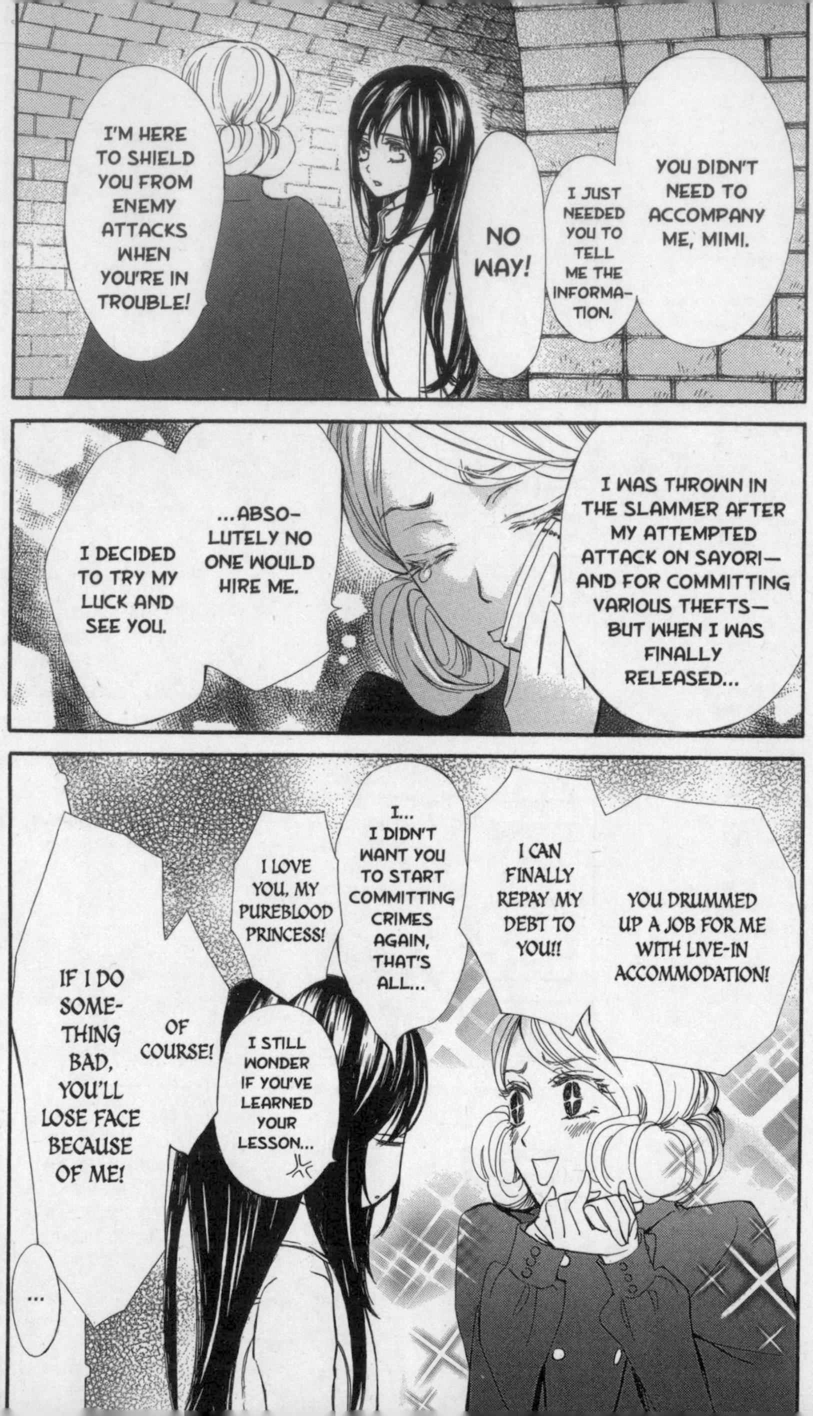
YOU DIDN'T NEED TO ACCOMPANY ME, MIMI.
I JUST NEEDED YOU TO TELL ME THE INFORMATION.
NO WAY!
I'M HERE TO SHIELD YOU FROM ENEMY ATTACKS WHEN YOU'RE IN TROUBLE!
I WAS THROWN IN THE SLAMMER AFTER MY ATTEMPTED ATTACK ON SAYORI—AND FOR COMMITTING VARIOUS THEFTS—BUT WHEN I WAS FINALLY RELEASED...
...ABSOLUTELY NO ONE WOULD HIRE ME.
I DECIDED TO TRY MY LUCK AND SEE YOU.
YOU DRUMMED UP A JOB FOR ME WITH LIVE-IN ACCOMMODATION!
I CAN FINALLY REPAY MY DEBT TO YOU!!
I... I DIDN'T WANT YOU TO START COMMITTING CRIMES AGAIN, THAT'S ALL...
I LOVE YOU, MY PUREBLOOD PRINCESS!
I STILL WONDER IF YOU'VE LEARNED YOUR LESSON...
OF COURSE!
IF I DO SOMETHING BAD, YOU'LL LOSE FACE BECAUSE OF ME!
...

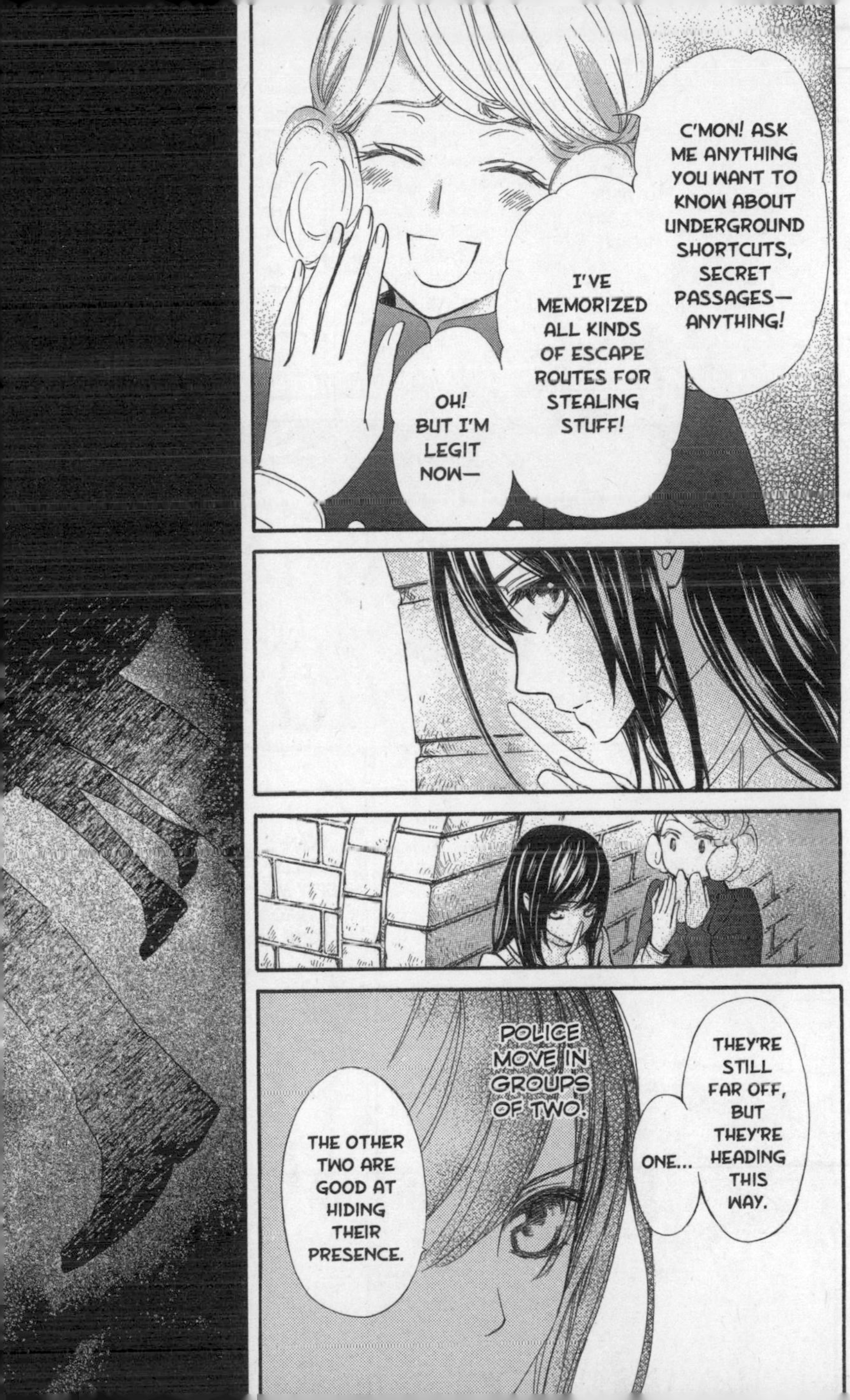
C'MON! ASK ME ANYTHING YOU WANT TO KNOW ABOUT UNDERGROUND SHORTCUTS, SECRET PASSAGES—ANYTHING!
I'VE MEMORIZED ALL KINDS OF ESCAPE ROUTES FOR STEALING STUFF!
OH! BUT I'M LEGIT NOW—
THEY'RE STILL FAR OFF, BUT THEY'RE HEADING THIS WAY.
ONE...
POLICE MOVE IN GROUPS OF TWO.
THE OTHER TWO ARE GOOD AT HIDING THEIR PRESENCE.

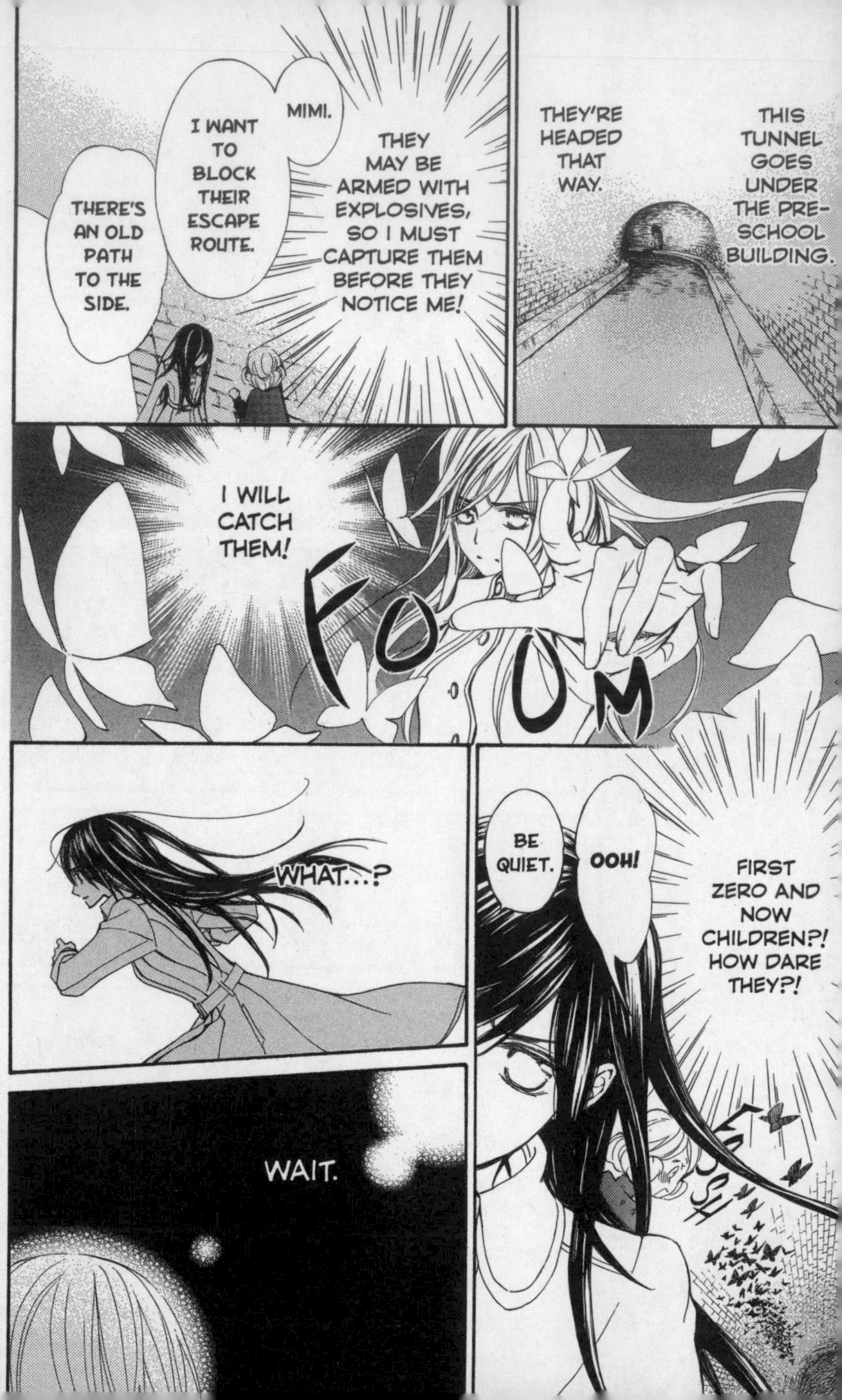
THIS TUNNEL GOES UNDER THE PRE-SCHOOL BUILDING.
THEY'RE HEADED THAT WAY.
THEY MAY BE ARMED WITH EXPLOSIVES, SO I MUST CAPTURE THEM BEFORE THEY NOTICE ME!
MIMI.
I WANT TO BLOCK THEIR ESCAPE ROUTE.
THERE'S AN OLD PATH TO THE SIDE.
I WILL CATCH THEM!
FOOM
FIRST ZERO AND NOW CHILDREN?! HOW DARE THEY?!
OOH!
BE QUIET.
WHAT...?
WAIT.

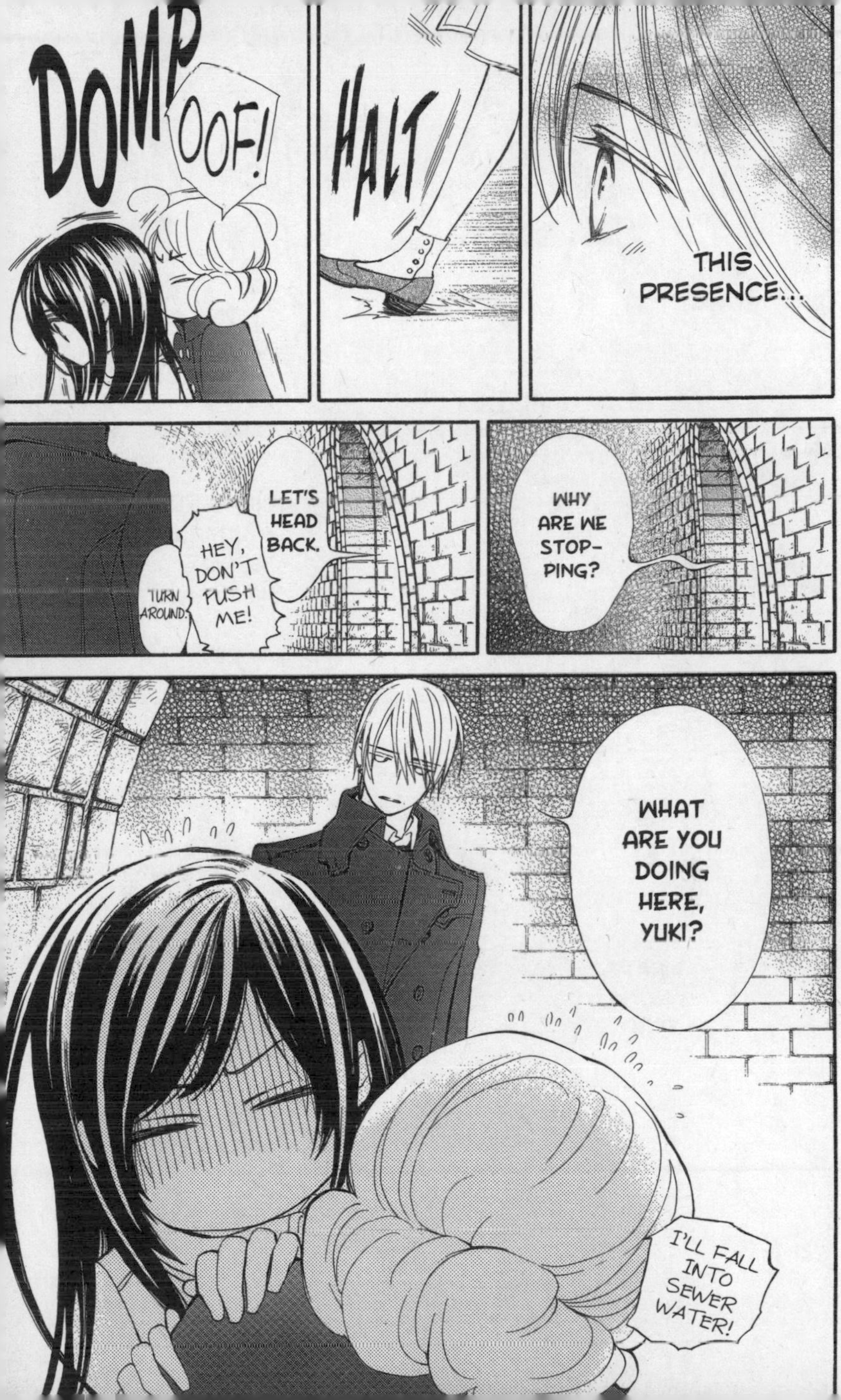
THIS PRESENCE...
HALT
DOMP
OOF!
WHY ARE WE STOP-PING?
LET'S HEAD BACK.
HEY, DON'T PUSH ME!
TURN AROUND.
WHAT ARE YOU DOING HERE, YUKI?
I'LL FALL INTO SEWER WATER!

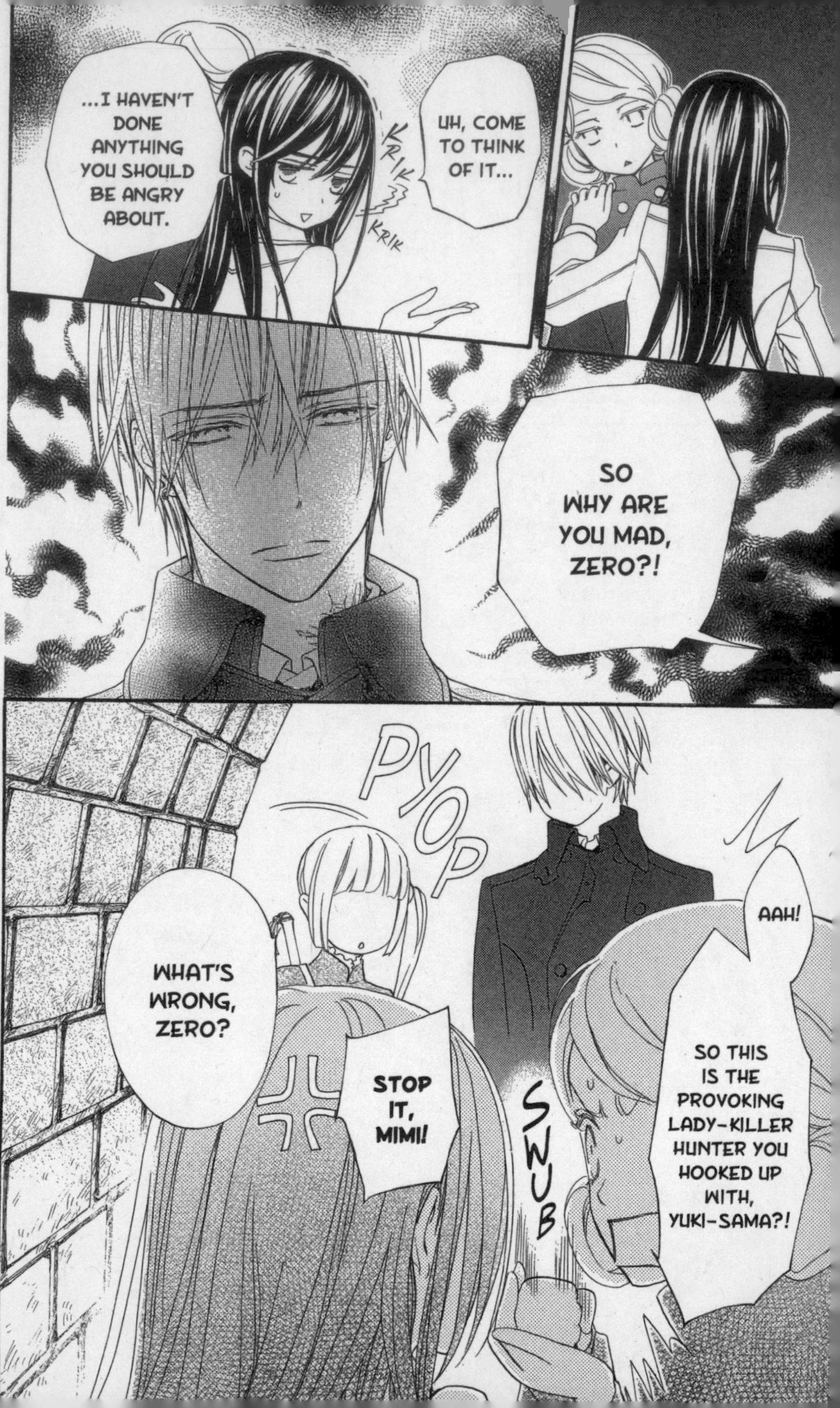
UH, COME TO THINK OF IT...
KRIK KRIK
...I HAVEN'T DONE ANYTHING YOU SHOULD BE ANGRY ABOUT.
KRIK
SO WHY ARE YOU MAD, ZERO?!
PYOP
AAH!
SO THIS IS THE PROVOKING LADY-KILLER HUNTER YOU HOOKED UP WITH, YUKI-SAMA?!
SWUB
STOP IT, MIMI!
WHAT'S WRONG, ZERO?

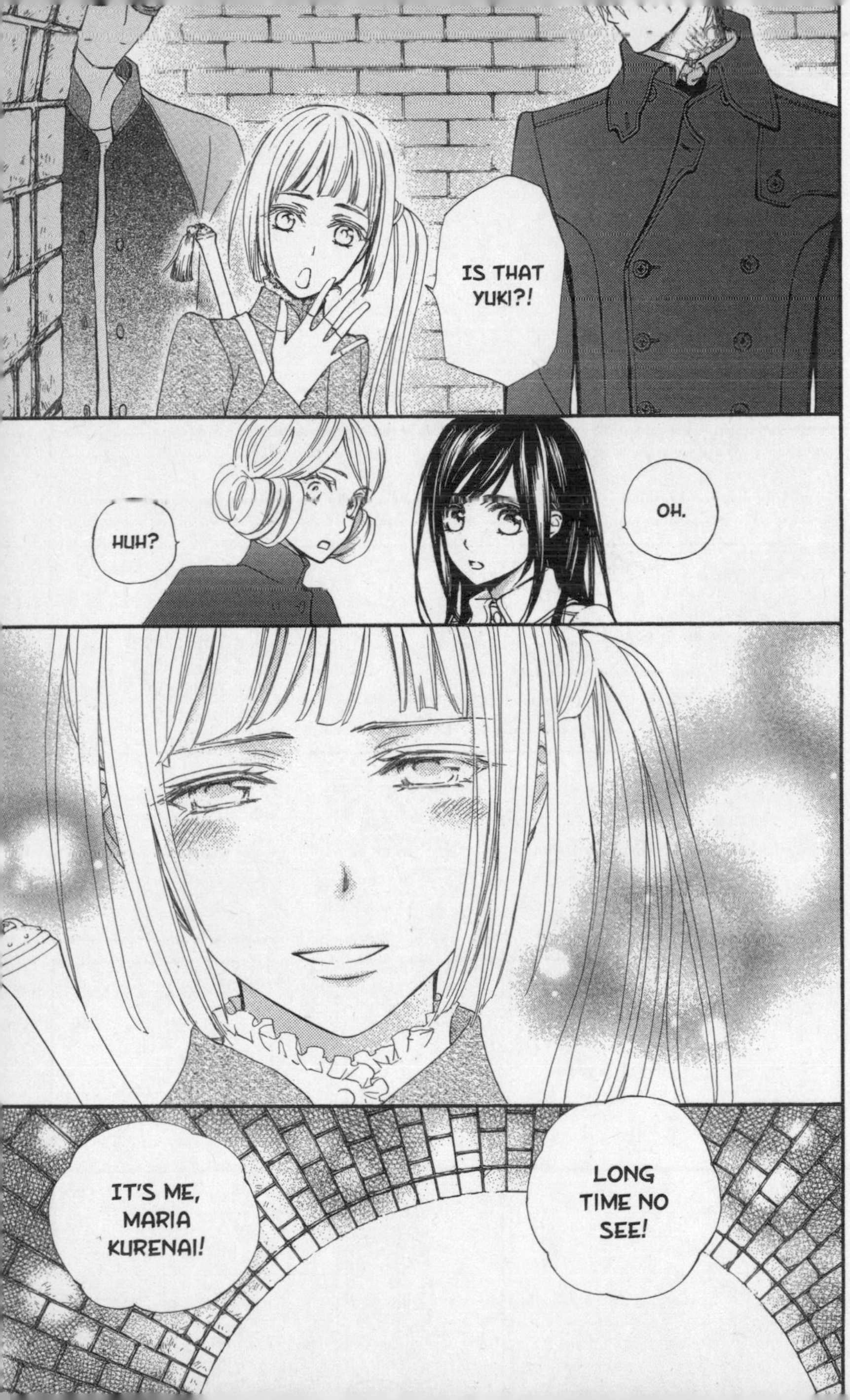
IS THAT YUKI?!
OH.
HUH?
LONG TIME NO SEE!
IT'S ME, MARIA KURENAI!

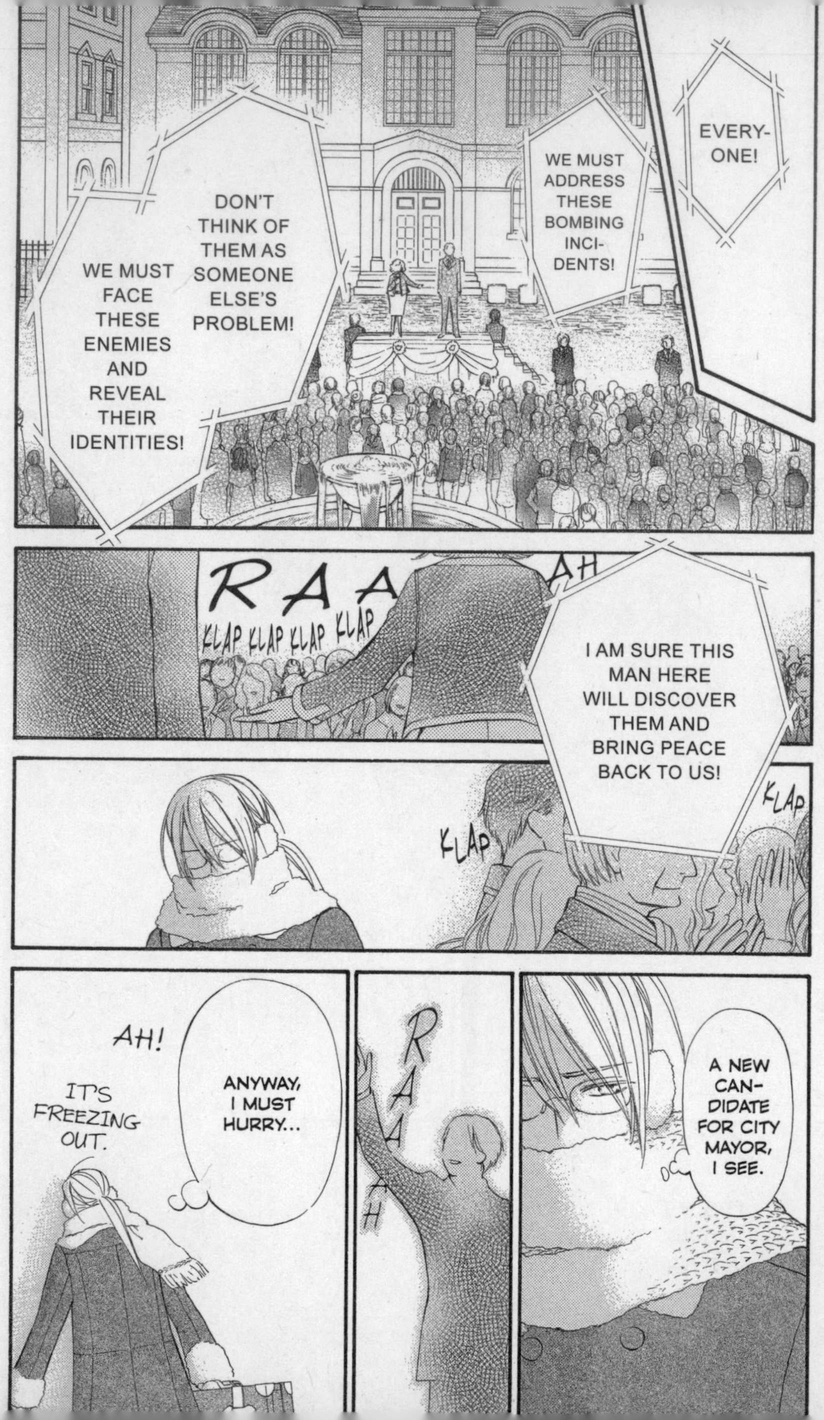
EVERY-ONE!
WE MUST ADDRESS THESE BOMBING INCI-DENTS!
DON'T THINK OF THEM AS SOMEONE ELSE'S PROBLEM!
WE MUST FACE THESE ENEMIES AND REVEAL THEIR IDENTITIES!
I AM SURE THIS MAN HERE WILL DISCOVER THEM AND BRING PEACE BACK TO US!
RAA
AH
KLAP KLAP KLAP KLAP
KLAP
KLAP
A NEW CAN-DIDATE FOR CITY MAYOR, I SEE.
RAAAH
ANYWAY, I MUST HURRY...
AH!
IT'S FREEZING OUT.

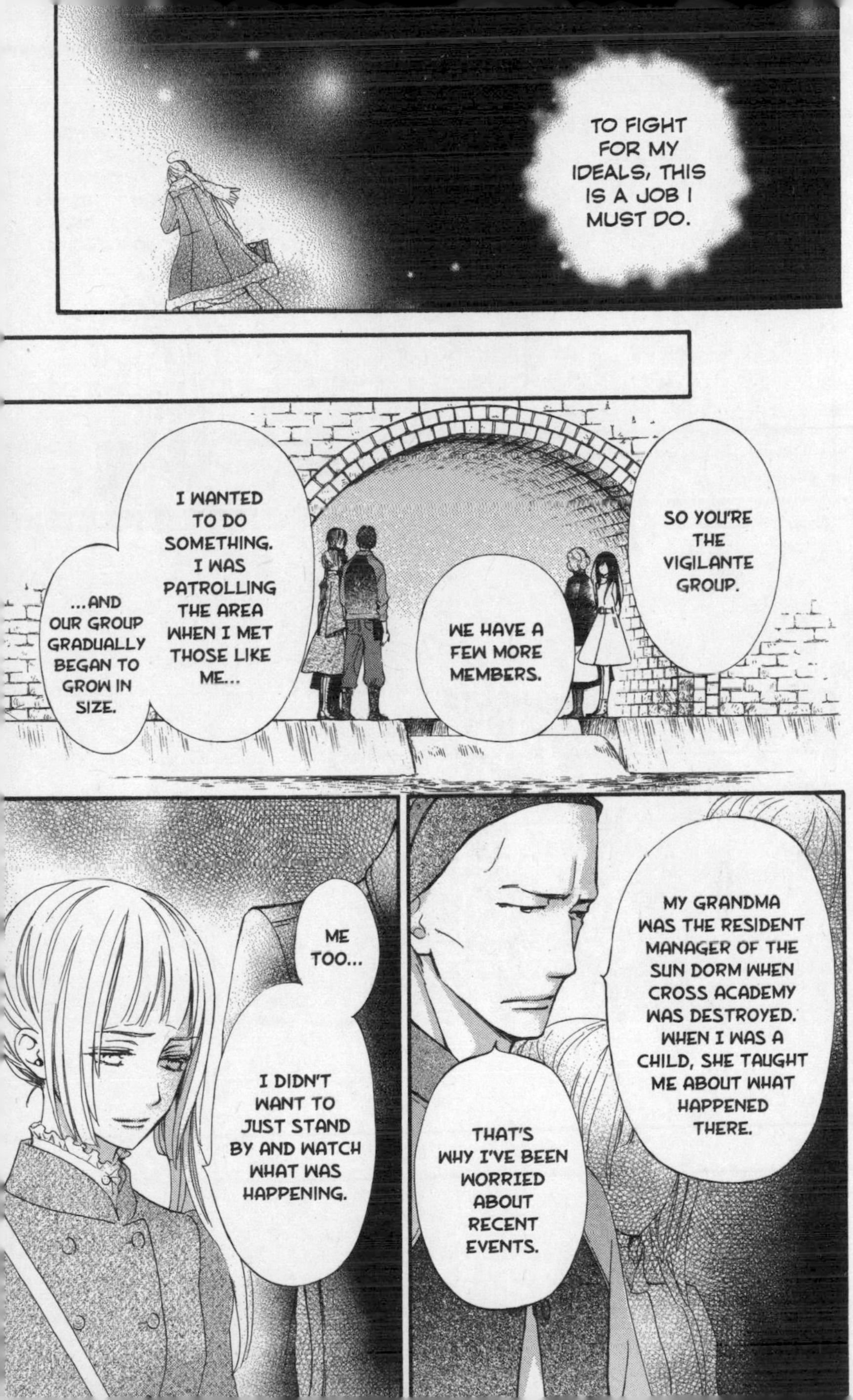
TO FIGHT FOR MY IDEALS, THIS IS A JOB I MUST DO.
SO YOU'RE THE VIGILANTE GROUP.
WE HAVE A FEW MORE MEMBERS.
I WANTED TO DO SOMETHING. I WAS PATROLLING THE AREA WHEN I MET THOSE LIKE ME...
...AND OUR GROUP GRADUALLY BEGAN TO GROW IN SIZE.
MY GRANDMA WAS THE RESIDENT MANAGER OF THE SUN DORM WHEN CROSS ACADEMY WAS DESTROYED. WHEN I WAS A CHILD, SHE TAUGHT ME ABOUT WHAT HAPPENED THERE.
THAT'S WHY I'VE BEEN WORRIED ABOUT RECENT EVENTS.
ME TOO...
I DIDN'T WANT TO JUST STAND BY AND WATCH WHAT WAS HAPPENING.

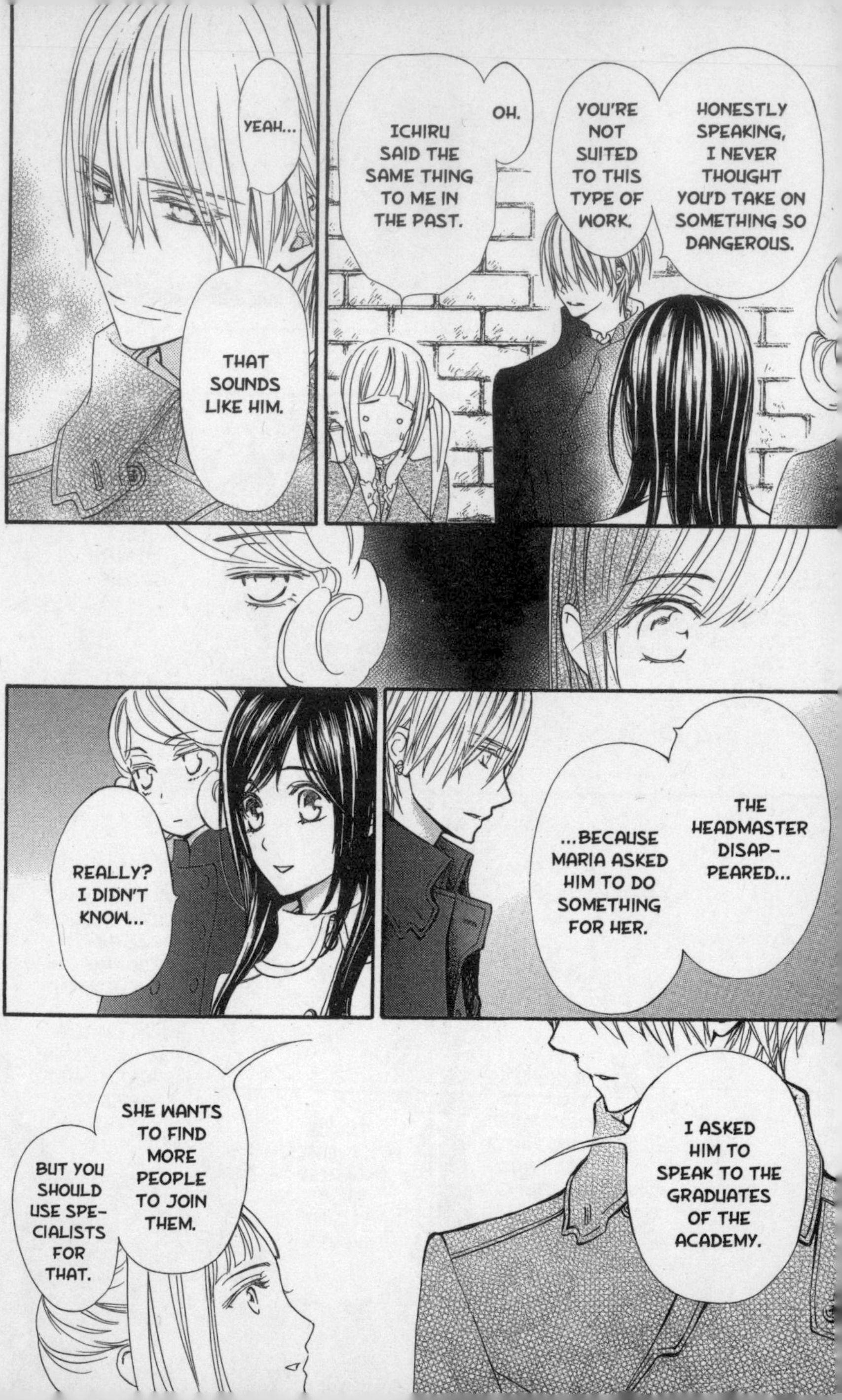
HONESTLY SPEAKING, I NEVER THOUGHT YOU'D TAKE ON SOMETHING SO DANGEROUS.
YOU'RE NOT SUITED TO THIS TYPE OF WORK.
OH.
ICHIRU SAID THE SAME THING TO ME IN THE PAST.
YEAH...
THAT SOUNDS LIKE HIM.
THE HEADMASTER DISAPPEARED...
...BECAUSE MARIA ASKED HIM TO DO SOMETHING FOR HER.
REALLY? I DIDN'T KNOW...
I ASKED HIM TO SPEAK TO THE GRADUATES OF THE ACADEMY.
SHE WANTS TO FIND MORE PEOPLE TO JOIN THEM.
BUT YOU SHOULD USE SPECIALISTS FOR THAT.

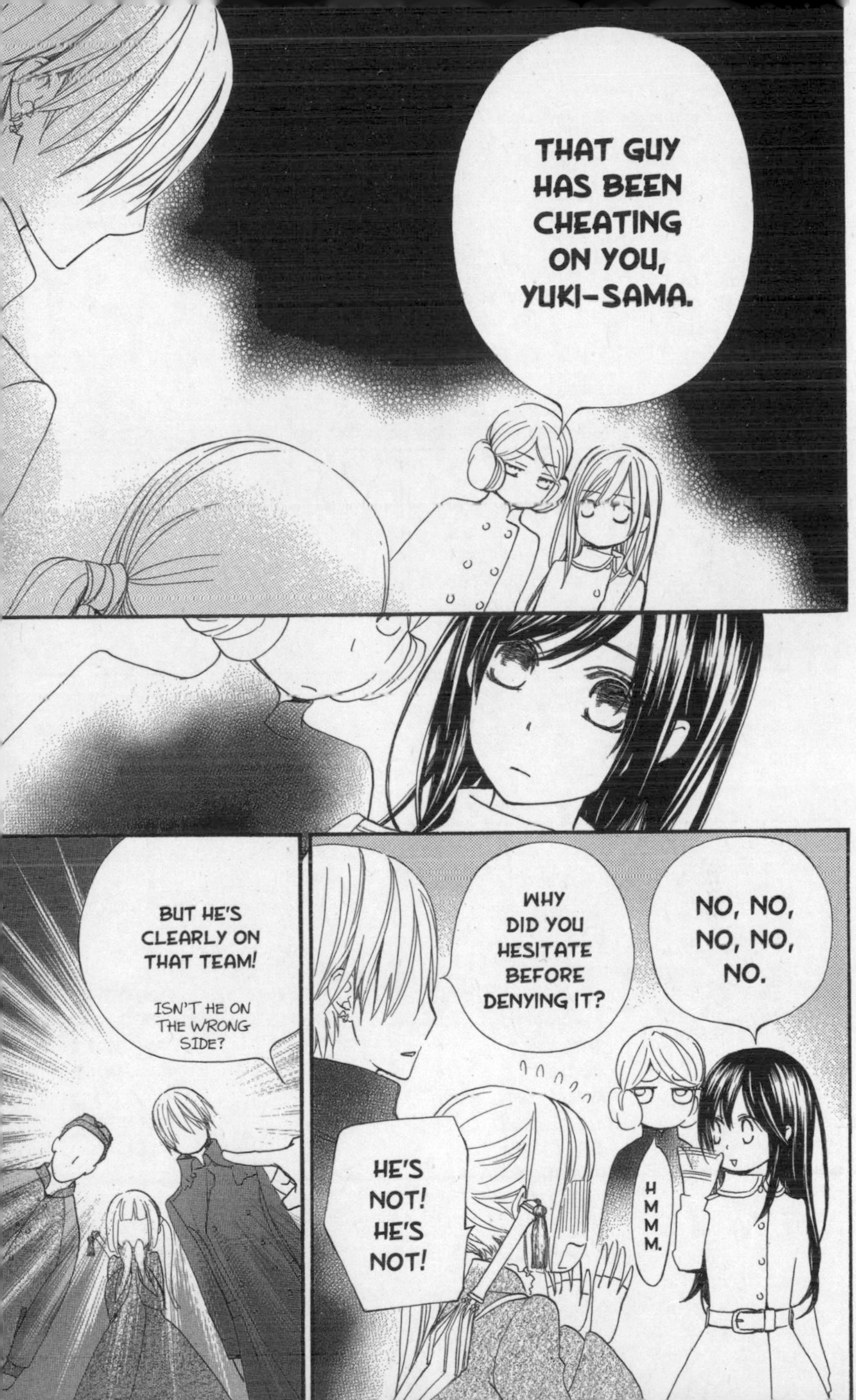
THAT GUY HAS BEEN CHEATING ON YOU, YUKI-SAMA.
NO, NO, NO, NO, NO.
WHY DID YOU HESITATE BEFORE DENYING IT?
HMMM.
HE'S NOT! HE'S NOT!
BUT HE'S CLEARLY ON THAT TEAM!
ISN'T HE ON THE WRONG SIDE?

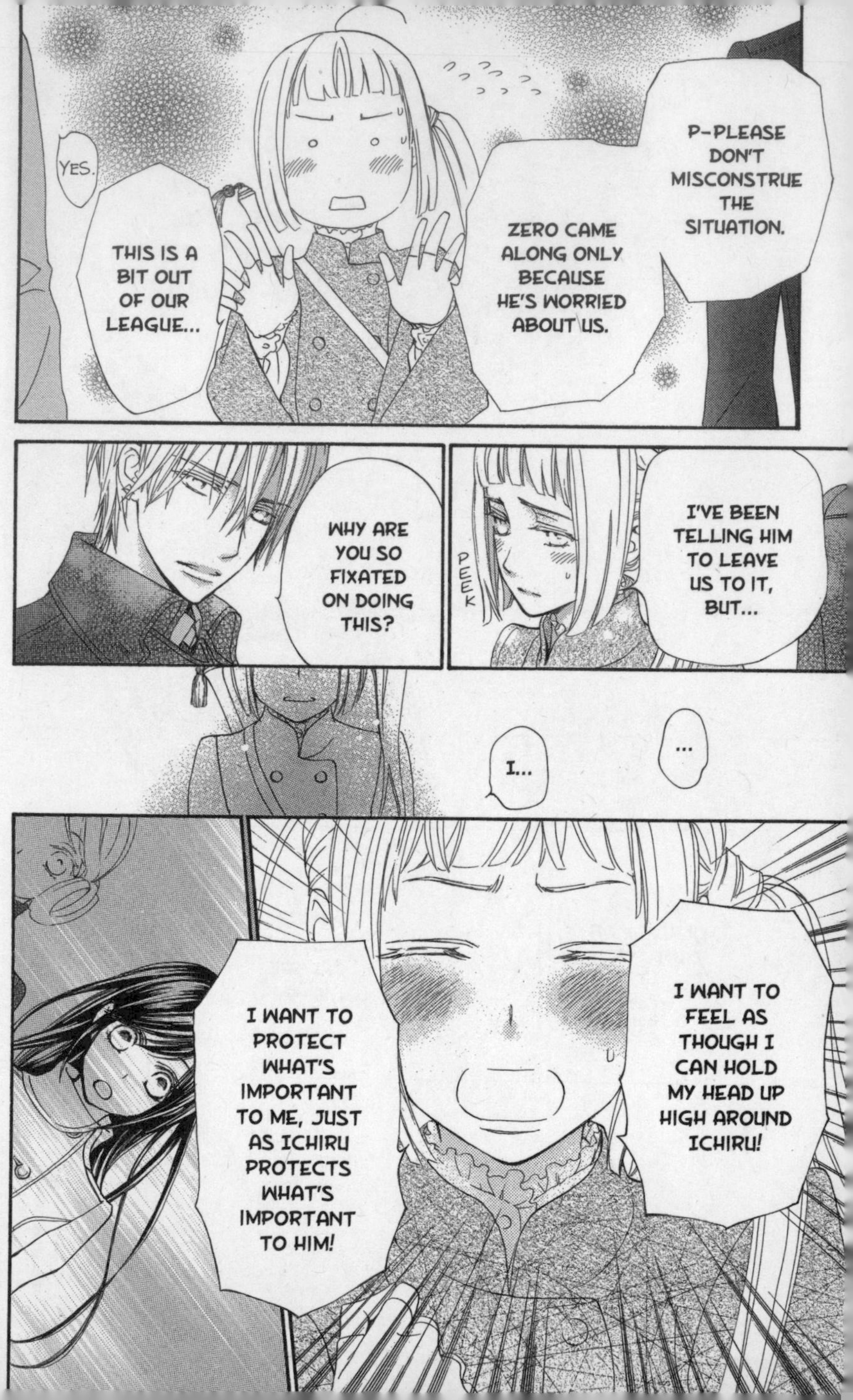
P-PLEASE DON'T MISCONSTRUE THE SITUATION.
ZERO CAME ALONG ONLY BECAUSE HE'S WORRIED ABOUT US.
YES.
THIS IS A BIT OUT OF OUR LEAGUE...
I'VE BEEN TELLING HIM TO LEAVE US TO IT, BUT...
PEEK
WHY ARE YOU SO FIXATED ON DOING THIS?
...
I...
I WANT TO FEEL AS THOUGH I CAN HOLD MY HEAD UP HIGH AROUND ICHIRU!
I WANT TO PROTECT WHAT'S IMPORTANT TO ME, JUST AS ICHIRU PROTECTS WHAT'S IMPORTANT TO HIM!

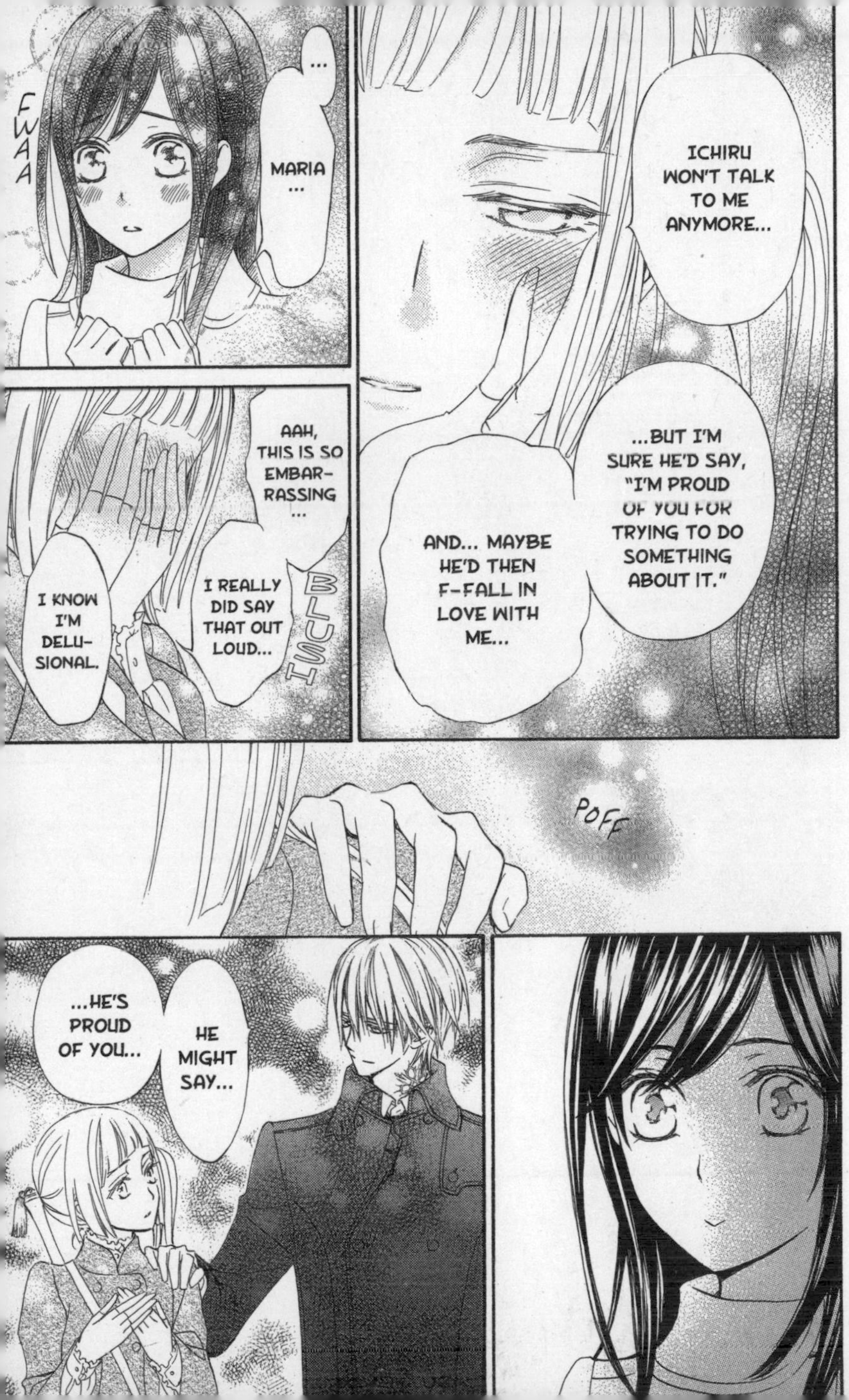
ICHIRU WON'T TALK TO ME ANYMORE...
...BUT I'M SURE HE'D SAY, "I'M PROUD OF YOU FOR TRYING TO DO SOMETHING ABOUT IT."
AND... MAYBE HE'D THEN F-FALL IN LOVE WITH ME...
...
MARIA ...
FWAAA
AAH, THIS IS SO EMBAR-RASSING ...
BLUSH
I REALLY DID SAY THAT OUT LOUD...
I KNOW I'M DELU-SIONAL.
POFF
HE MIGHT SAY...
...HE'S PROUD OF YOU...

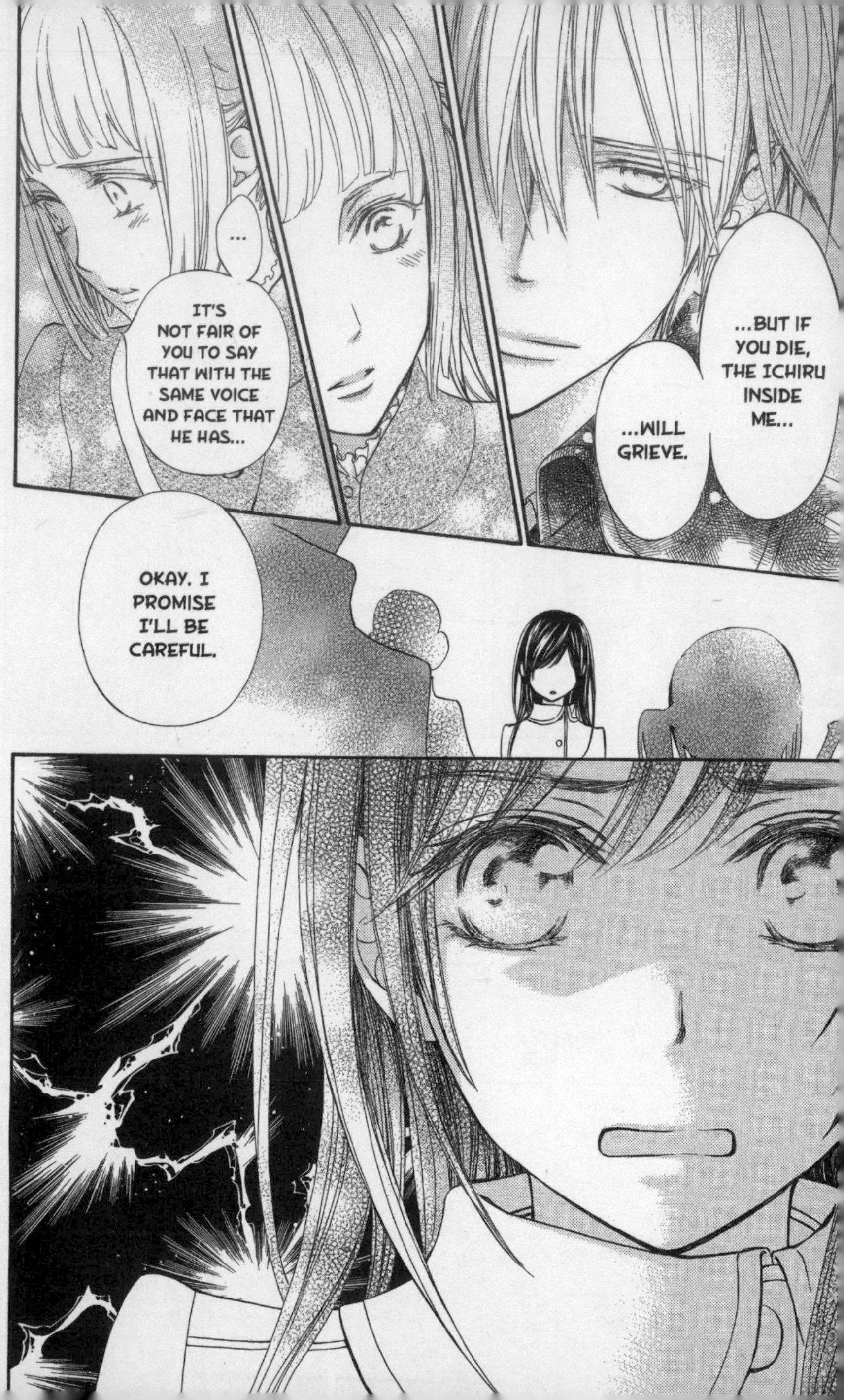
...BUT IF YOU DIE, THE ICHIRU INSIDE ME...
...WILL GRIEVE.
...
IT'S NOT FAIR OF YOU TO SAY THAT WITH THE SAME VOICE AND FACE THAT HE HAS...
OKAY. I PROMISE I'LL BE CAREFUL.

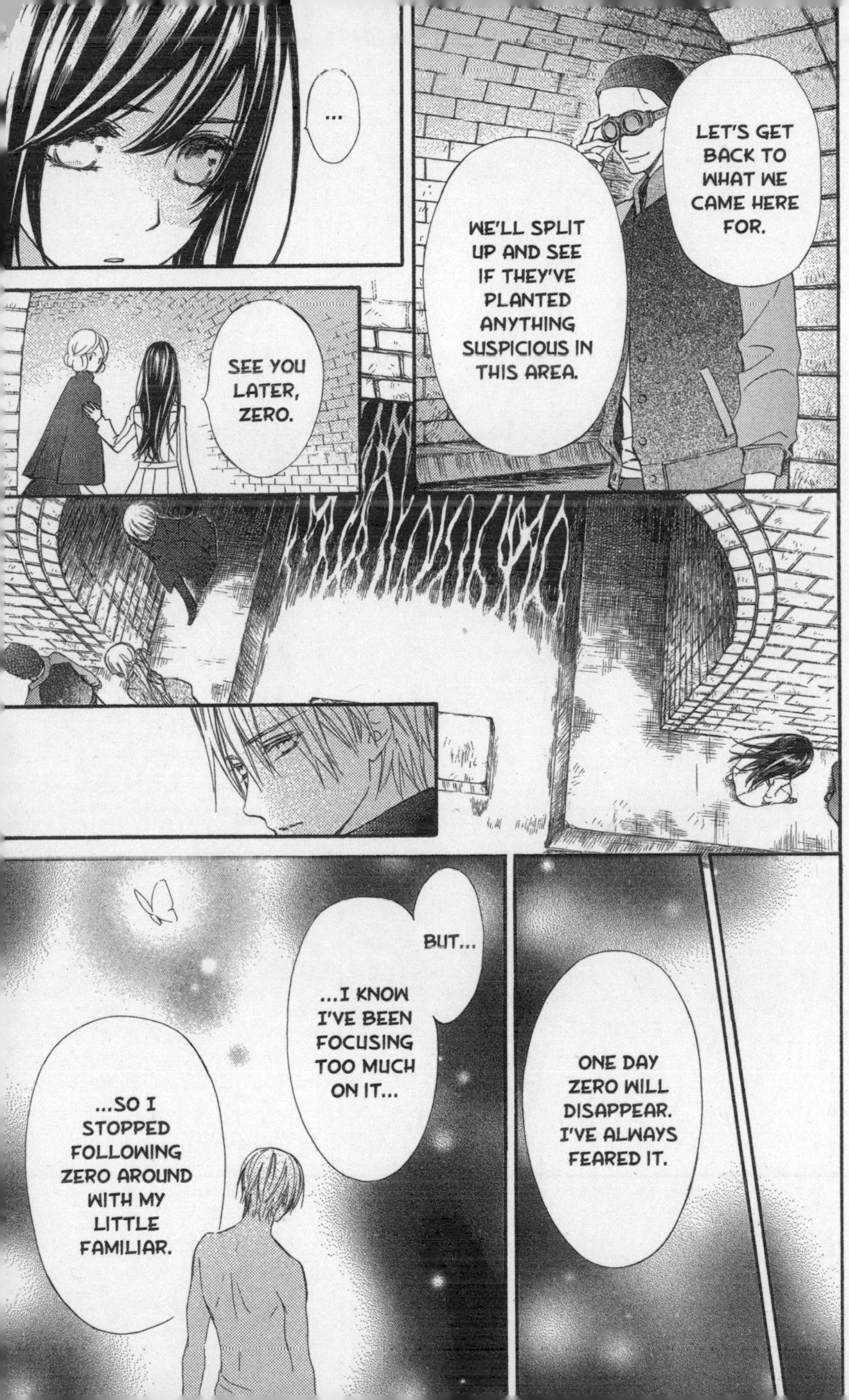
LET'S GET BACK TO WHAT WE CAME HERE FOR.
WE'LL SPLIT UP AND SEE IF THEY'VE PLANTED ANYTHING SUSPICIOUS IN THIS AREA.
...
SEE YOU LATER, ZERO.
ONE DAY ZERO WILL DISAPPEAR. I'VE ALWAYS FEARED IT.
BUT...
...I KNOW I'VE BEEN FOCUSING TOO MUCH ON IT...
...SO I STOPPED FOLLOWING ZERO AROUND WITH MY LITTLE FAMILIAR.

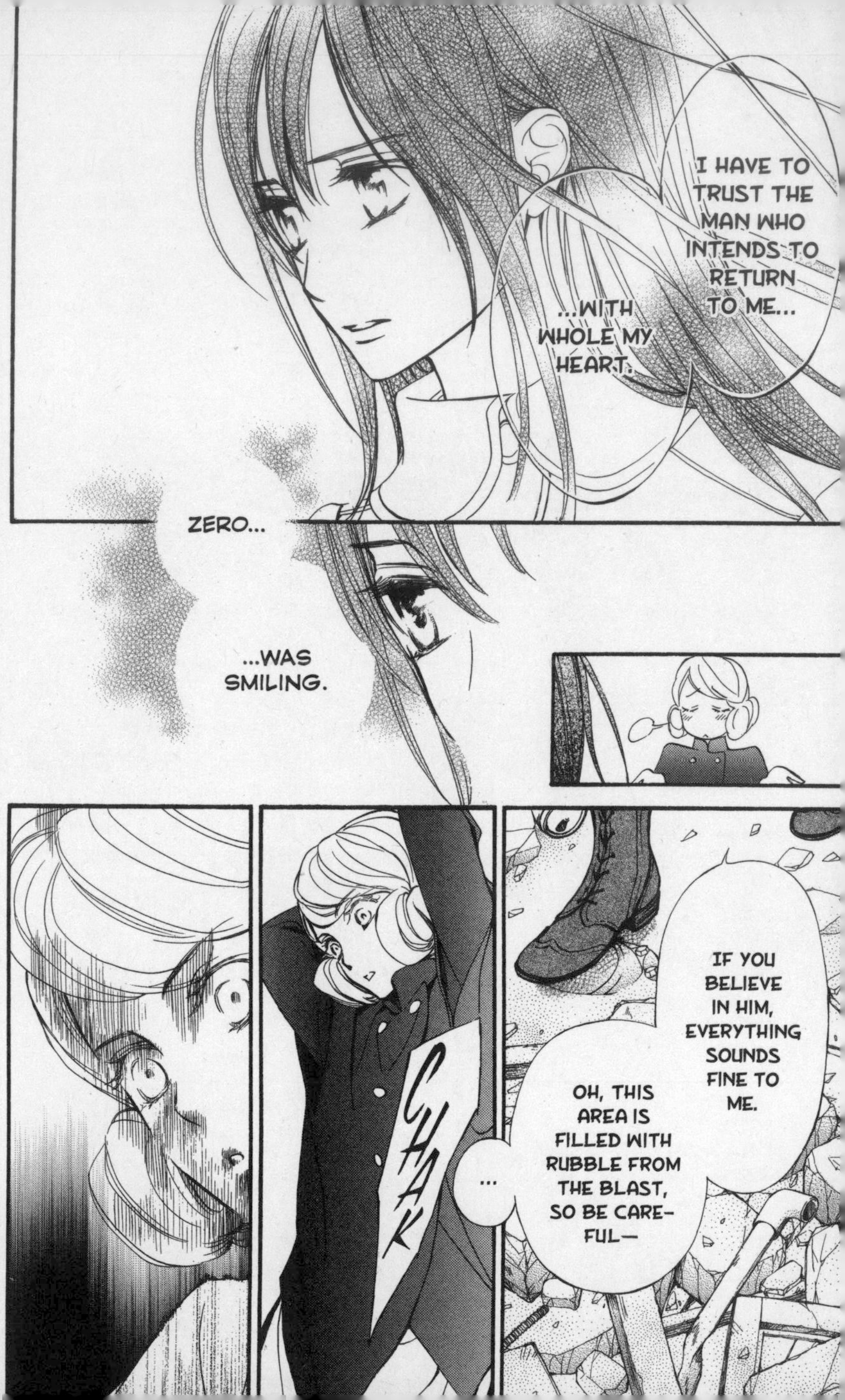
I HAVE TO TRUST THE MAN WHO INTENDS TO RETURN TO ME...
...WITH WHOLE MY HEART.
ZERO...
...WAS SMILING.
IF YOU BELIEVE IN HIM, EVERYTHING SOUNDS FINE TO ME.
OH, THIS AREA IS FILLED WITH RUBBLE FROM THE BLAST, SO BE CARE-FUL—
...
CHAK

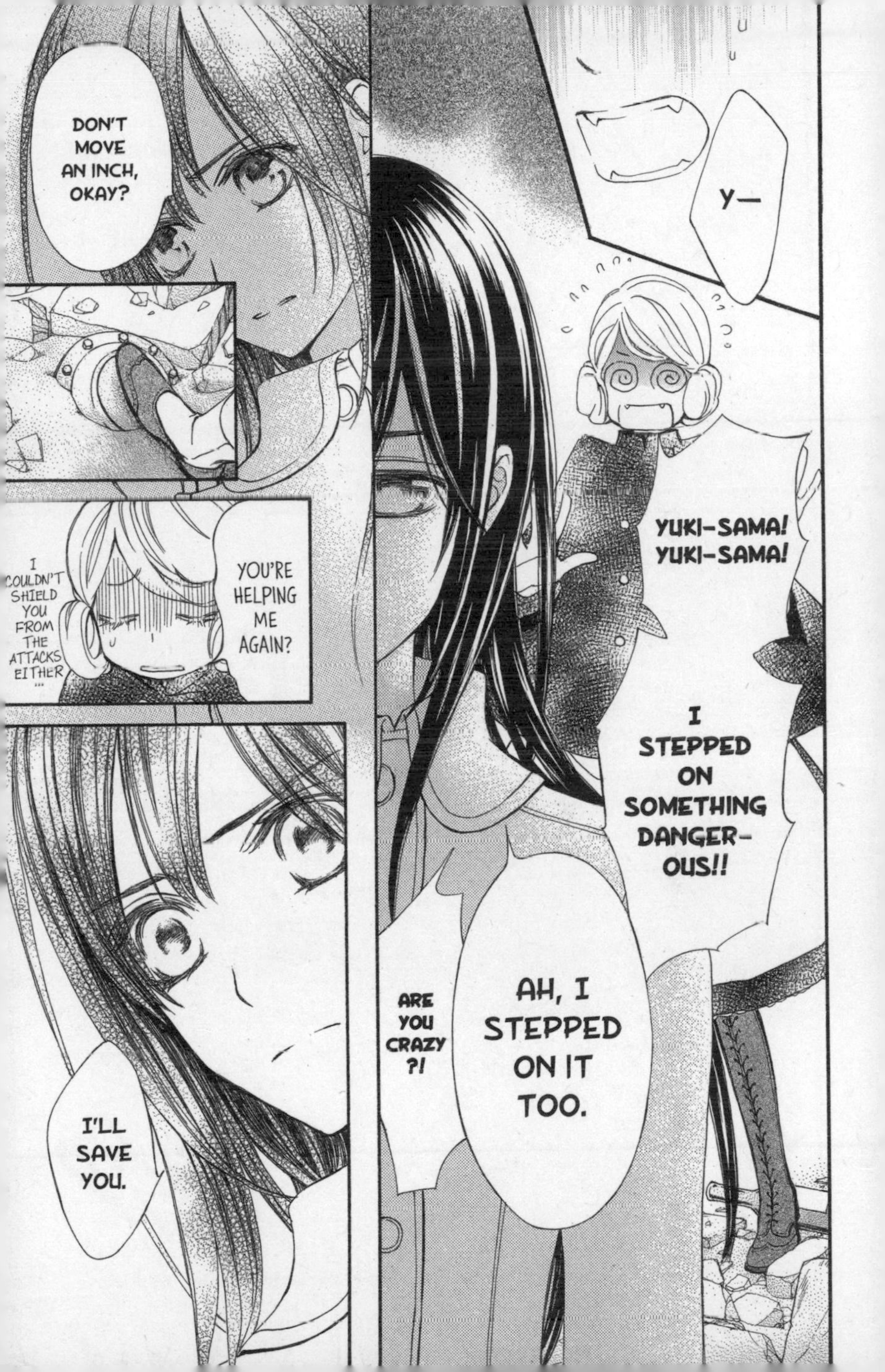
Y—
YUKI-SAMA! YUKI-SAMA!
I STEPPED ON SOMETHING DANGER-OUS!!
AH, I STEPPED ON IT TOO.
ARE YOU CRAZY?!
DON'T MOVE AN INCH, OKAY?
YOU'RE HELPING ME AGAIN?
I COULDN'T SHIELD YOU FROM THE ATTACKS EITHER...
I'LL SAVE YOU.

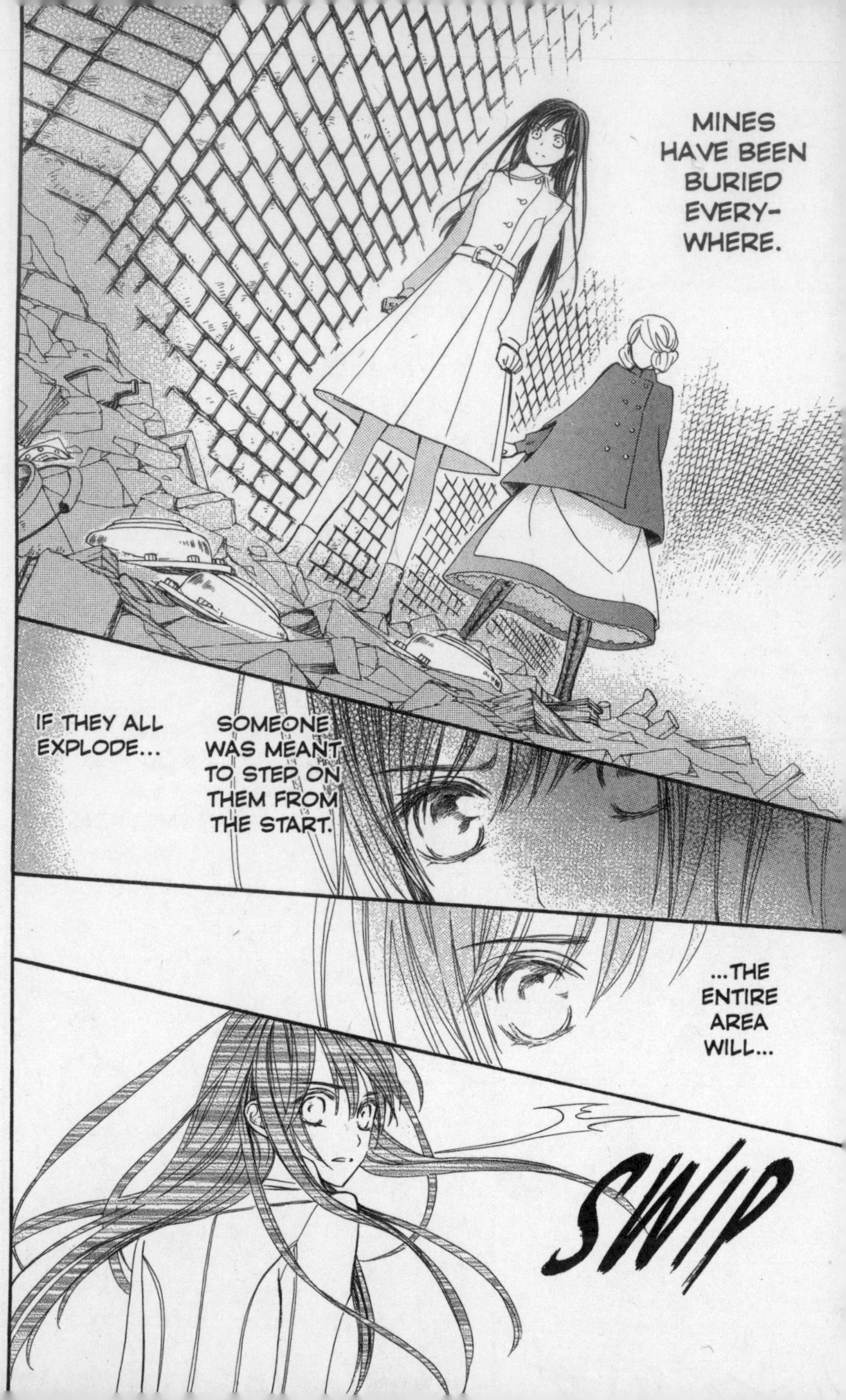
MINES HAVE BEEN BURIED EVERY-WHERE.
SOMEONE WAS MEANT TO STEP ON THEM FROM THE START.
IF THEY ALL EXPLODE...
...THE ENTIRE AREA WILL...
SWIP

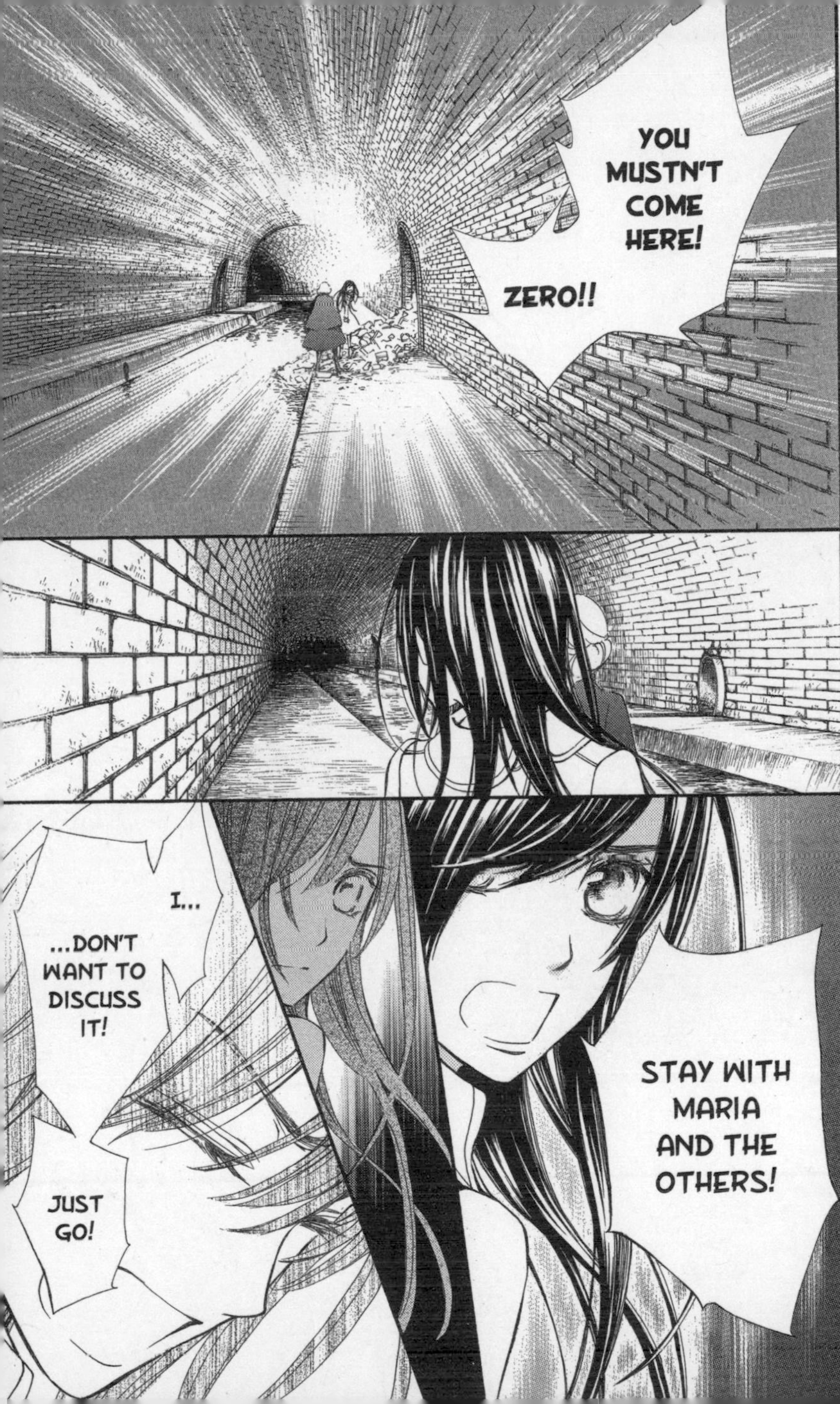
YOU MUSTN'T COME HERE!
ZERO!!
STAY WITH MARIA AND THE OTHERS!
I...
...DON'T WANT TO DISCUSS IT!
JUST GO!

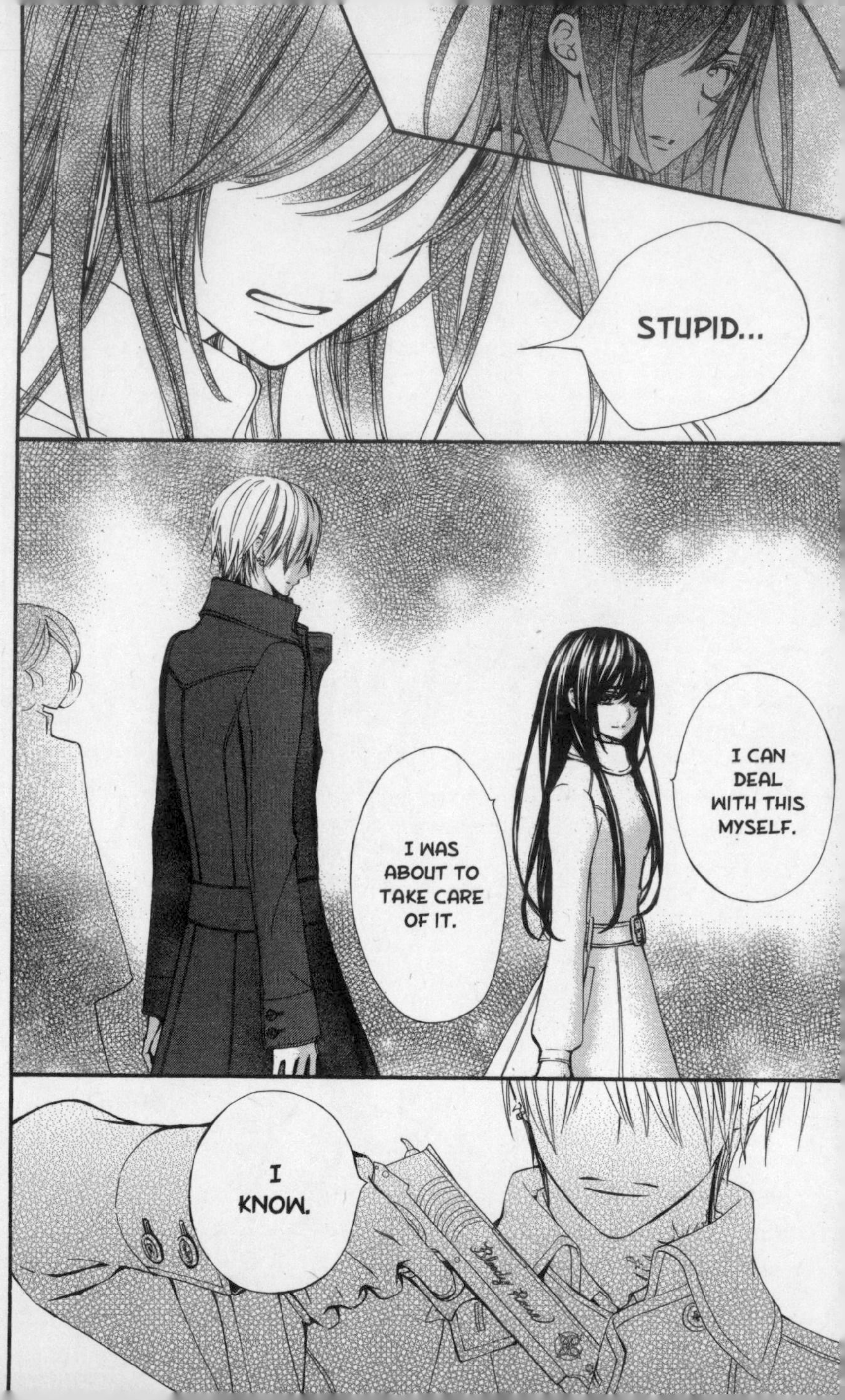
STUPID...
I CAN DEAL WITH THIS MYSELF.
I WAS ABOUT TO TAKE CARE OF IT.
I KNOW.
Bloody Rose

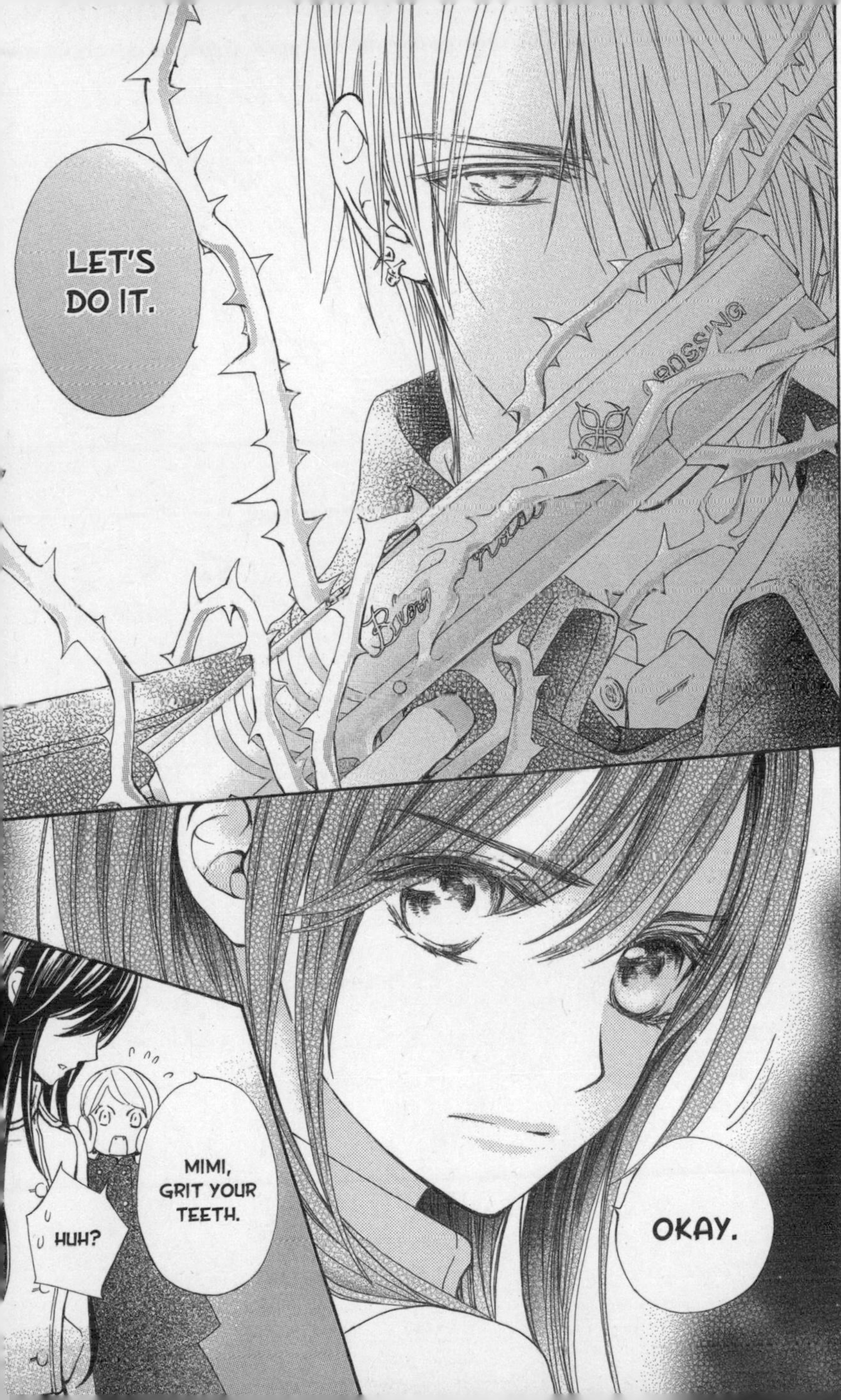
LET'S DO IT.
OKAY.
MIMI, GRIT YOUR TEETH.
HUH?

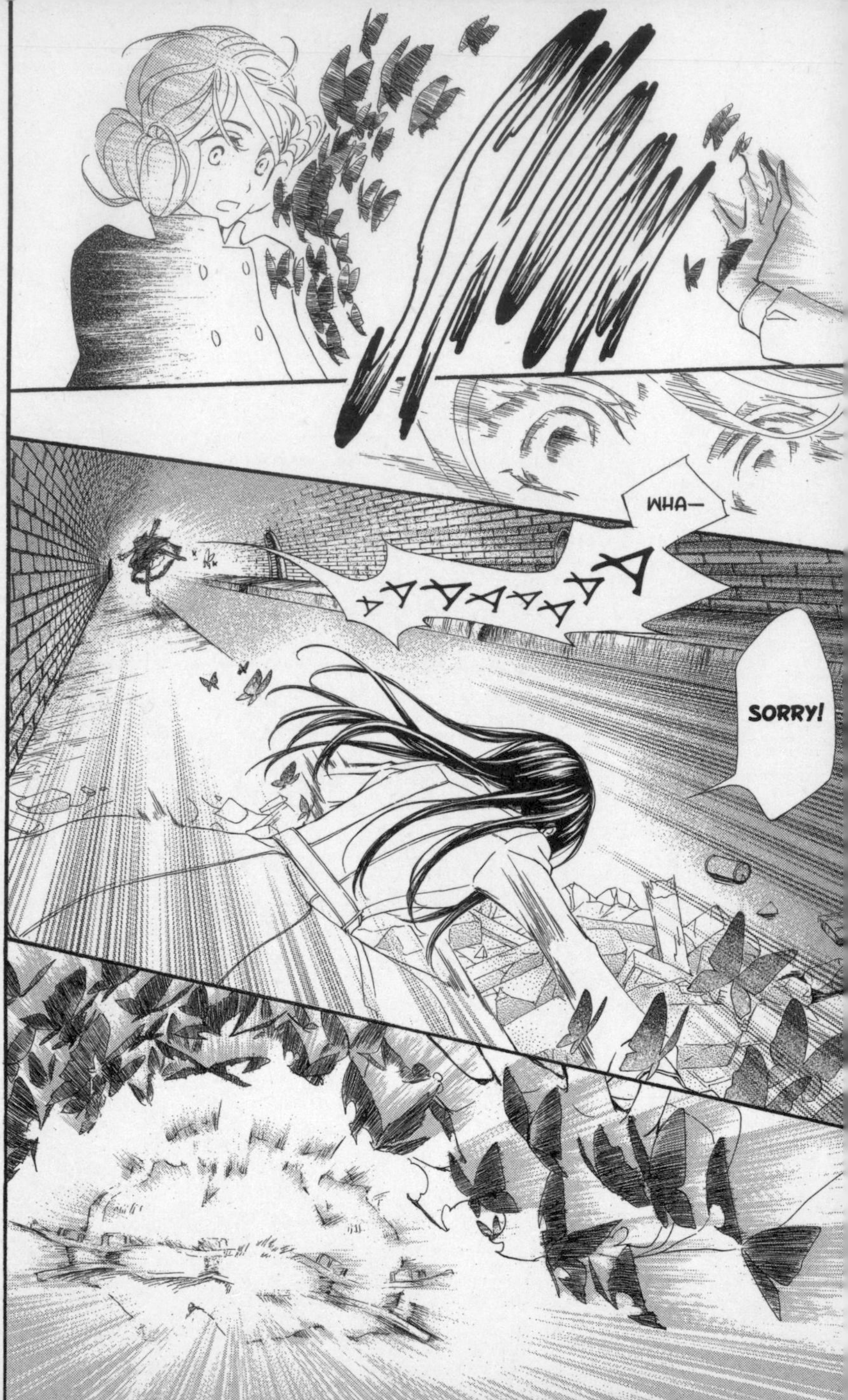
WHA—
AAAAAAAAA
SORRY!

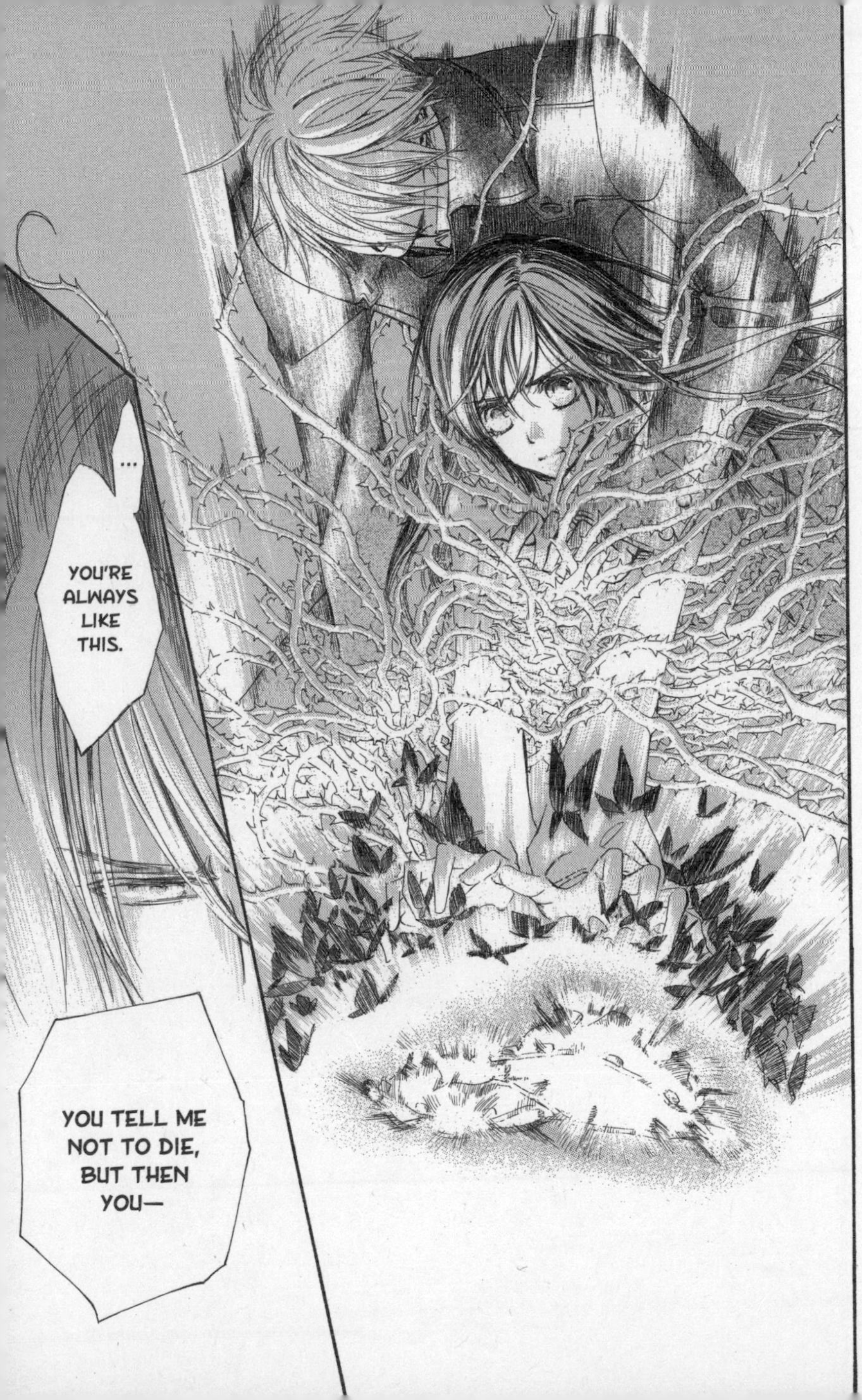
...
YOU'RE ALWAYS LIKE THIS.
YOU TELL ME NOT TO DIE, BUT THEN YOU—

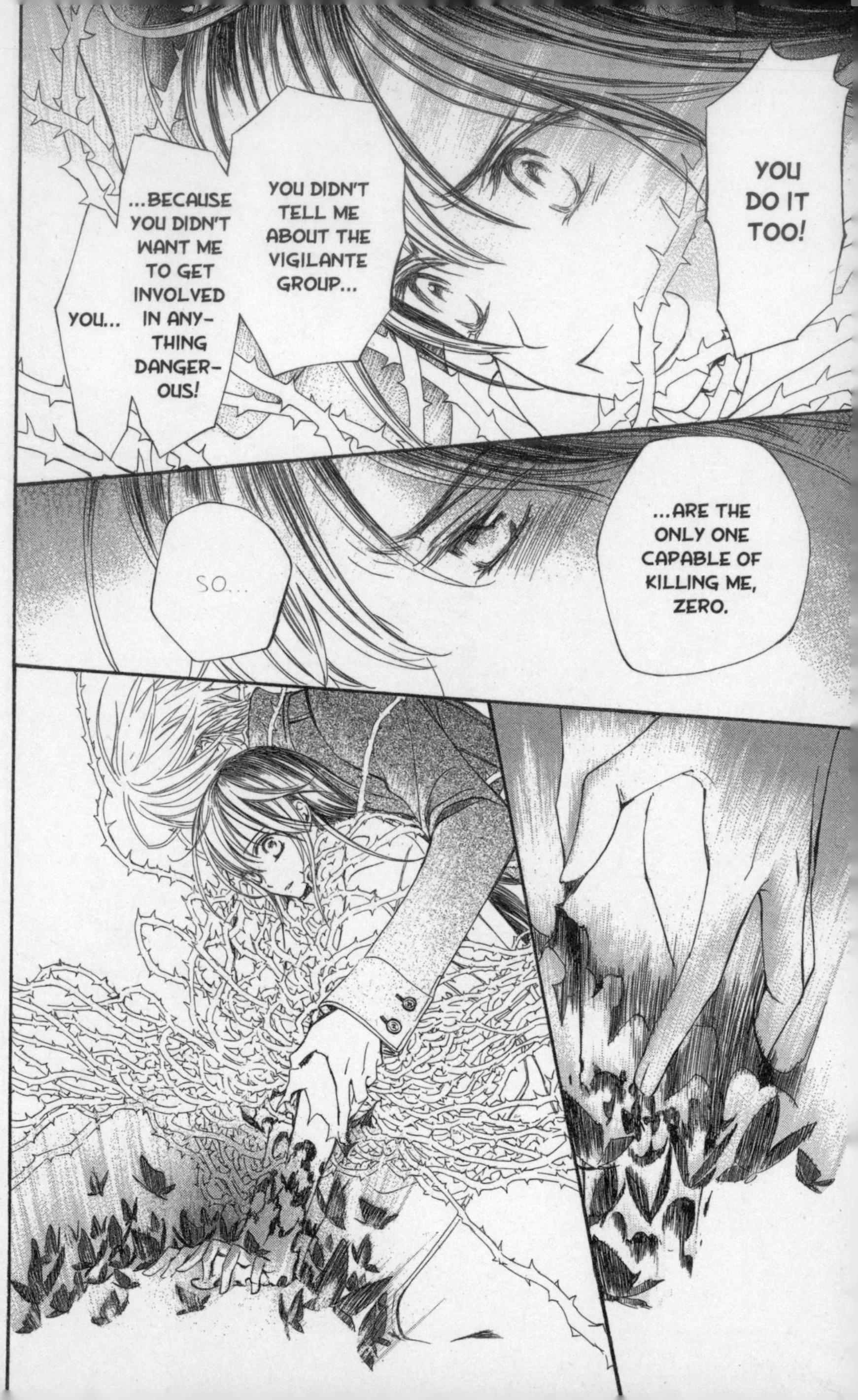
YOU DO IT TOO!
YOU DIDN'T TELL ME ABOUT THE VIGILANTE GROUP...
...BECAUSE YOU DIDN'T WANT ME TO GET INVOLVED IN ANYTHING DANGEROUS!
YOU...
...ARE THE ONLY ONE CAPABLE OF KILLING ME, ZERO.
SO...

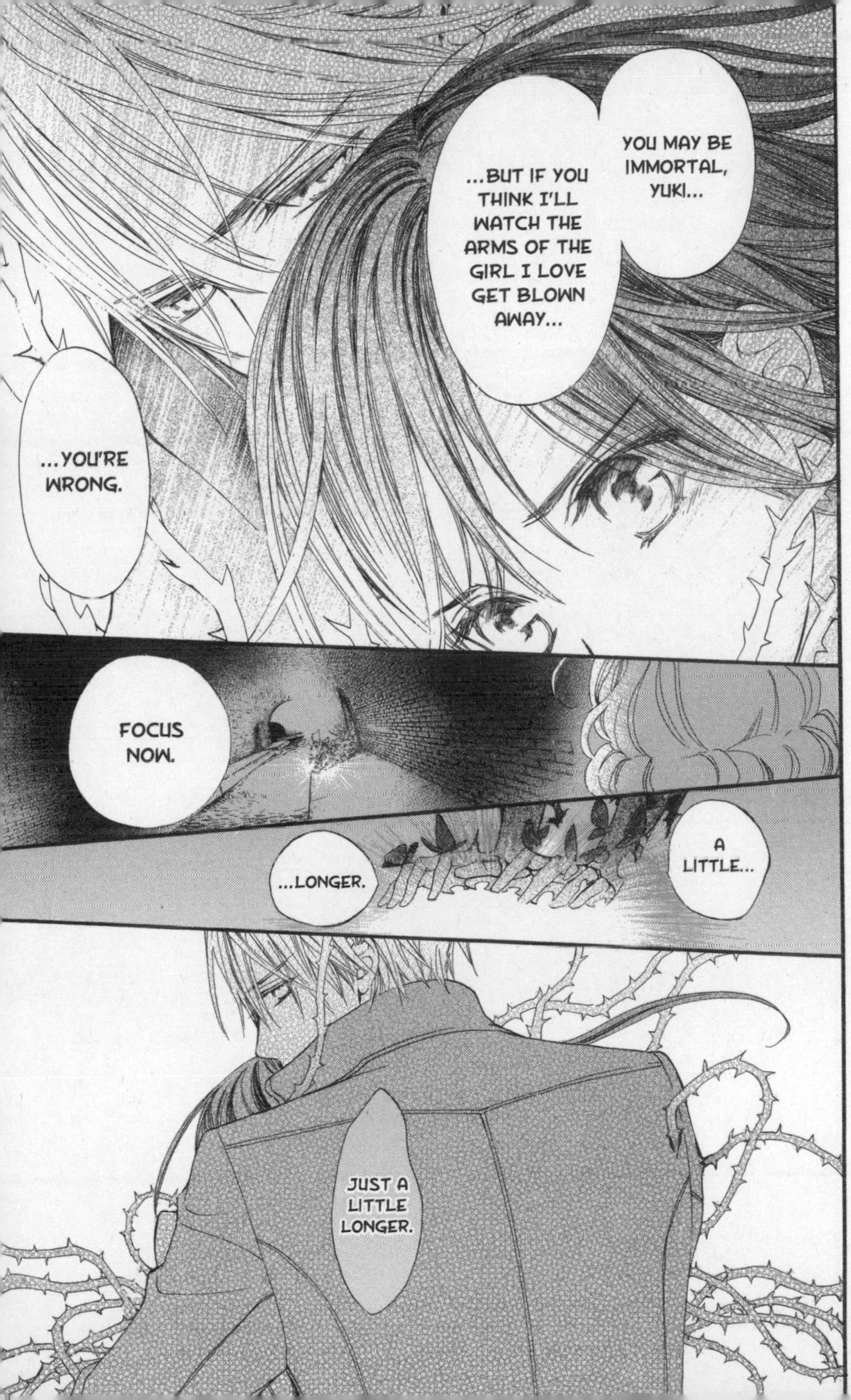
YOU MAY BE IMMORTAL, YUKI...
...BUT IF YOU THINK I'LL WATCH THE ARMS OF THE GIRL I LOVE GET BLOWN AWAY...
...YOU'RE WRONG.
FOCUS NOW.
A LITTLE...
...LONGER.
JUST A LITTLE LONGER.

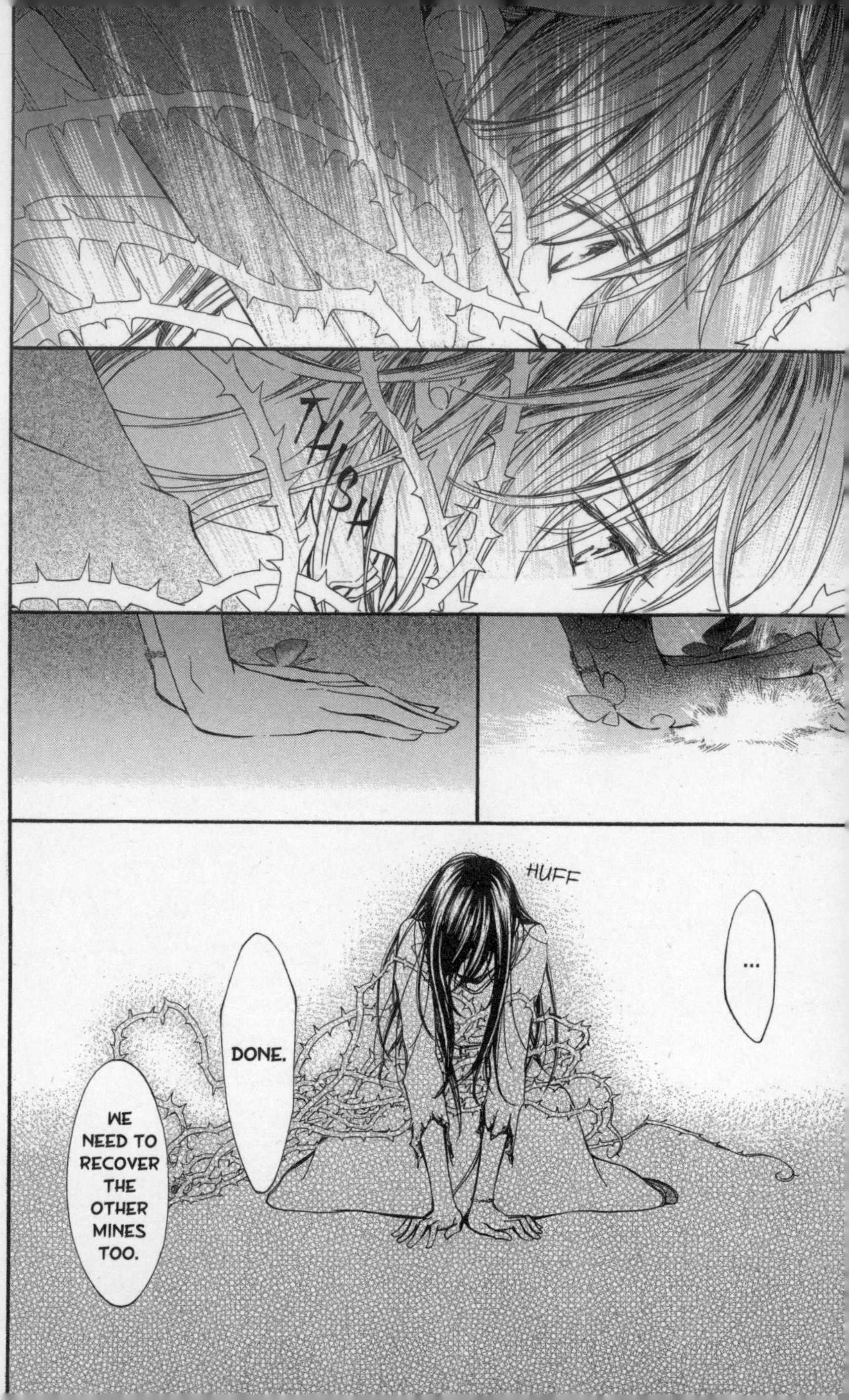
THSH
HUFF
...
DONE.
WE NEED TO RECOVER THE OTHER MINES TOO.

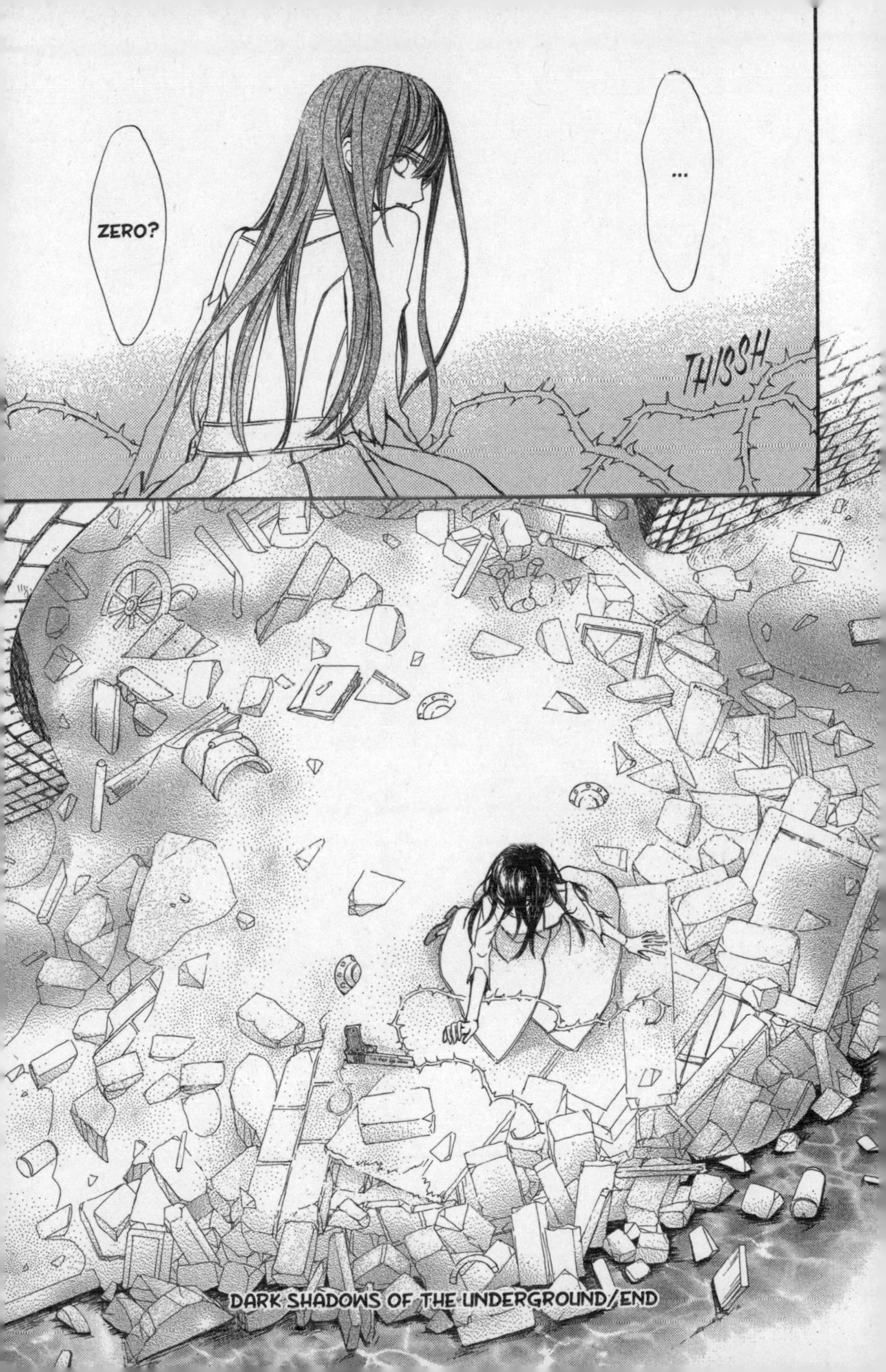
...
ZERO?
THISSH
DARK SHADOWS OF THE UNDERGROUND/END

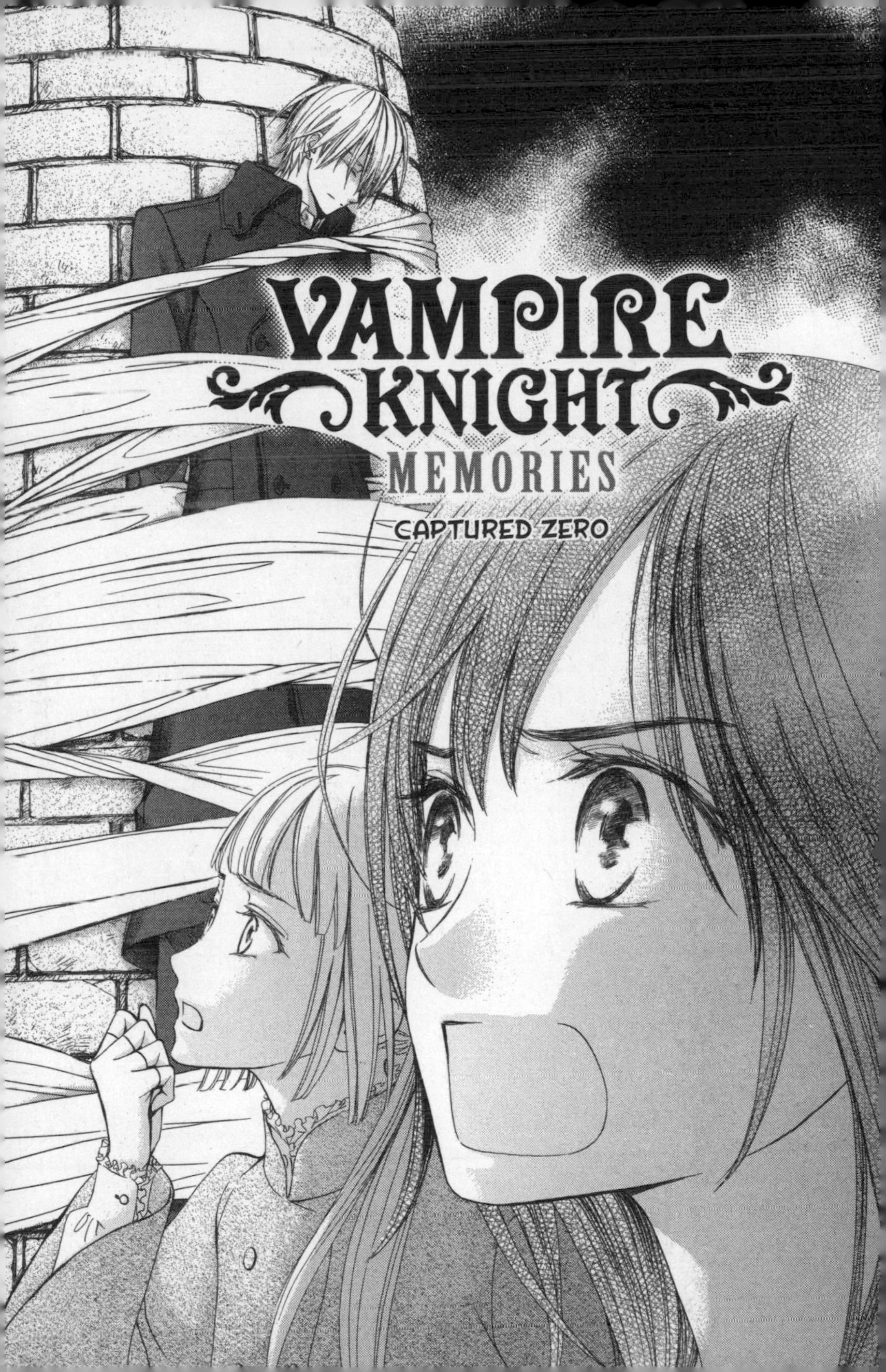
VAMPIRE KNIGHT
MEMORIES
CAPTURED ZERO

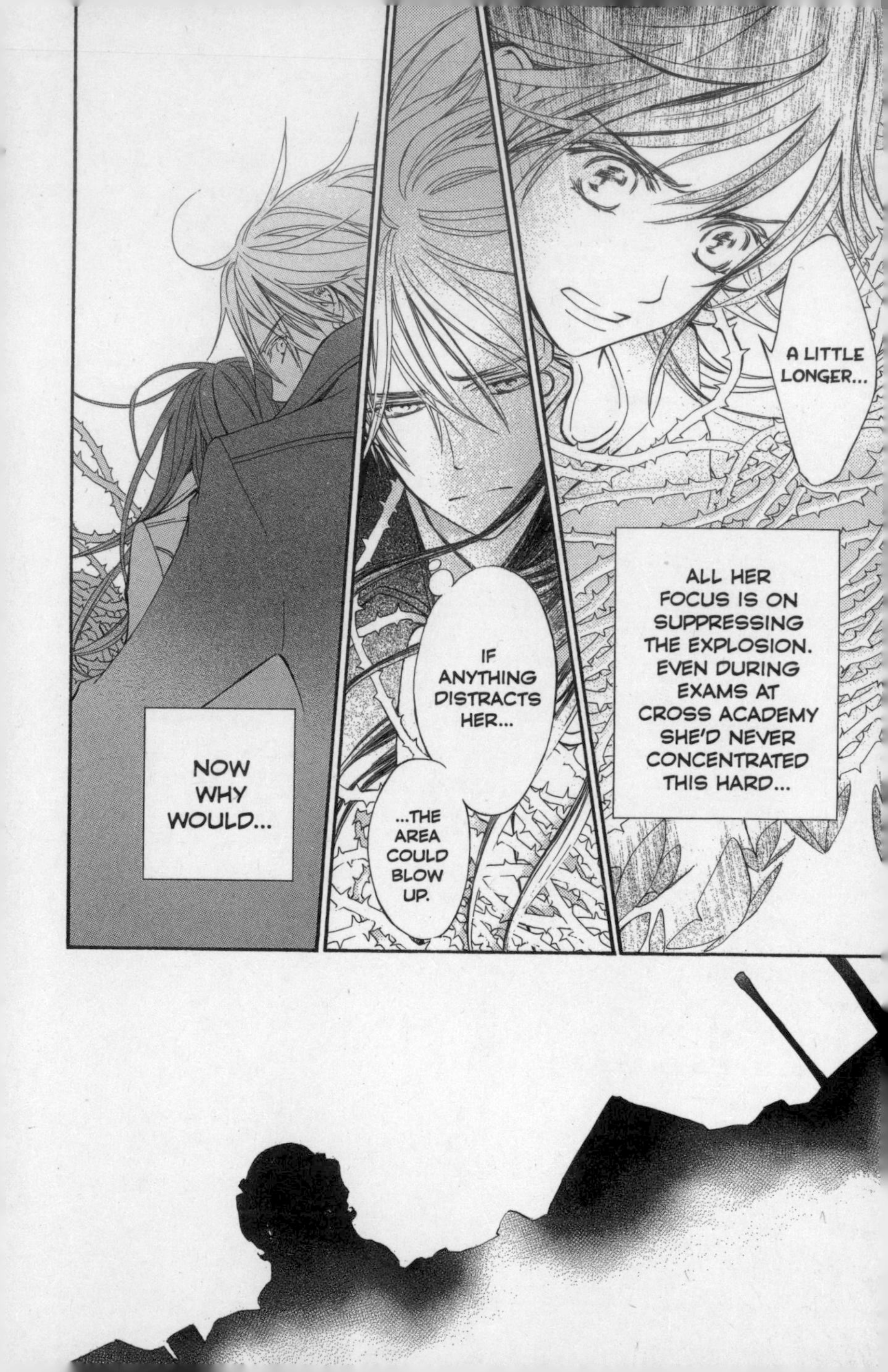
A LITTLE LONGER...
ALL HER FOCUS IS ON SUPPRESSING THE EXPLOSION. EVEN DURING EXAMS AT CROSS ACADEMY SHE'D NEVER CONCENTRATED THIS HARD...
IF ANYTHING DISTRACTS HER...
...THE AREA COULD BLOW UP.
NOW WHY WOULD...

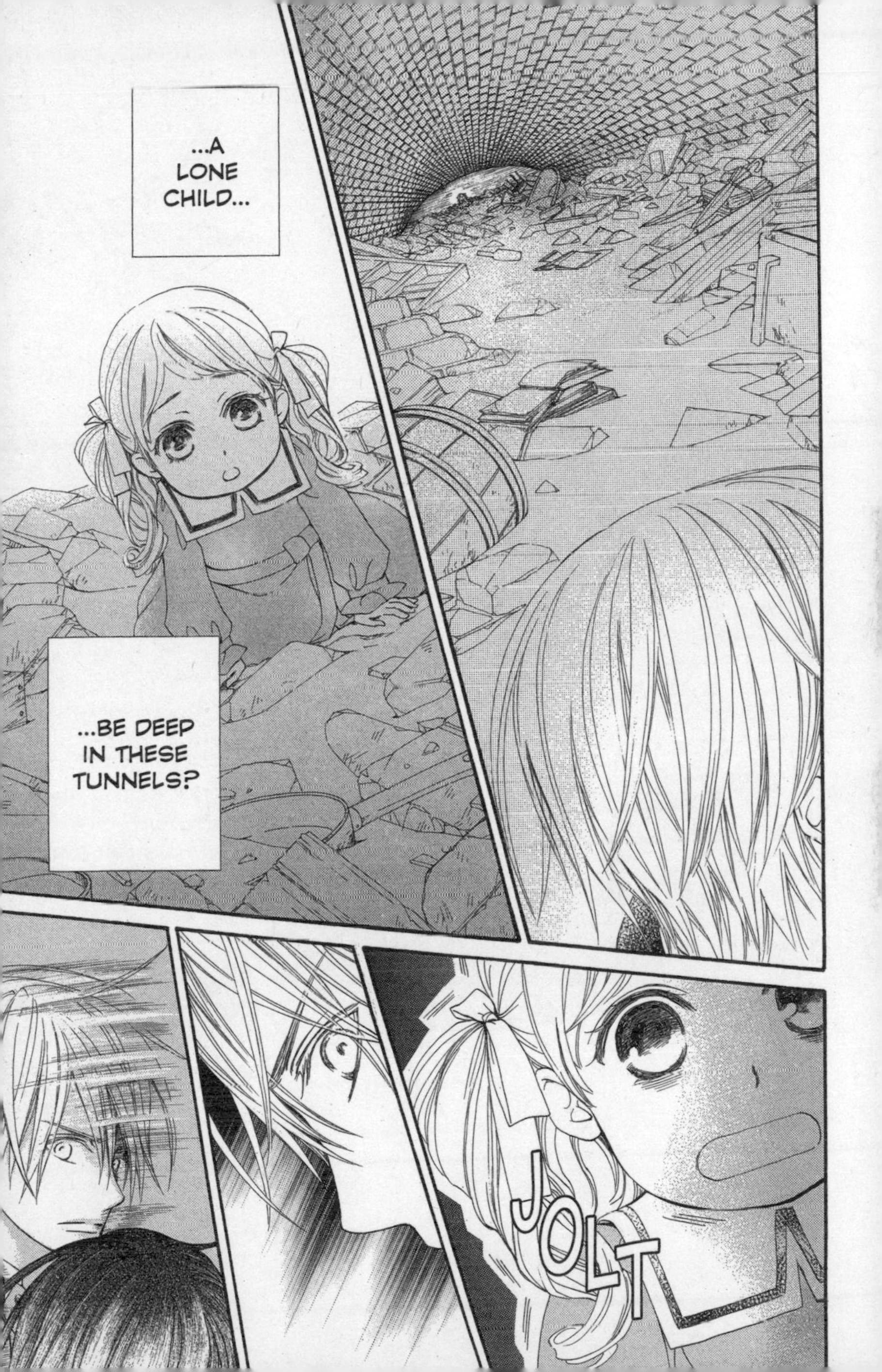
...A LONE CHILD...
...BE DEEP IN THESE TUNNELS?
JOLT

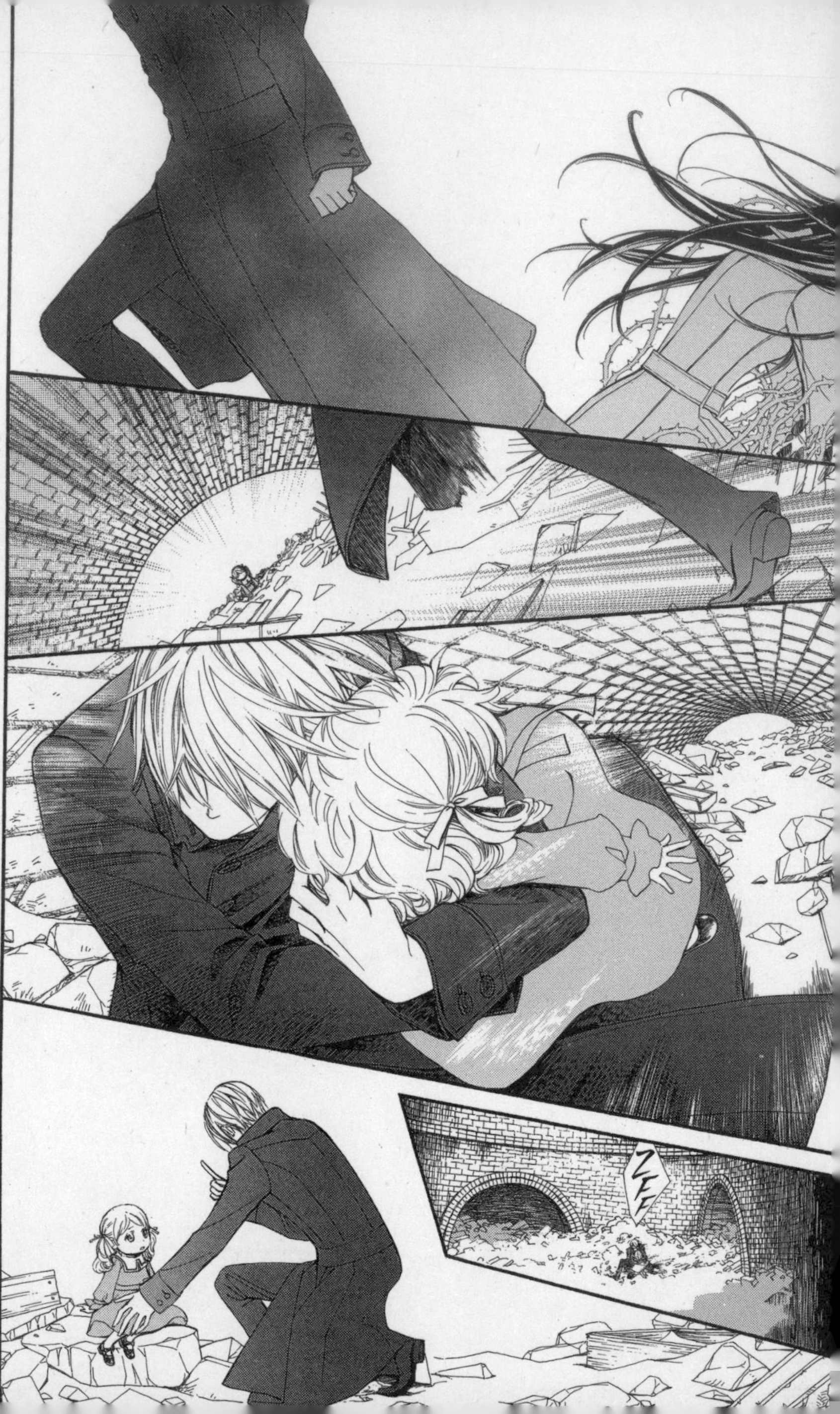
ZFFF

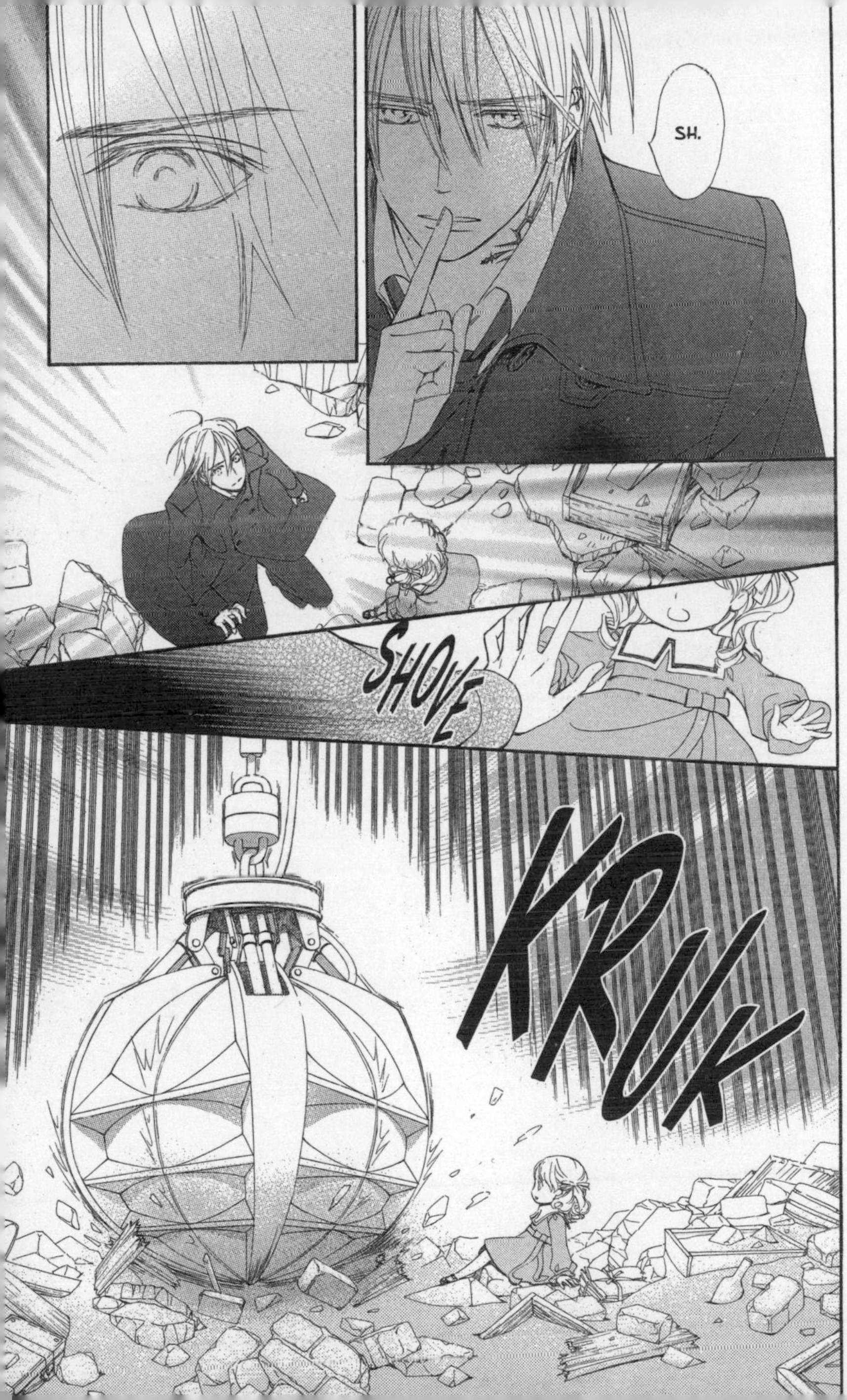
SH.
SHOVE
KRUK

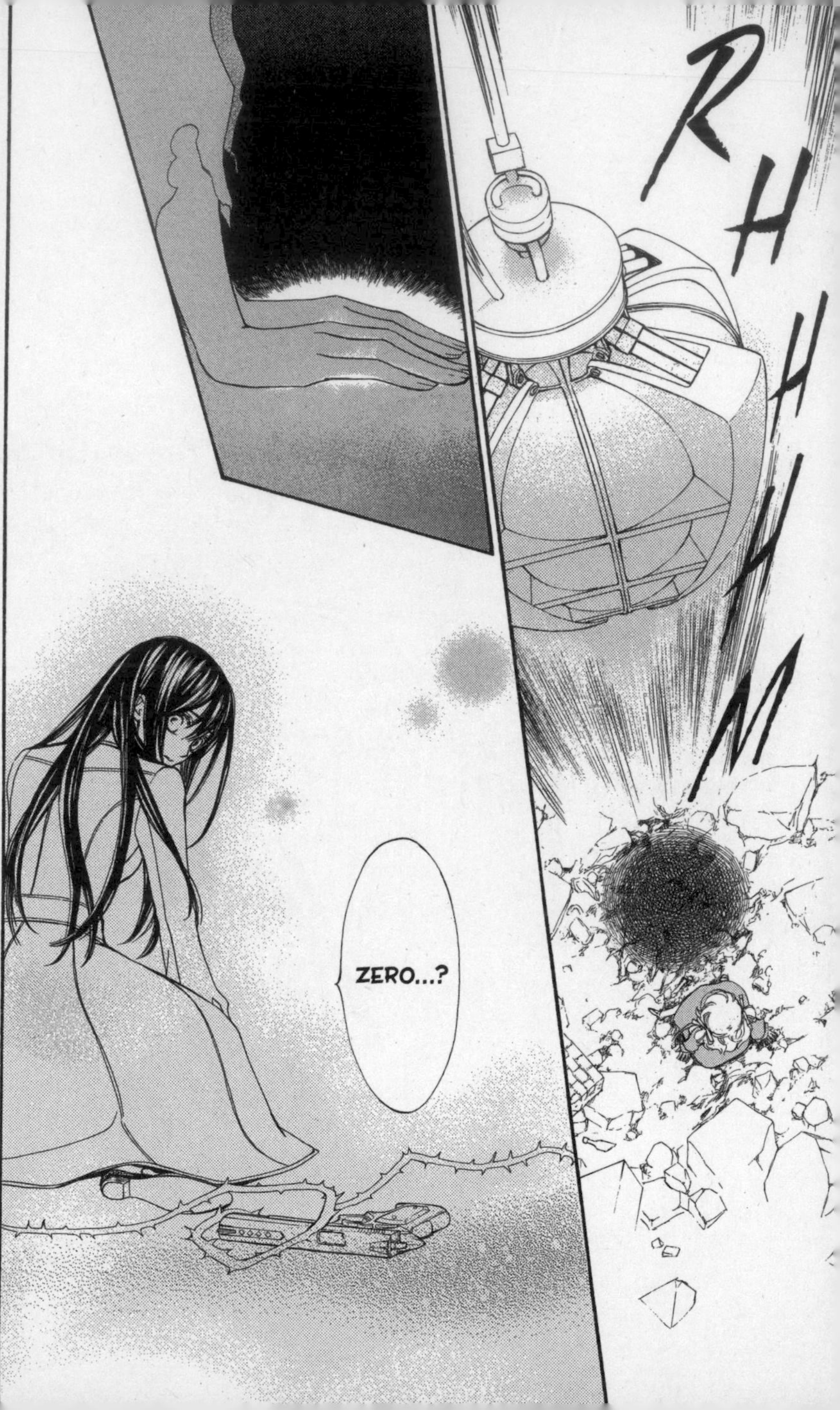
RHHHHM
ZERO...?

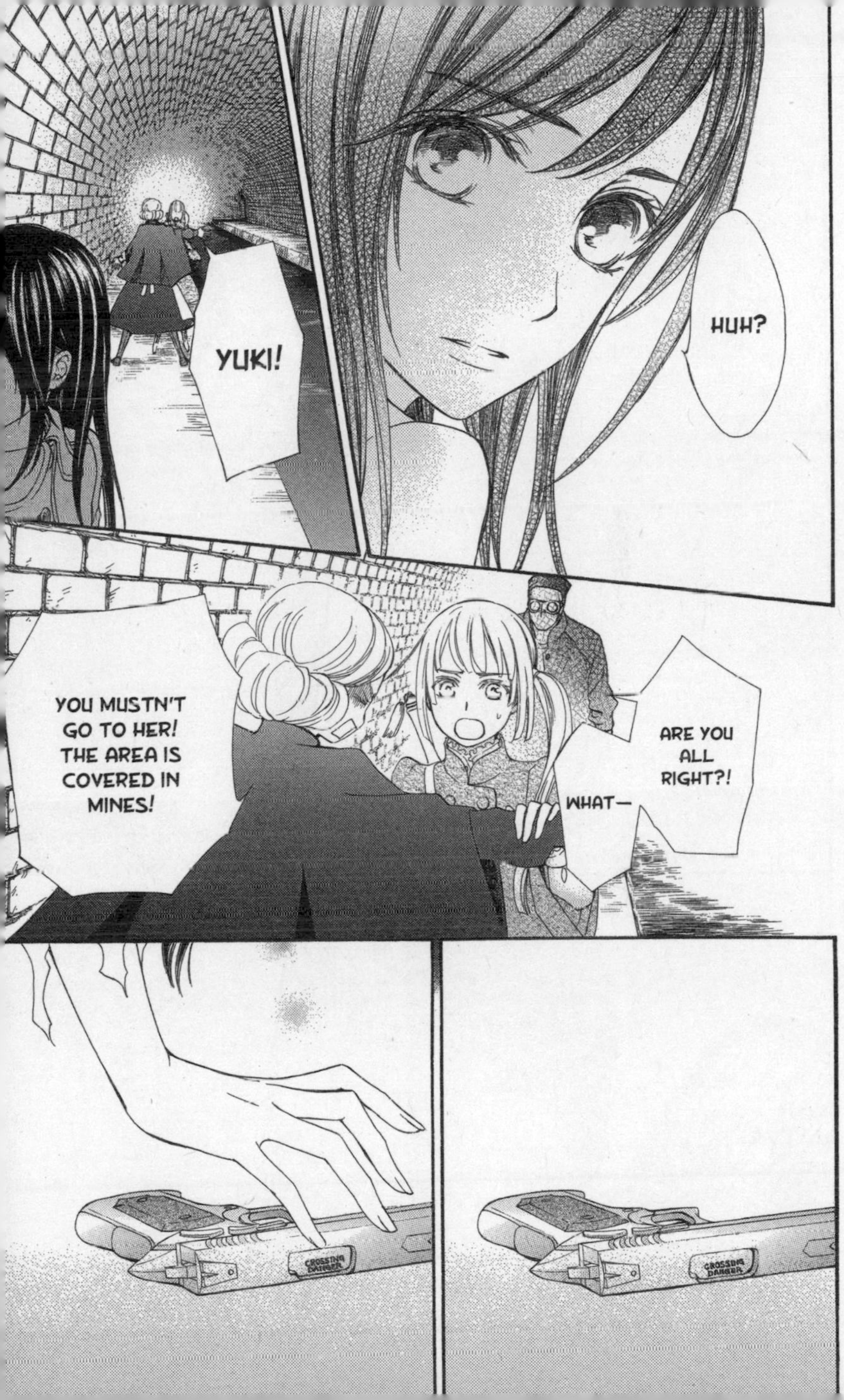
HUH?
YUKI!
ARE YOU ALL RIGHT?!
WHAT—
YOU MUSTN'T GO TO HER! THE AREA IS COVERED IN MINES!
CROSSING DANGER
CROSSING DANGER

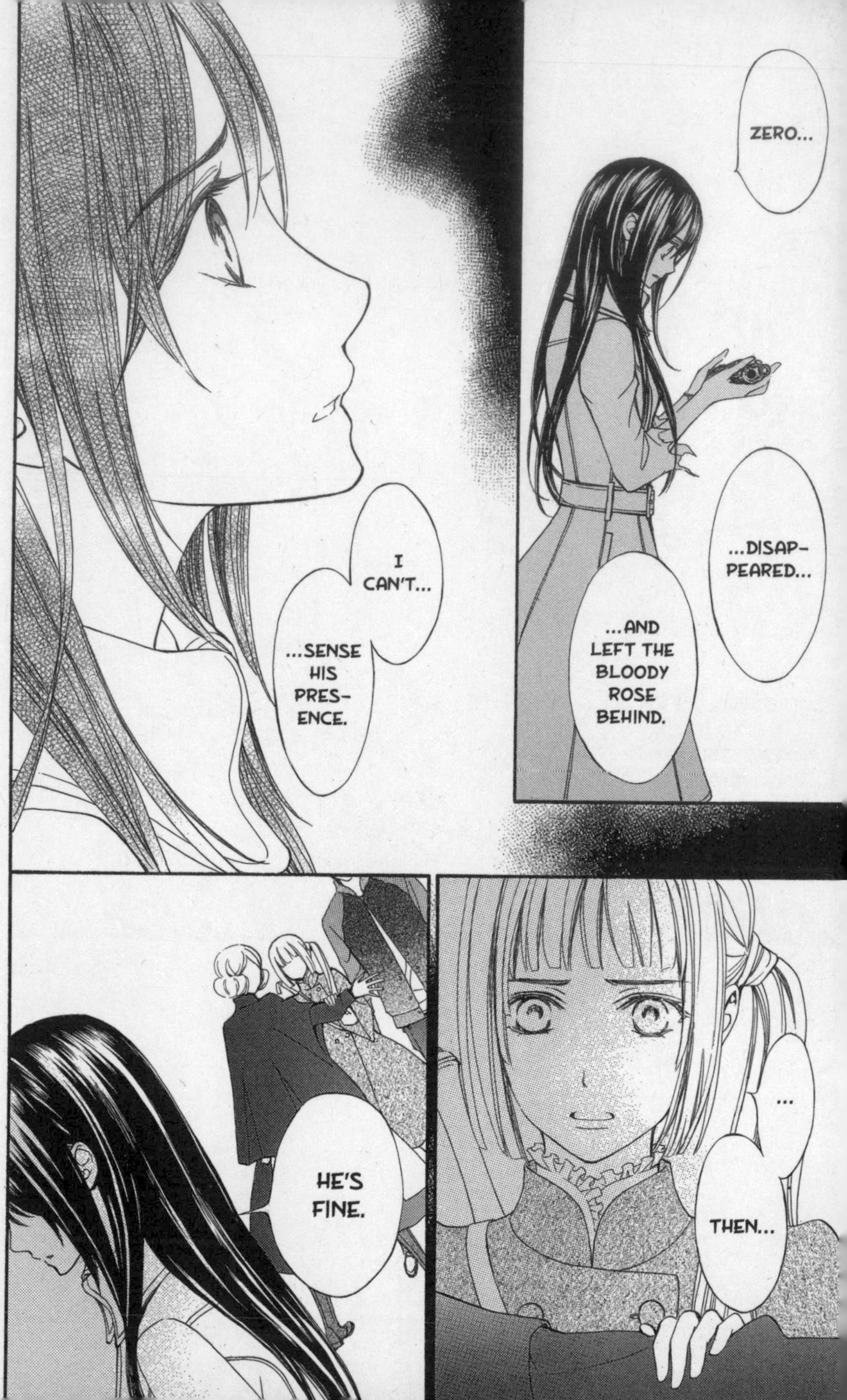
ZERO...
...DISAP-PEARED...
...AND LEFT THE BLOODY ROSE BEHIND.
I CAN'T...
...SENSE HIS PRES-ENCE.
...
THEN...
HE'S FINE.

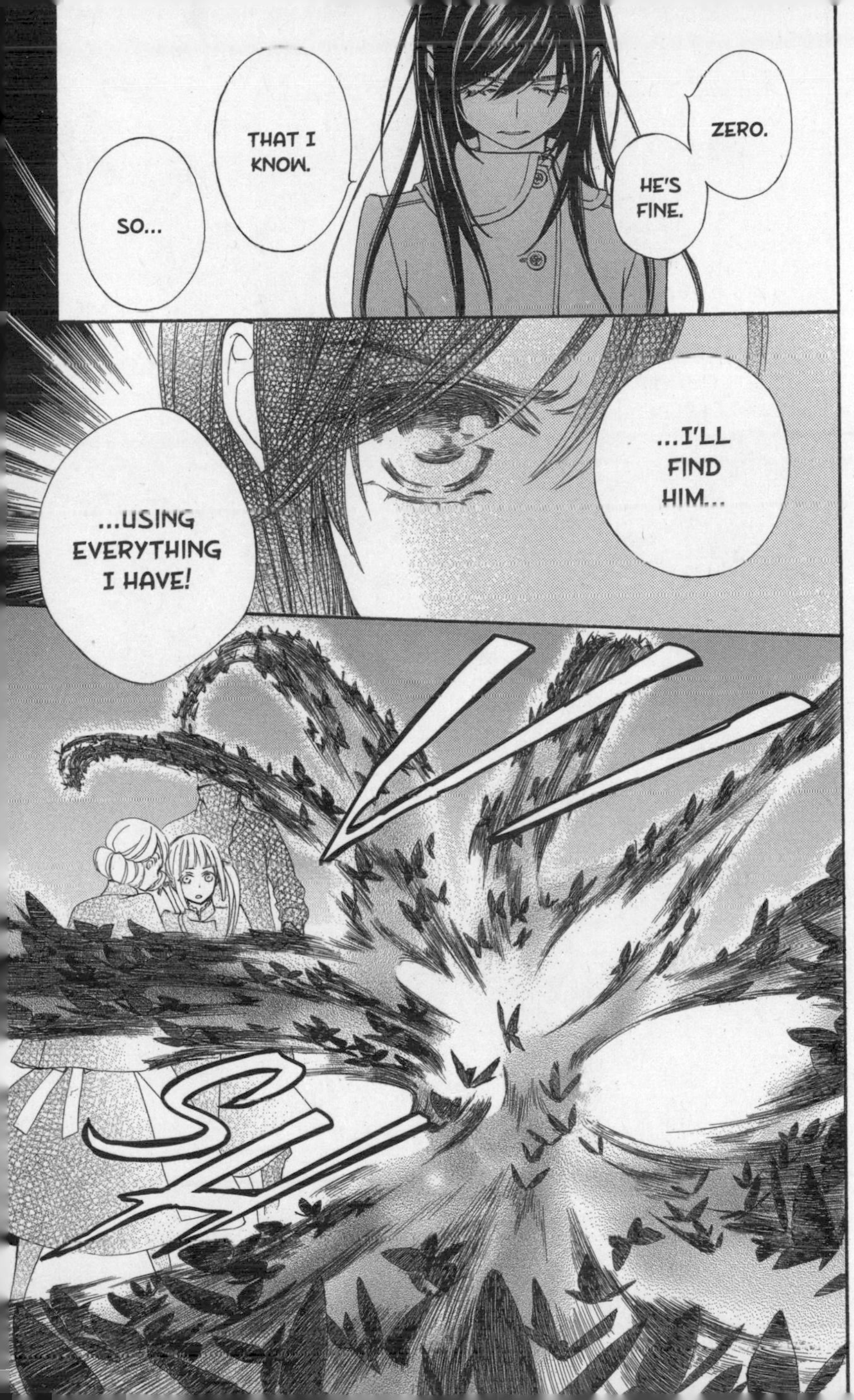
ZERO.
HE'S FINE.
THAT I KNOW.
SO...
...I'LL FIND HIM...
...USING EVERYTHING I HAVE!
SH

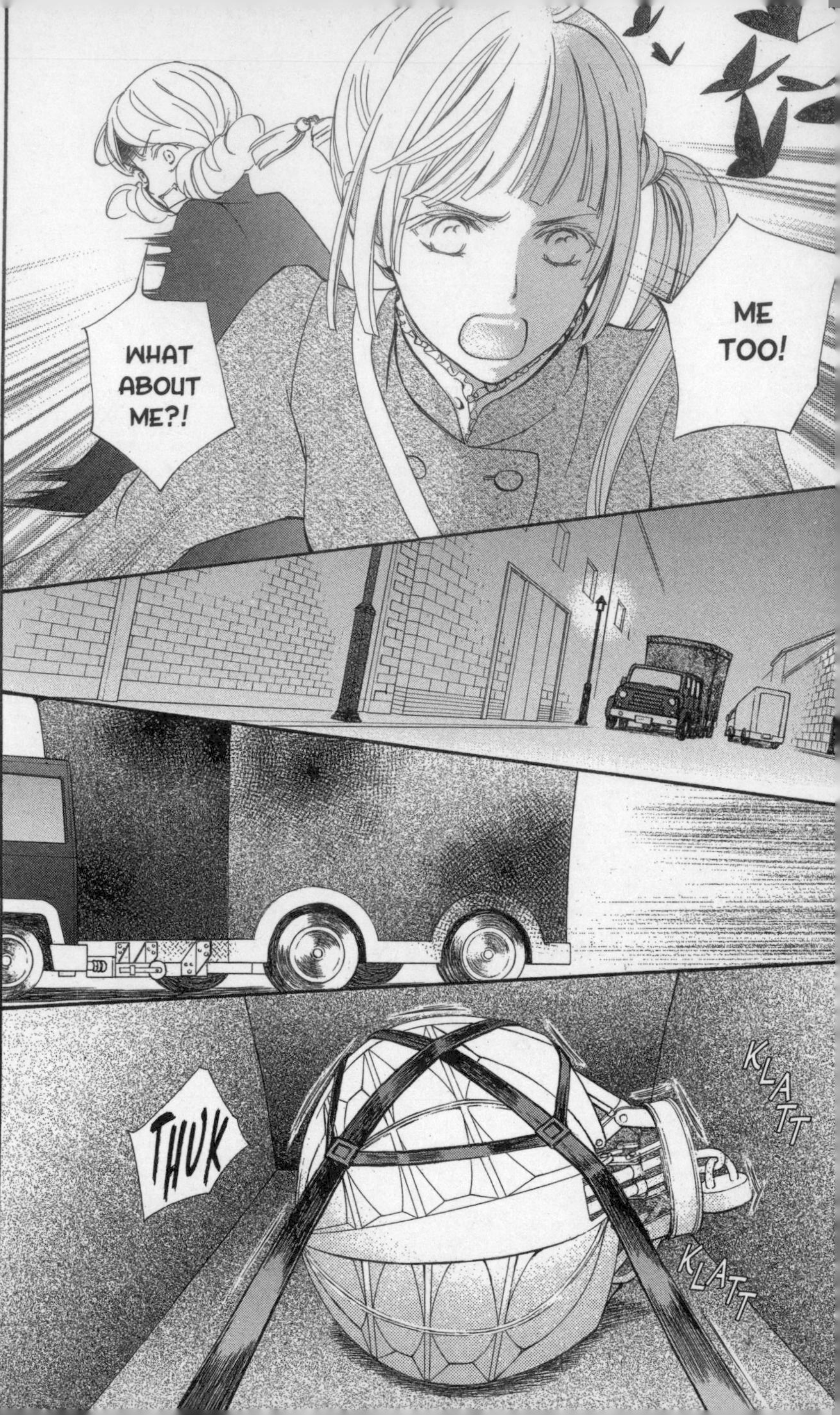
ME TOO!
WHAT ABOUT ME?!
KLATT
THUK
KLATT

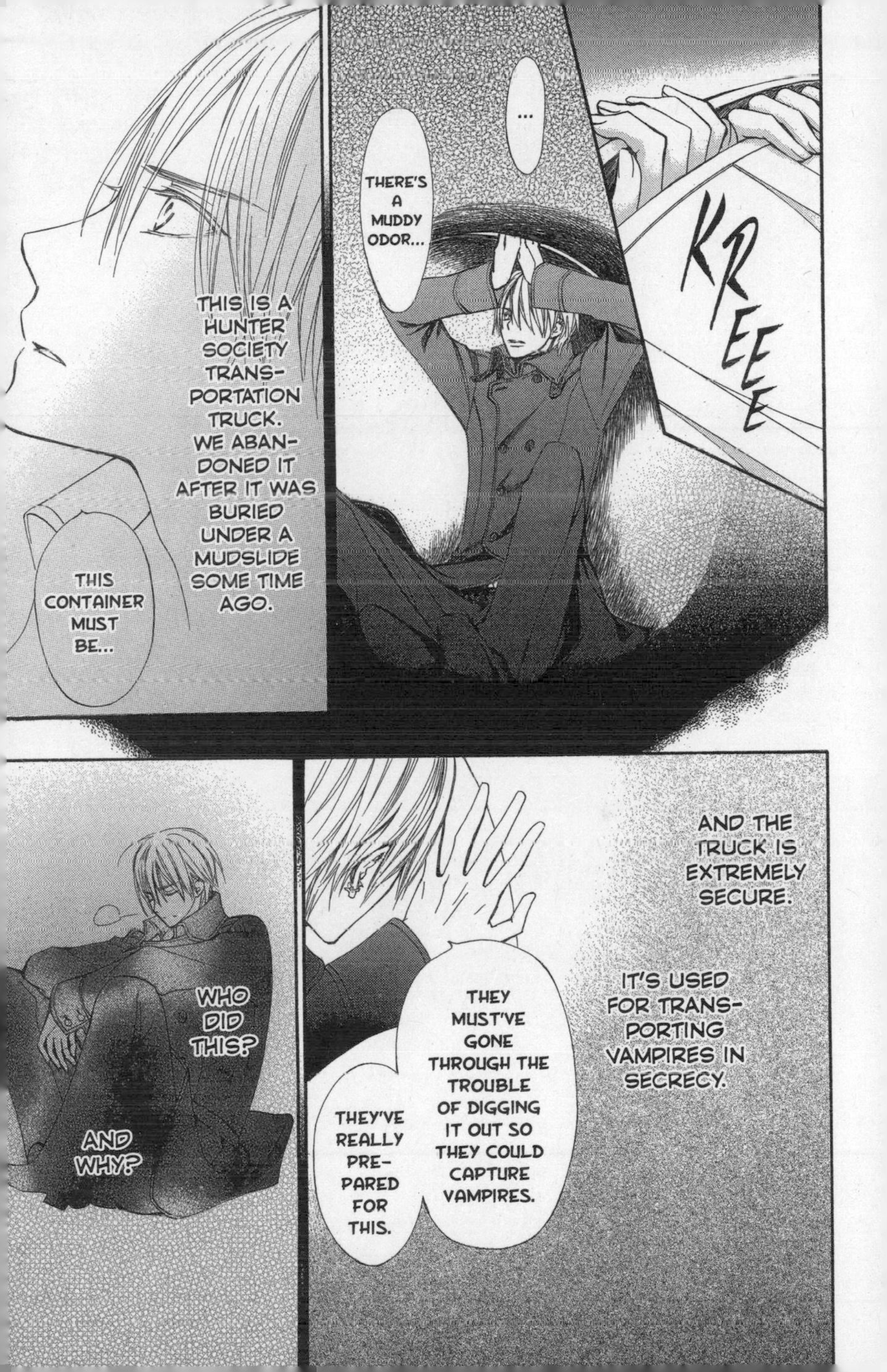
KREEE
...
THERE'S A MUDDY ODOR...
THIS CONTAINER MUST BE...
THIS IS A HUNTER SOCIETY TRANSPORTATION TRUCK. WE ABANDONED IT AFTER IT WAS BURIED UNDER A MUDSLIDE SOME TIME AGO.
AND THE TRUCK IS EXTREMELY SECURE.
IT'S USED FOR TRANSPORTING VAMPIRES IN SECRECY.
THEY MUST'VE GONE THROUGH THE TROUBLE OF DIGGING IT OUT SO THEY COULD CAPTURE VAMPIRES.
THEY'VE REALLY PREPARED FOR THIS.
WHO DID THIS?
AND WHY?

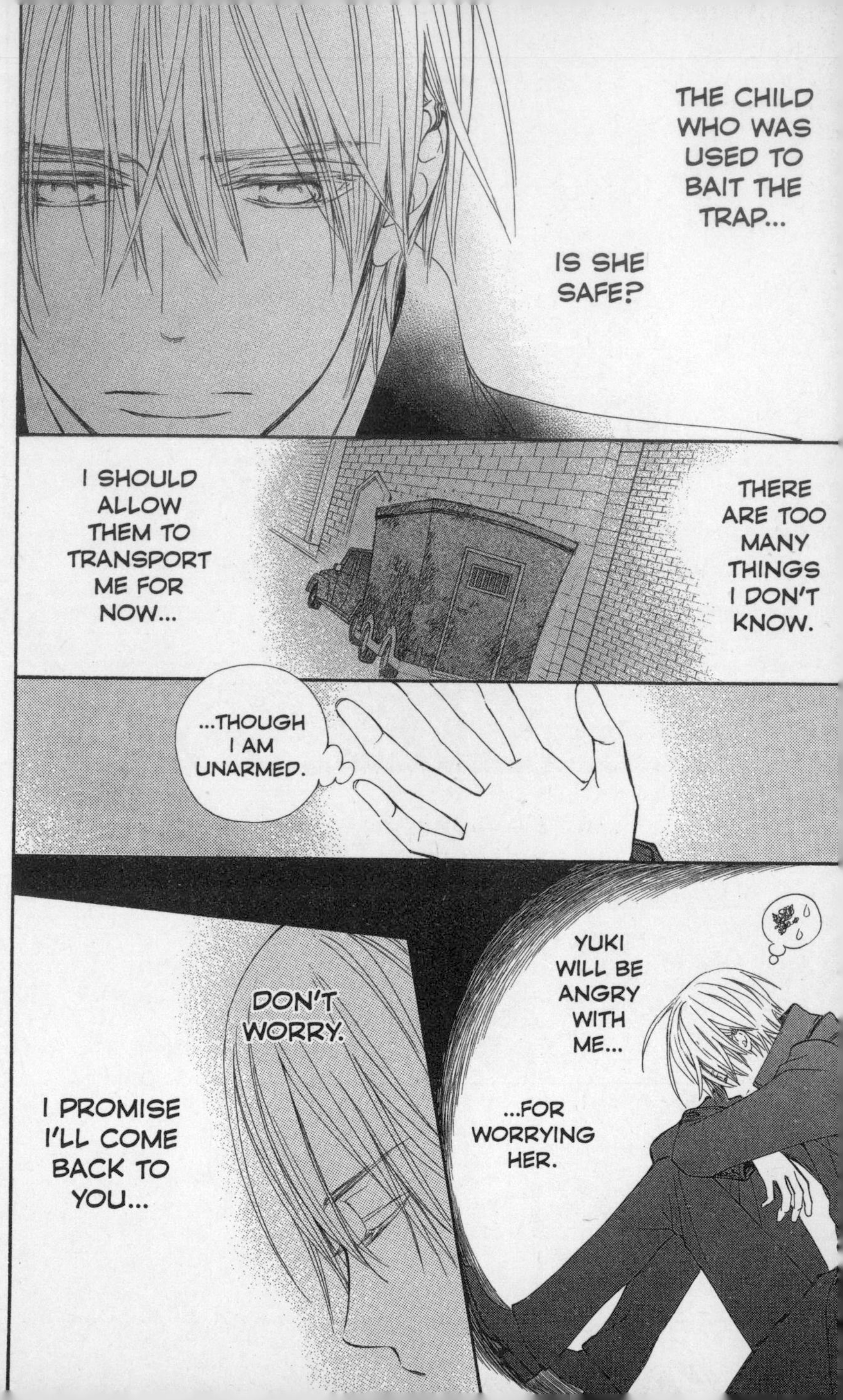
THE CHILD WHO WAS USED TO BAIT THE TRAP...
IS SHE SAFE?
THERE ARE TOO MANY THINGS I DON'T KNOW.
I SHOULD ALLOW THEM TO TRANSPORT ME FOR NOW...
...THOUGH I AM UNARMED.
YUKI WILL BE ANGRY WITH ME...
...FOR WORRYING HER.
DON'T WORRY.
I PROMISE I'LL COME BACK TO YOU...

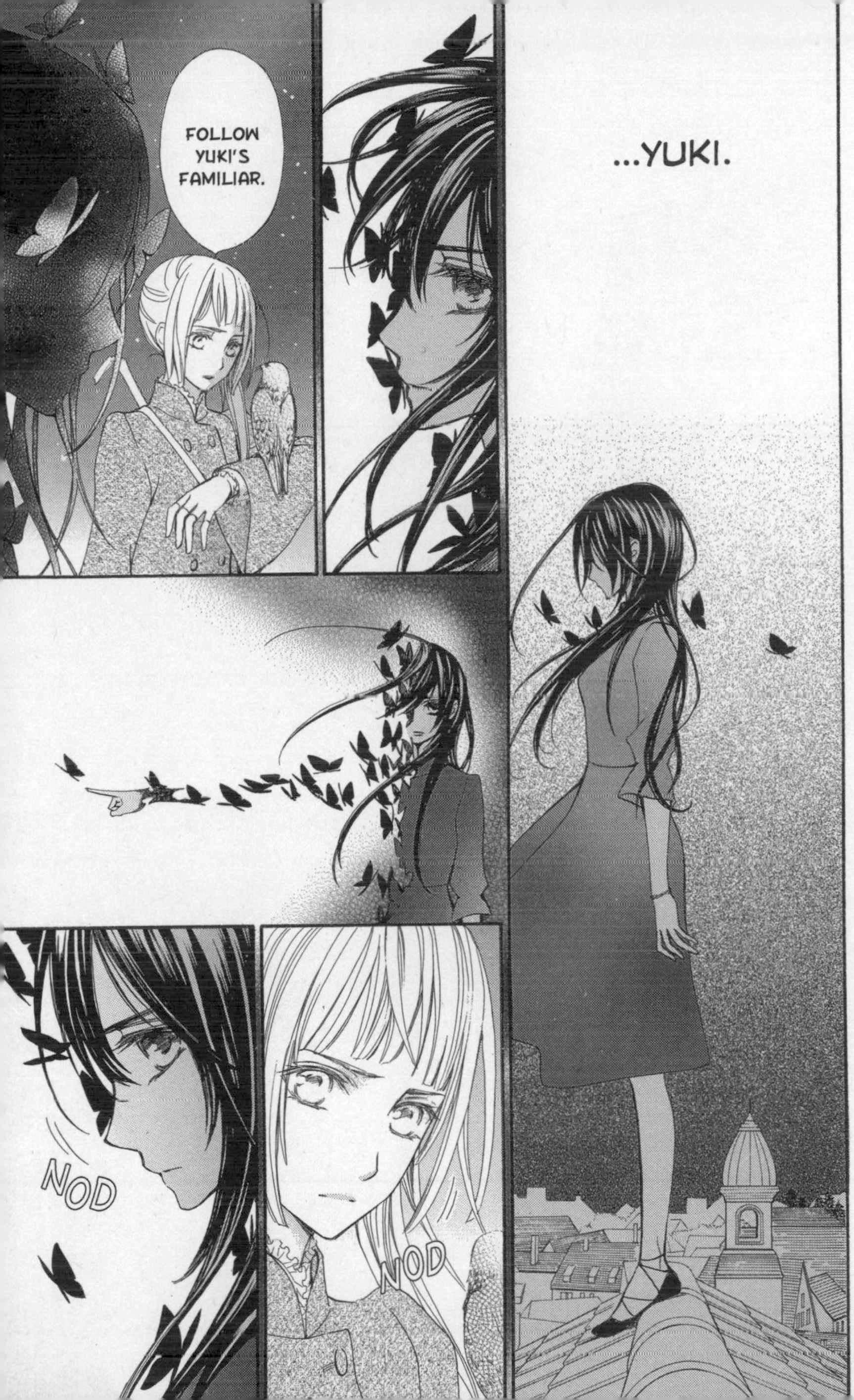
...YUKI.
FOLLOW YUKI'S FAMILIAR.
NOD
NOD

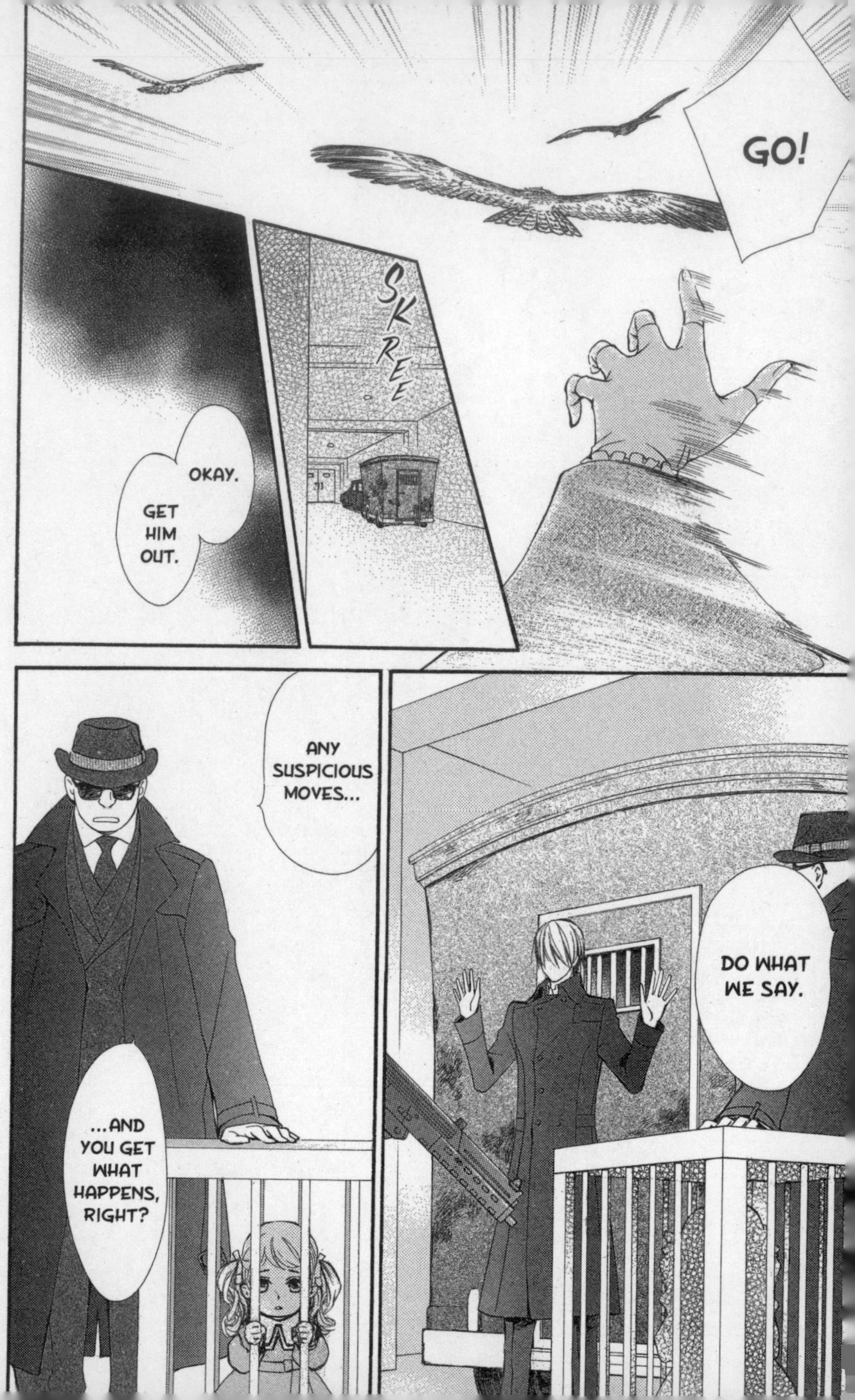
GO!
SKREE
OKAY.
GET HIM OUT.
DO WHAT WE SAY.
ANY SUSPICIOUS MOVES...
...AND YOU GET WHAT HAPPENS, RIGHT?

Ⅱ

There are four chapters recorded on the drama CD that comes with the special edition. Three of them I created for the drama CD. The other one has been restructured, so it may sound new to your ear. I reedited the entire chapter to make it shorter, and I think it's become quite interesting.

And~

The voice actors breathed life into it. It was the same cast as the anime from ten years ago, along with some new voices. I visited the studio to watch them record and screamed, "Everyone absolutely has to hear this!!!" inside my mind. That's what this drama CD is like.

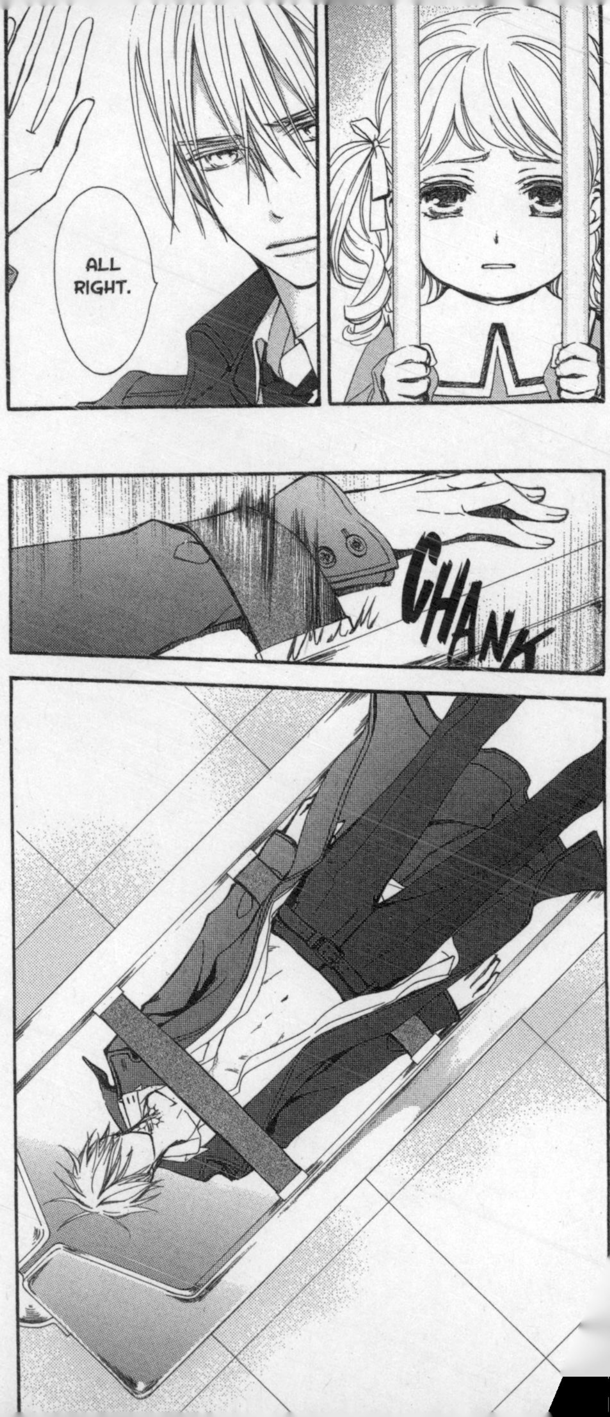
ALL RIGHT.
CHANK

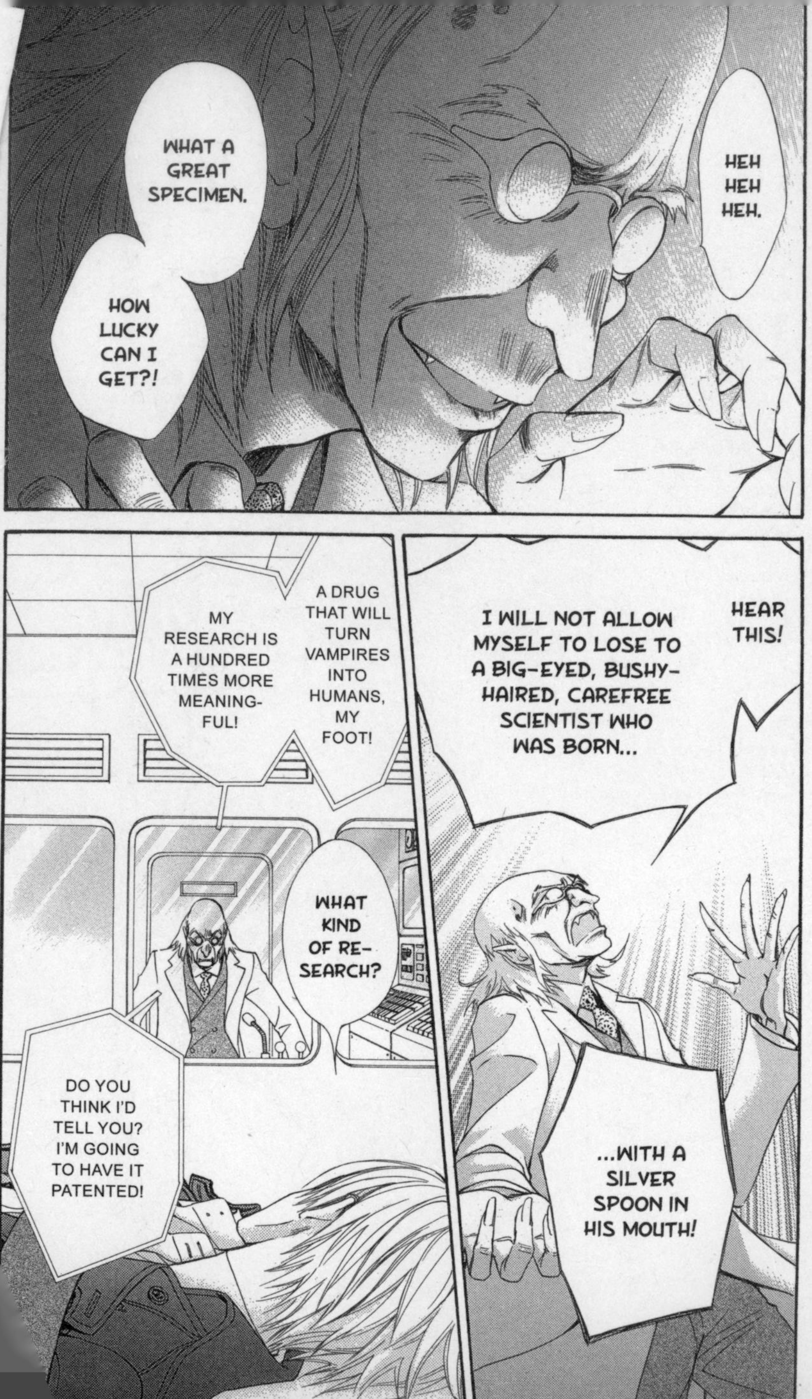
HEH HEH HEH.
WHAT A GREAT SPECIMEN.
HOW LUCKY CAN I GET?!
HEAR THIS!
I WILL NOT ALLOW MYSELF TO LOSE TO A BIG-EYED, BUSHY-HAIRED, CAREFREE SCIENTIST WHO WAS BORN...
...WITH A SILVER SPOON IN HIS MOUTH!
A DRUG THAT WILL TURN VAMPIRES INTO HUMANS, MY FOOT!
MY RESEARCH IS A HUNDRED TIMES MORE MEANING-FUL!
WHAT KIND OF RE-SEARCH?
DO YOU THINK I'D TELL YOU? I'M GOING TO HAVE IT PATENTED!

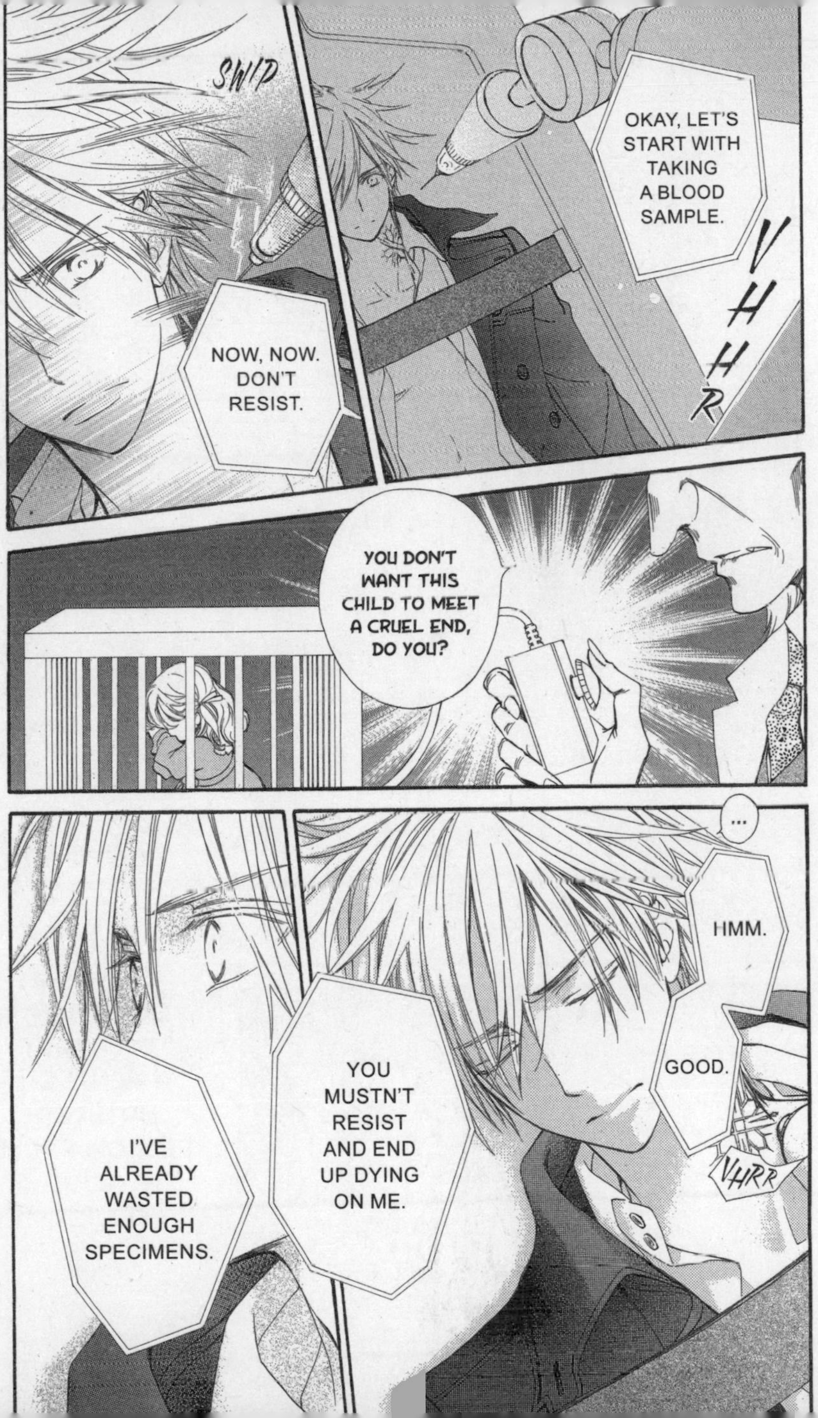
OKAY, LET'S START WITH TAKING A BLOOD SAMPLE.
VHHR
SWIP
NOW, NOW. DON'T RESIST.
YOU DON'T WANT THIS CHILD TO MEET A CRUEL END, DO YOU?
...
HMM.
GOOD.
VHRR
YOU MUSTN'T RESIST AND END UP DYING ON ME.
I'VE ALREADY WASTED ENOUGH SPECIMENS.

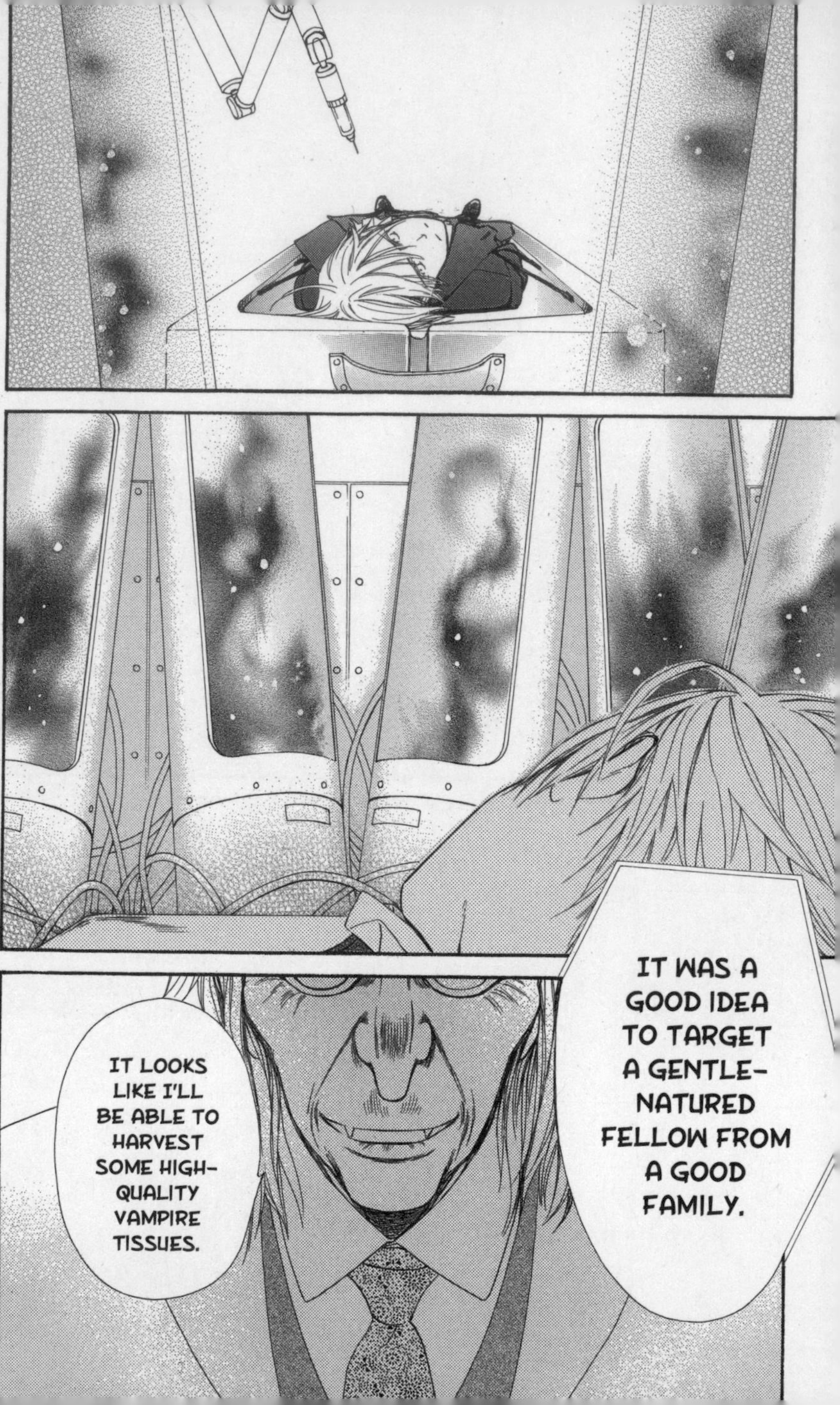
IT WAS A GOOD IDEA TO TARGET A GENTLE-NATURED FELLOW FROM A GOOD FAMILY.
IT LOOKS LIKE I'LL BE ABLE TO HARVEST SOME HIGH-QUALITY VAMPIRE TISSUES.

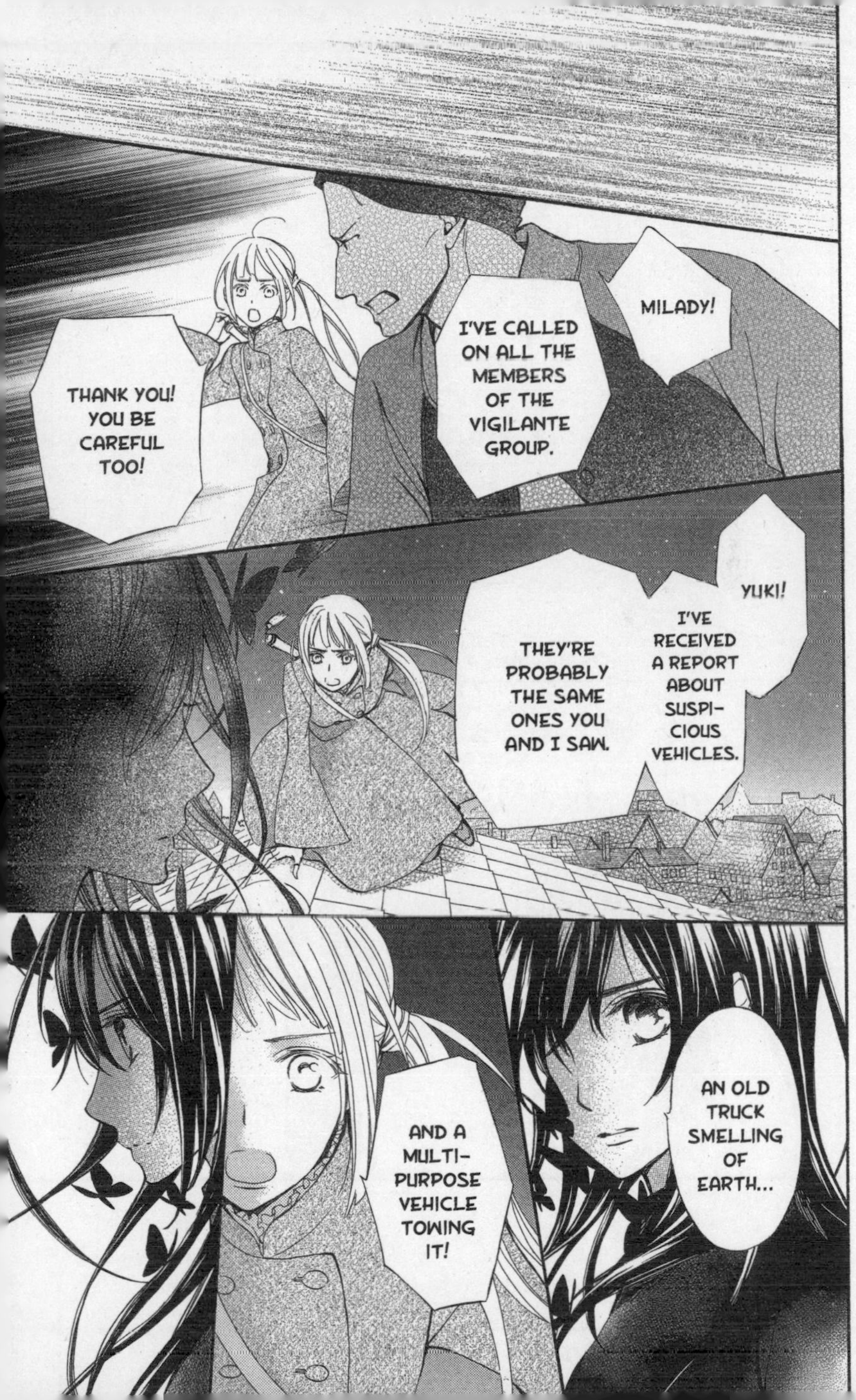
MILADY!
I'VE CALLED ON ALL THE MEMBERS OF THE VIGILANTE GROUP.
THANK YOU! YOU BE CAREFUL TOO!
YUKI!
I'VE RECEIVED A REPORT ABOUT SUSPICIOUS VEHICLES.
THEY'RE PROBABLY THE SAME ONES YOU AND I SAW.
AN OLD TRUCK SMELLING OF EARTH...
AND A MULTIPURPOSE VEHICLE TOWING IT!

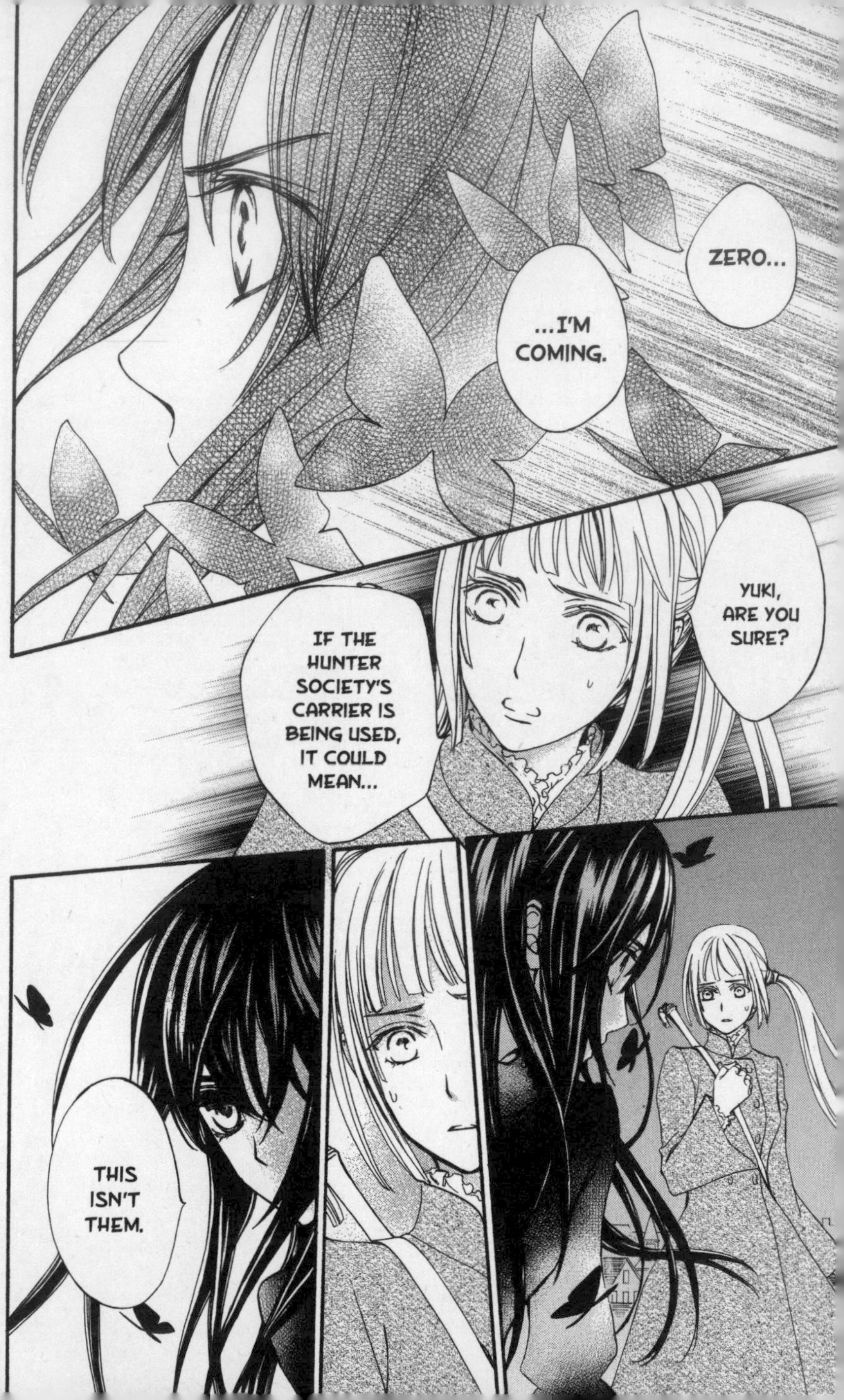
ZERO...
...I'M COMING.
YUKI, ARE YOU SURE?
IF THE HUNTER SOCIETY'S CARRIER IS BEING USED, IT COULD MEAN...
THIS ISN'T THEM.

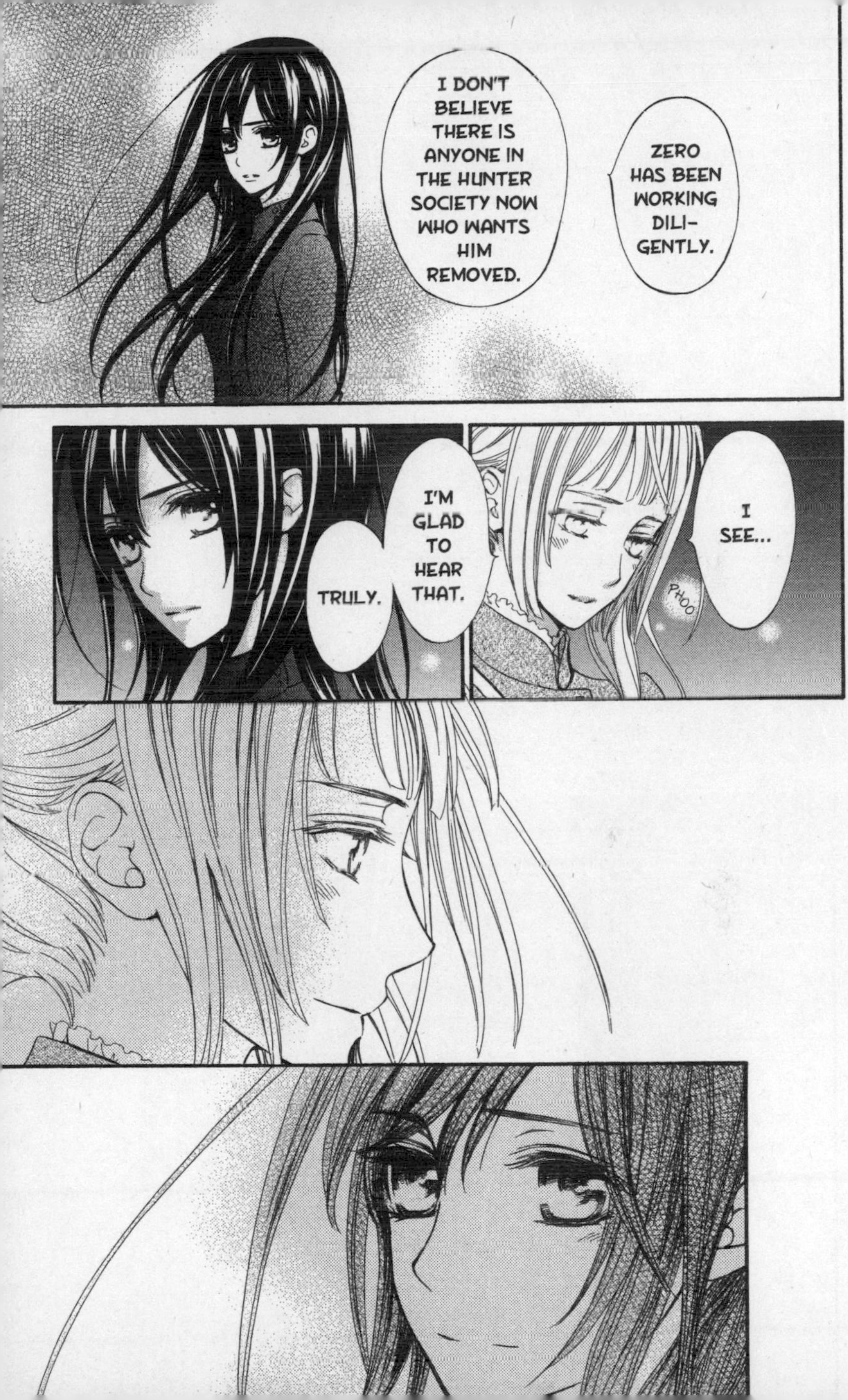
ZERO HAS BEEN WORKING DILI- GENTLY.
I DON'T BELIEVE THERE IS ANYONE IN THE HUNTER SOCIETY NOW WHO WANTS HIM REMOVED.
I SEE...
PHOO
I'M GLAD TO HEAR THAT.
TRULY.

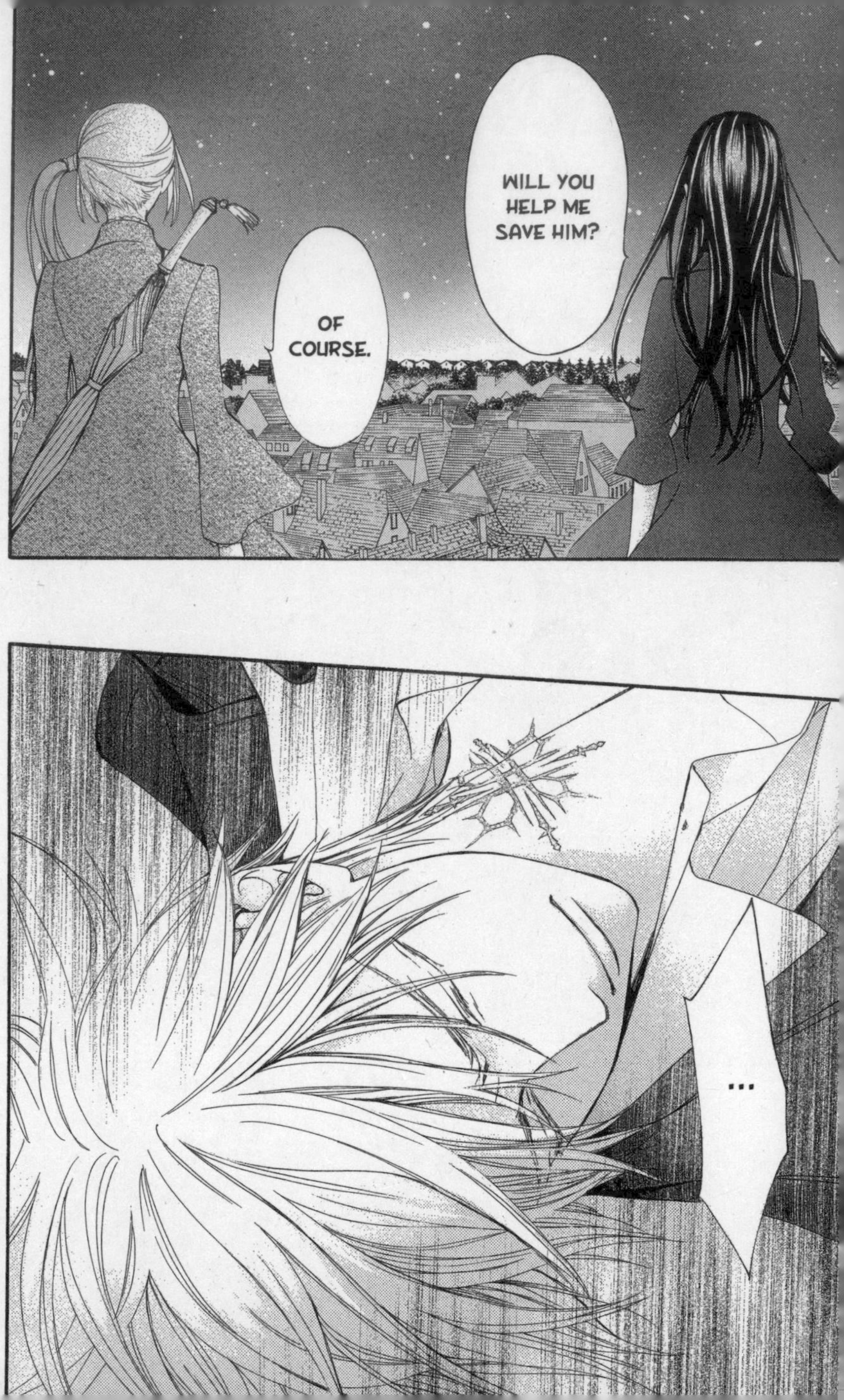
WILL YOU HELP ME SAVE HIM?
OF COURSE.
...

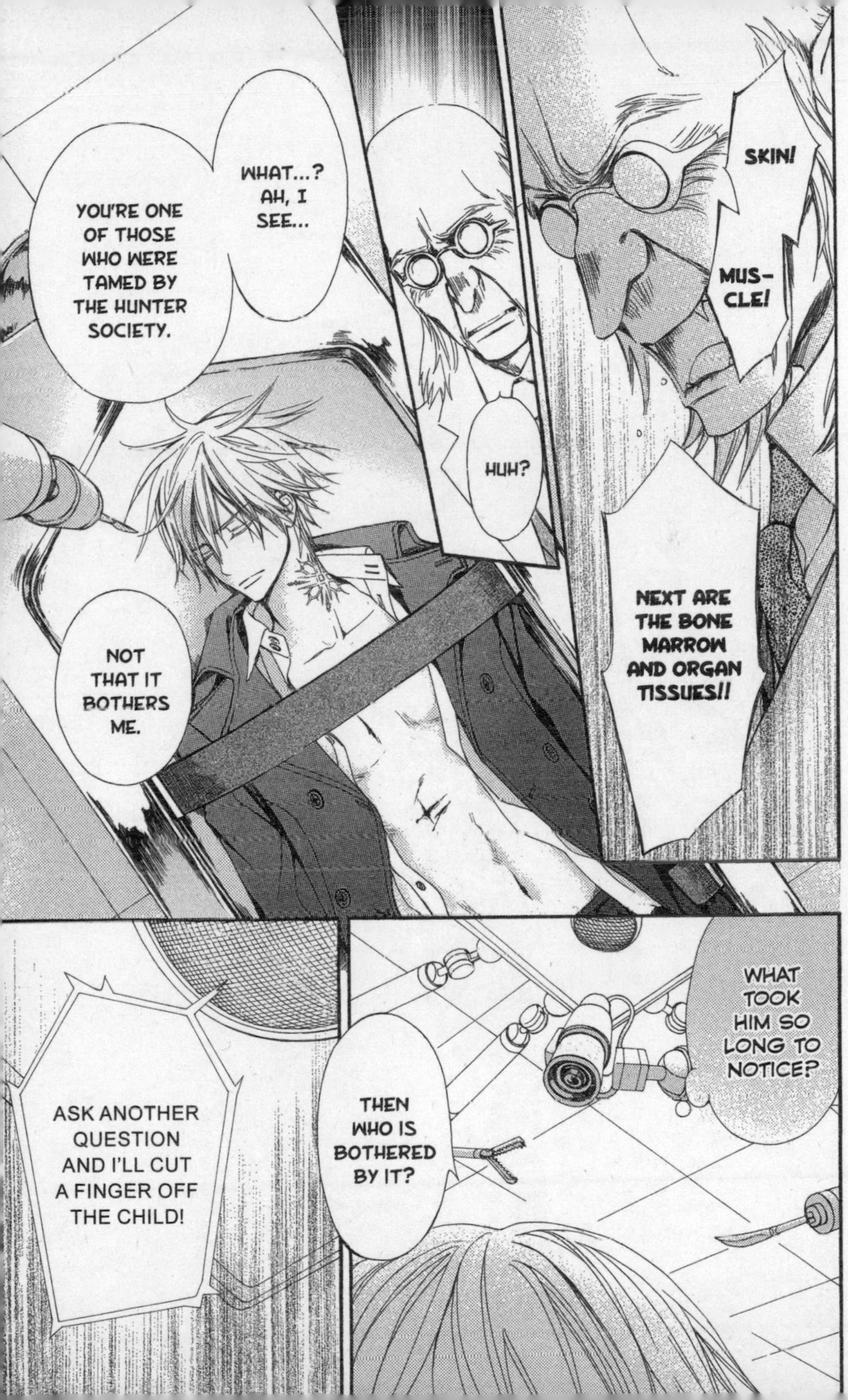
SKIN!
MUS-CLE!
NEXT ARE THE BONE MARROW AND ORGAN TISSUES!!
HUH?
WHAT...? AH, I SEE...
YOU'RE ONE OF THOSE WHO WERE TAMED BY THE HUNTER SOCIETY.
NOT THAT IT BOTHERS ME.
WHAT TOOK HIM SO LONG TO NOTICE?
THEN WHO IS BOTHERED BY IT?
ASK ANOTHER QUESTION AND I'LL CUT A FINGER OFF THE CHILD!

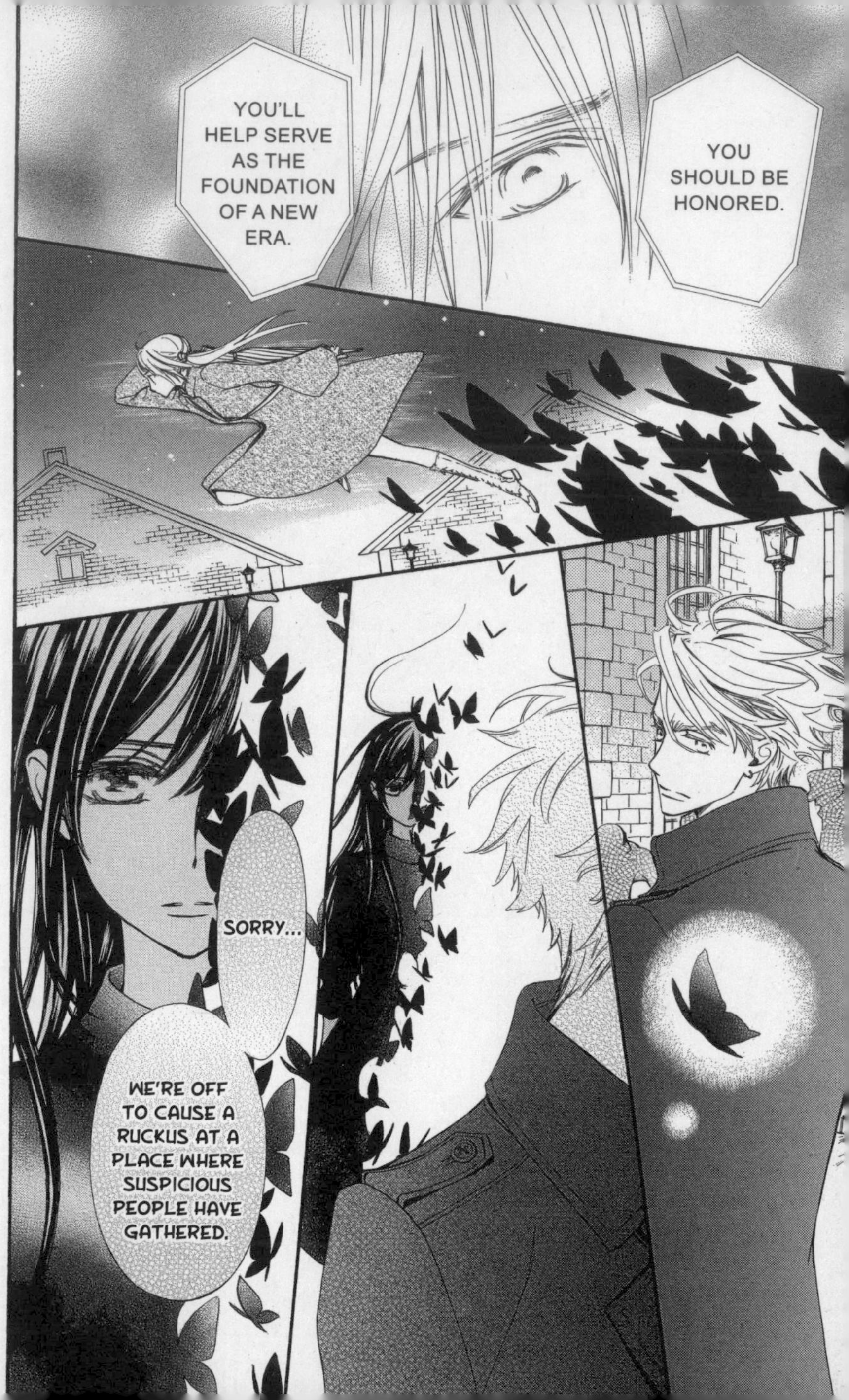
YOU SHOULD BE HONORED.
YOU'LL HELP SERVE AS THE FOUNDATION OF A NEW ERA.
SORRY...
WE'RE OFF TO CAUSE A RUCKUS AT A PLACE WHERE SUSPICIOUS PEOPLE HAVE GATHERED.

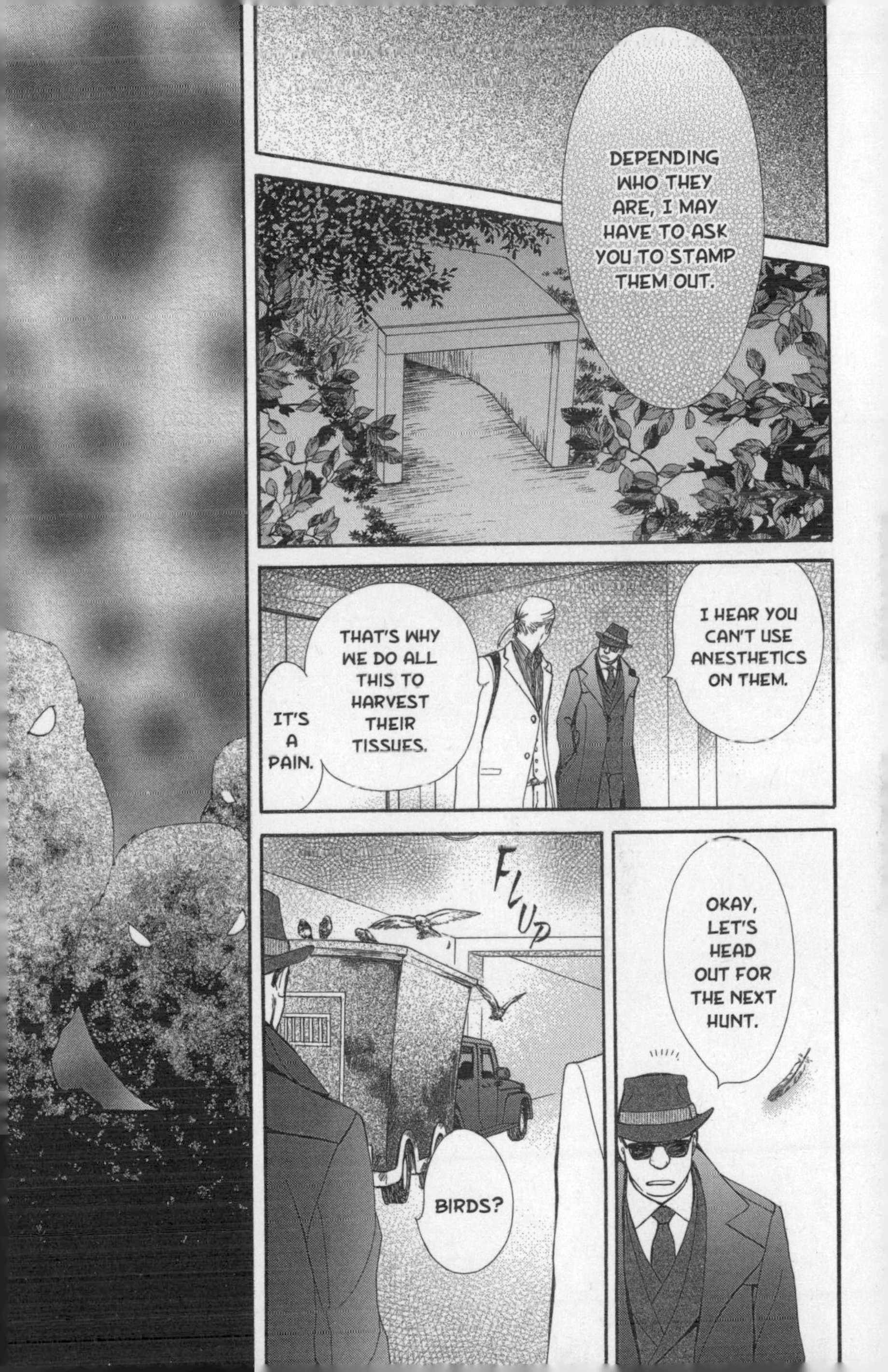
DEPENDING WHO THEY ARE, I MAY HAVE TO ASK YOU TO STAMP THEM OUT.
I HEAR YOU CAN'T USE ANESTHETICS ON THEM.
THAT'S WHY WE DO ALL THIS TO HARVEST THEIR TISSUES.
IT'S A PAIN.
OKAY, LET'S HEAD OUT FOR THE NEXT HUNT.
FLUP
BIRDS?

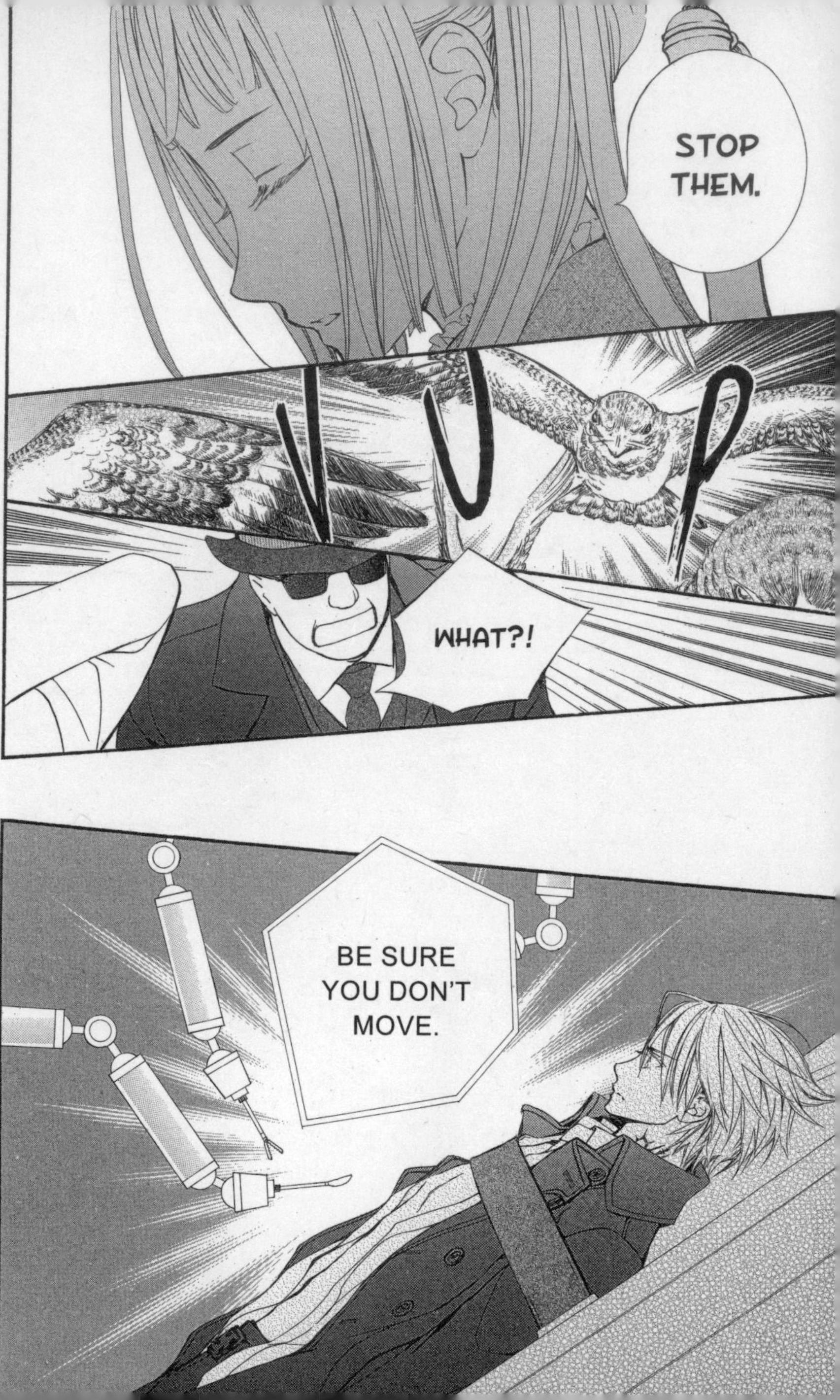
STOP THEM.
WHAT?!
BE SURE YOU DON'T MOVE.

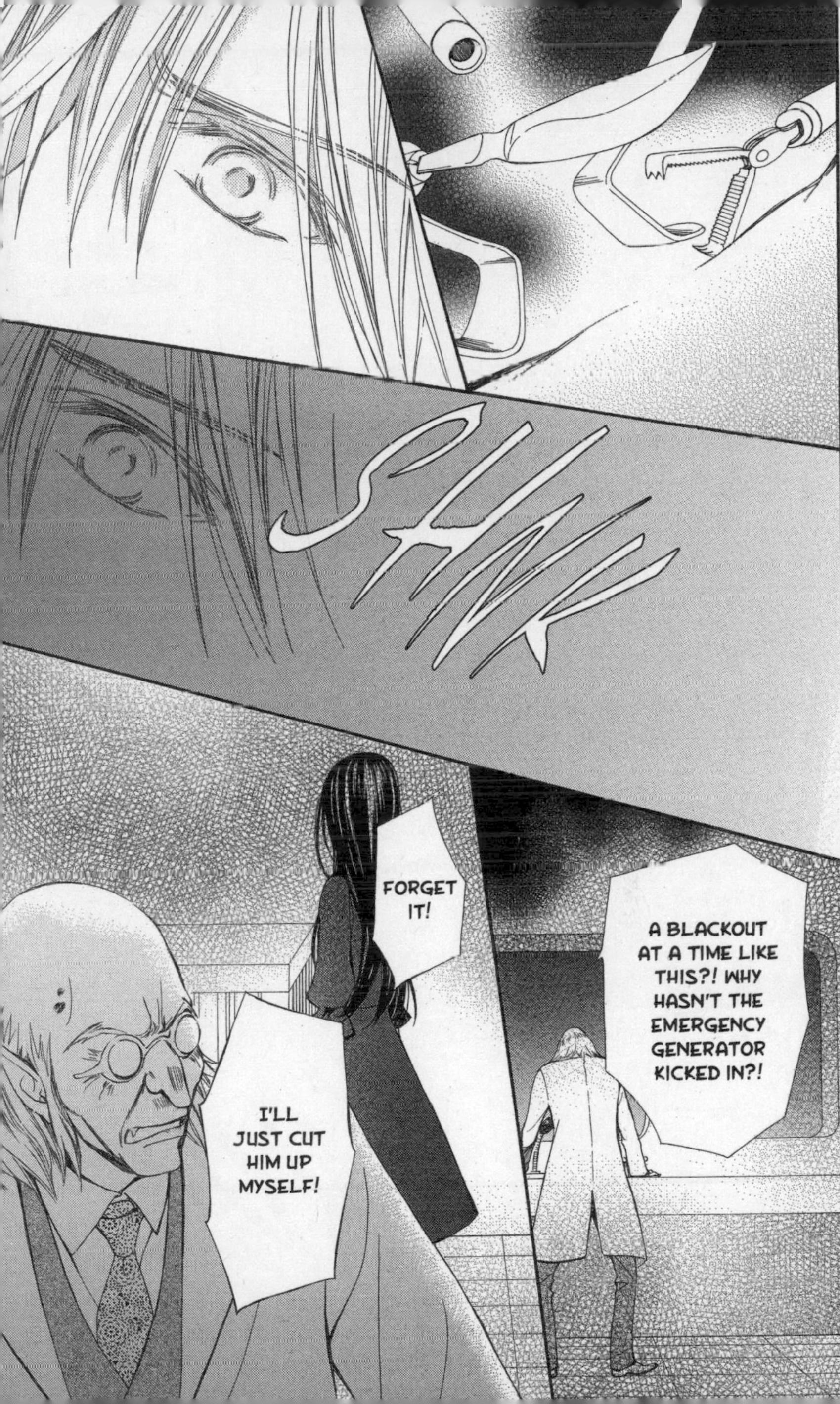
SHAAK
A BLACKOUT AT A TIME LIKE THIS?! WHY HASN'T THE EMERGENCY GENERATOR KICKED IN?!
FORGET IT!
I'LL JUST CUT HIM UP MYSELF!

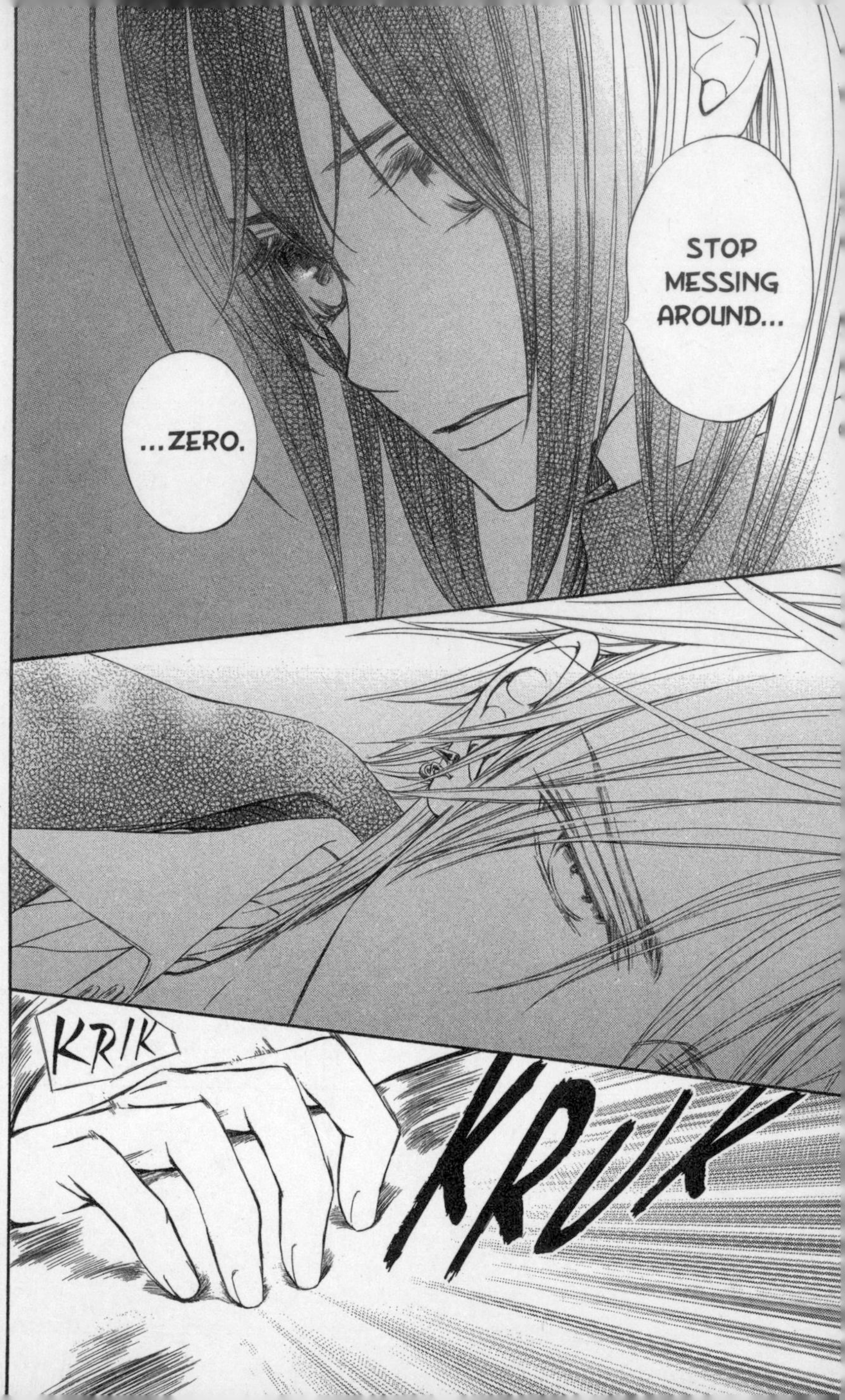
STOP MESSING AROUND...
...ZERO.
KRIK
KRUK

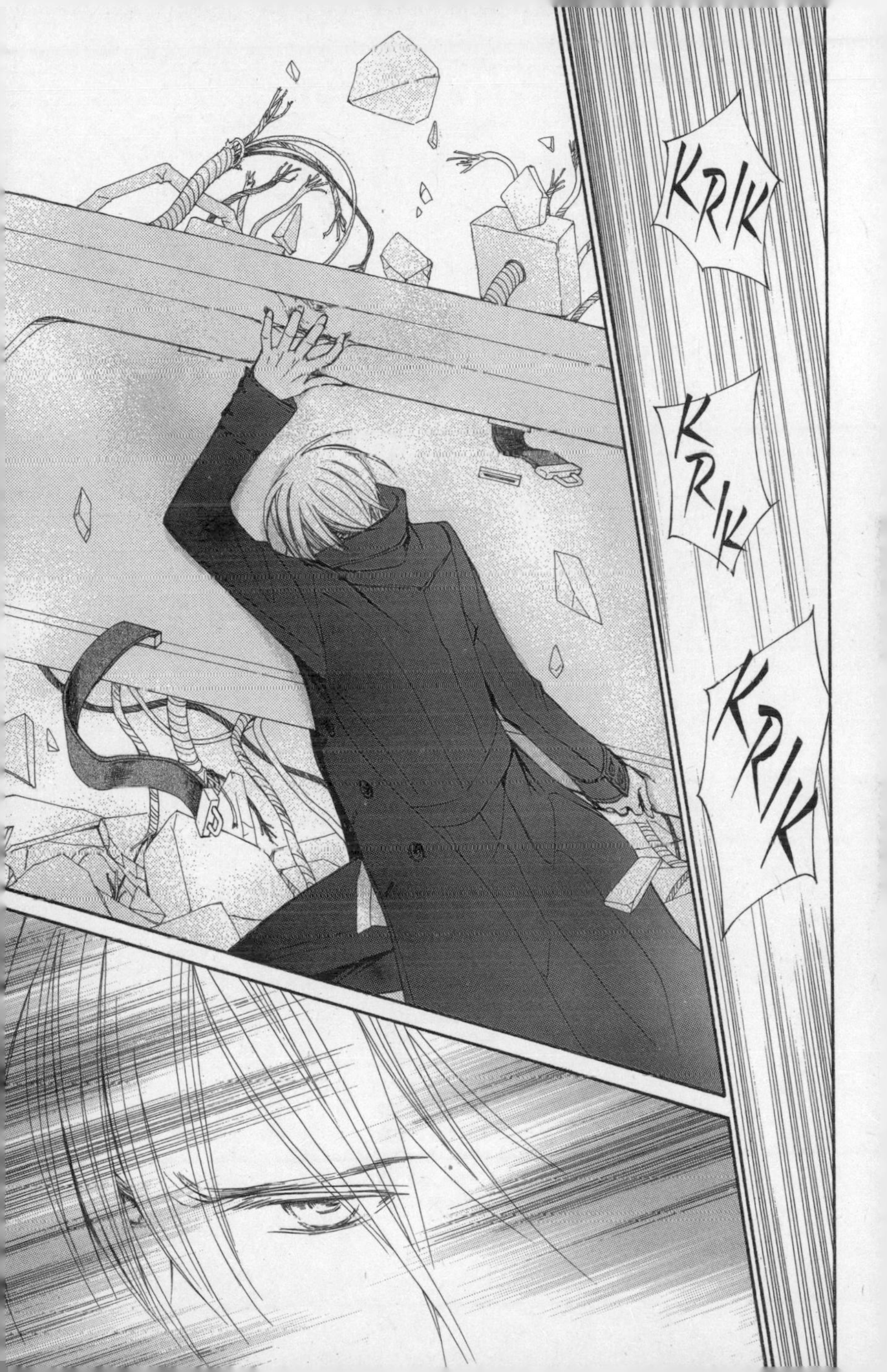
KRIK
KRIK
KRIK

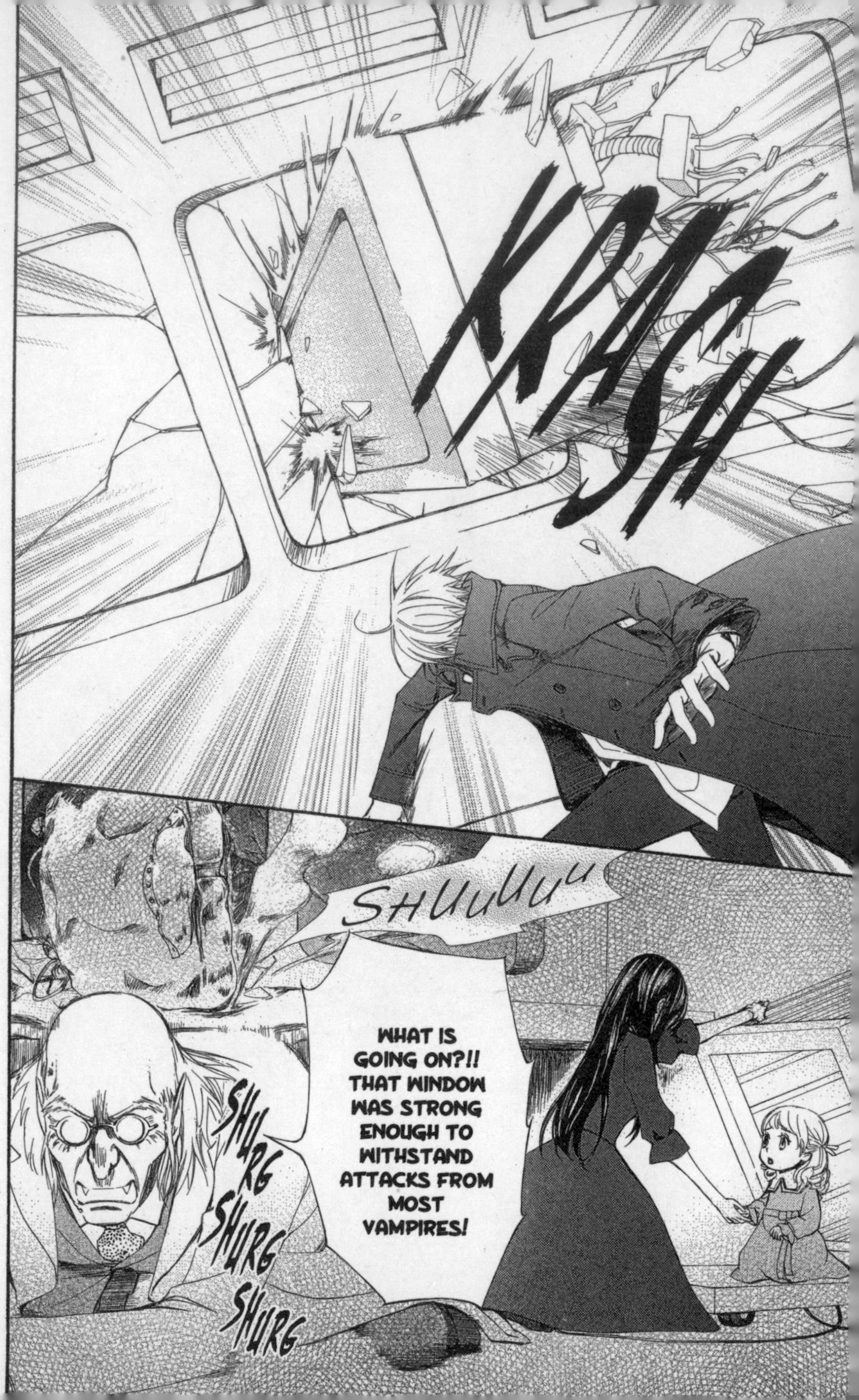
KRASH
SHUUUUU
WHAT IS GOING ON?!! THAT WINDOW WAS STRONG ENOUGH TO WITHSTAND ATTACKS FROM MOST VAMPIRES!
SHURG SHURG SHURG SHURG

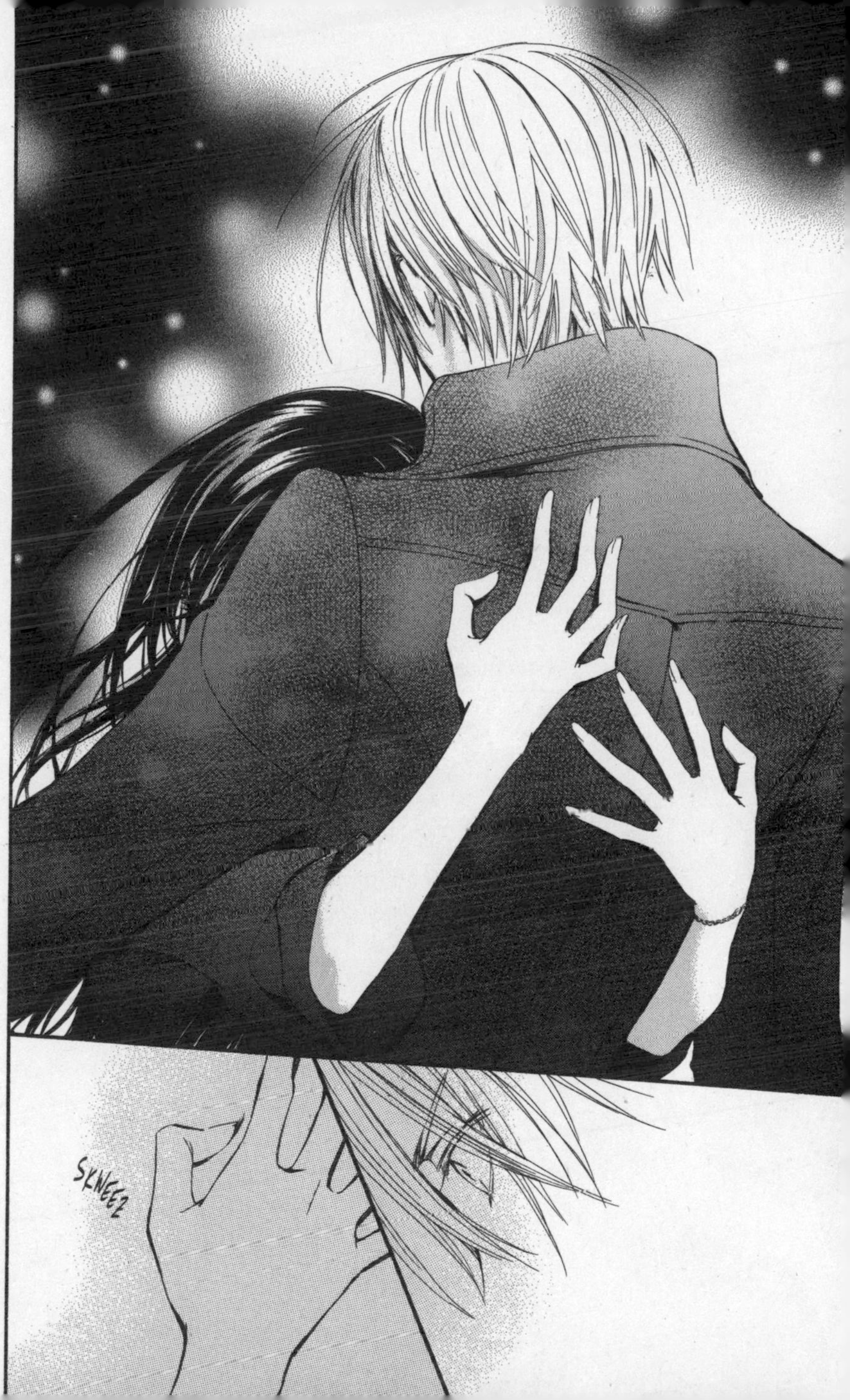
SKWEEZ

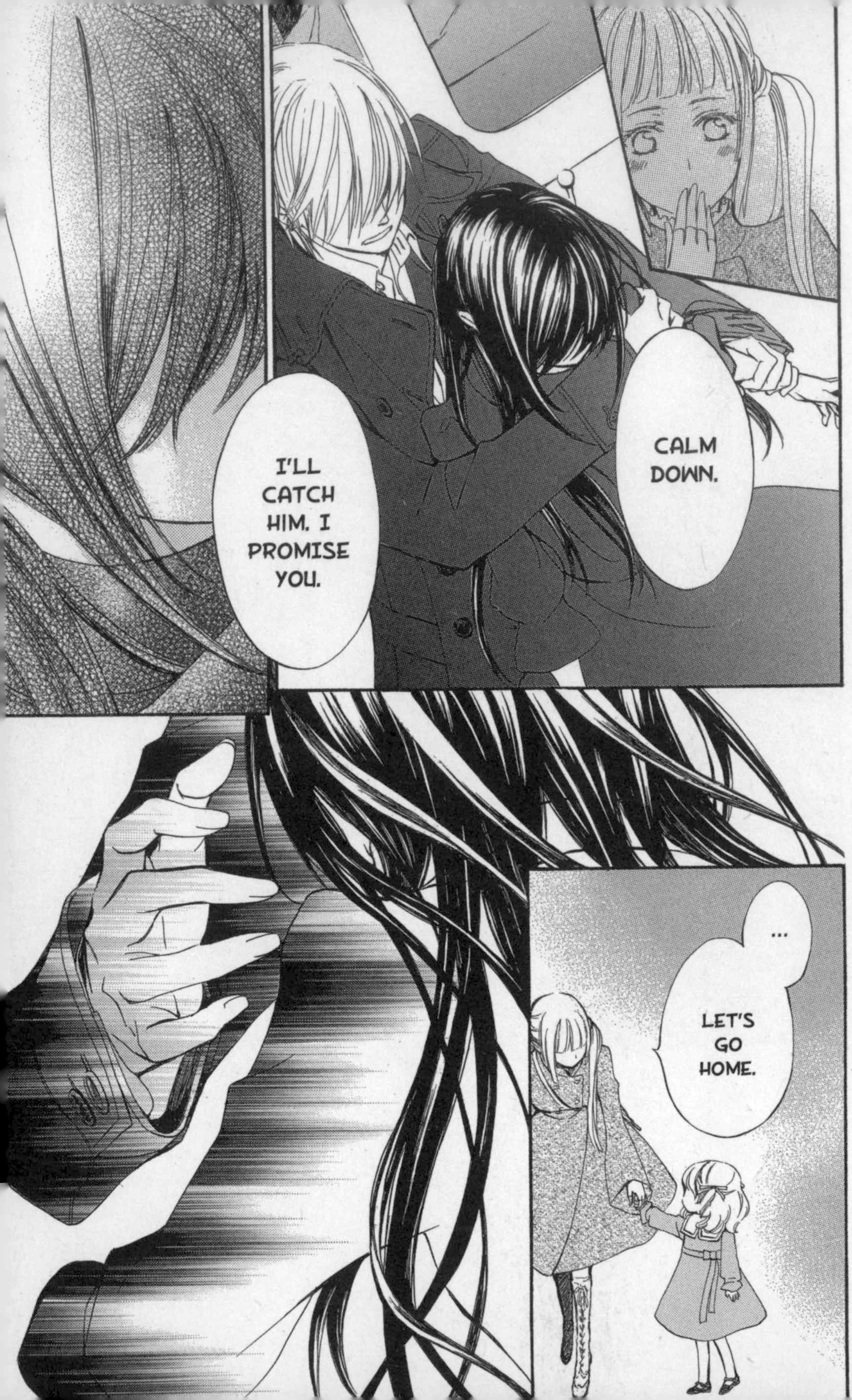
CALM DOWN.
I'LL CATCH HIM. I PROMISE YOU.
...
LET'S GO HOME.

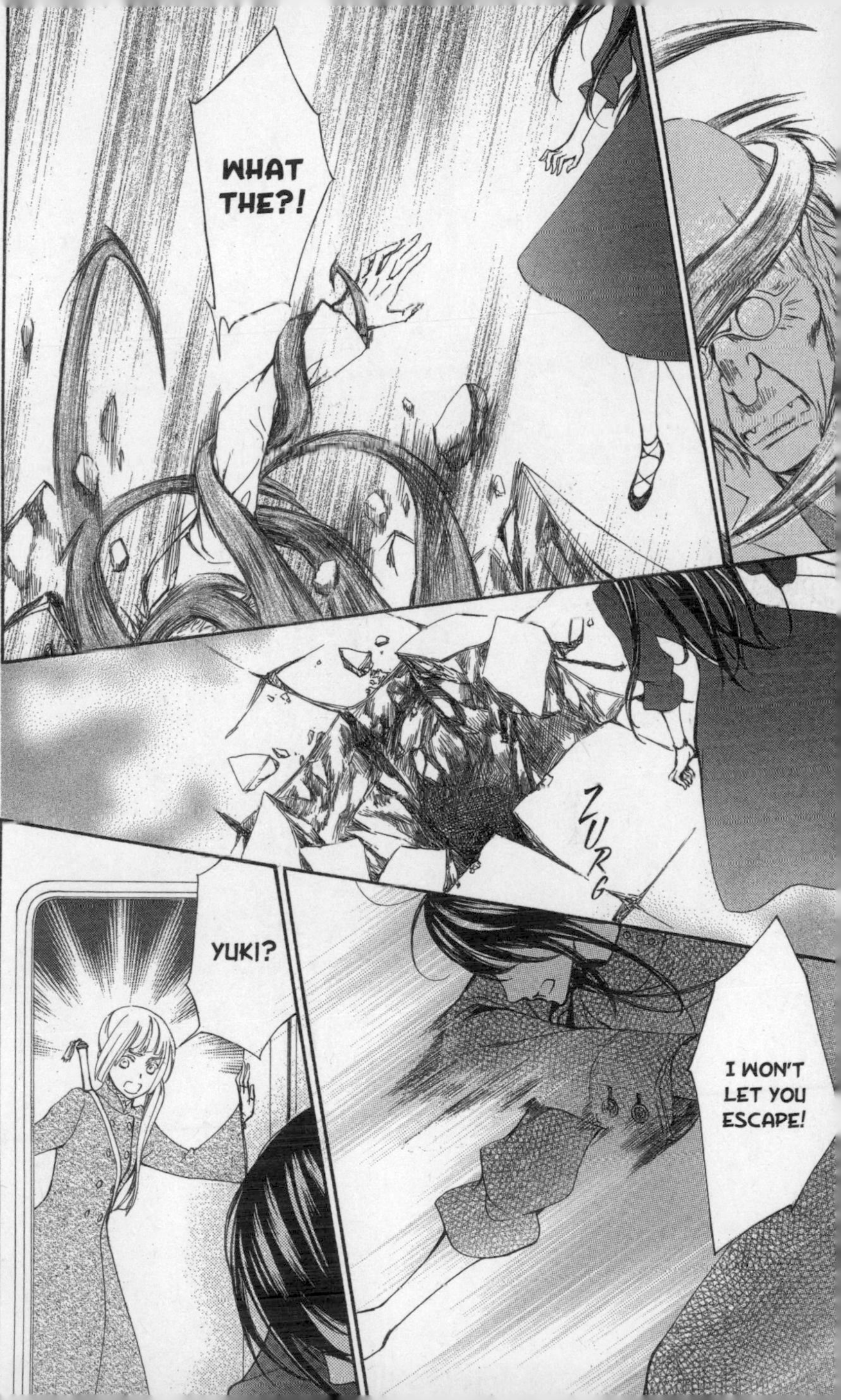
WHAT THE?!
ZURG
I WON'T LET YOU ESCAPE!
YUKI?

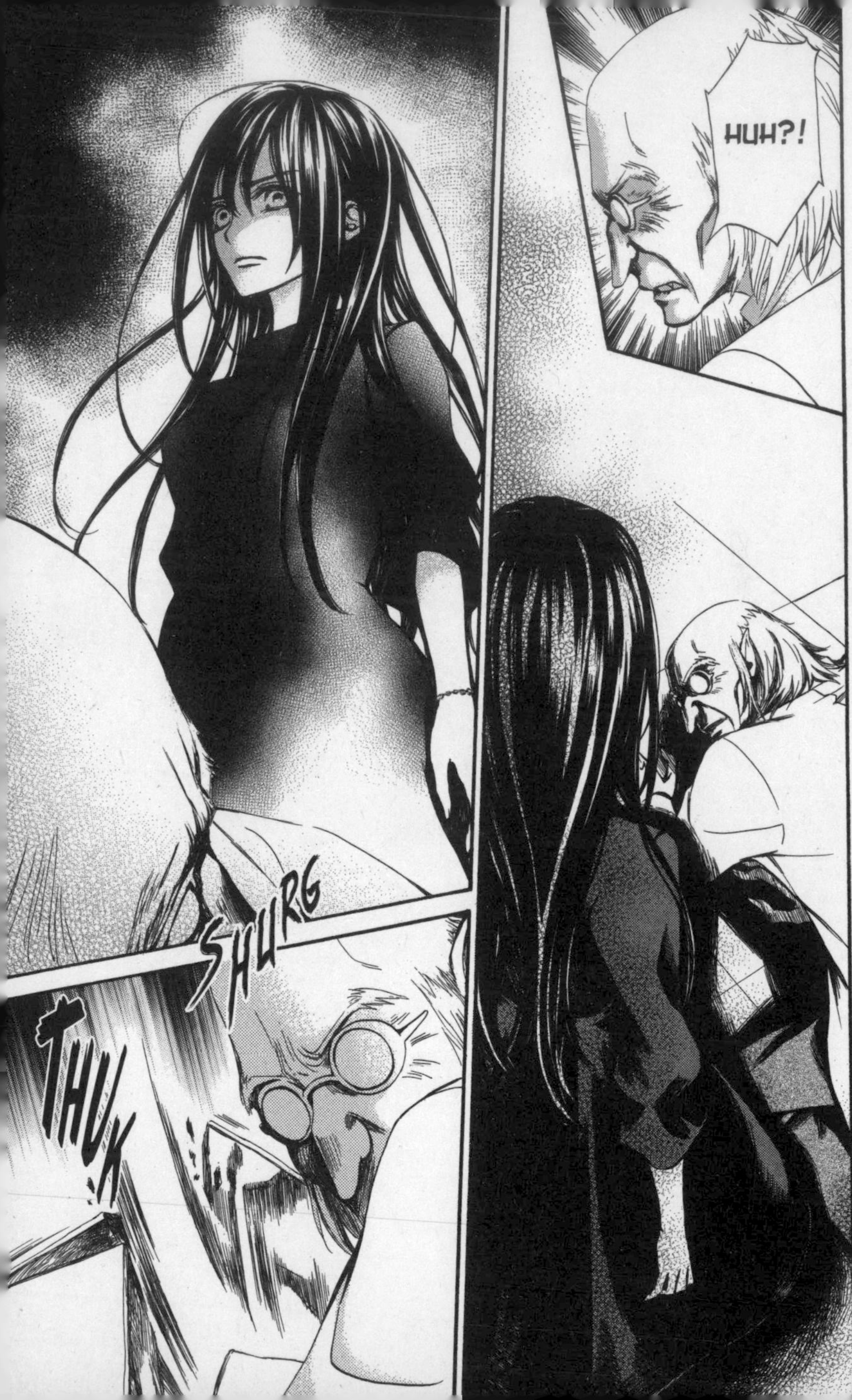
HUH?!
SHURG
THUK

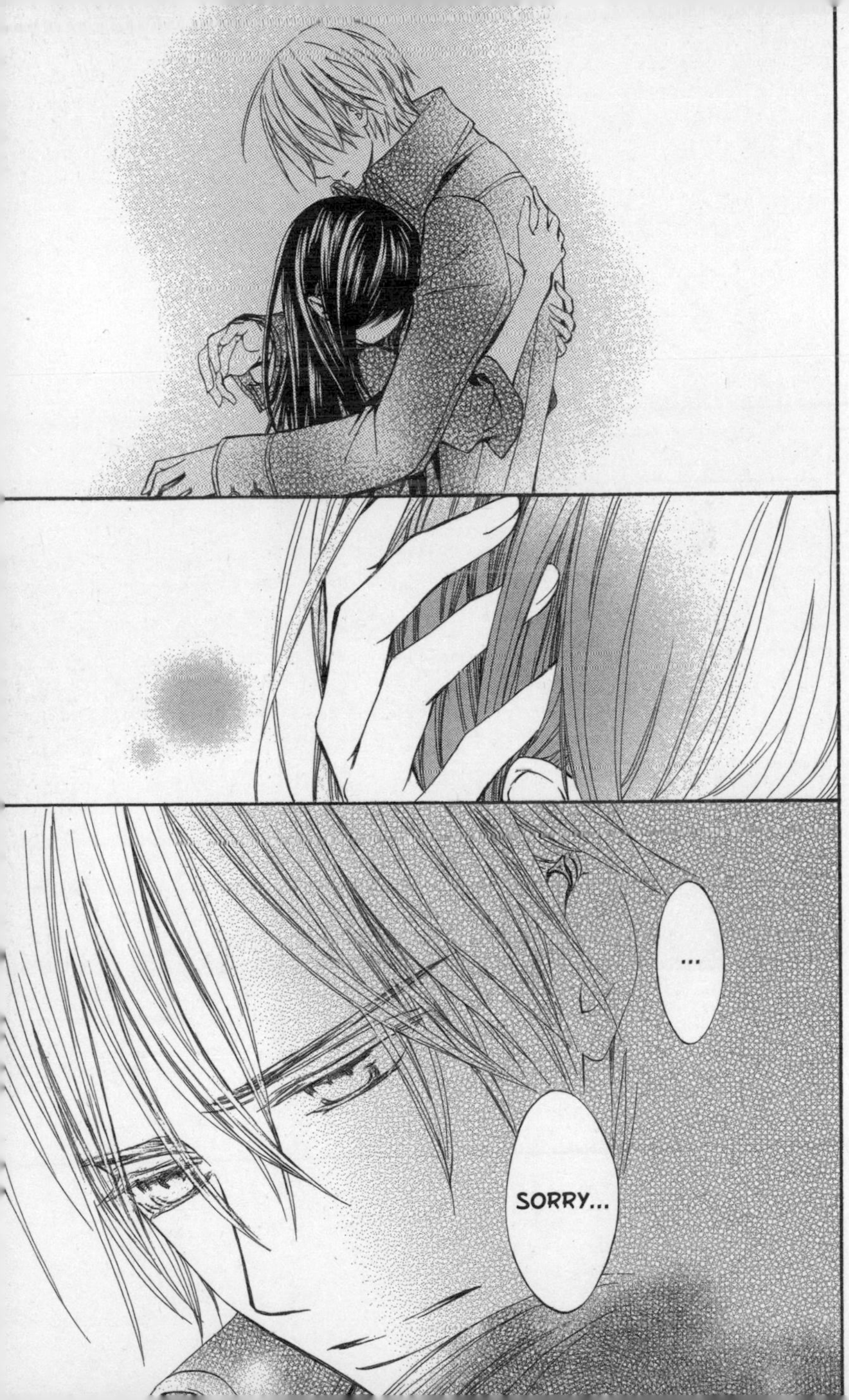
...
SORRY...

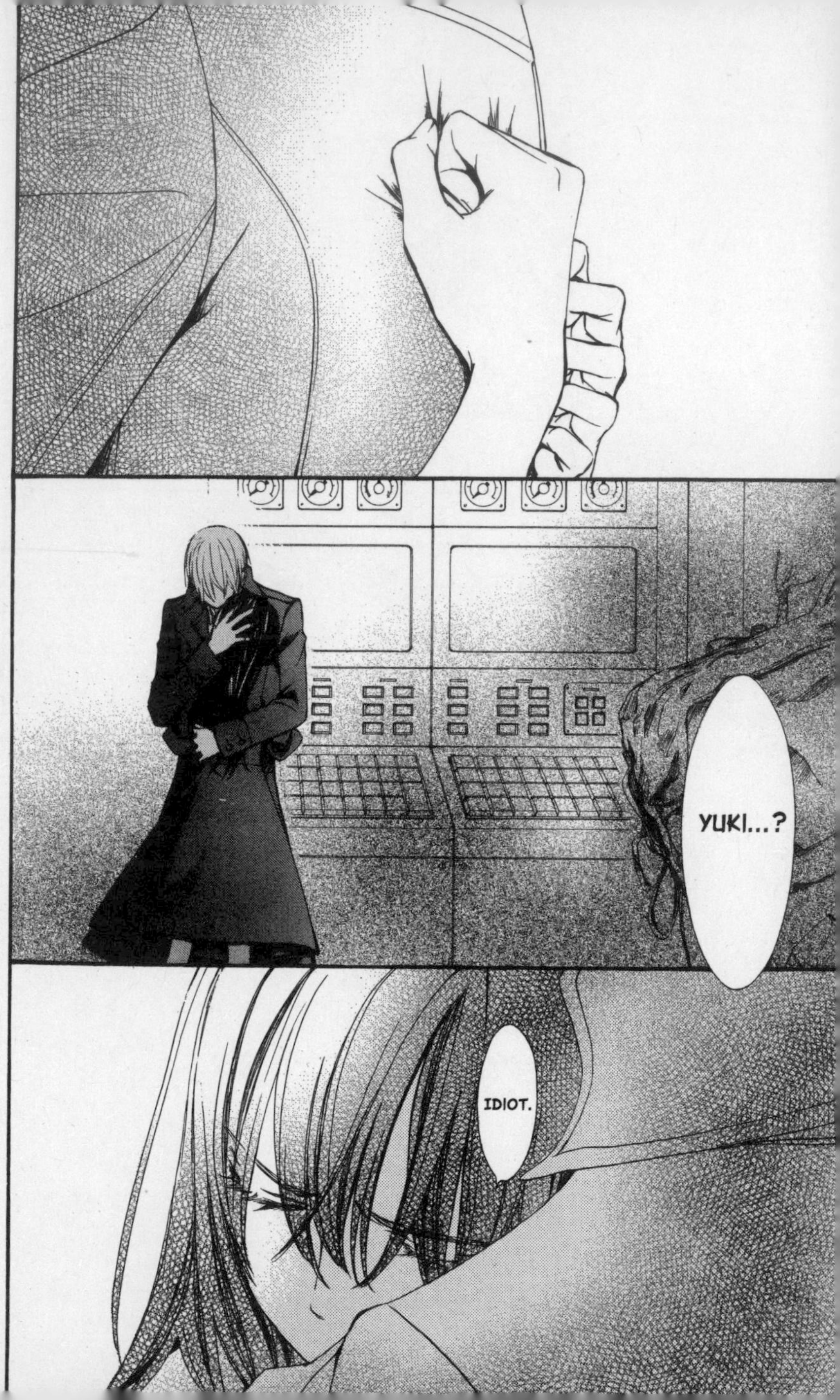
YUKI...?
IDIOT.

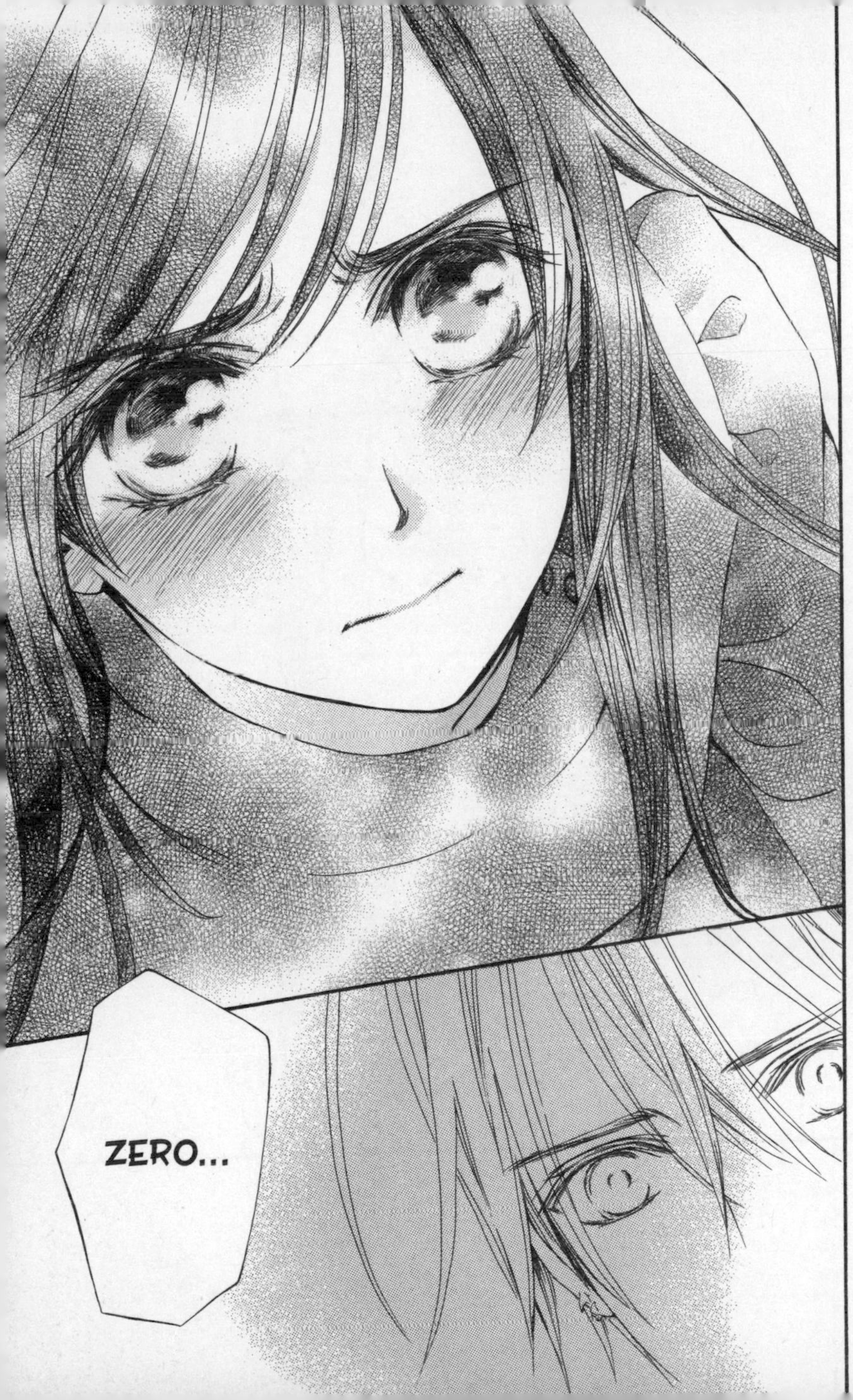
ZERO...

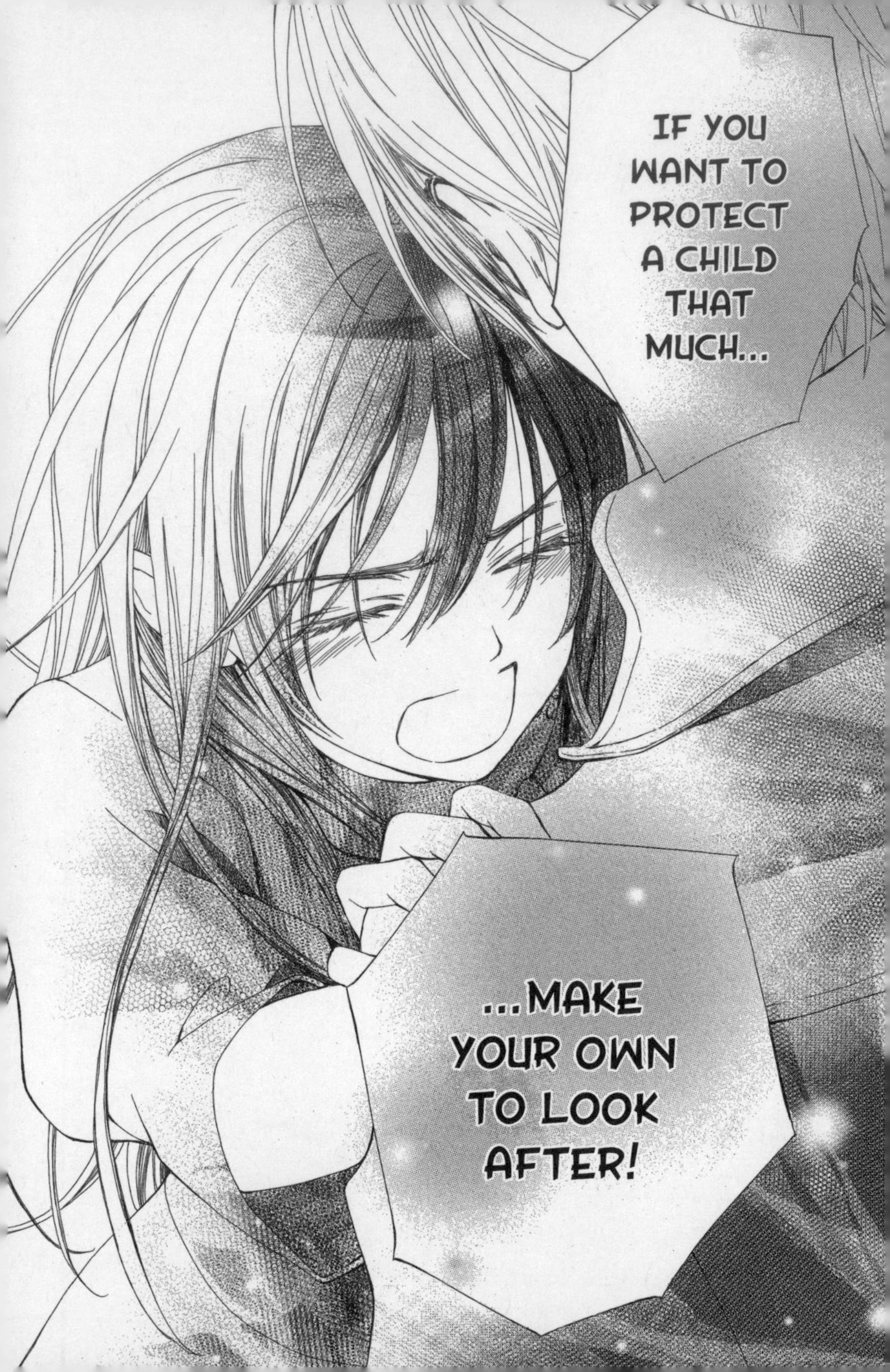
IF YOU WANT TO PROTECT A CHILD THAT MUCH...
...MAKE YOUR OWN TO LOOK AFTER!

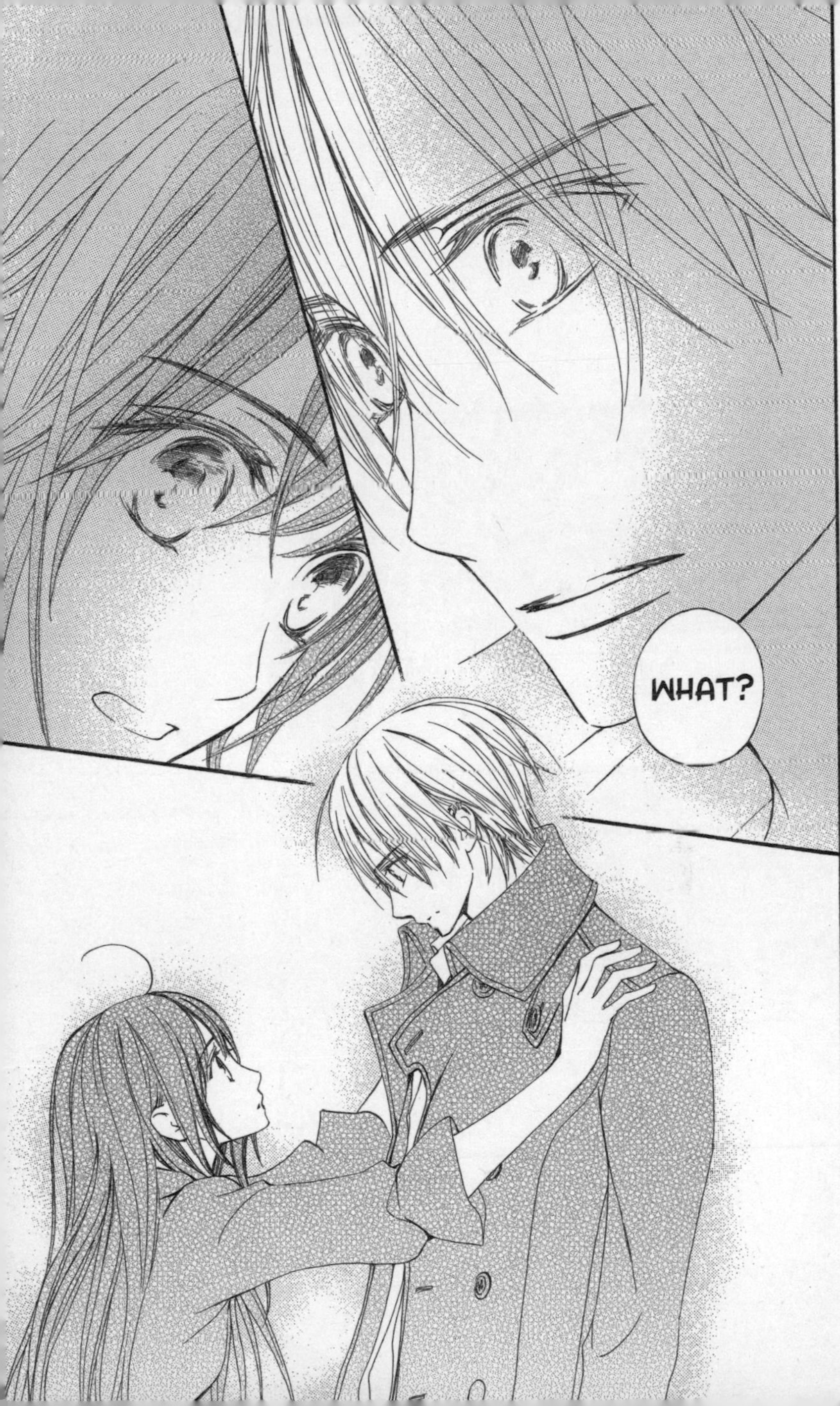
WHAT?

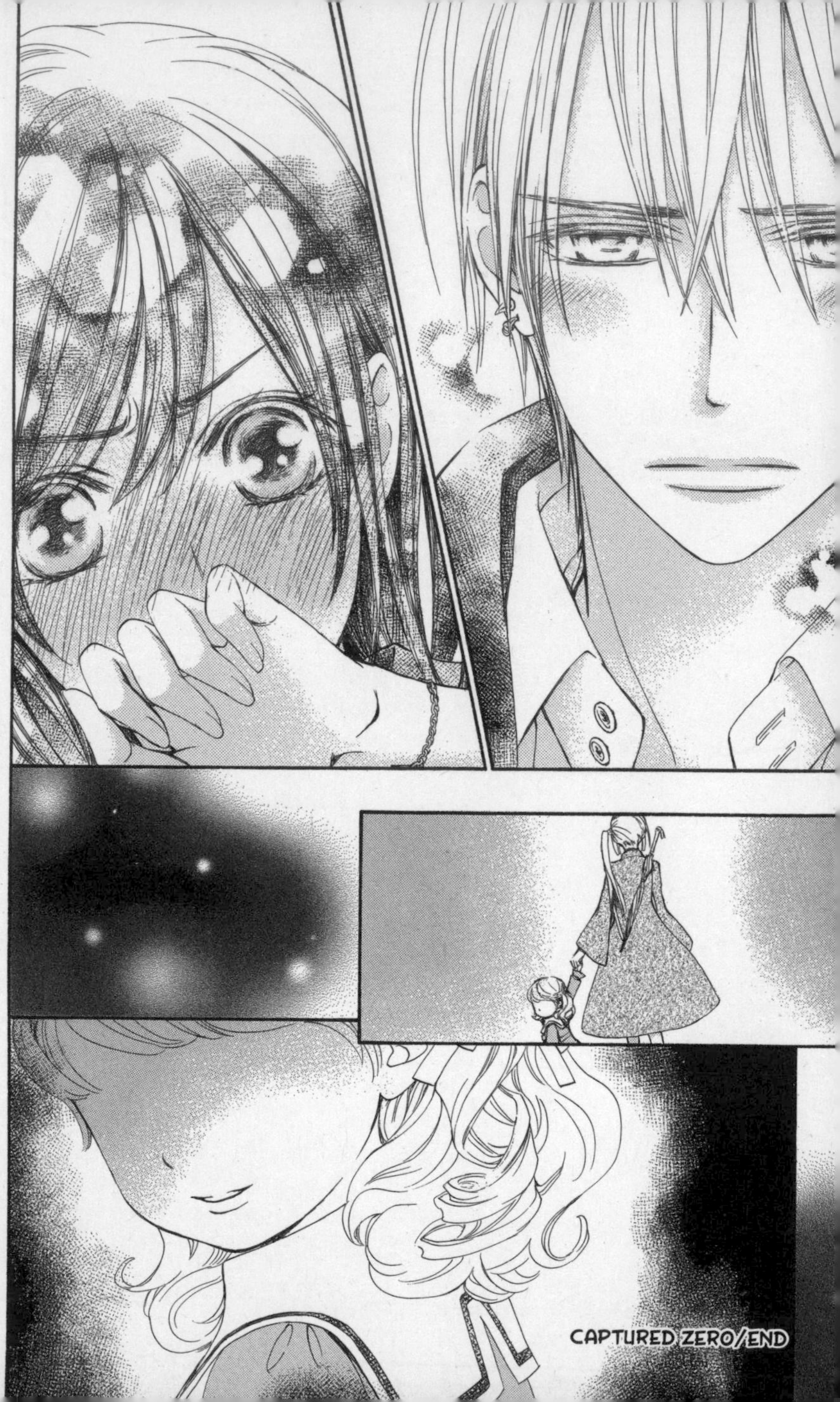
CAPTURED ZERO/END

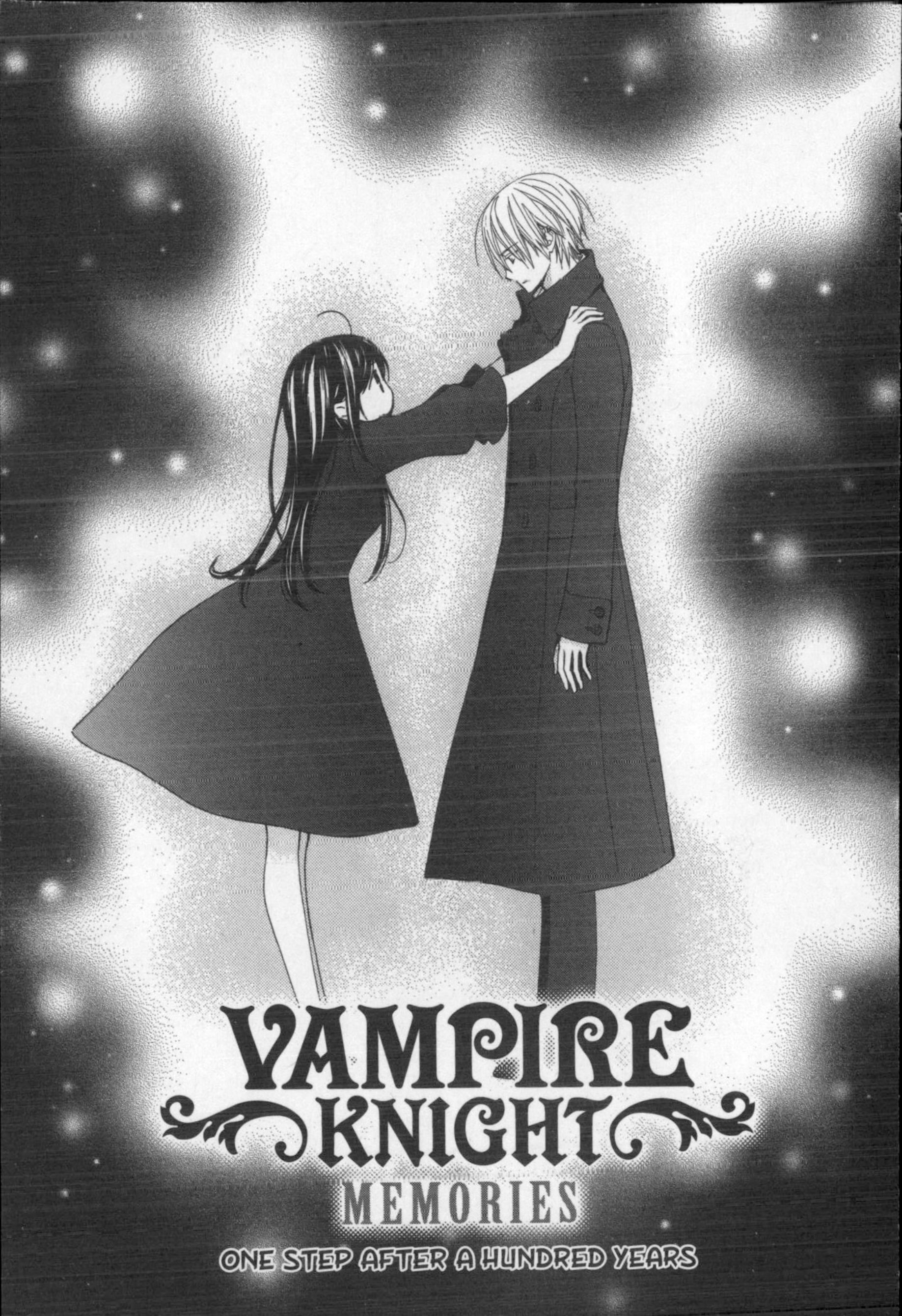
VAMPIRE KNIGHT
MEMORIES
ONE STEP AFTER A HUNDRED YEARS

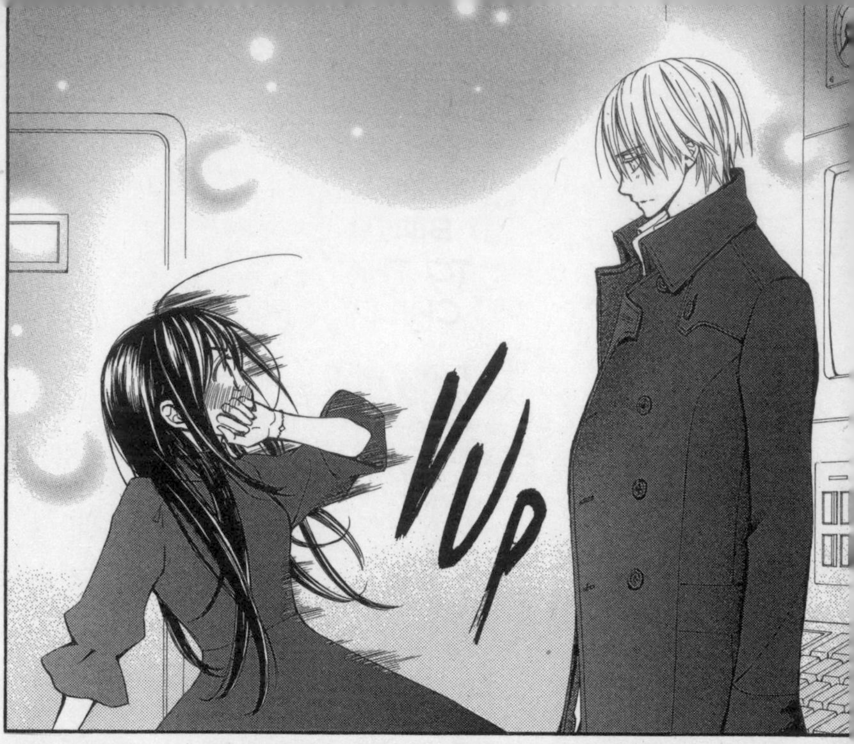
VUP
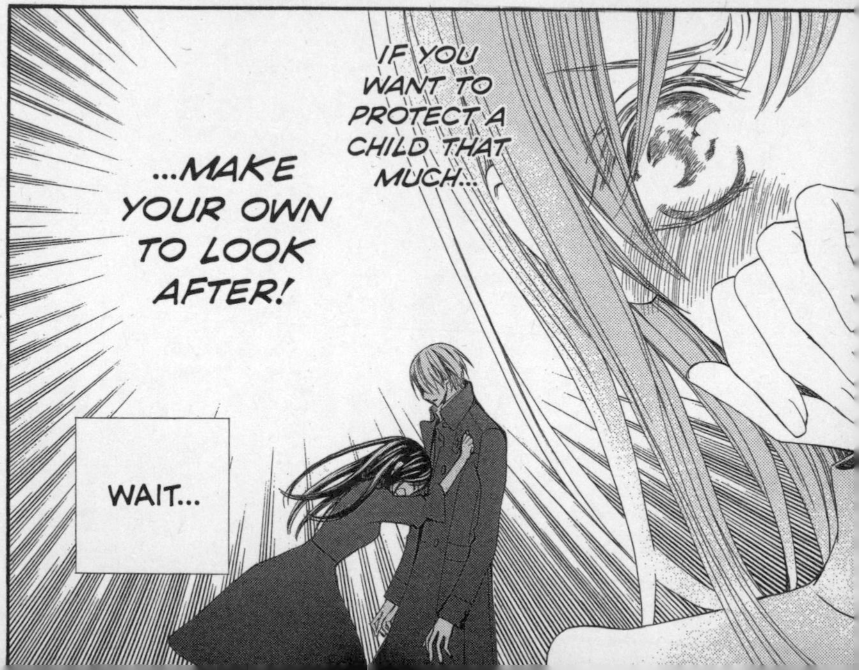
IF YOU WANT TO PROTECT A CHILD THAT MUCH...
...MAKE YOUR OWN TO LOOK AFTER!
WAIT...

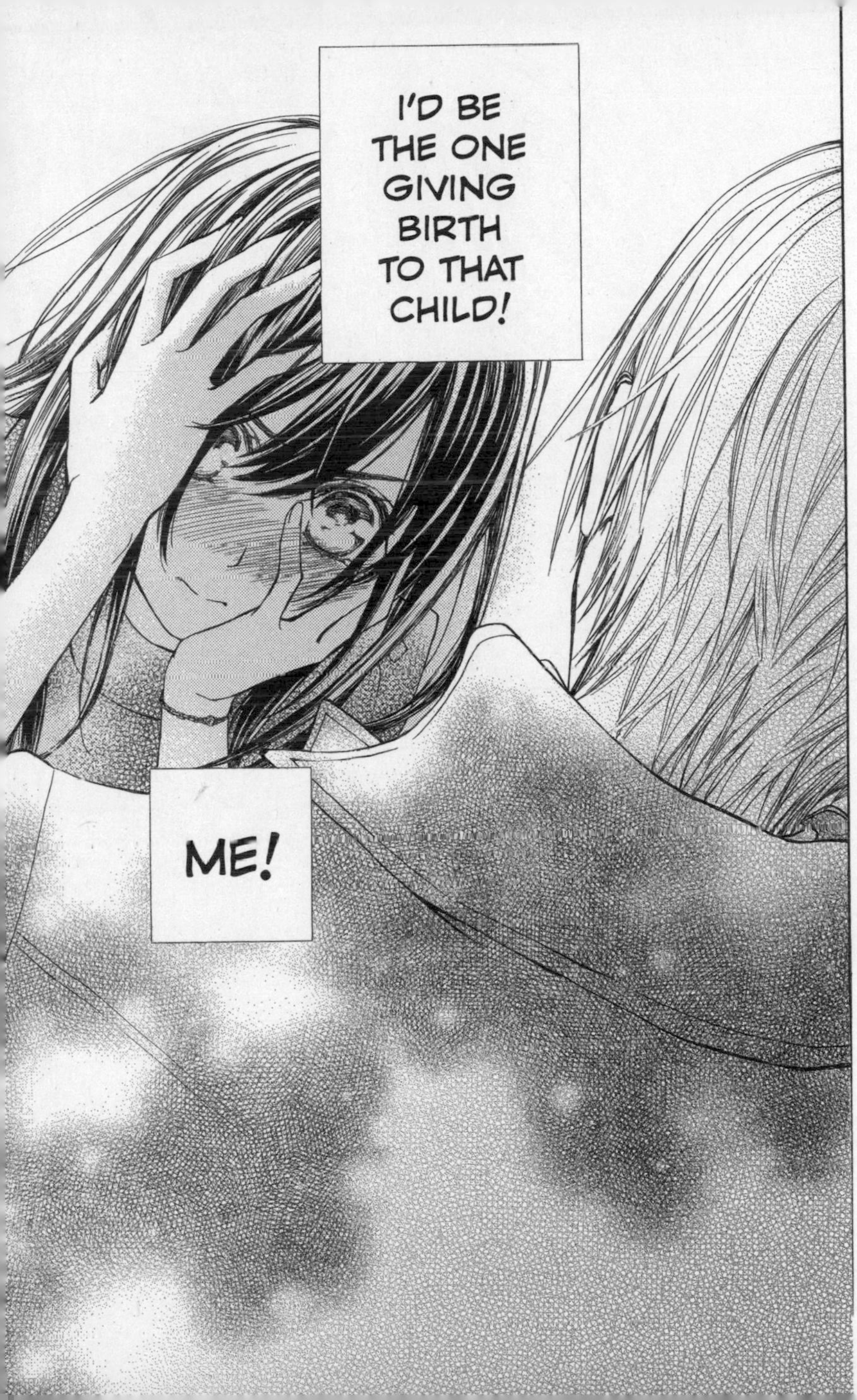
I'D BE THE ONE GIVING BIRTH TO THAT CHILD!
ME!

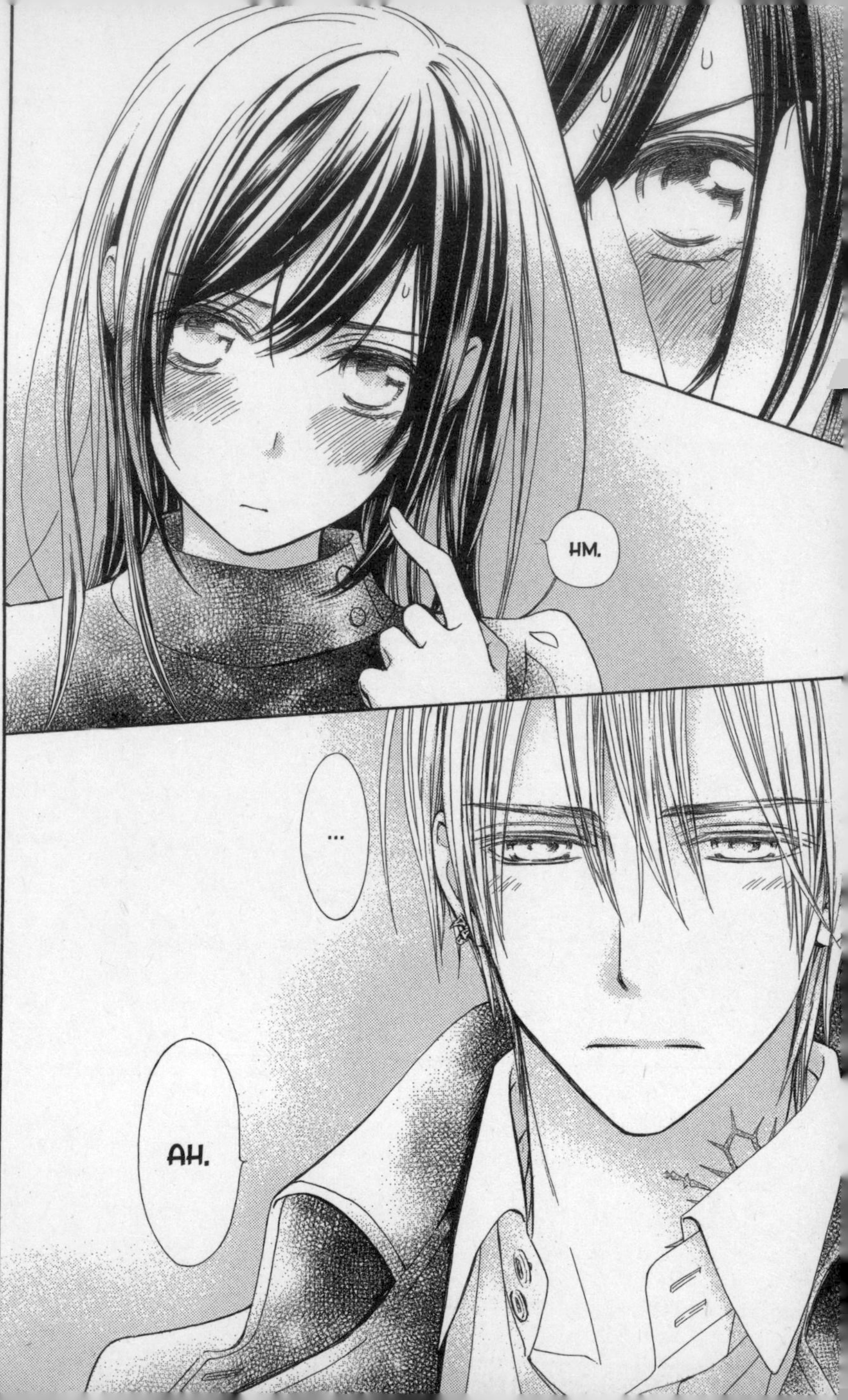
HM.
...
AH.

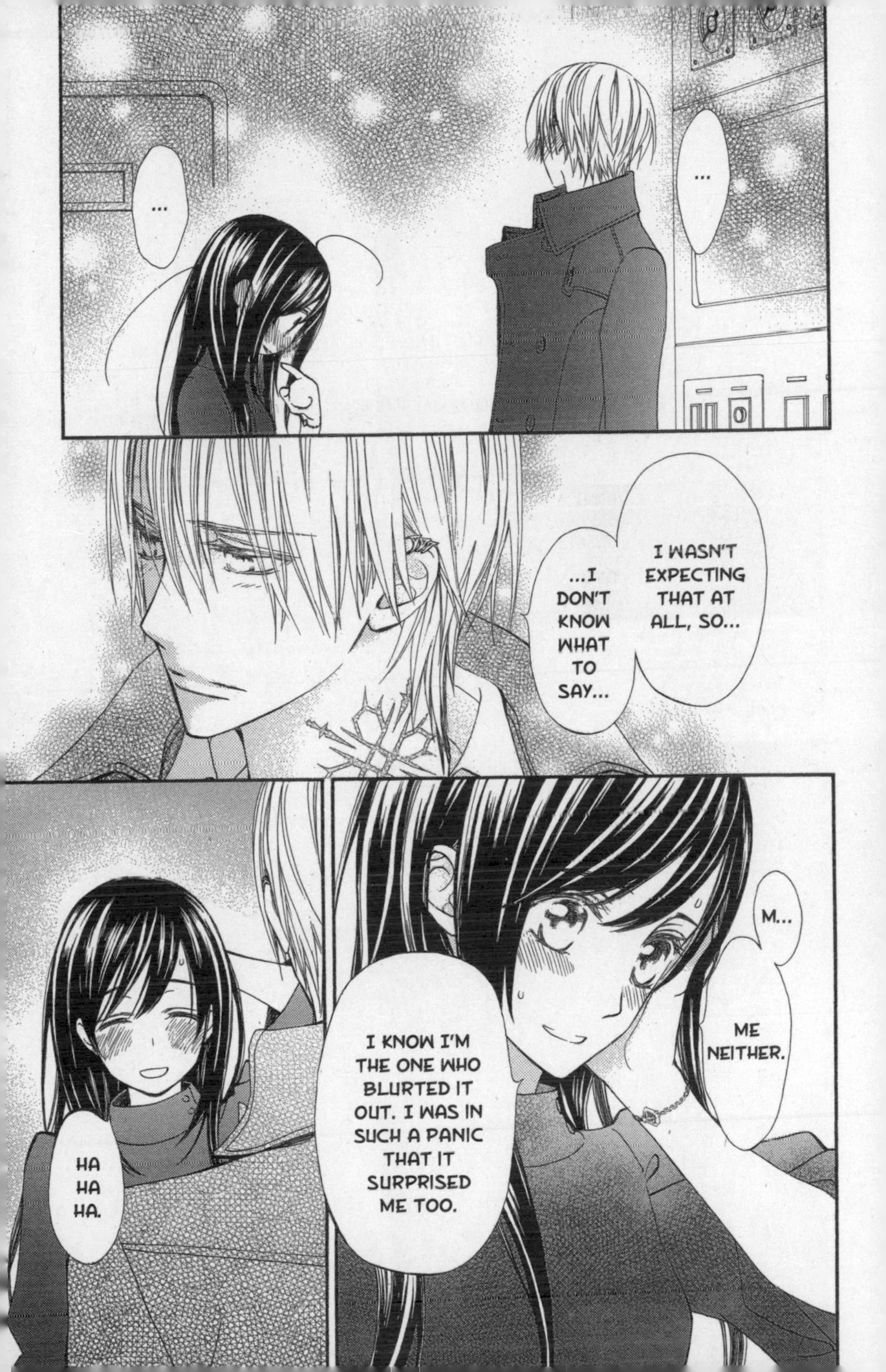
...
...
I WASN'T EXPECTING THAT AT ALL, SO...
...I DON'T KNOW WHAT TO SAY...
M...
ME NEITHER.
I KNOW I'M THE ONE WHO BLURTED IT OUT. I WAS IN SUCH A PANIC THAT IT SURPRISED ME TOO.
HA HA HA.

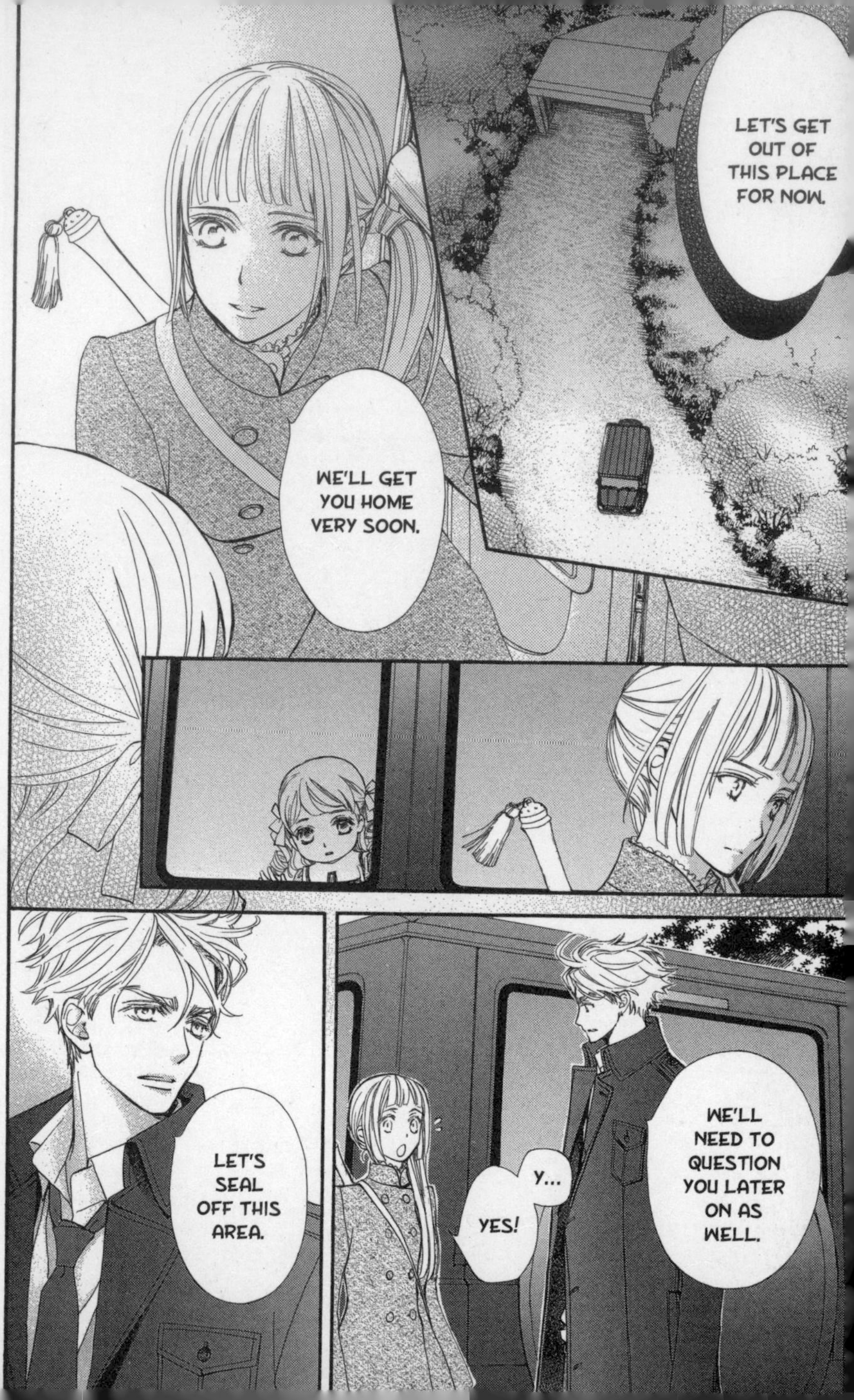
LET'S GET OUT OF THIS PLACE FOR NOW.
WE'LL GET YOU HOME VERY SOON.
WE'LL NEED TO QUESTION YOU LATER ON AS WELL.
Y...
YES!
LET'S SEAL OFF THIS AREA.

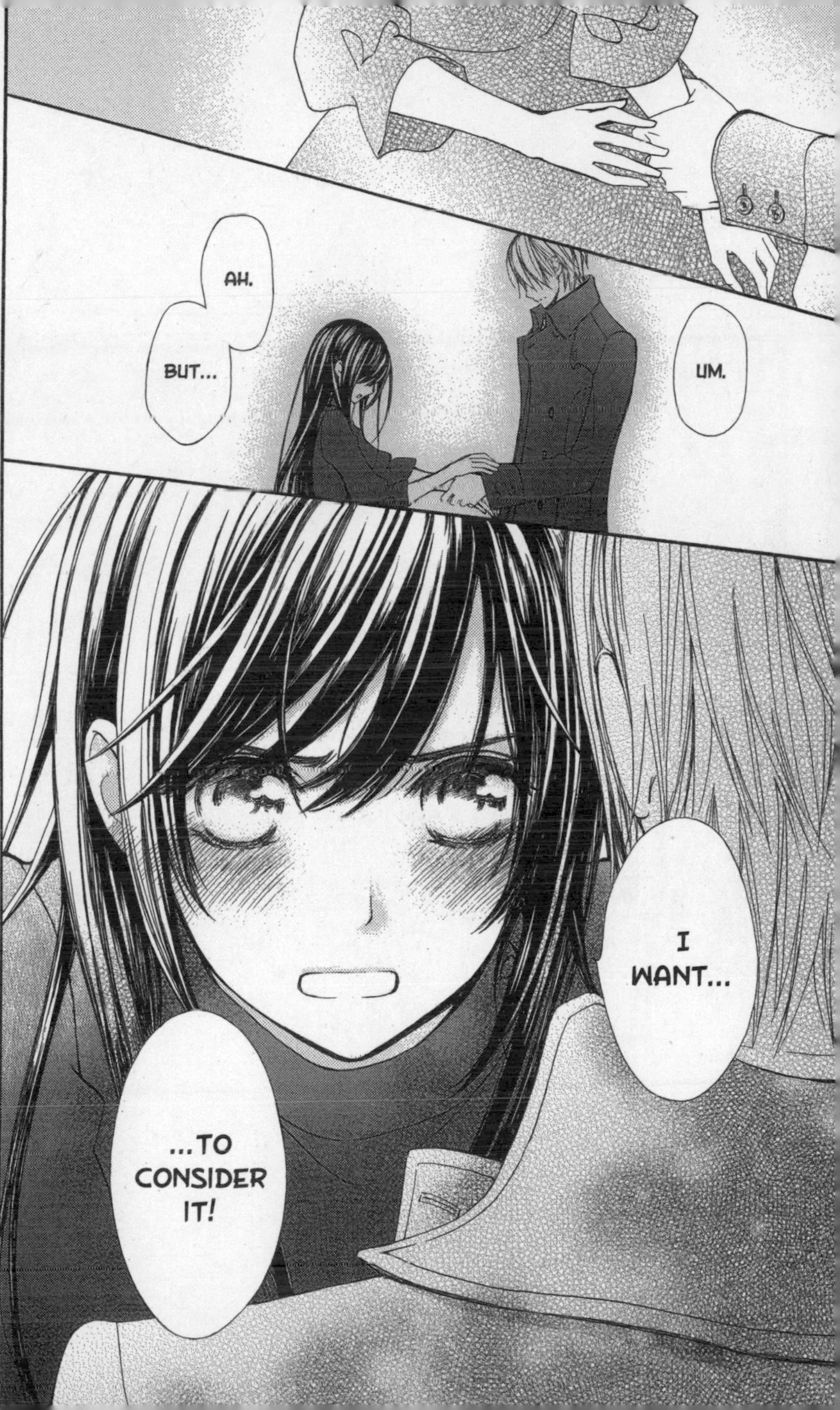
UM.
AH.
BUT...
I WANT...
...TO CONSIDER IT!

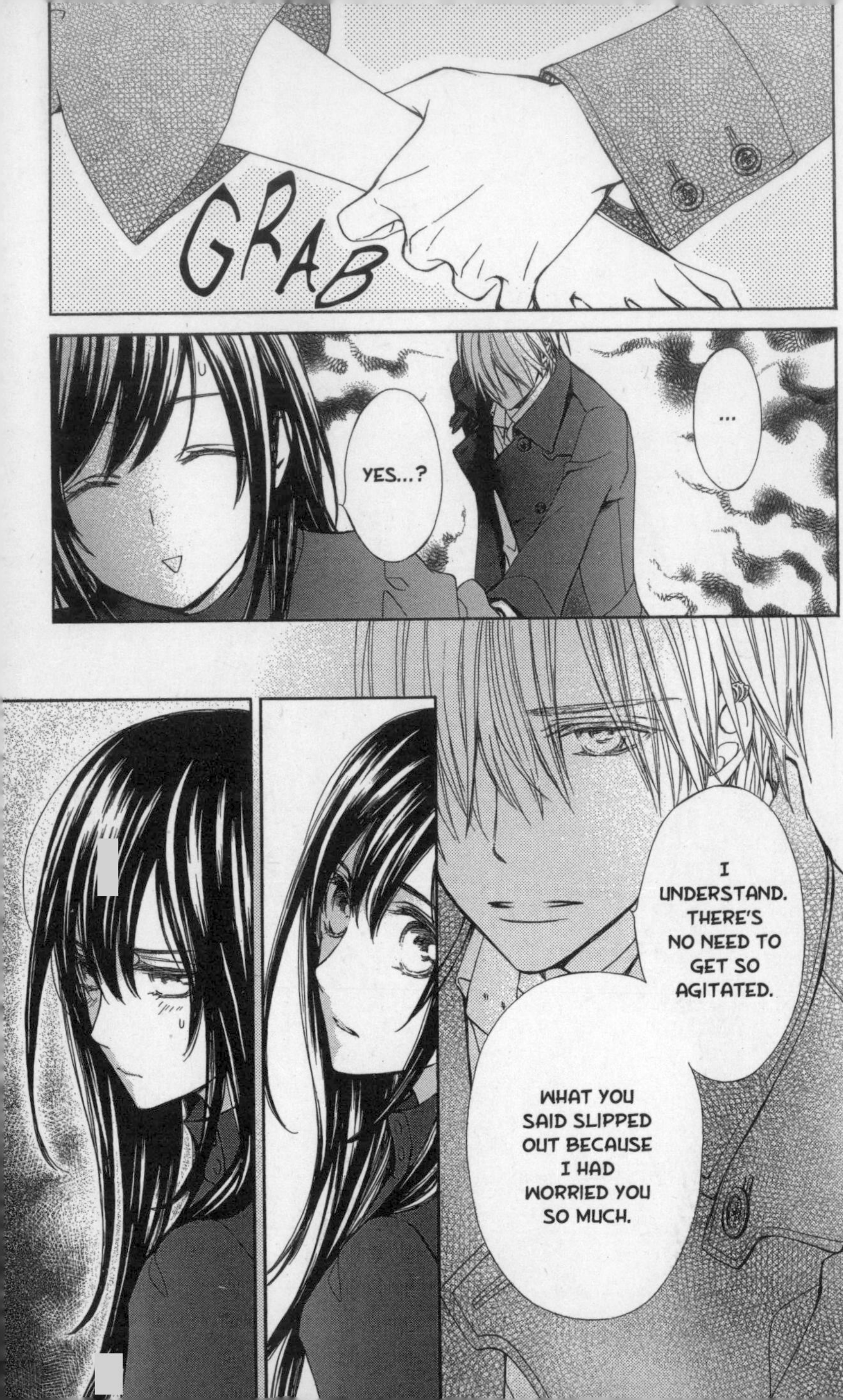
GRAB
...
YES...?
I UNDERSTAND. THERE'S NO NEED TO GET SO AGITATED.
WHAT YOU SAID SLIPPED OUT BECAUSE I HAD WORRIED YOU SO MUCH.

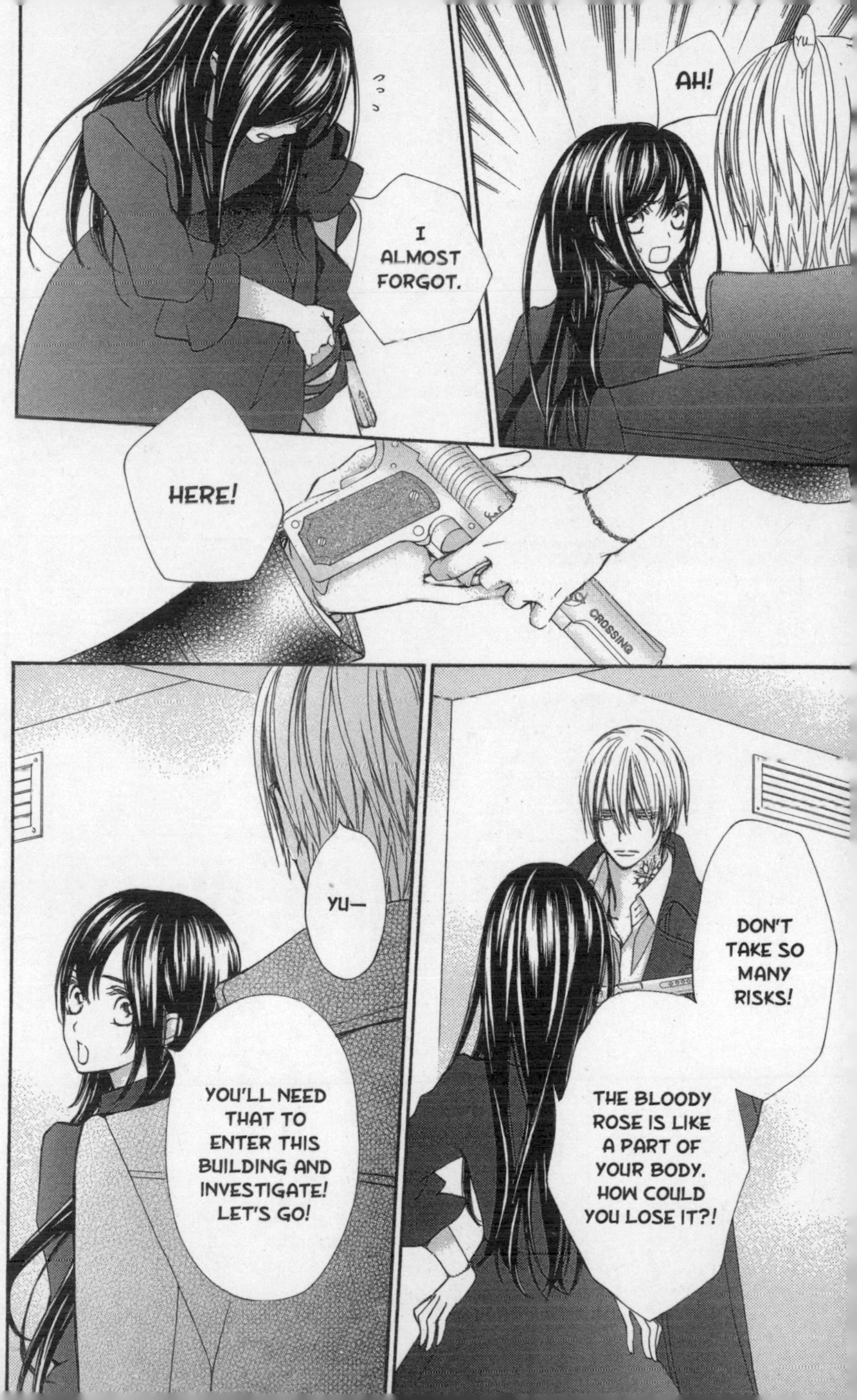
YU...
AH!
I ALMOST FORGOT.
HERE!
CROSSING
DON'T TAKE SO MANY RISKS!
THE BLOODY ROSE IS LIKE A PART OF YOUR BODY. HOW COULD YOU LOSE IT?!
YU—
YOU'LL NEED THAT TO ENTER THIS BUILDING AND INVESTIGATE! LET'S GO!

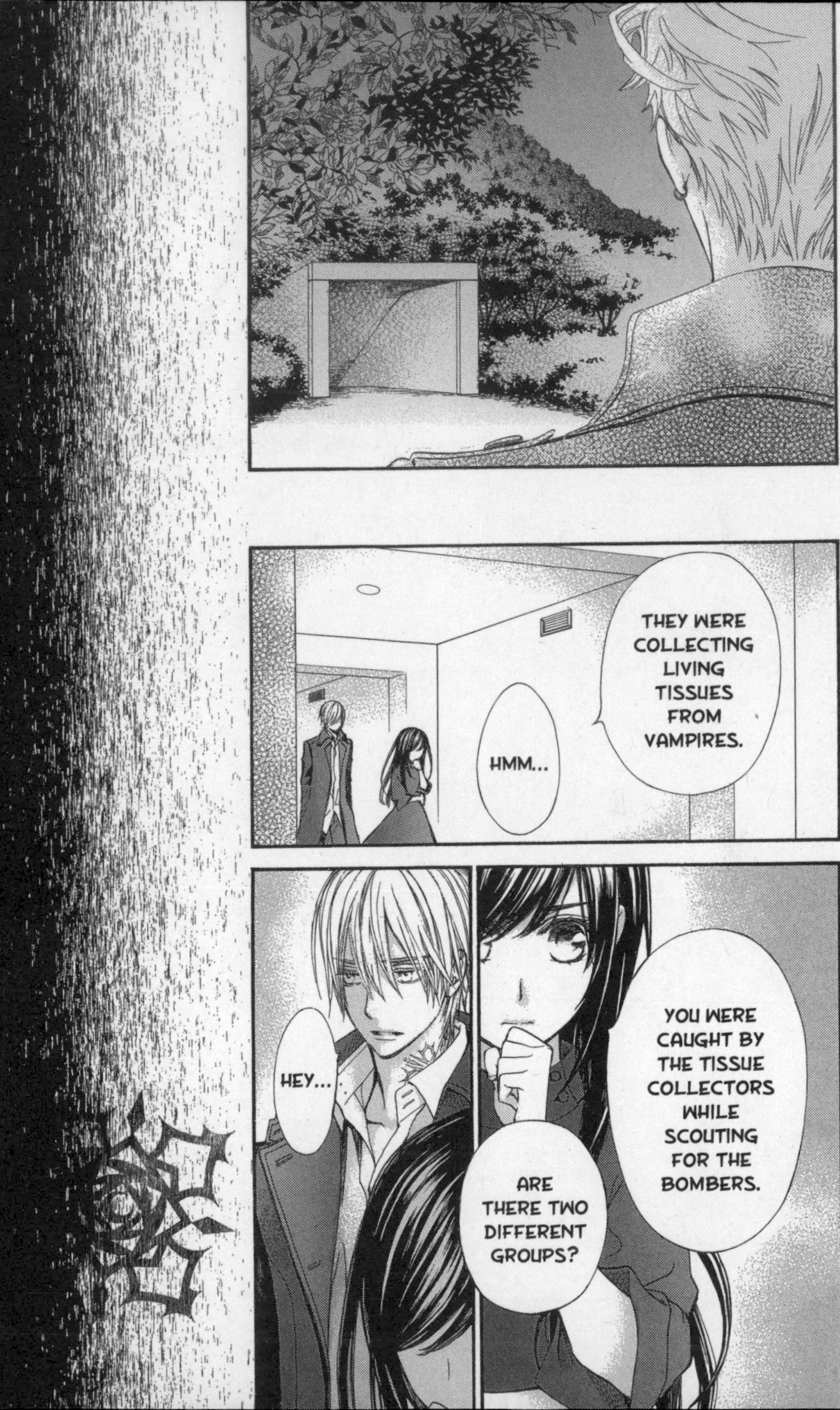
THEY WERE COLLECTING LIVING TISSUES FROM VAMPIRES.
HMM...
YOU WERE CAUGHT BY THE TISSUE COLLECTORS WHILE SCOUTING FOR THE BOMBERS.
HEY...
ARE THERE TWO DIFFERENT GROUPS?

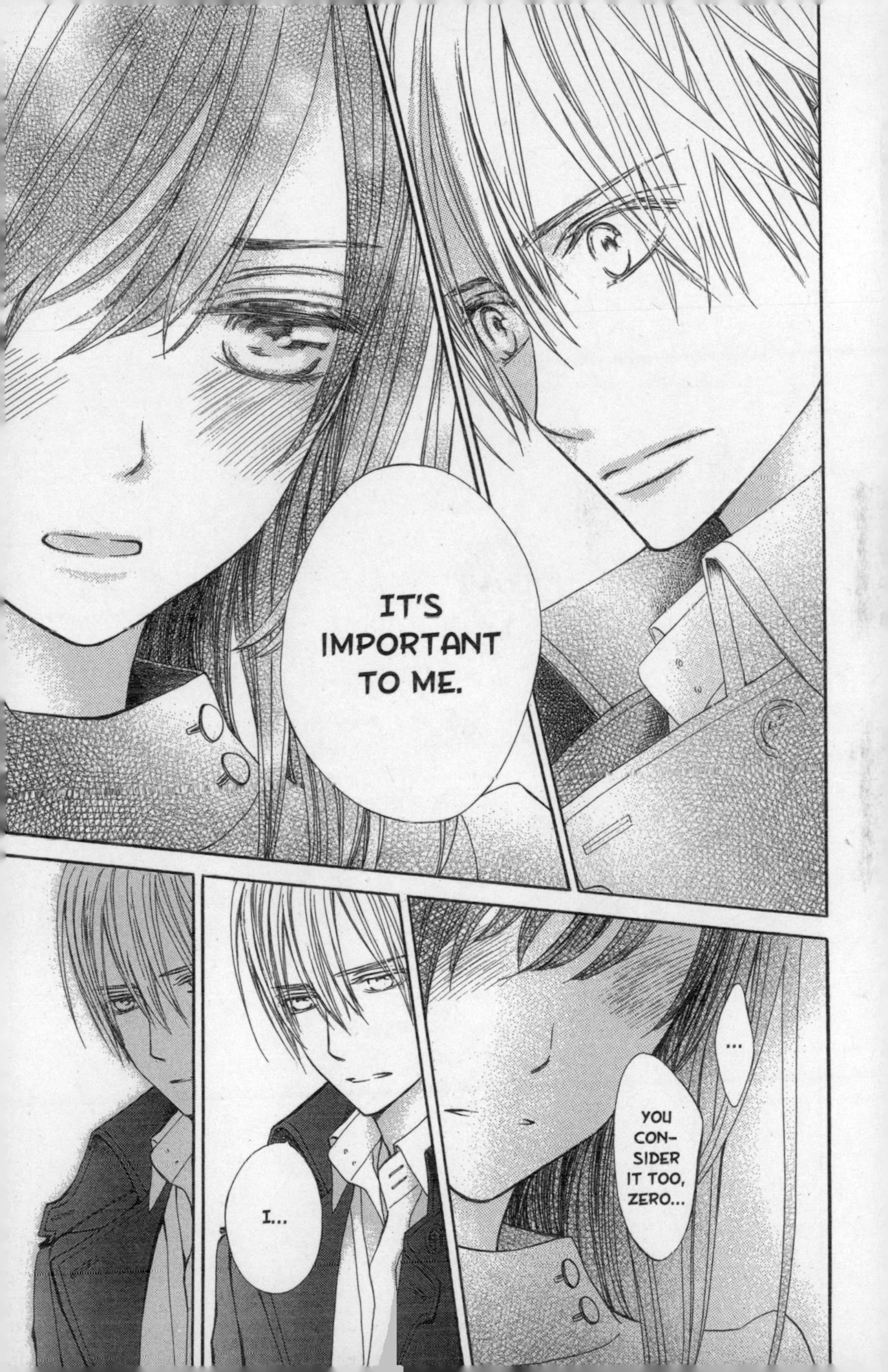
IT'S IMPORTANT TO ME.
...
YOU CONSIDER IT TOO, ZERO...
I...

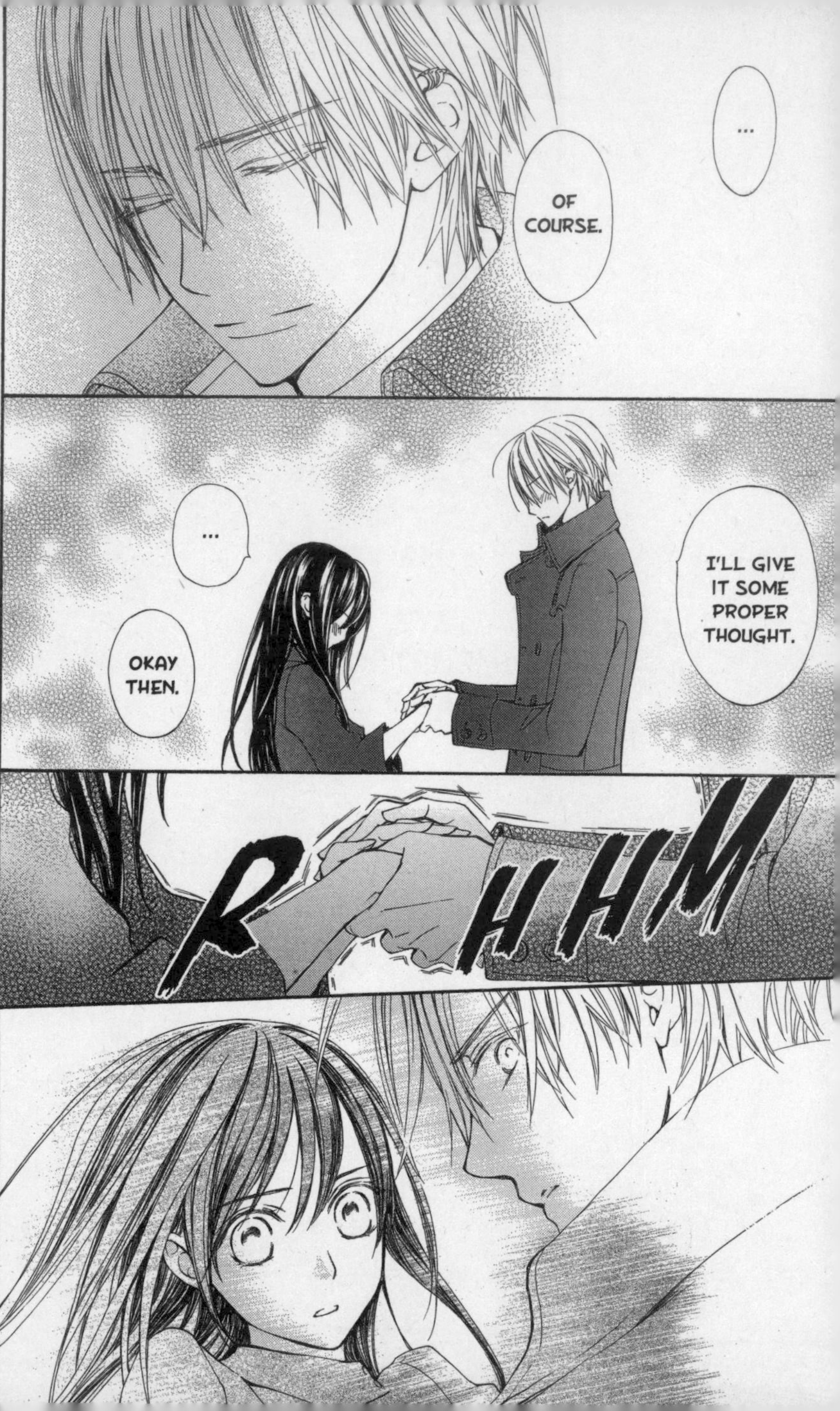
...
OF COURSE.
I'LL GIVE IT SOME PROPER THOUGHT.
...
OKAY THEN.
RHHM

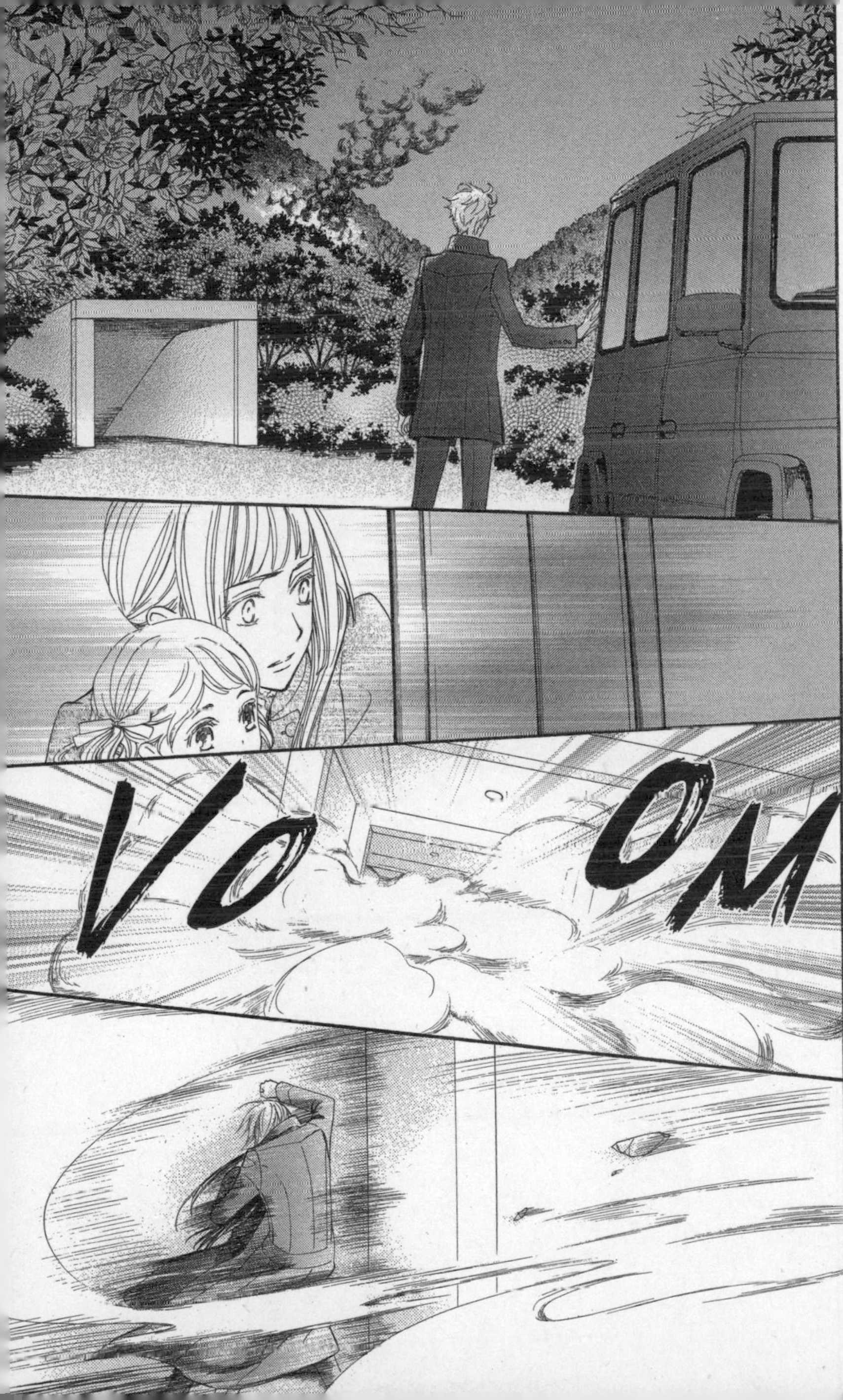
VOOM

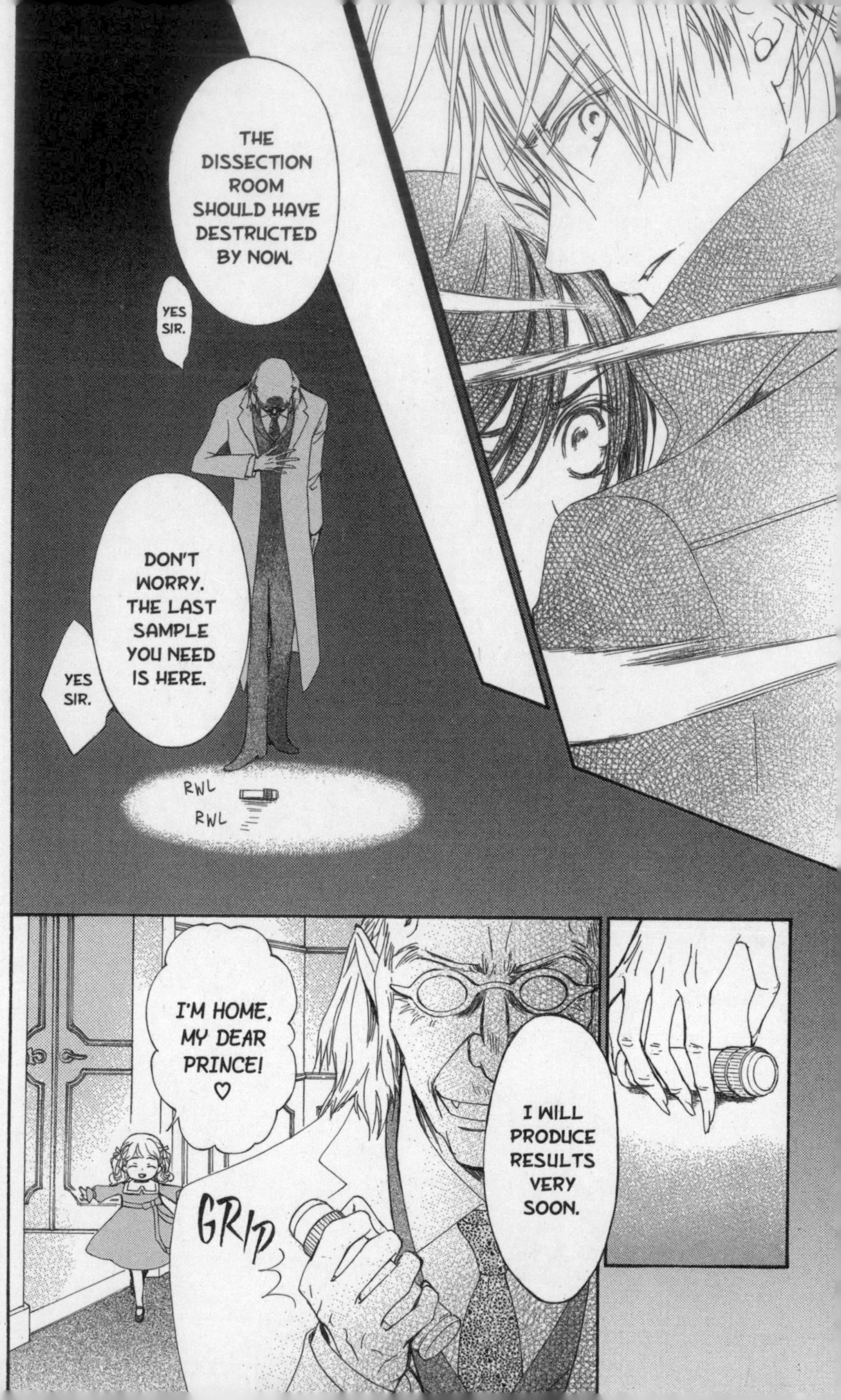
THE DISSECTION ROOM SHOULD HAVE DESTRUCTED BY NOW.
YES SIR.
DON'T WORRY. THE LAST SAMPLE YOU NEED IS HERE.
YES SIR.
RWL
RWL
I WILL PRODUCE RESULTS VERY SOON.
GRIP
I'M HOME, MY DEAR PRINCE! ♡

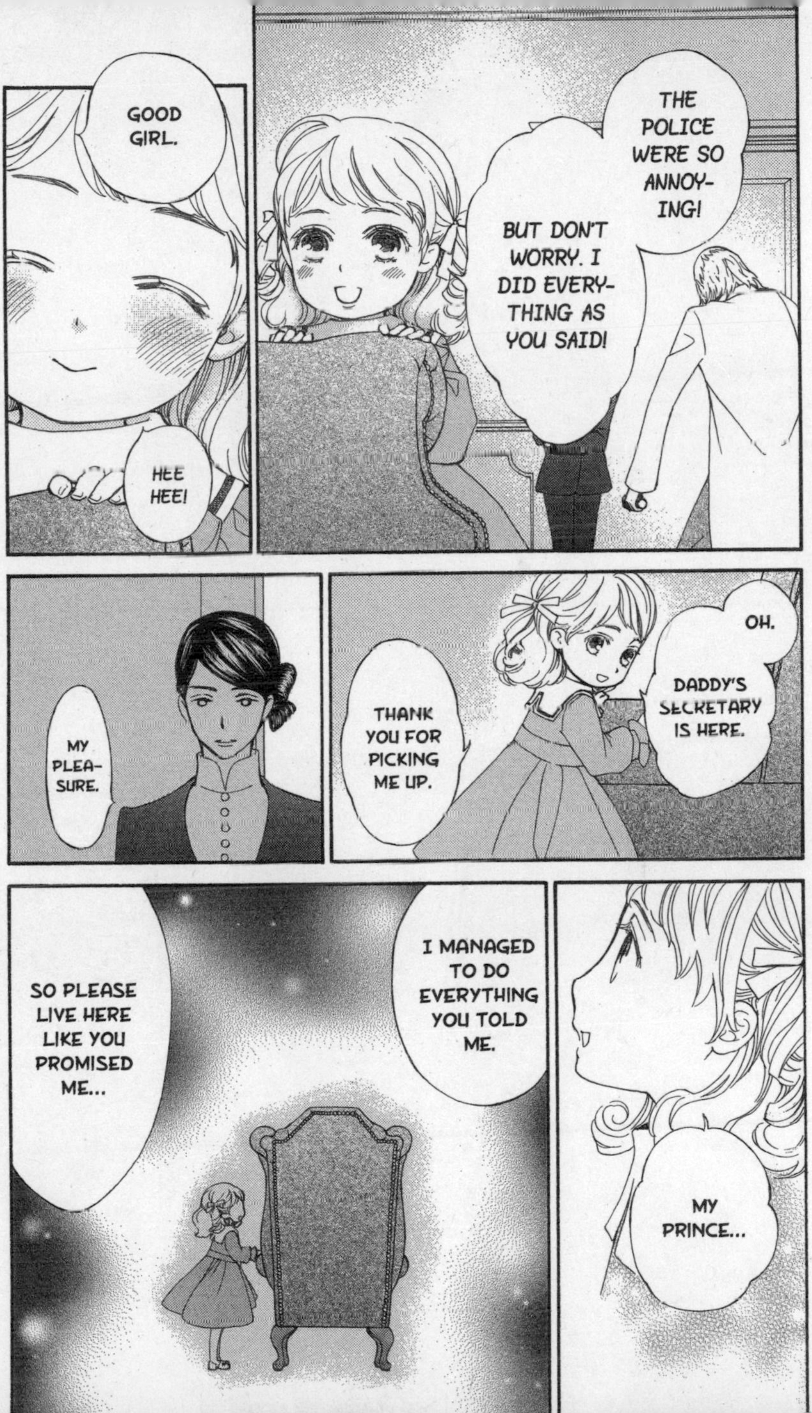
THE POLICE WERE SO ANNOY-ING!
BUT DON'T WORRY. I DID EVERY-THING AS YOU SAID!
GOOD GIRL.
HEE HEE!
OH.
DADDY'S SECRETARY IS HERE.
THANK YOU FOR PICKING ME UP.
MY PLEA-SURE.
MY PRINCE...
I MANAGED TO DO EVERYTHING YOU TOLD ME.
SO PLEASE LIVE HERE LIKE YOU PROMISED ME...

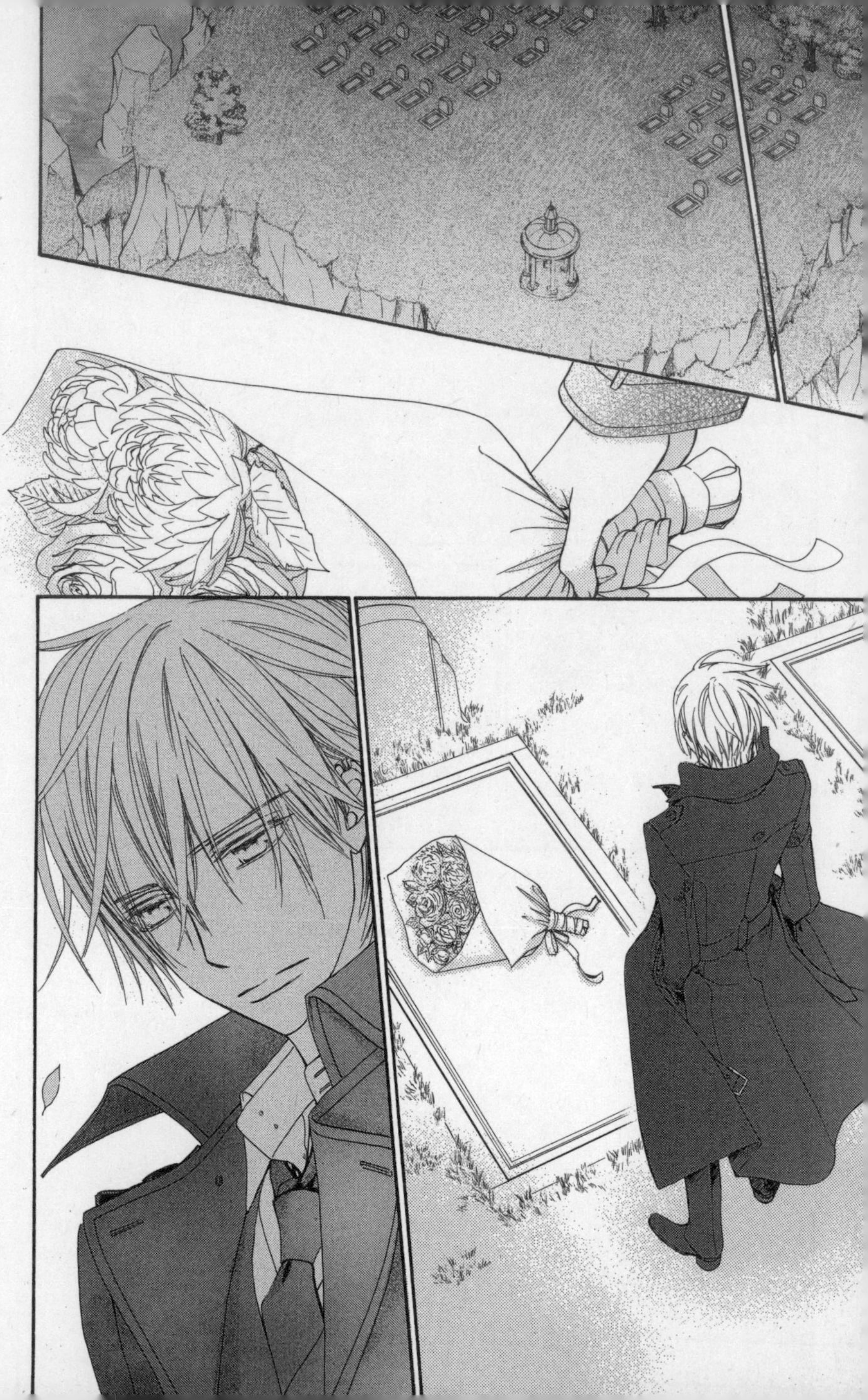

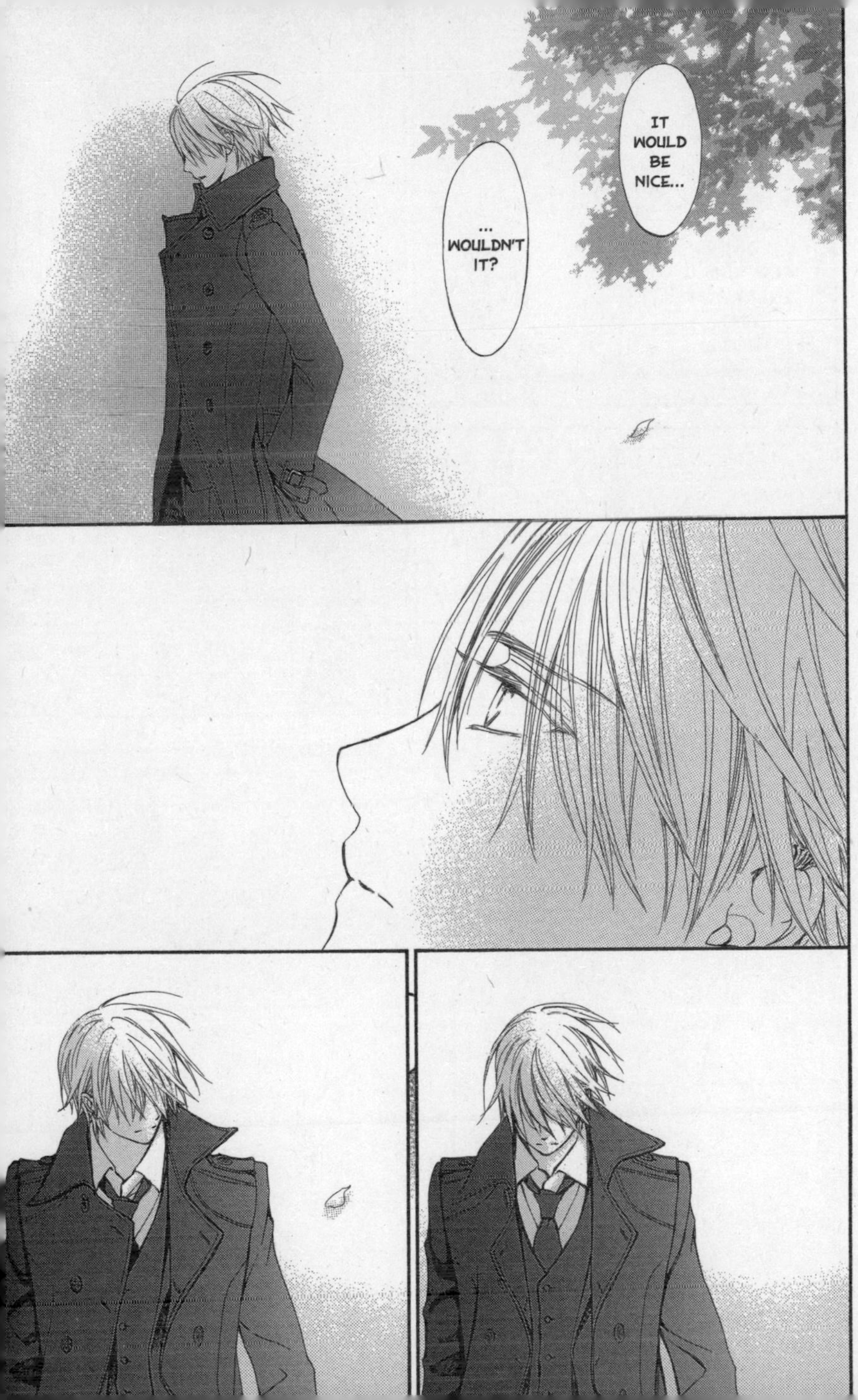
IT WOULD BE NICE...
... WOULDN'T IT?

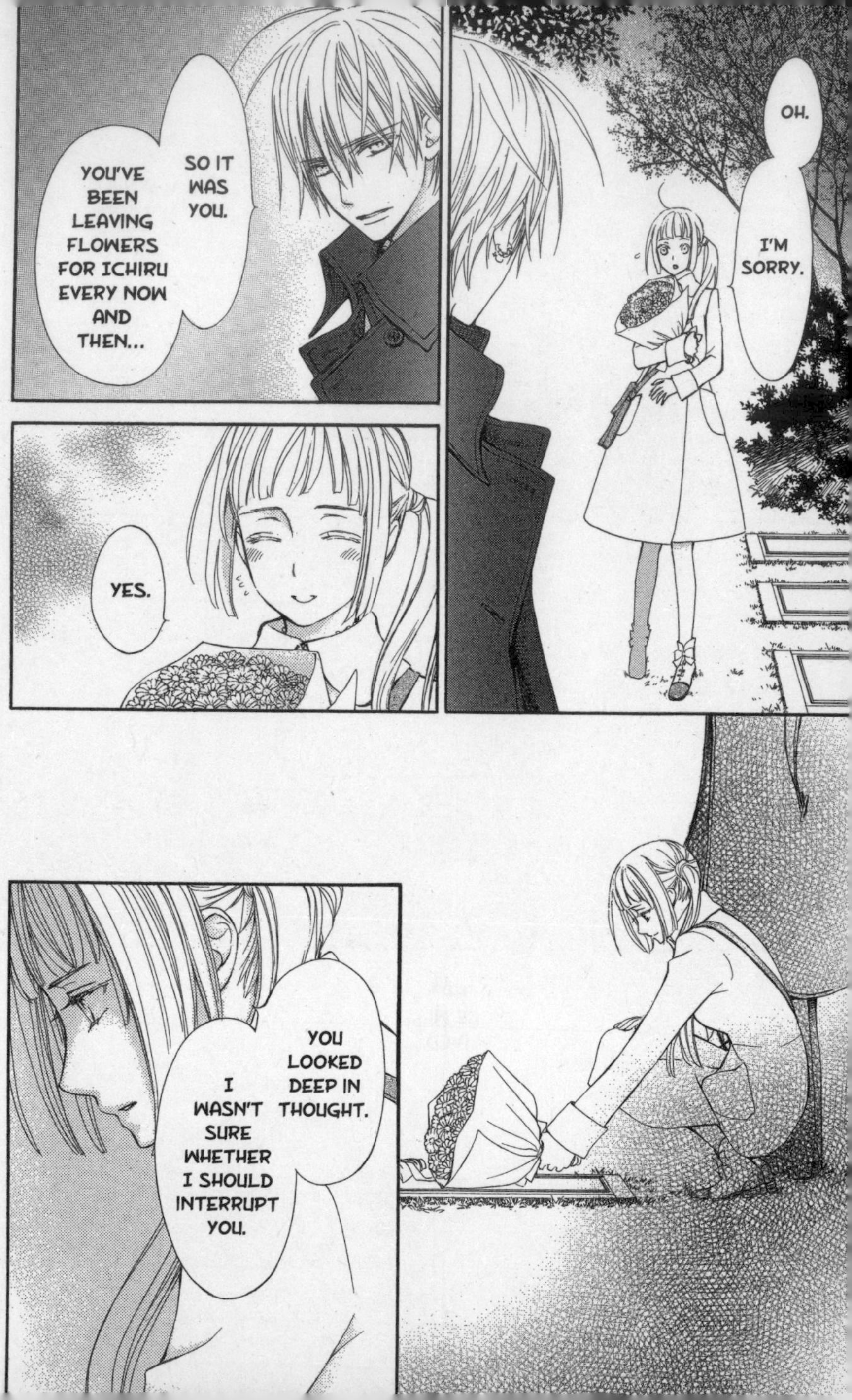
OH.
I'M SORRY.
SO IT WAS YOU.
YOU'VE BEEN LEAVING FLOWERS FOR ICHIRU EVERY NOW AND THEN...
YES.
YOU LOOKED DEEP IN THOUGHT.
I WASN'T SURE WHETHER I SHOULD INTERRUPT YOU.

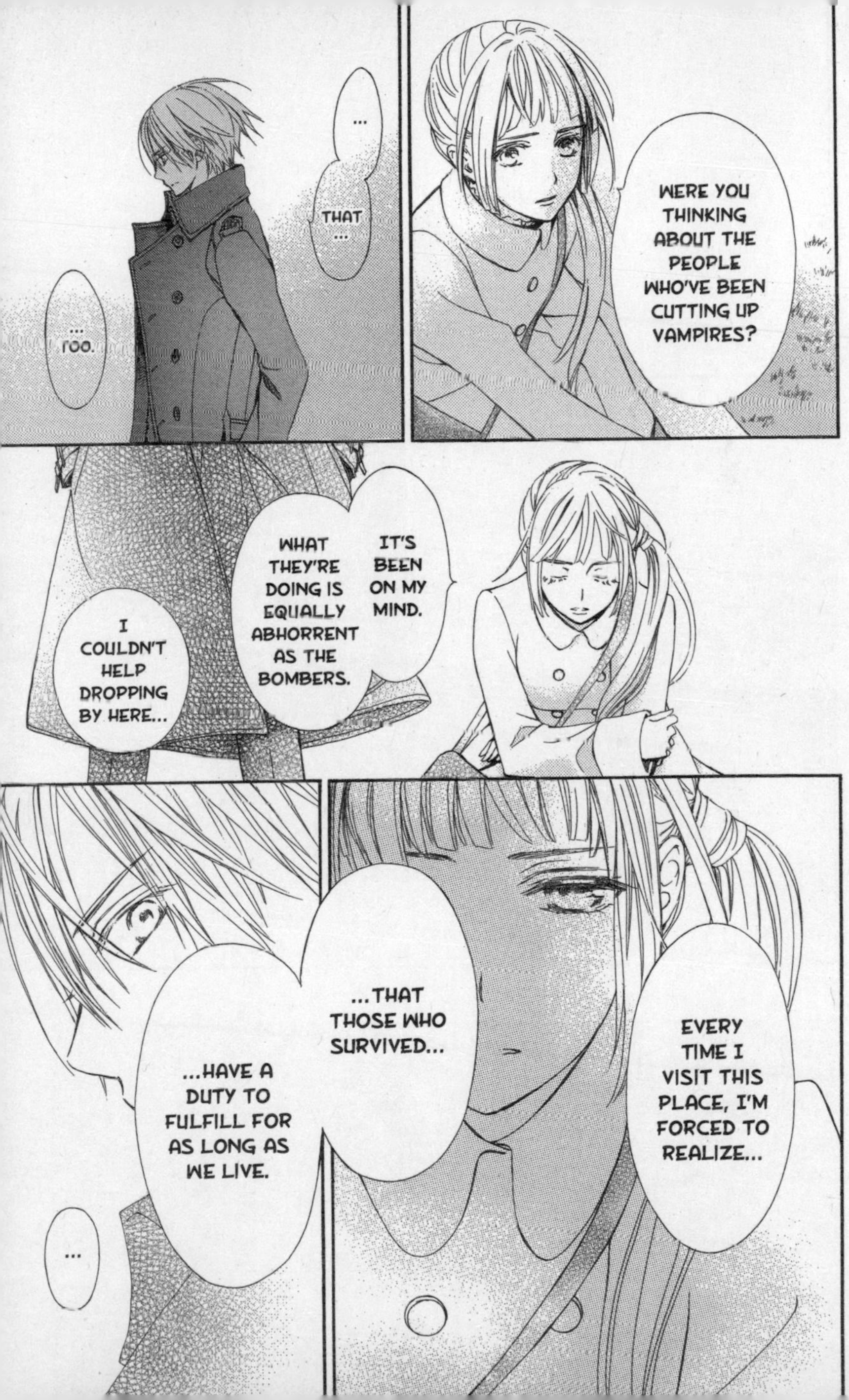
WERE YOU THINKING ABOUT THE PEOPLE WHO'VE BEEN CUTTING UP VAMPIRES?
...
THAT...
...TOO.
IT'S BEEN ON MY MIND.
WHAT THEY'RE DOING IS EQUALLY ABHORRENT AS THE BOMBERS.
I COULDN'T HELP DROPPING BY HERE...
EVERY TIME I VISIT THIS PLACE, I'M FORCED TO REALIZE...
...THAT THOSE WHO SURVIVED...
...HAVE A DUTY TO FULFILL FOR AS LONG AS WE LIVE.
...

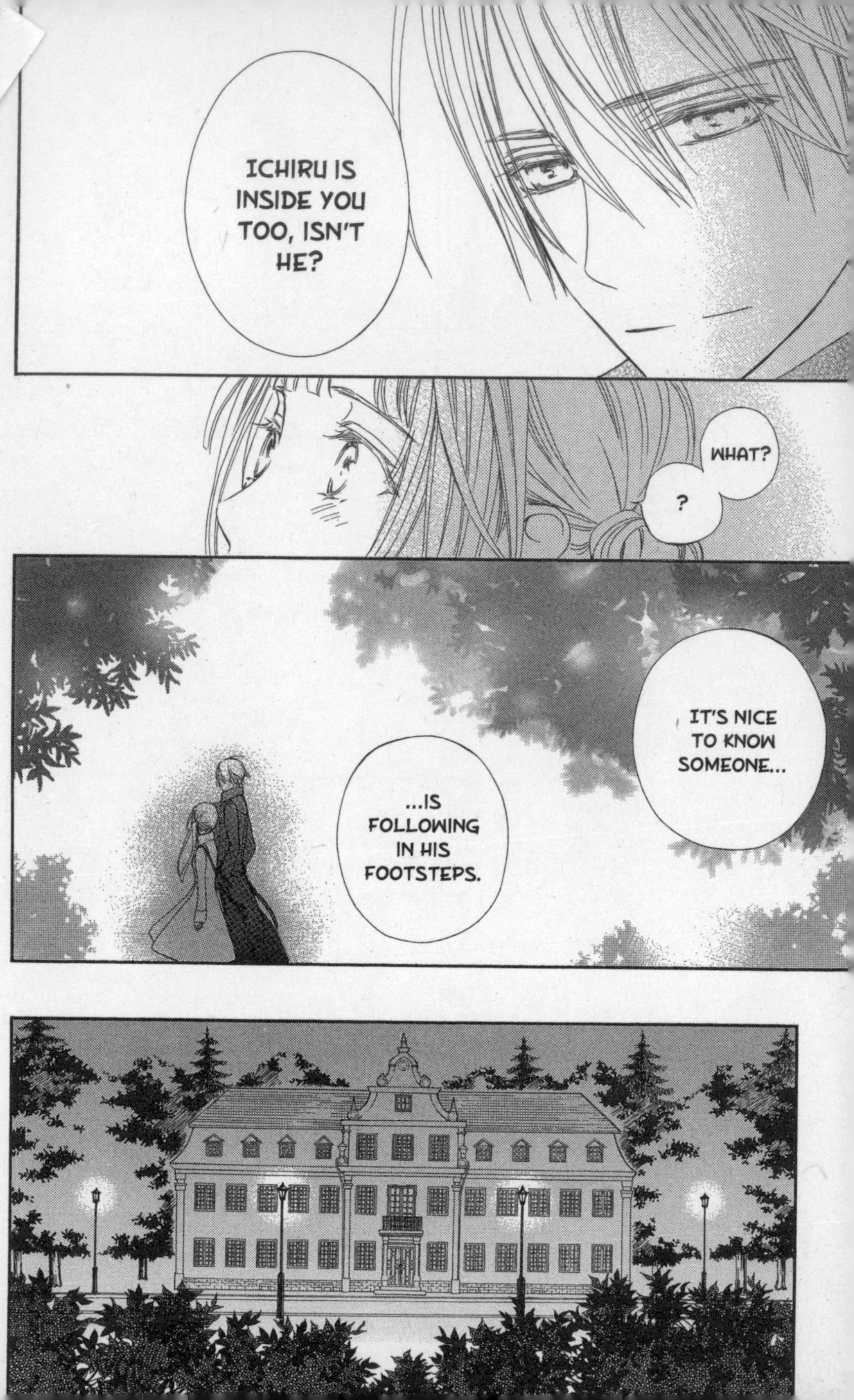
ICHIRU IS INSIDE YOU TOO, ISN'T HE?
WHAT?
?
IT'S NICE TO KNOW SOMEONE...
...IS FOLLOWING IN HIS FOOTSTEPS.

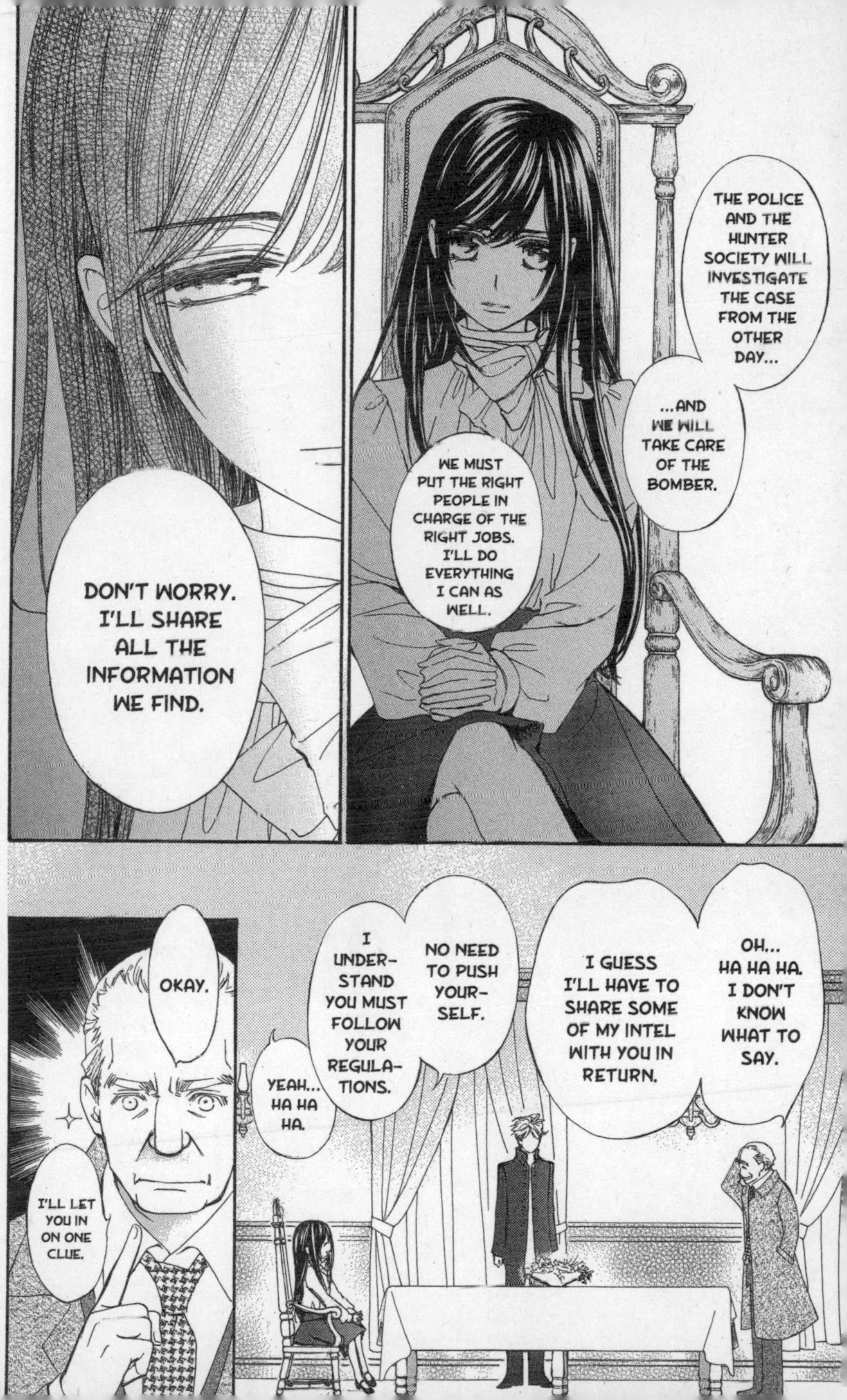
THE POLICE AND THE HUNTER SOCIETY WILL INVESTIGATE THE CASE FROM THE OTHER DAY...
...AND WE WILL TAKE CARE OF THE BOMBER.
WE MUST PUT THE RIGHT PEOPLE IN CHARGE OF THE RIGHT JOBS. I'LL DO EVERYTHING I CAN AS WELL.
DON'T WORRY. I'LL SHARE ALL THE INFORMATION WE FIND.
OH... HA HA HA. I DON'T KNOW WHAT TO SAY.
I GUESS I'LL HAVE TO SHARE SOME OF MY INTEL WITH YOU IN RETURN.
NO NEED TO PUSH YOURSELF.
I UNDERSTAND YOU MUST FOLLOW YOUR REGULATIONS.
YEAH... HA HA HA.
OKAY.
I'LL LET YOU IN ON ONE CLUE.

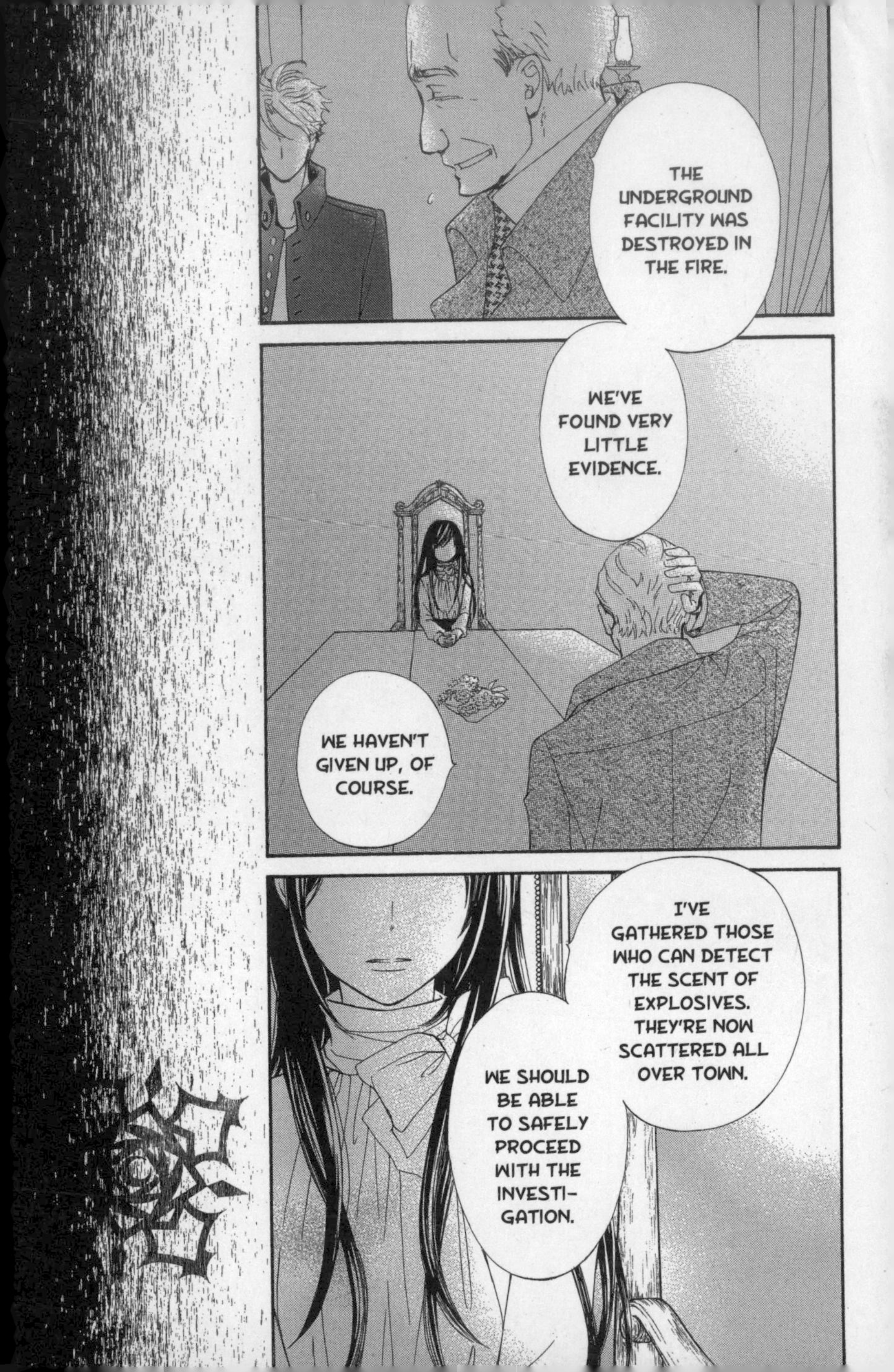
THE UNDERGROUND FACILITY WAS DESTROYED IN THE FIRE.
WE'VE FOUND VERY LITTLE EVIDENCE.
WE HAVEN'T GIVEN UP, OF COURSE.
I'VE GATHERED THOSE WHO CAN DETECT THE SCENT OF EXPLOSIVES. THEY'RE NOW SCATTERED ALL OVER TOWN.
WE SHOULD BE ABLE TO SAFELY PROCEED WITH THE INVESTI-GATION.

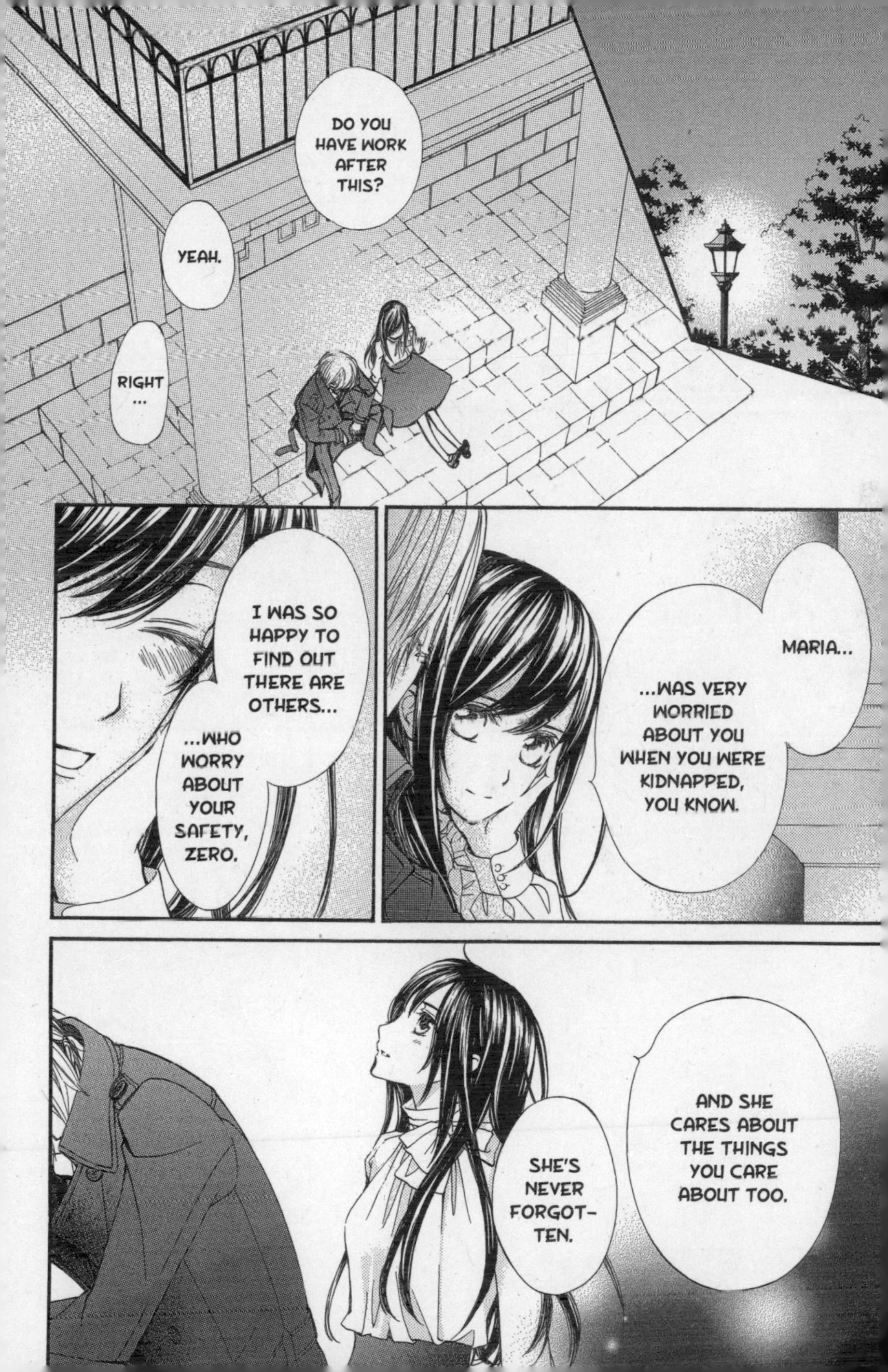
DO YOU HAVE WORK AFTER THIS?
YEAH.
RIGHT...
MARIA...
...WAS VERY WORRIED ABOUT YOU WHEN YOU WERE KIDNAPPED, YOU KNOW.
I WAS SO HAPPY TO FIND OUT THERE ARE OTHERS...
...WHO WORRY ABOUT YOUR SAFETY, ZERO.
AND SHE CARES ABOUT THE THINGS YOU CARE ABOUT TOO.
SHE'S NEVER FORGOT-TEN.

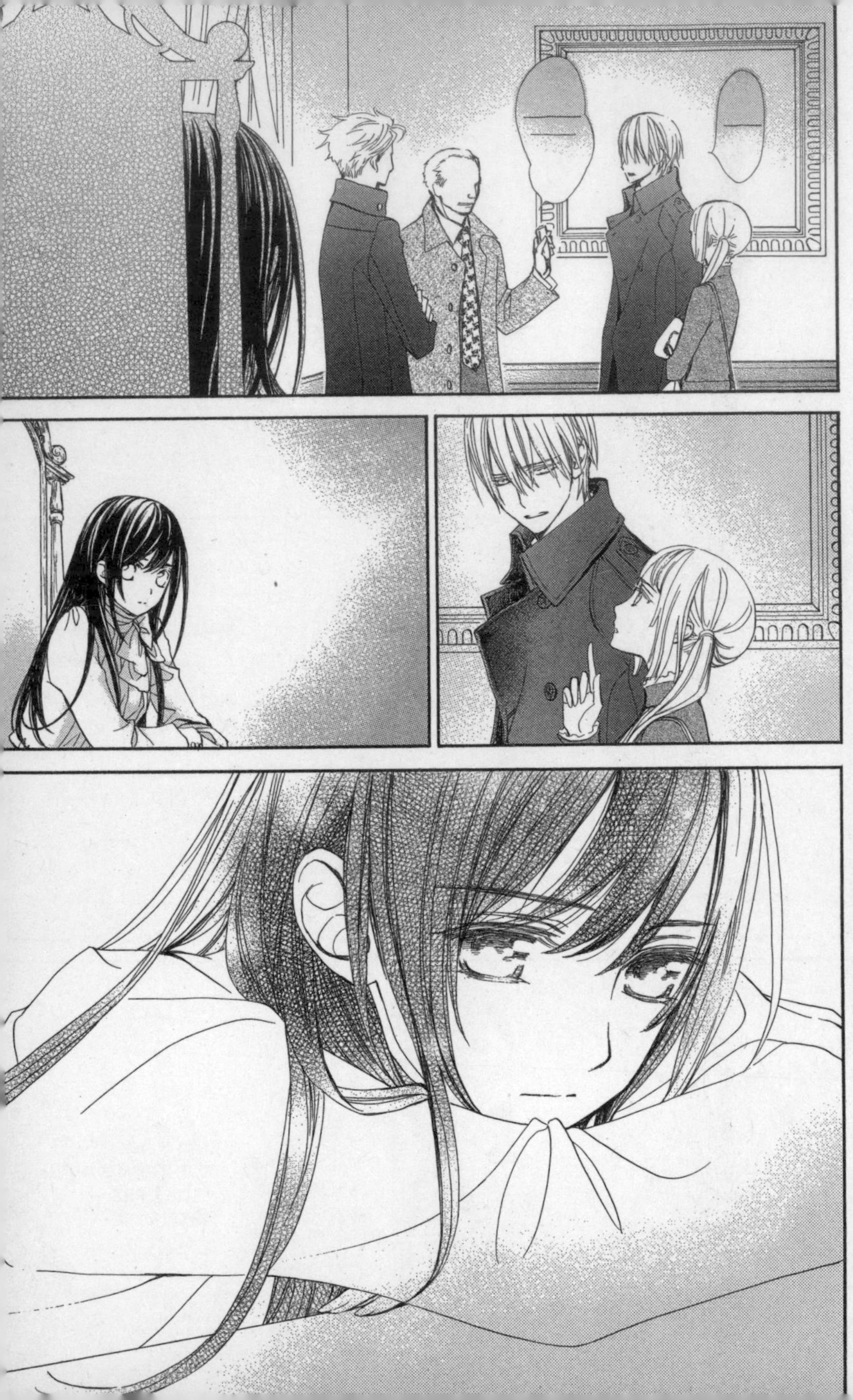

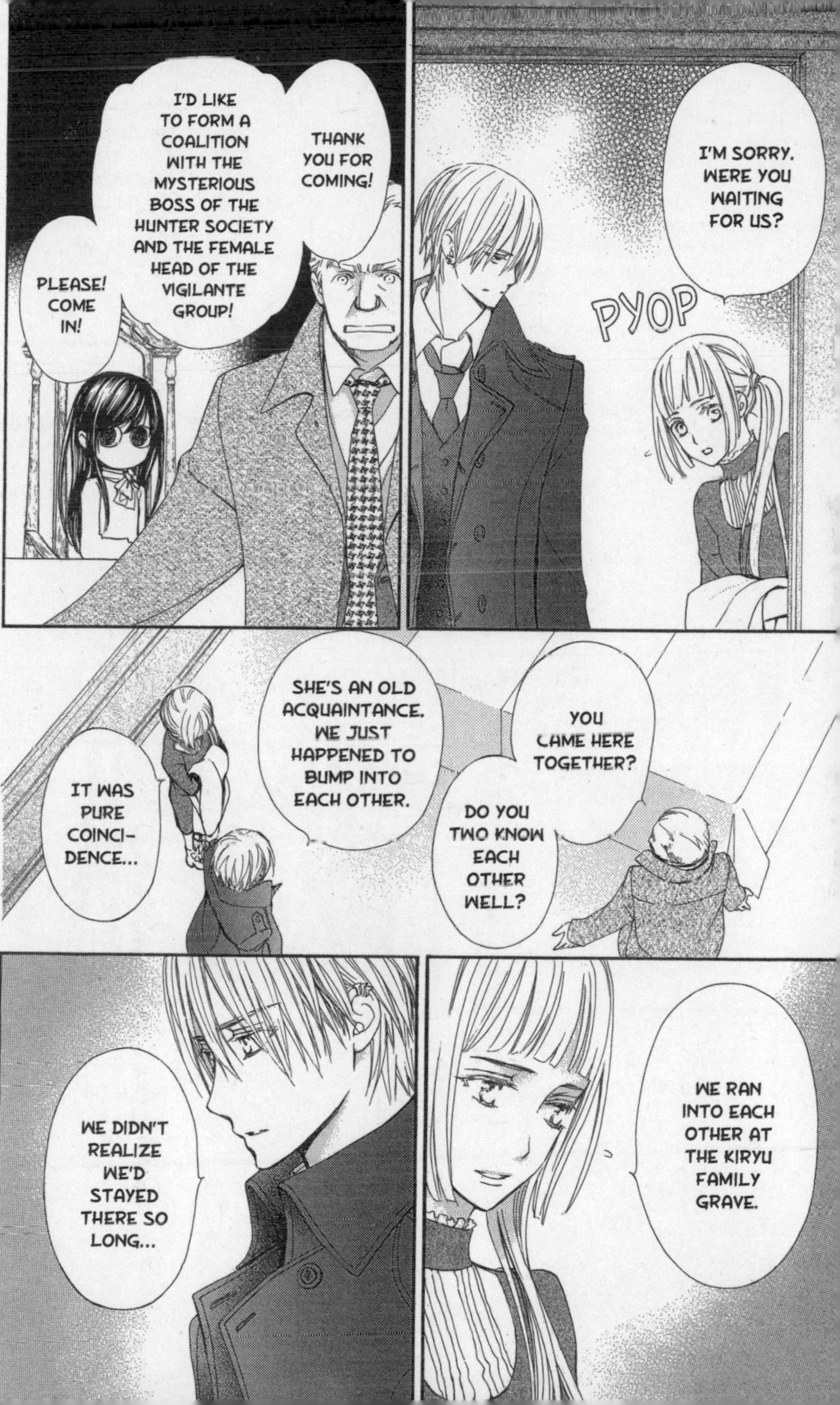
I'M SORRY. WERE YOU WAITING FOR US?
PYOP
THANK YOU FOR COMING!
I'D LIKE TO FORM A COALITION WITH THE MYSTERIOUS BOSS OF THE HUNTER SOCIETY AND THE FEMALE HEAD OF THE VIGILANTE GROUP!
PLEASE! COME IN!
YOU CAME HERE TOGETHER?
DO YOU TWO KNOW EACH OTHER WELL?
SHE'S AN OLD ACQUAINTANCE. WE JUST HAPPENED TO BUMP INTO EACH OTHER.
IT WAS PURE COINCIDENCE...
WE RAN INTO EACH OTHER AT THE KIRYU FAMILY GRAVE.
WE DIDN'T REALIZE WE'D STAYED THERE SO LONG...

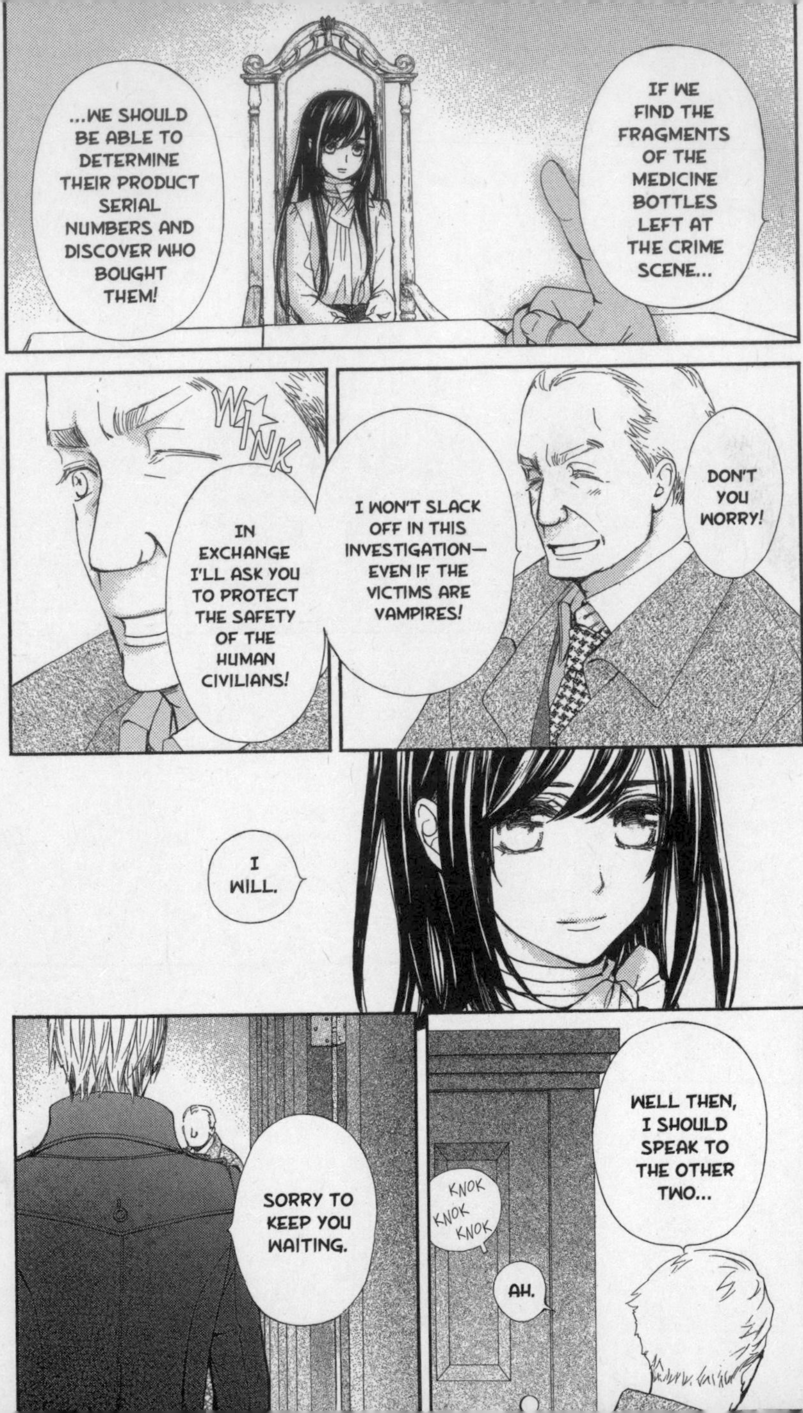
IF WE FIND THE FRAGMENTS OF THE MEDICINE BOTTLES LEFT AT THE CRIME SCENE...
...WE SHOULD BE ABLE TO DETERMINE THEIR PRODUCT SERIAL NUMBERS AND DISCOVER WHO BOUGHT THEM!
DON'T YOU WORRY!
I WON'T SLACK OFF IN THIS INVESTIGATION—EVEN IF THE VICTIMS ARE VAMPIRES!
WINK
IN EXCHANGE I'LL ASK YOU TO PROTECT THE SAFETY OF THE HUMAN CIVILIANS!
I WILL.
WELL THEN, I SHOULD SPEAK TO THE OTHER TWO...
KNOK KNOK KNOK
AH.
SORRY TO KEEP YOU WAITING.

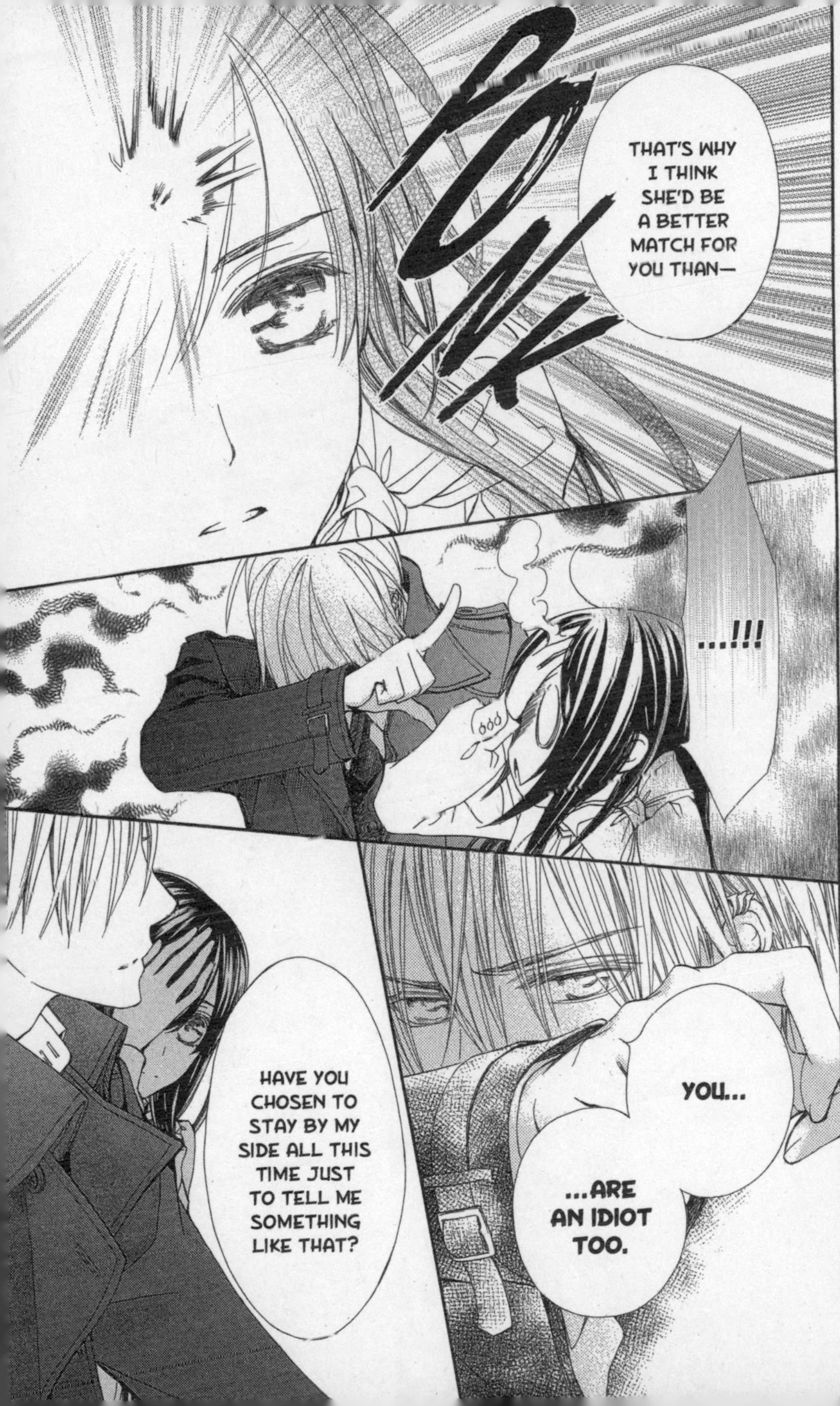
THAT'S WHY I THINK SHE'D BE A BETTER MATCH FOR YOU THAN—
BONK
...!!!
YOU...
...ARE AN IDIOT TOO.
HAVE YOU CHOSEN TO STAY BY MY SIDE ALL THIS TIME JUST TO TELL ME SOMETHING LIKE THAT?

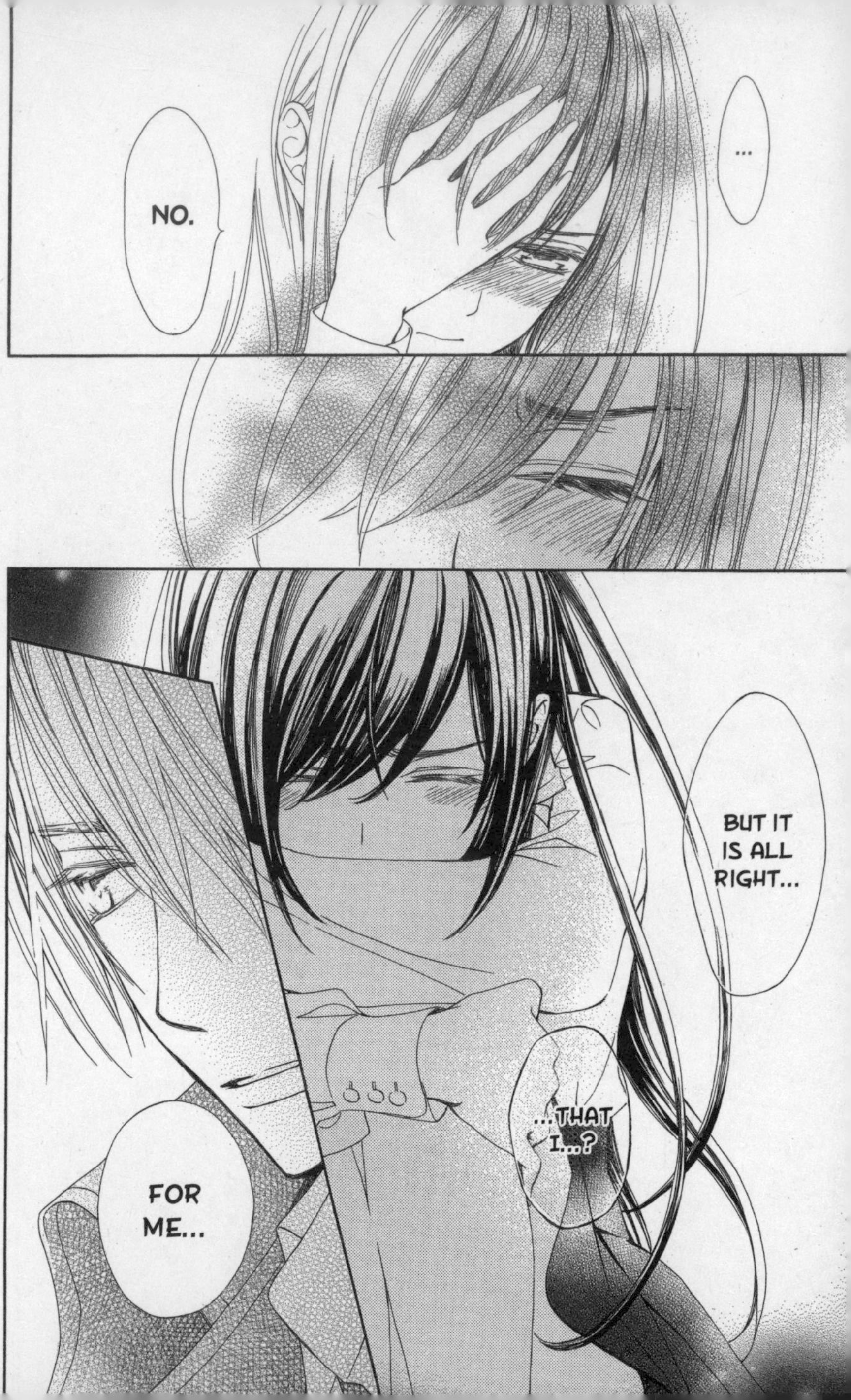
...
NO.
BUT IT IS ALL RIGHT...
...THAT I...?
FOR ME...

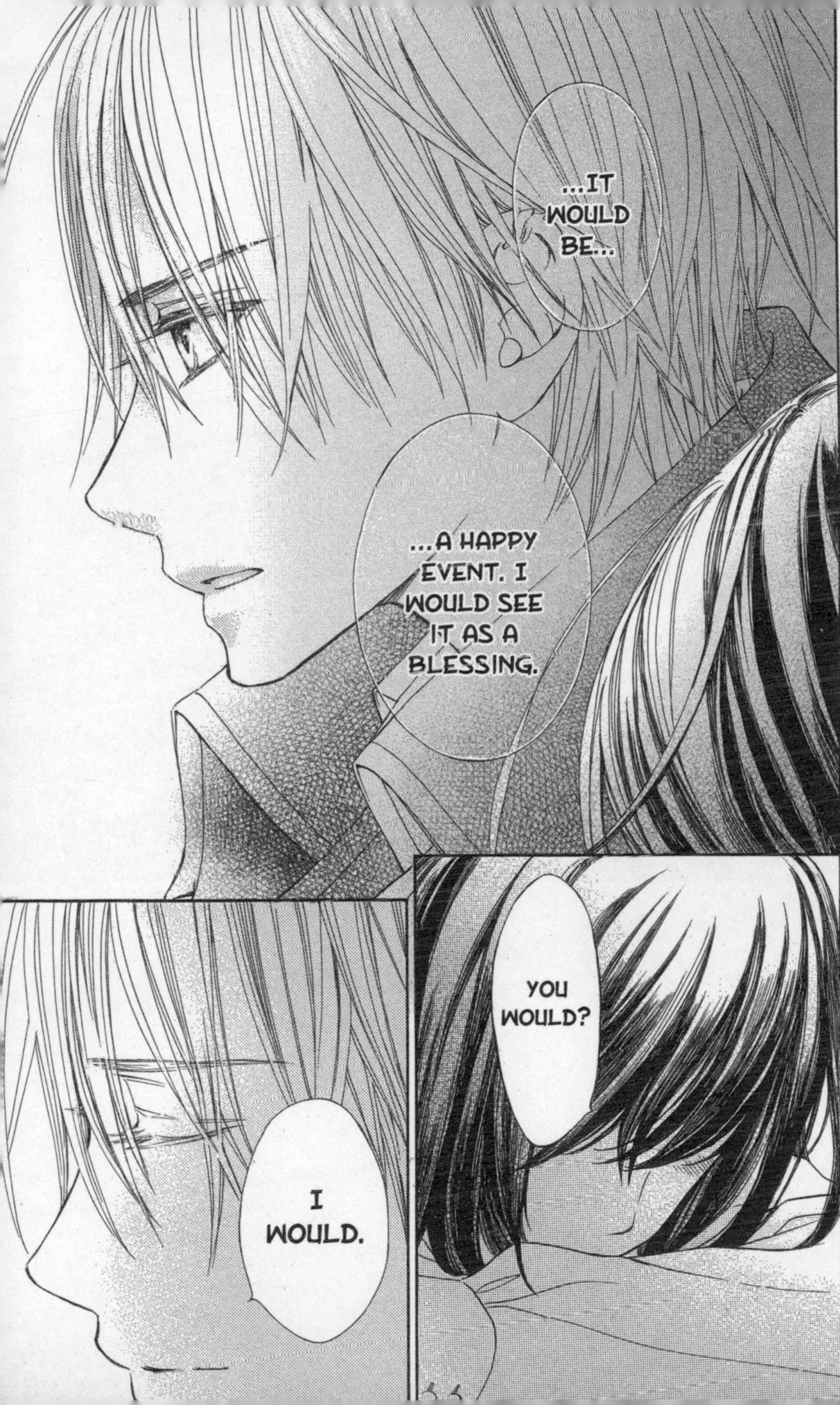
...IT WOULD BE...
...A HAPPY EVENT. I WOULD SEE IT AS A BLESSING.
YOU WOULD?
I WOULD.

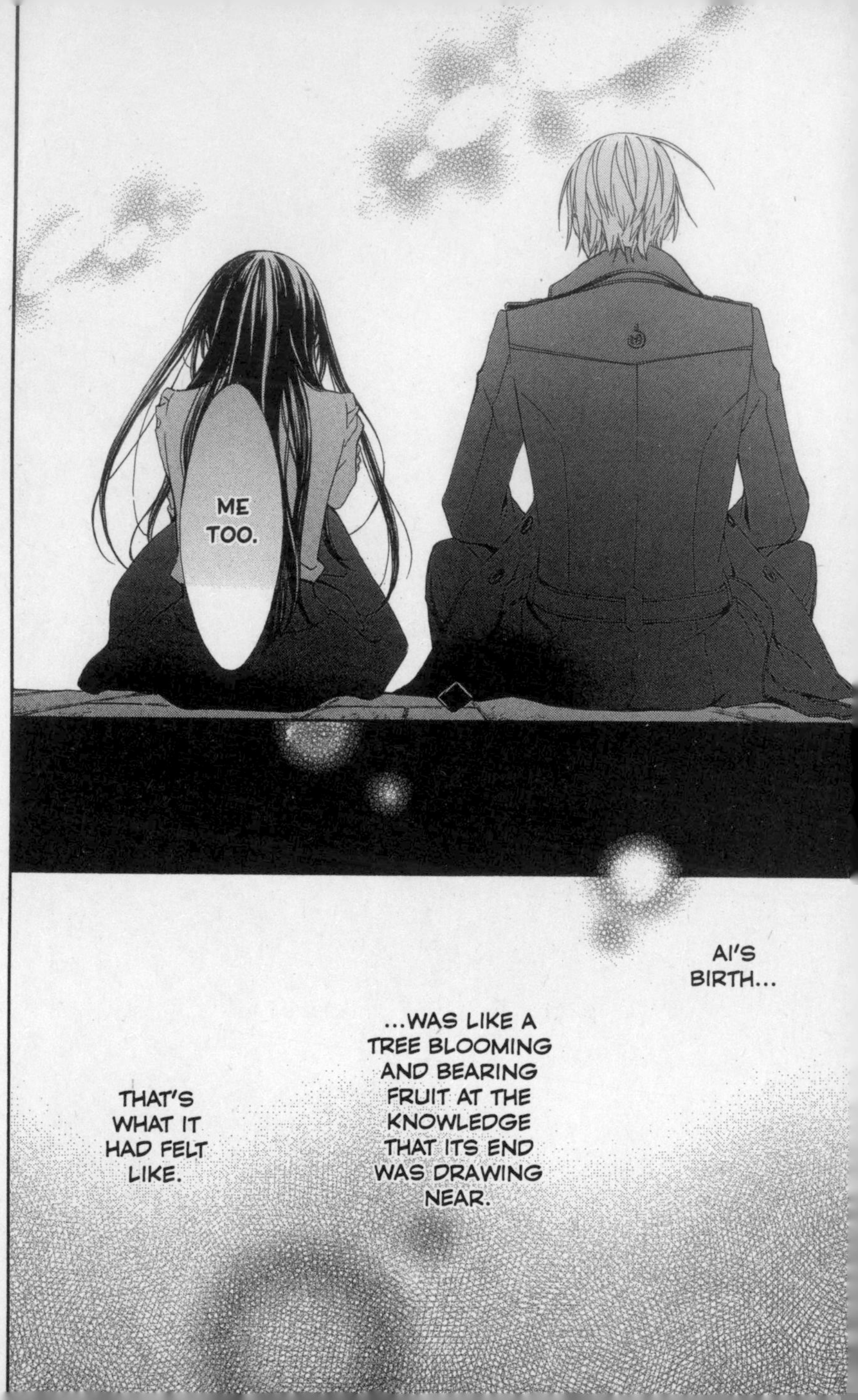
ME TOO.
AI'S BIRTH...
...WAS LIKE A TREE BLOOMING AND BEARING FRUIT AT THE KNOWLEDGE THAT ITS END WAS DRAWING NEAR.
THAT'S WHAT IT HAD FELT LIKE.

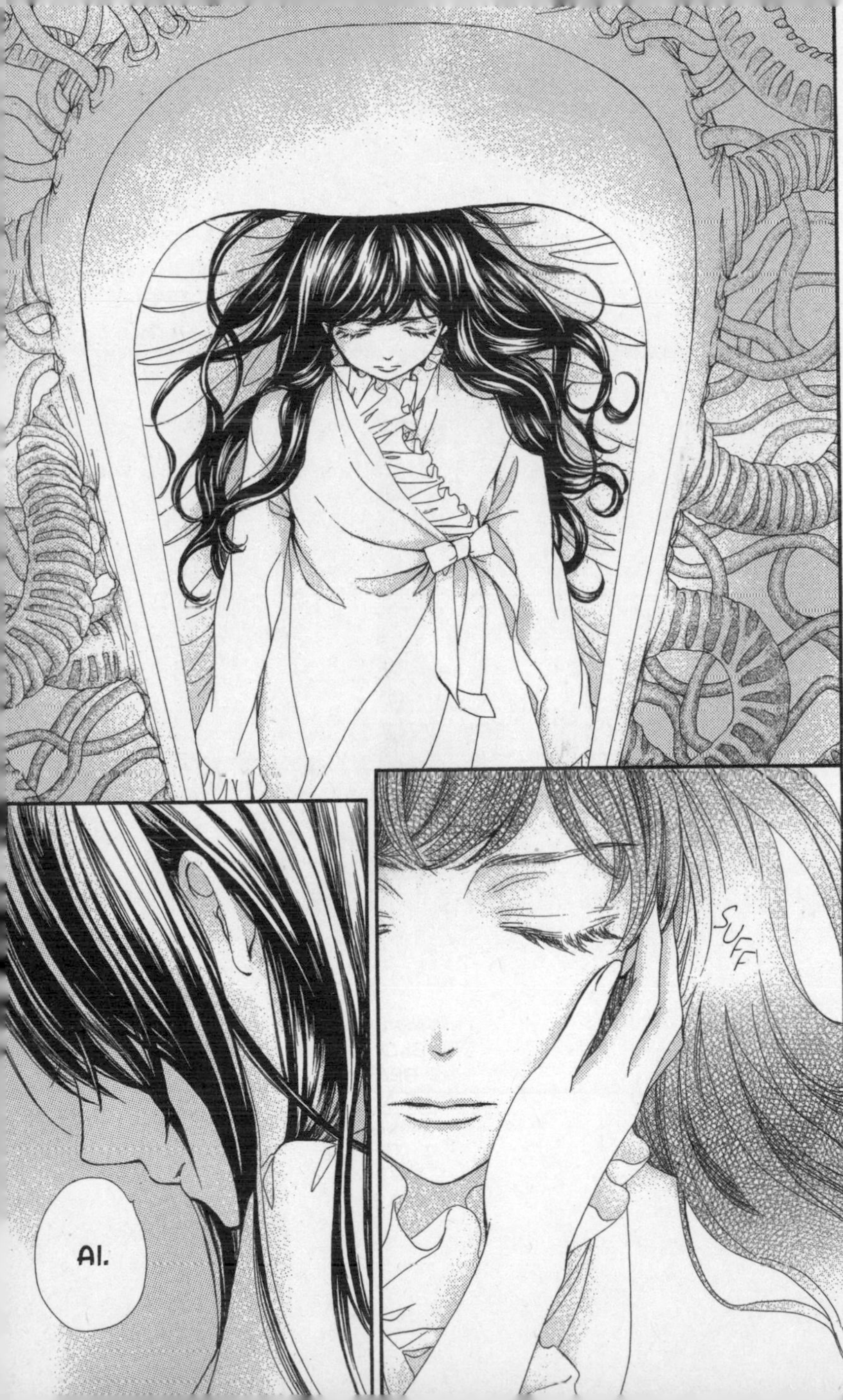
SUFF
AI.

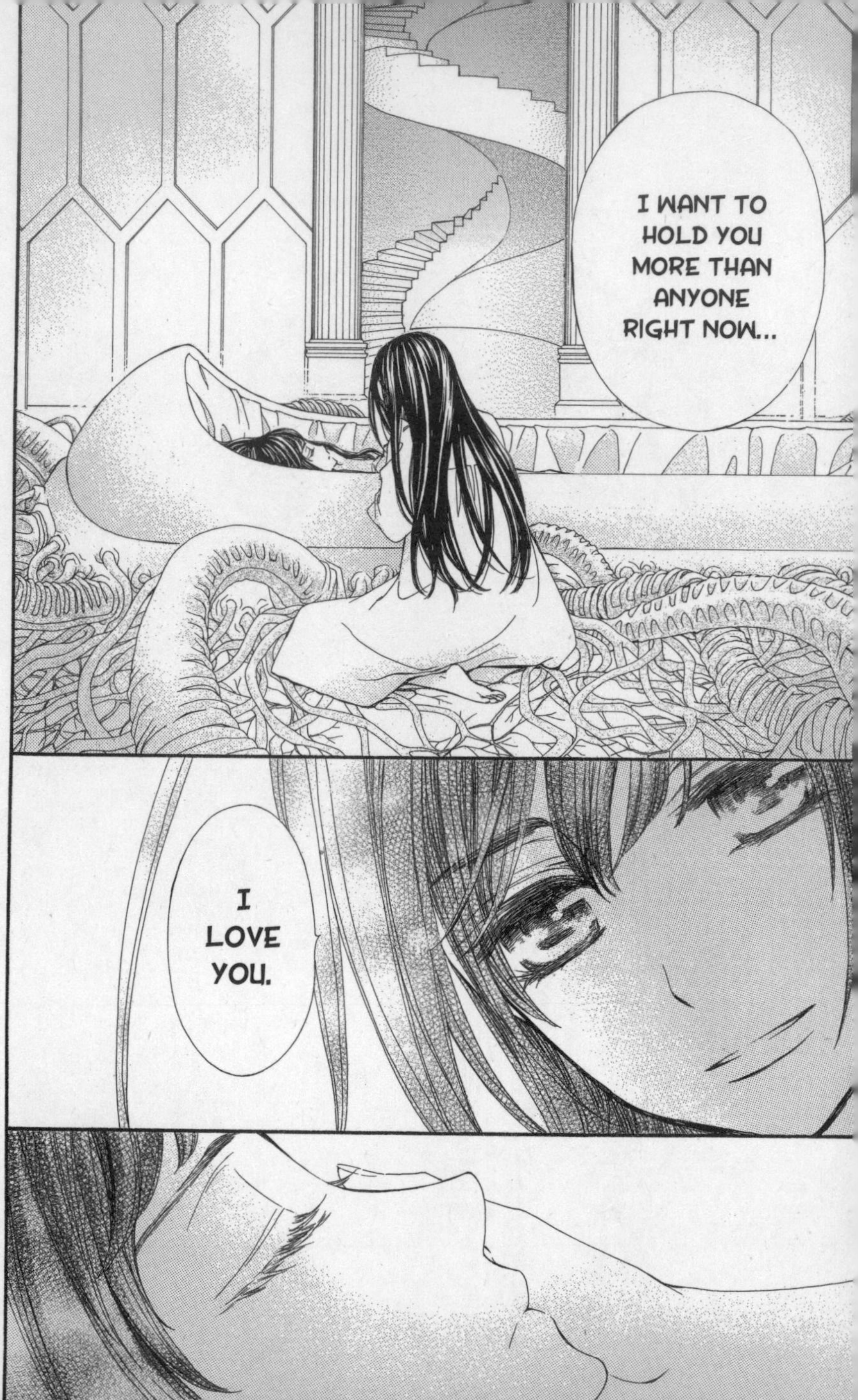
I WANT TO HOLD YOU MORE THAN ANYONE RIGHT NOW...
I LOVE YOU.

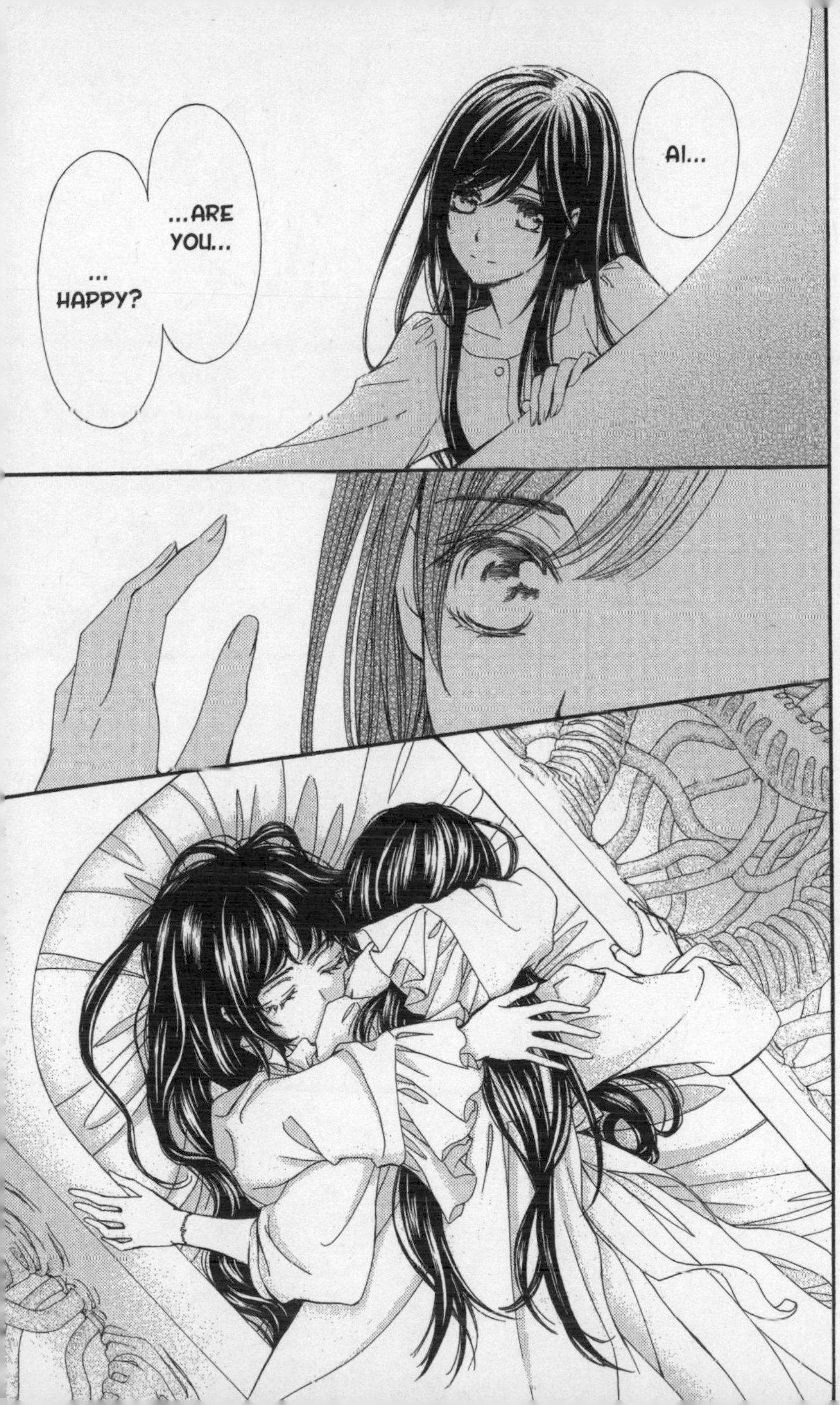
AI...
...ARE YOU... ...HAPPY?

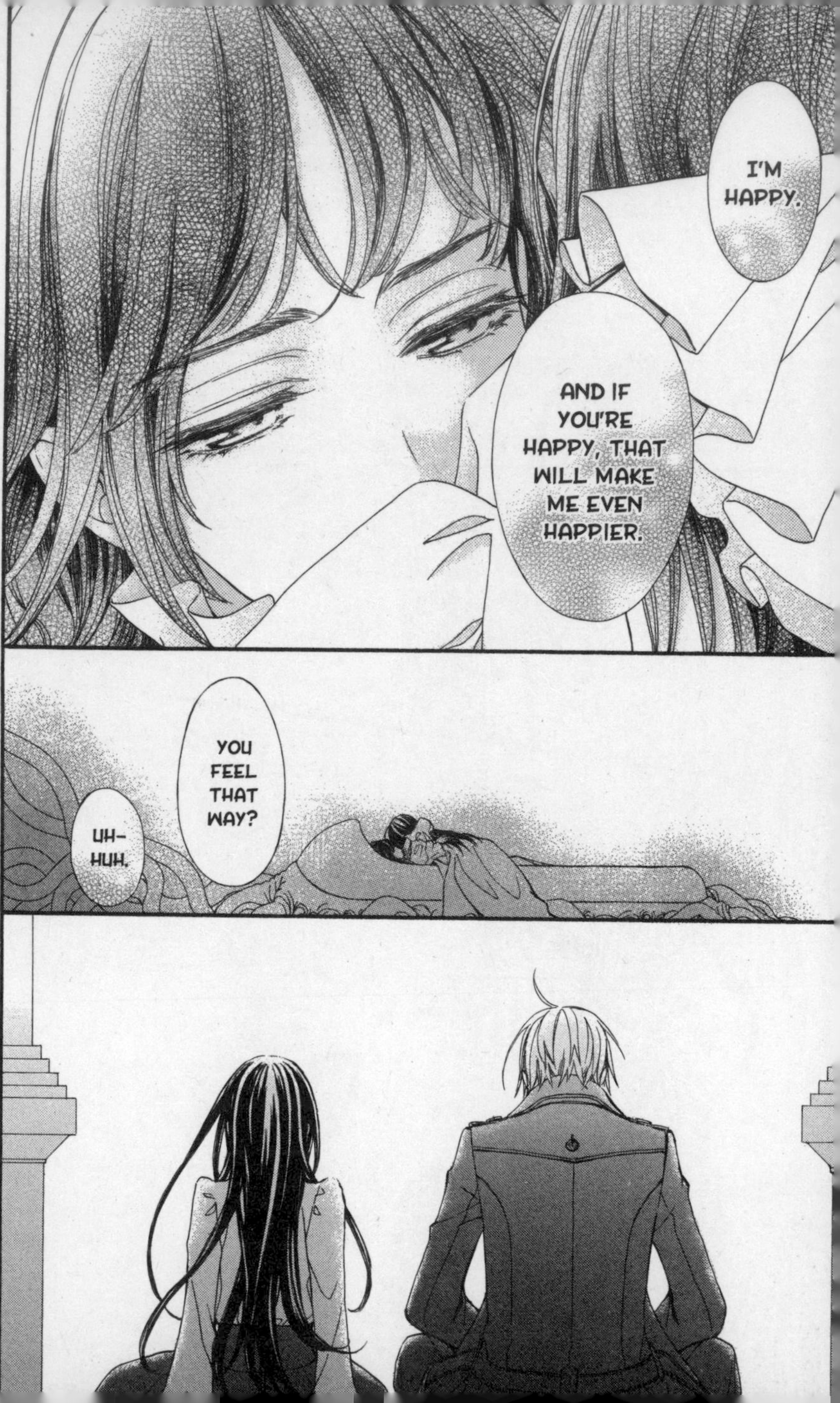
I'M HAPPY.
AND IF YOU'RE HAPPY, THAT WILL MAKE ME EVEN HAPPIER.
YOU FEEL THAT WAY?
UH-HUH.

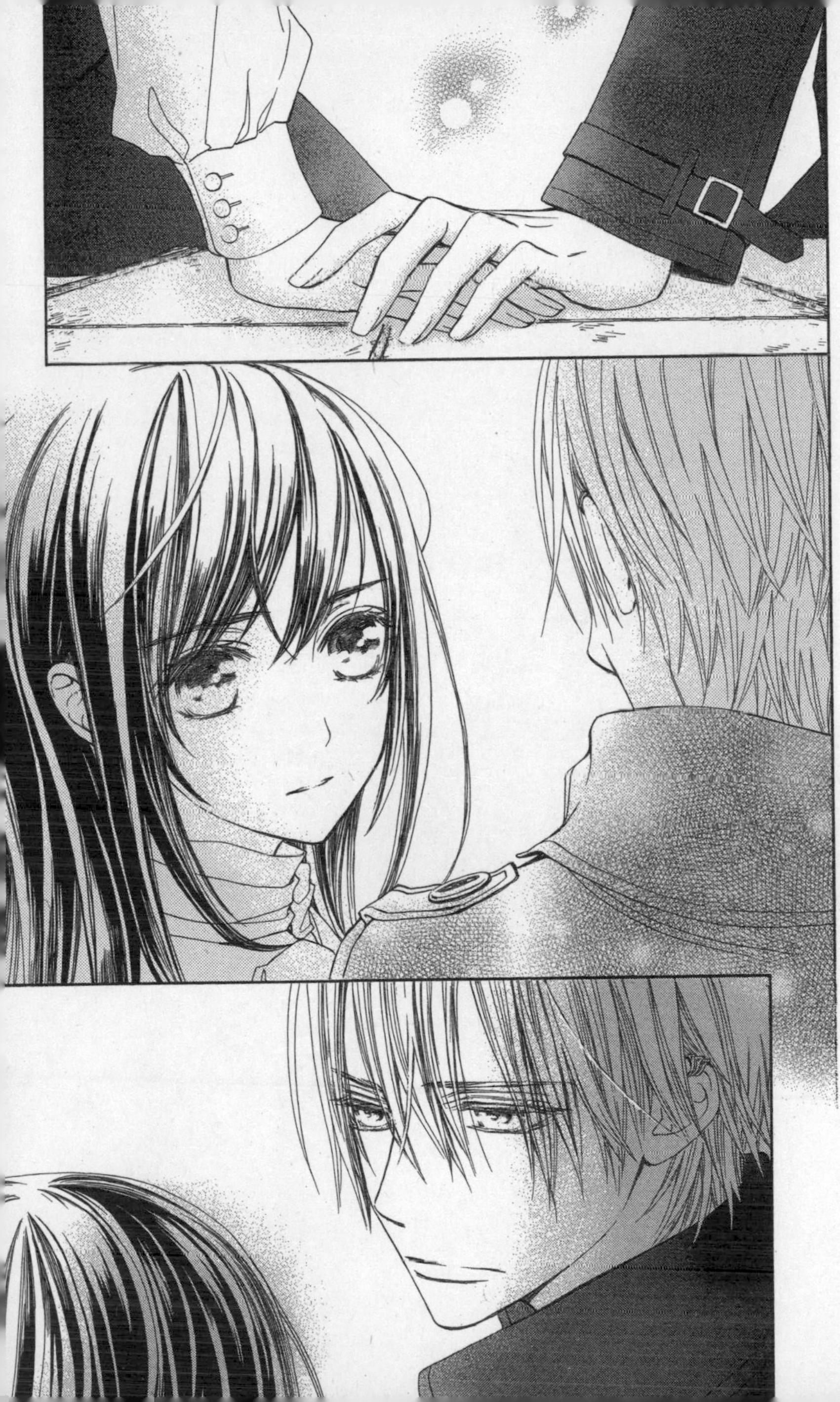

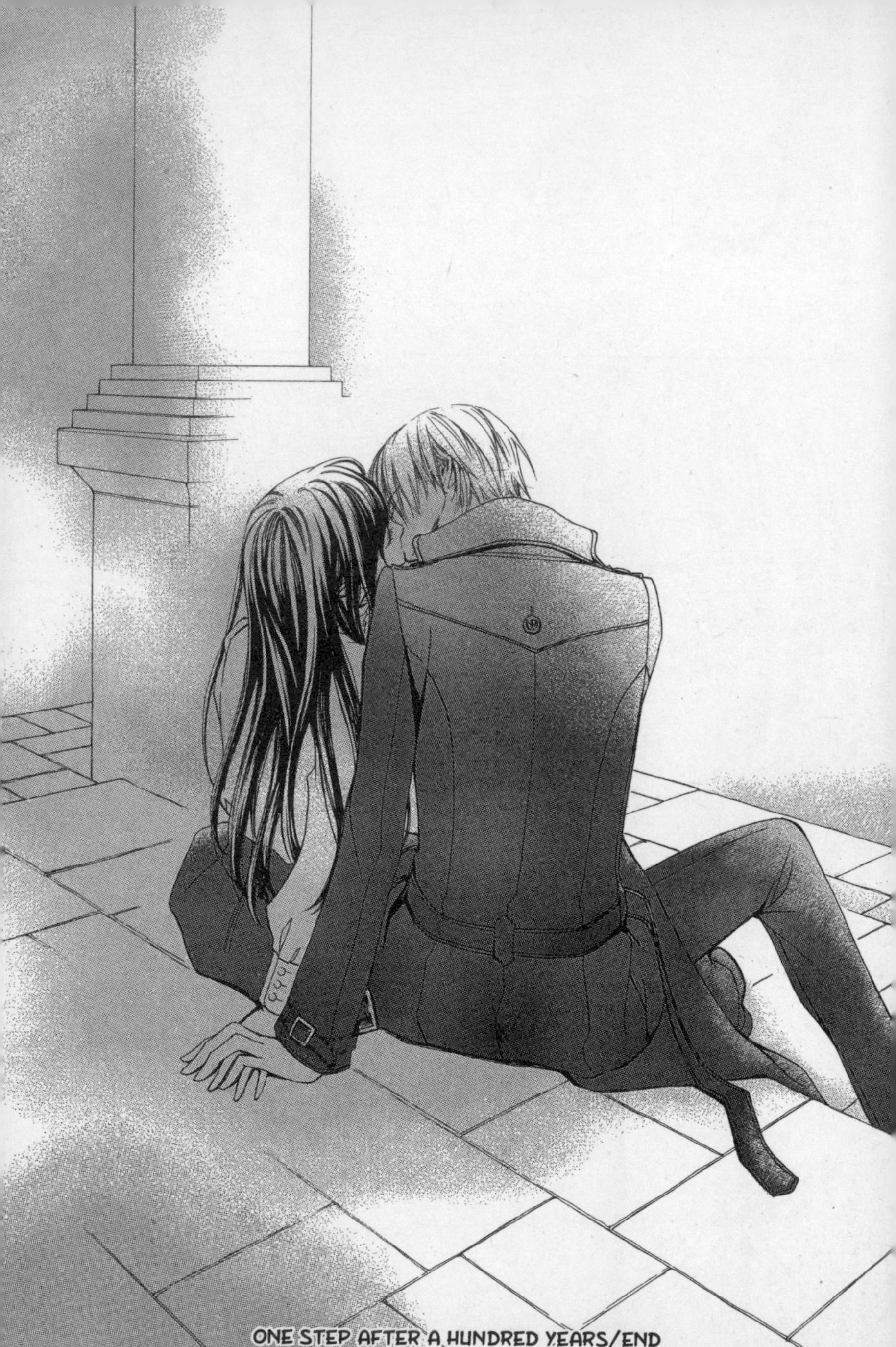

ONE STEP AFTER A HUNDRED YEARS/END

VAMPIRE KNIGHT MEMORIES

THE HOPE INSIDE A PHOTO ALBUM

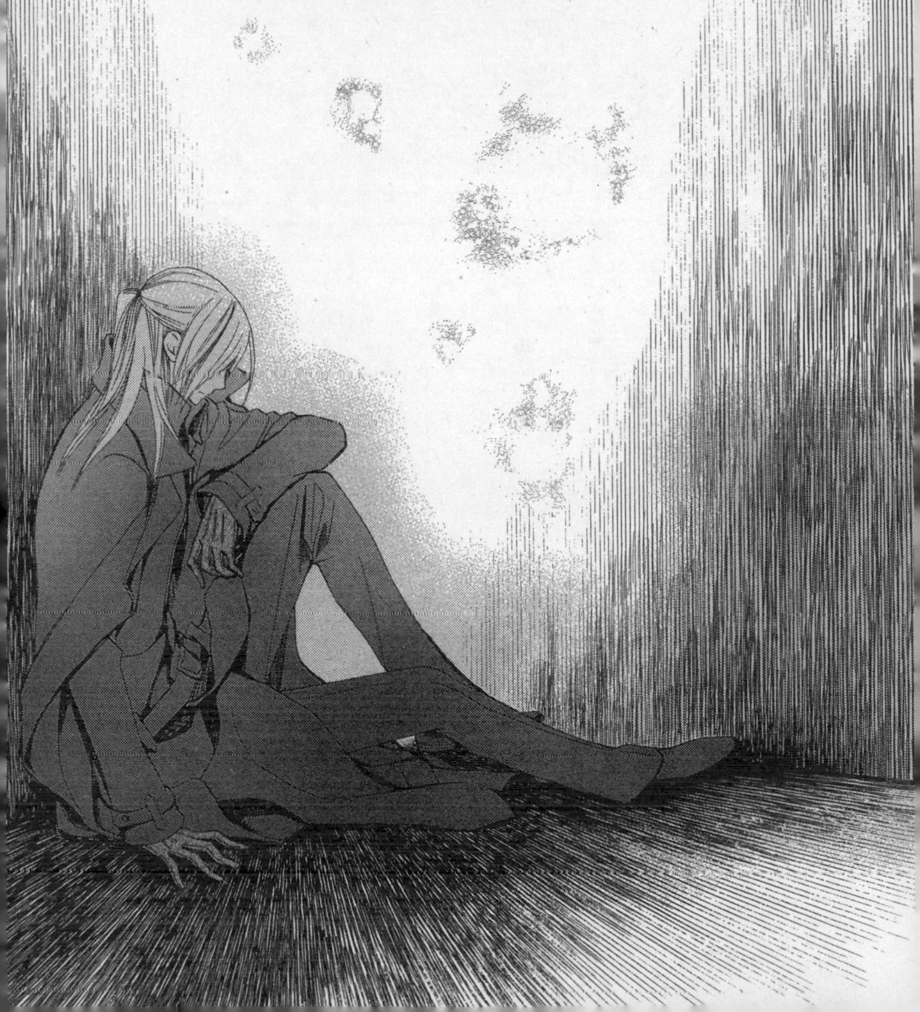

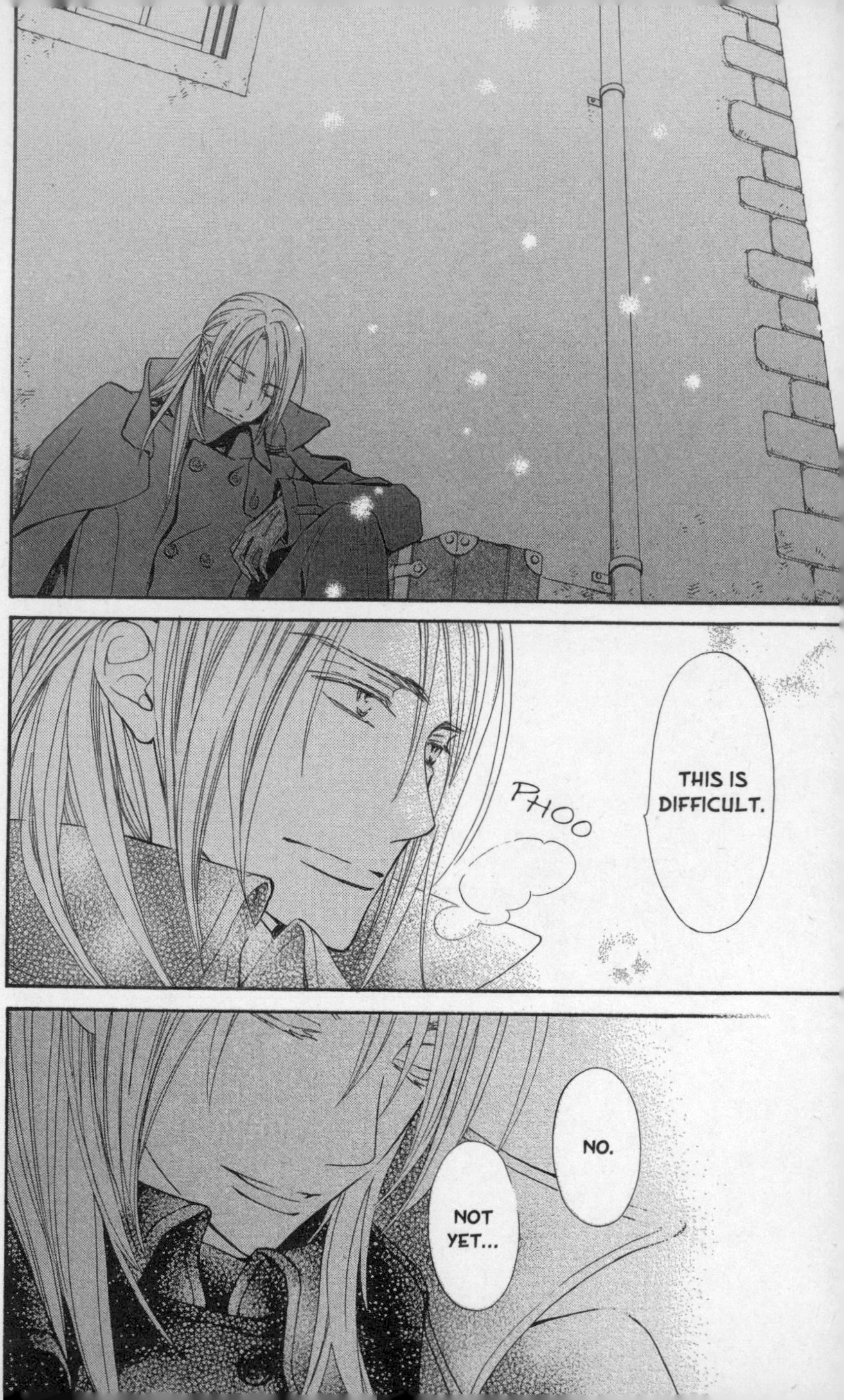
THIS IS DIFFICULT.
PHOO
NO.
NOT YET...

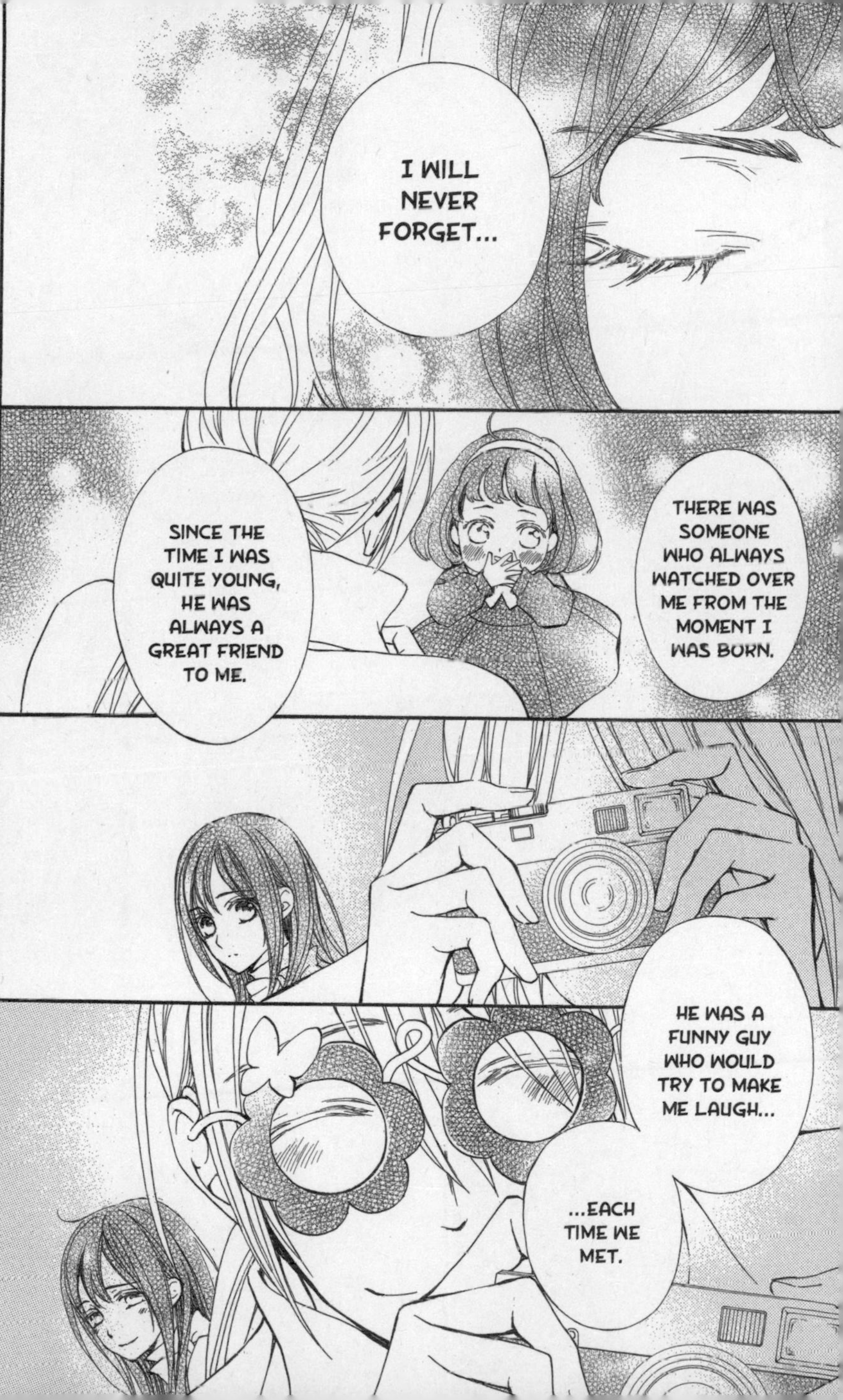
I WILL NEVER FORGET...
THERE WAS SOMEONE WHO ALWAYS WATCHED OVER ME FROM THE MOMENT I WAS BORN.
SINCE THE TIME I WAS QUITE YOUNG, HE WAS ALWAYS A GREAT FRIEND TO ME.
HE WAS A FUNNY GUY WHO WOULD TRY TO MAKE ME LAUGH...
...EACH TIME WE MET.

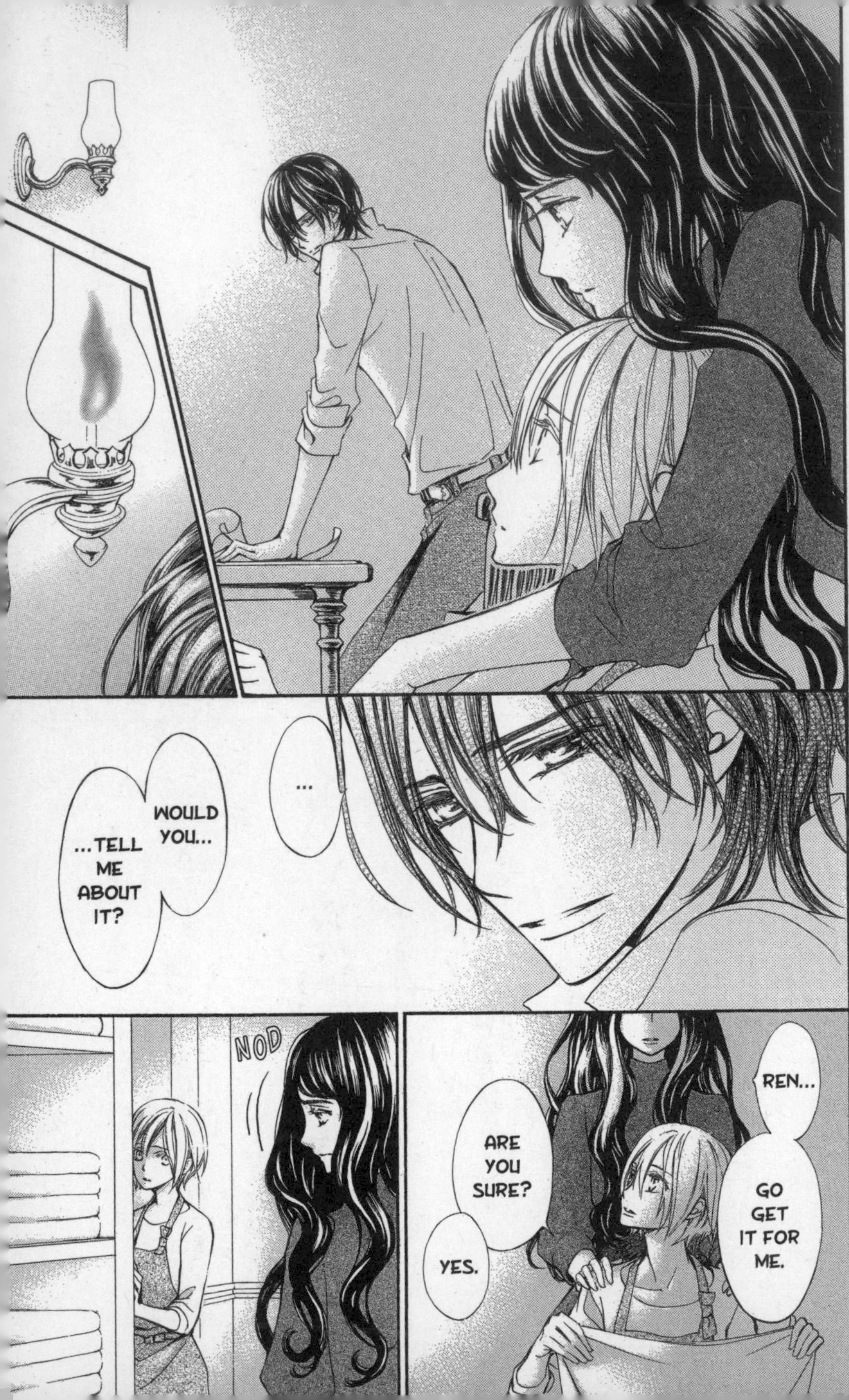
...
WOULD YOU...
...TELL ME ABOUT IT?
REN...
GO GET IT FOR ME.
ARE YOU SURE?
YES.
NOD

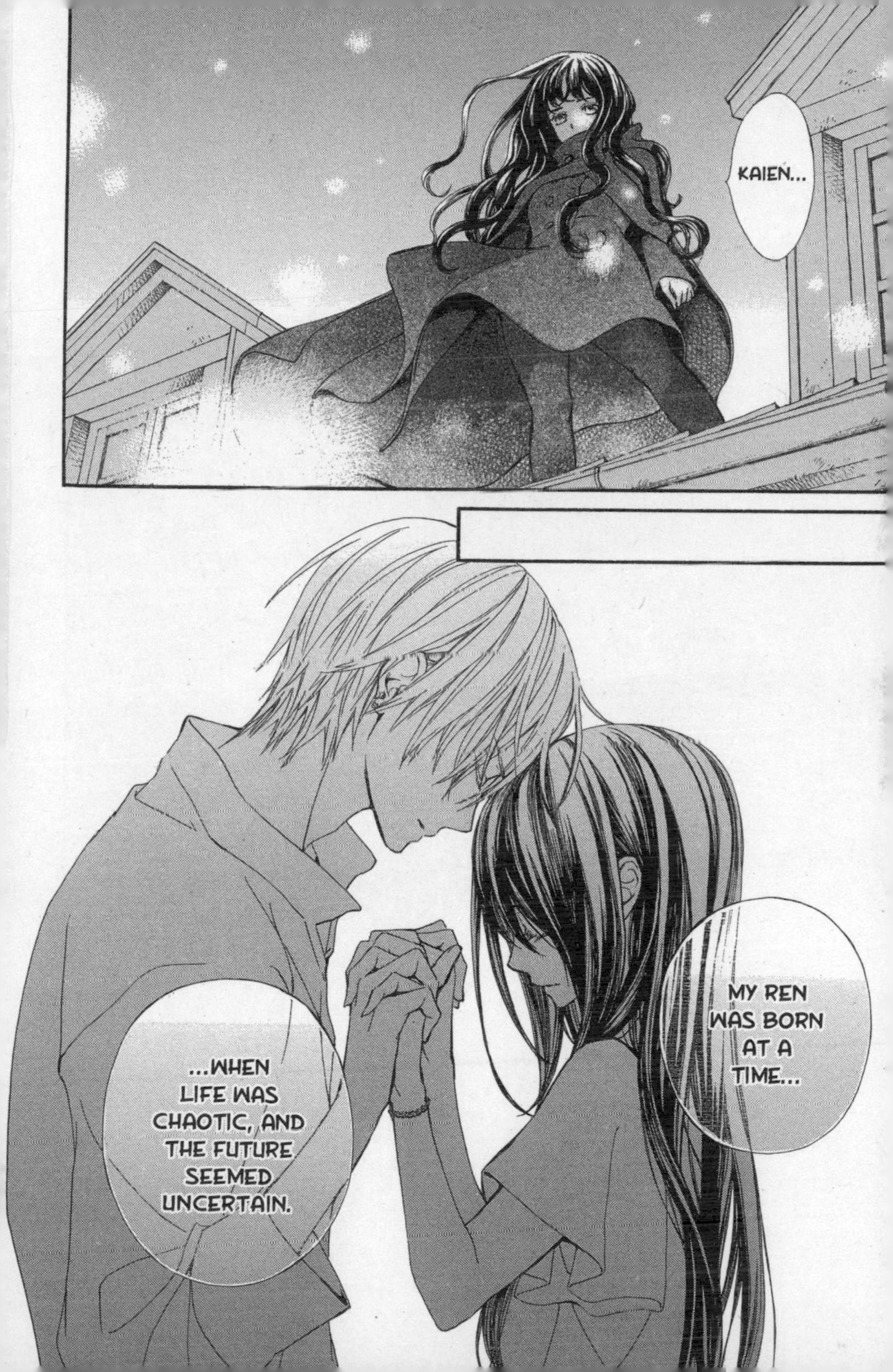
KAIEN...
MY REN WAS BORN AT A TIME...
...WHEN LIFE WAS CHAOTIC, AND THE FUTURE SEEMED UNCERTAIN.

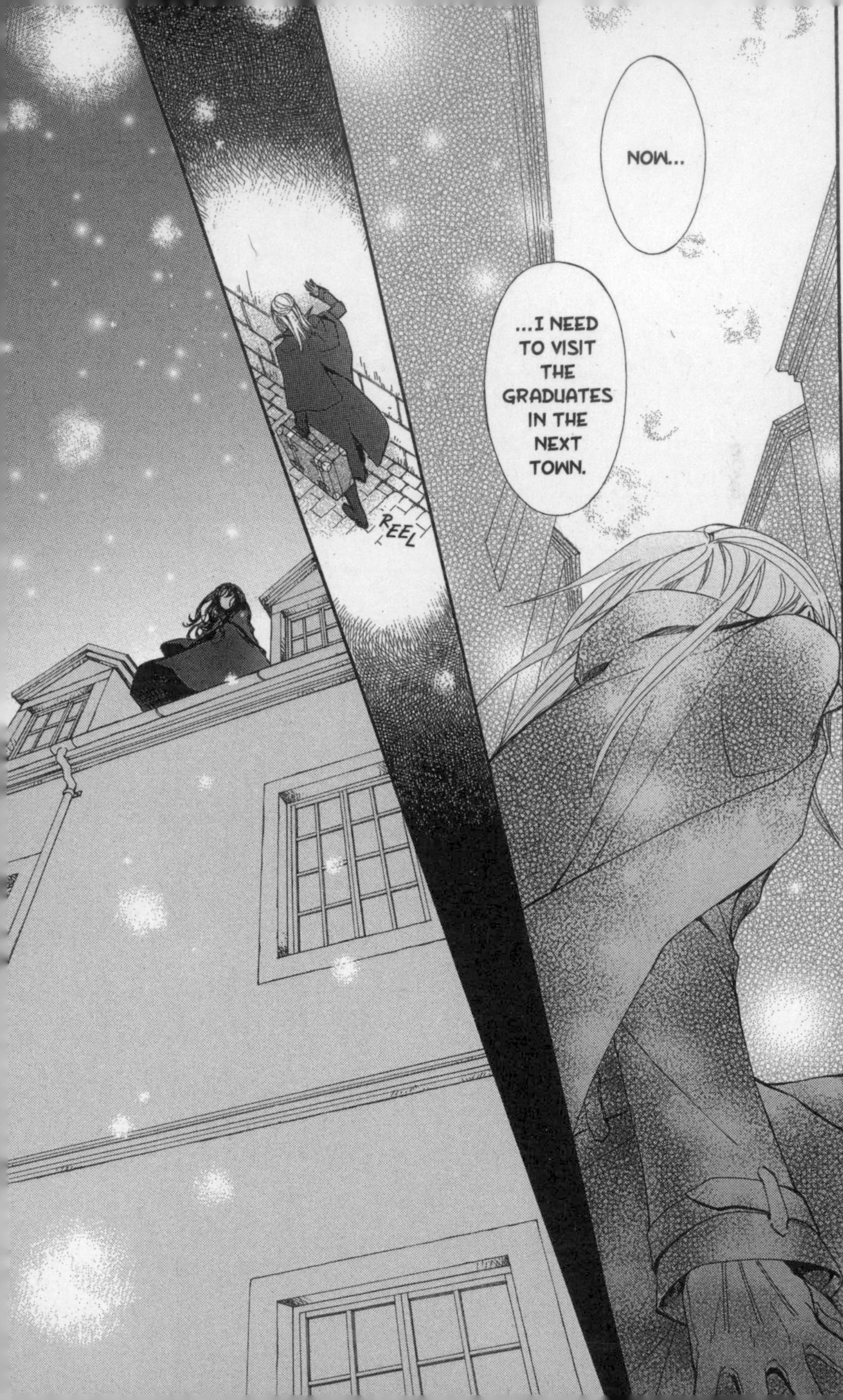
NOW...
...I NEED TO VISIT THE GRADUATES IN THE NEXT TOWN.
REEL

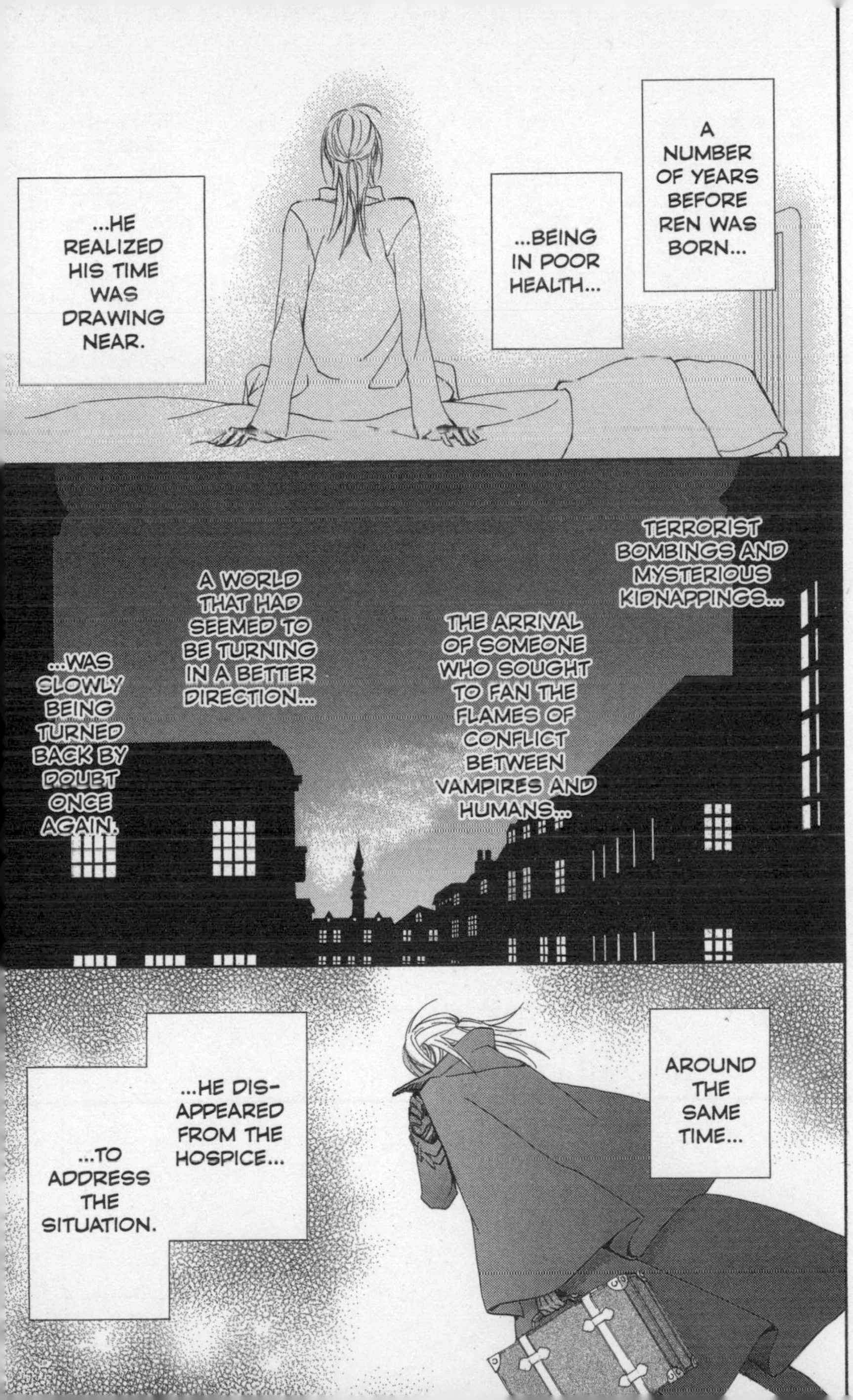
A NUMBER OF YEARS BEFORE REN WAS BORN...
...BEING IN POOR HEALTH...
...HE REALIZED HIS TIME WAS DRAWING NEAR.
TERRORIST BOMBINGS AND MYSTERIOUS KIDNAPPINGS...
THE ARRIVAL OF SOMEONE WHO SOUGHT TO FAN THE FLAMES OF CONFLICT BETWEEN VAMPIRES AND HUMANS...
A WORLD THAT HAD SEEMED TO BE TURNING IN A BETTER DIRECTION...
...WAS SLOWLY BEING TURNED BACK BY DOUBT ONCE AGAIN.
AROUND THE SAME TIME...
...HE DIS-APPEARED FROM THE HOSPICE...
...TO ADDRESS THE SITUATION.

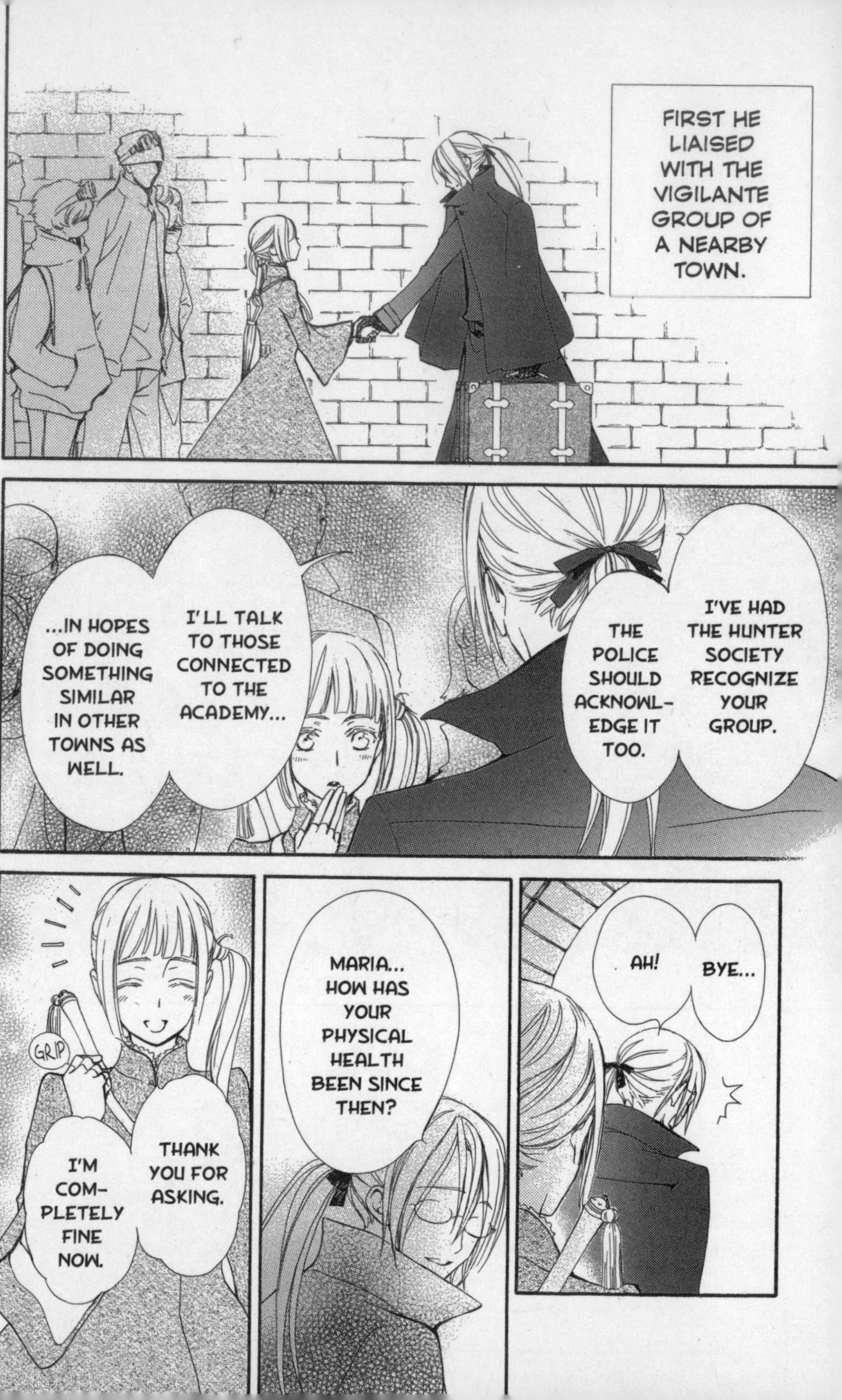
FIRST HE LIAISED WITH THE VIGILANTE GROUP OF A NEARBY TOWN.
I'VE HAD THE HUNTER SOCIETY RECOGNIZE YOUR GROUP.
THE POLICE SHOULD ACKNOWL-EDGE IT TOO.
I'LL TALK TO THOSE CONNECTED TO THE ACADEMY...
...IN HOPES OF DOING SOMETHING SIMILAR IN OTHER TOWNS AS WELL.
BYE...
AH!
MARIA... HOW HAS YOUR PHYSICAL HEALTH BEEN SINCE THEN?
GRIP
THANK YOU FOR ASKING.
I'M COM-PLETELY FINE NOW.

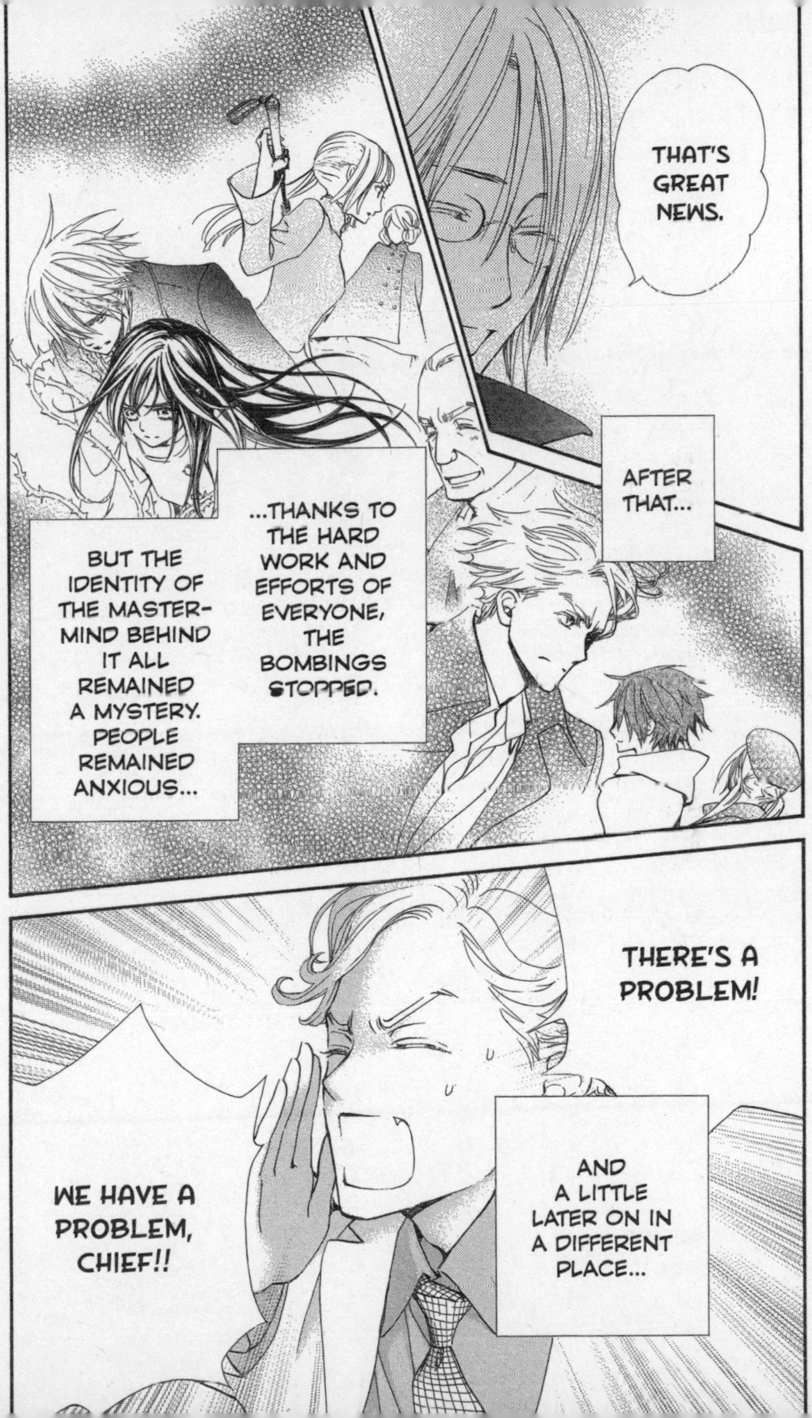
THAT'S GREAT NEWS.
AFTER THAT...
...THANKS TO THE HARD WORK AND EFFORTS OF EVERYONE, THE BOMBINGS STOPPED.
BUT THE IDENTITY OF THE MASTER-MIND BEHIND IT ALL REMAINED A MYSTERY. PEOPLE REMAINED ANXIOUS...
THERE'S A PROBLEM!
AND A LITTLE LATER ON IN A DIFFERENT PLACE...
WE HAVE A PROBLEM, CHIEF!!

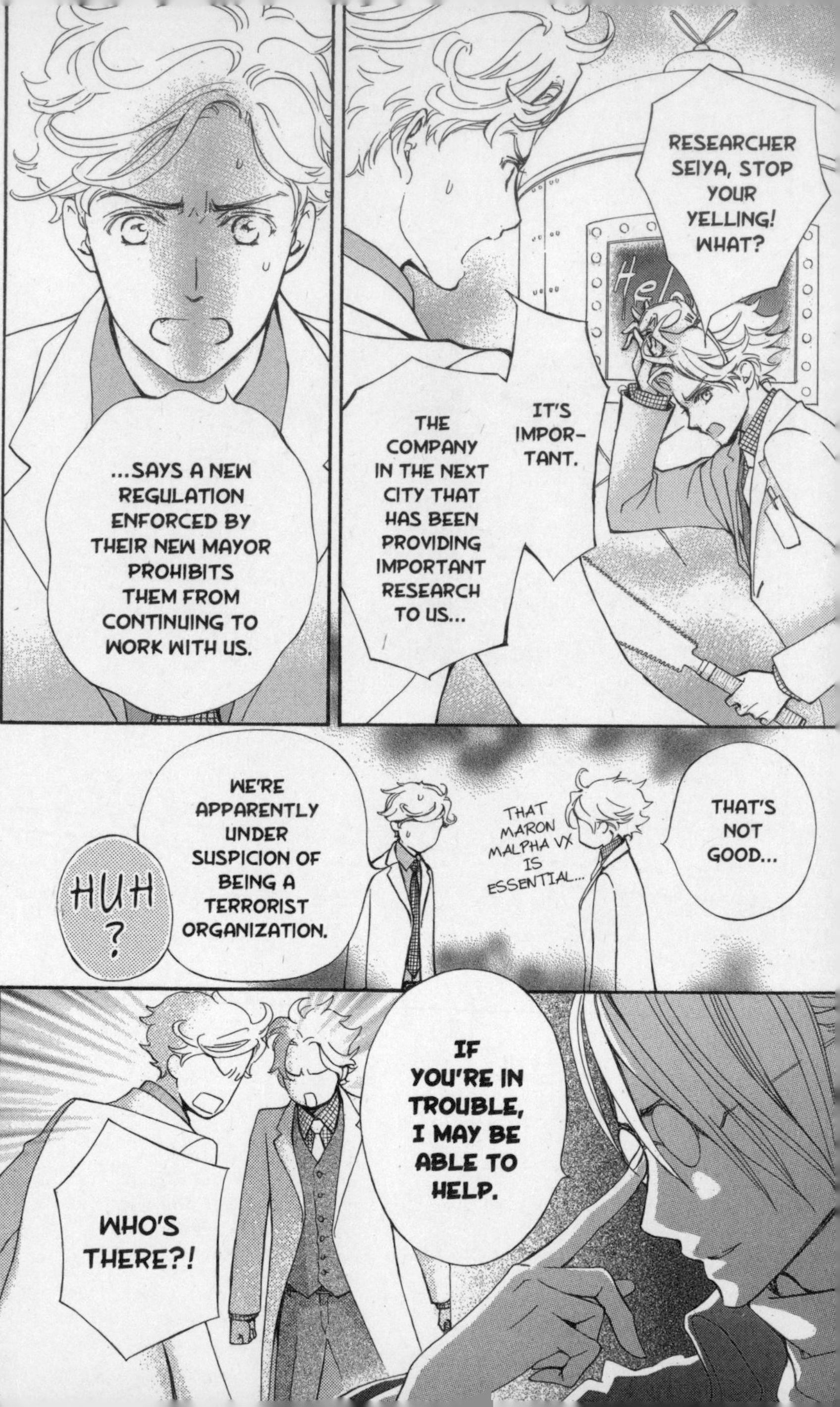
RESEARCHER SEIYA, STOP YOUR YELLING! WHAT?
IT'S IMPOR-TANT.
THE COMPANY IN THE NEXT CITY THAT HAS BEEN PROVIDING IMPORTANT RESEARCH TO US...
...SAYS A NEW REGULATION ENFORCED BY THEIR NEW MAYOR PROHIBITS THEM FROM CONTINUING TO WORK WITH US.
THAT'S NOT GOOD...
THAT MARON MALPHA VX IS ESSENTIAL...
WE'RE APPARENTLY UNDER SUSPICION OF BEING A TERRORIST ORGANIZATION.
HUH?
IF YOU'RE IN TROUBLE, I MAY BE ABLE TO HELP.
WHO'S THERE?!

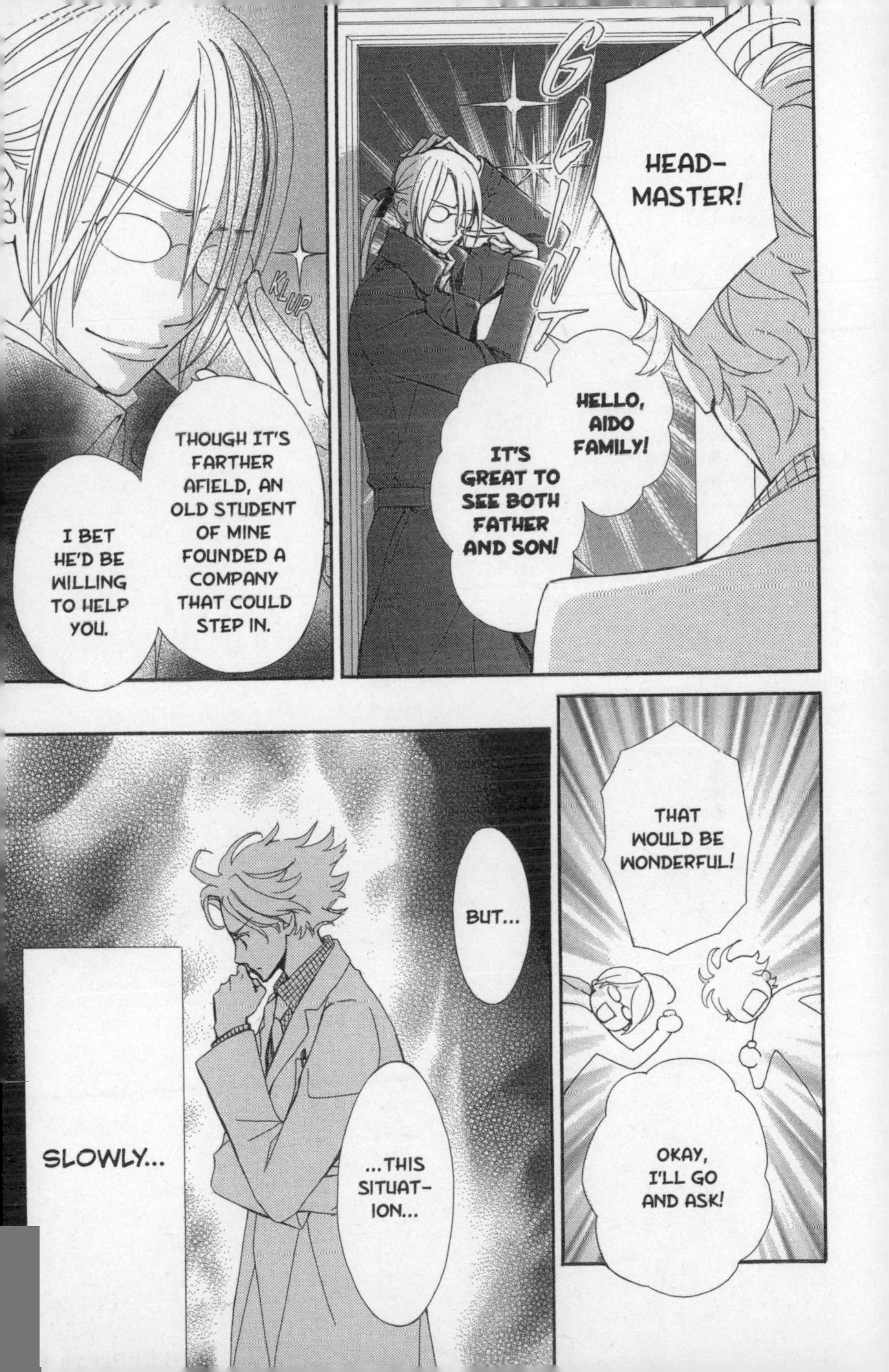
HEAD-MASTER!
GLINT
HELLO, AIDO FAMILY!
IT'S GREAT TO SEE BOTH FATHER AND SON!
KLUP
THOUGH IT'S FARTHER AFIELD, AN OLD STUDENT OF MINE FOUNDED A COMPANY THAT COULD STEP IN.
I BET HE'D BE WILLING TO HELP YOU.
THAT WOULD BE WONDERFUL!
OKAY, I'LL GO AND ASK!
BUT...
...THIS SITUAT-ION...
SLOWLY...

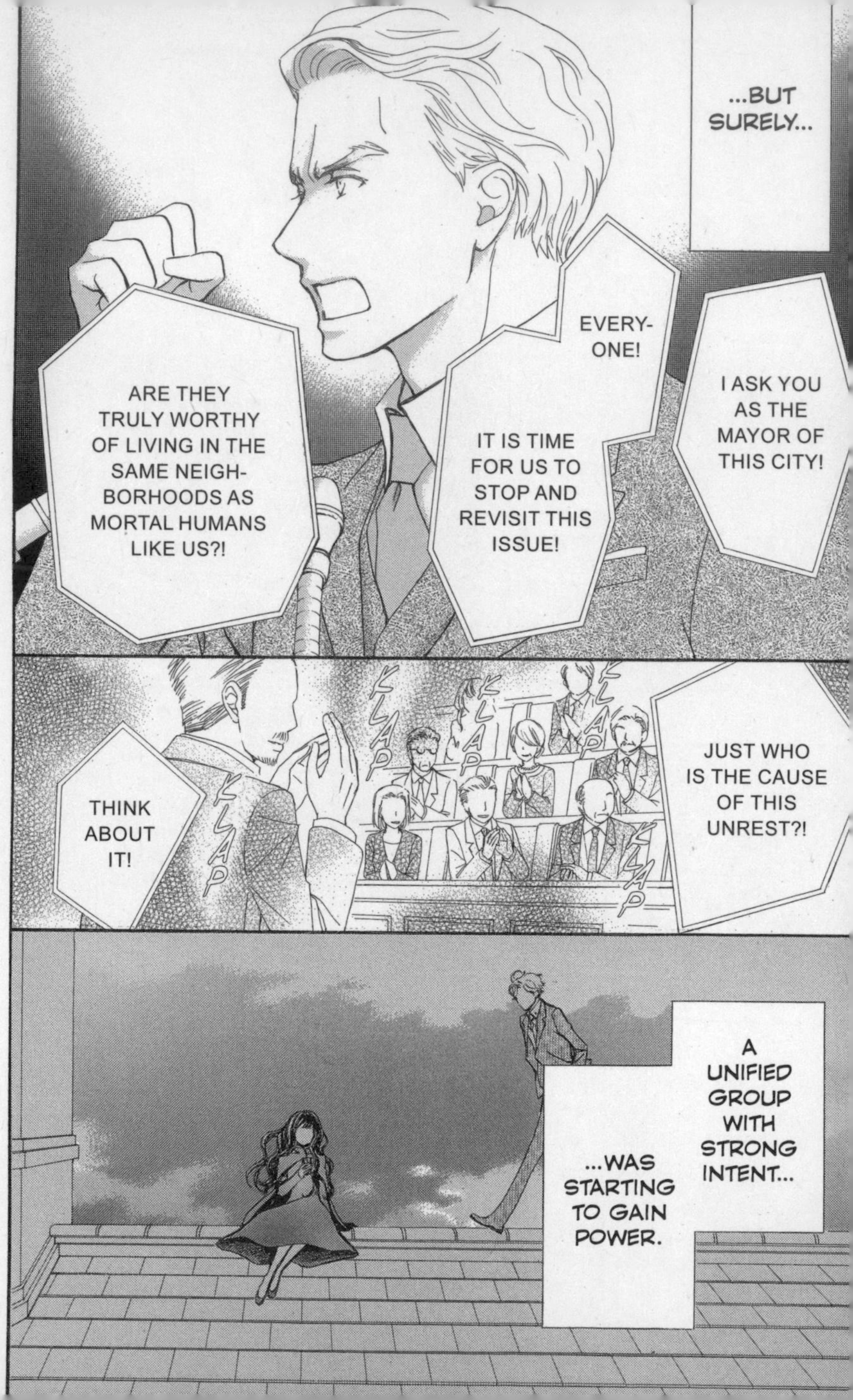
...BUT SURELY...
I ASK YOU AS THE MAYOR OF THIS CITY!
EVERY-ONE!
IT IS TIME FOR US TO STOP AND REVISIT THIS ISSUE!
ARE THEY TRULY WORTHY OF LIVING IN THE SAME NEIGH-BORHOODS AS MORTAL HUMANS LIKE US?!
JUST WHO IS THE CAUSE OF THIS UNREST?!
KLAP
KLAP
KLAP
KLAP
KLAP
KLAP
THINK ABOUT IT!
A UNIFIED GROUP WITH STRONG INTENT...
...WAS STARTING TO GAIN POWER.

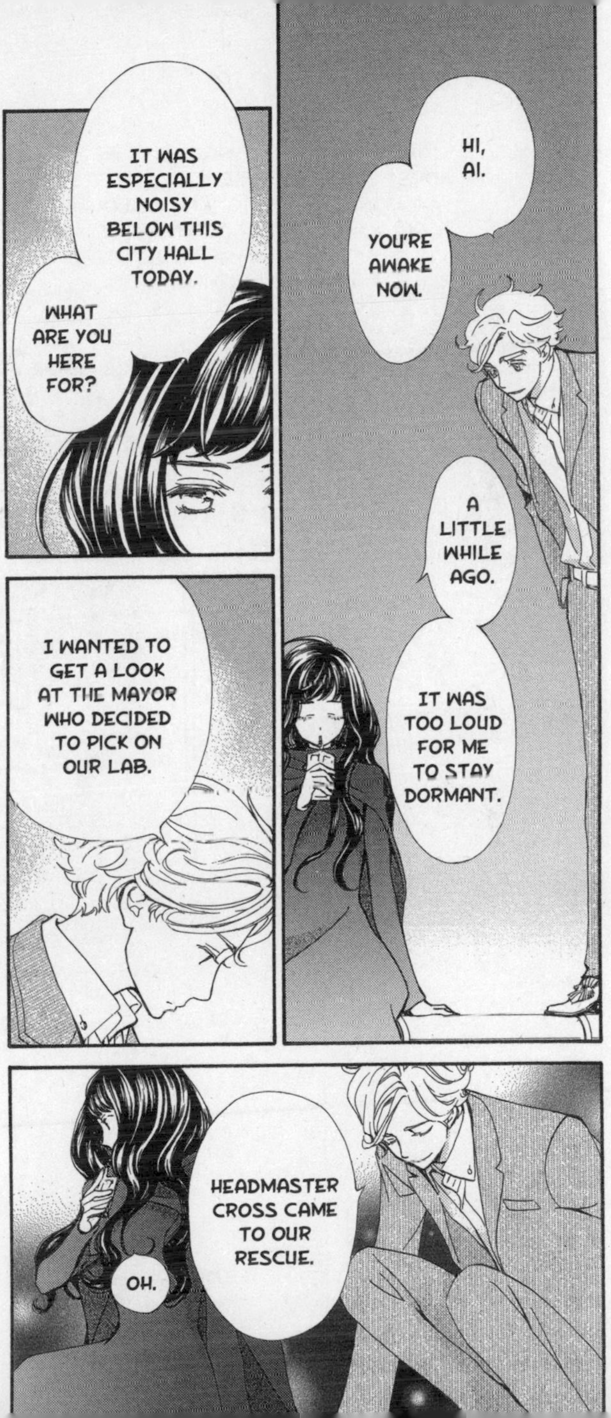
HI, AI.
YOU'RE AWAKE NOW.
A LITTLE WHILE AGO.
IT WAS TOO LOUD FOR ME TO STAY DORMANT.
IT WAS ESPECIALLY NOISY BELOW THIS CITY HALL TODAY.
WHAT ARE YOU HERE FOR?
I WANTED TO GET A LOOK AT THE MAYOR WHO DECIDED TO PICK ON OUR LAB.
HEADMASTER CROSS CAME TO OUR RESCUE.
OH.

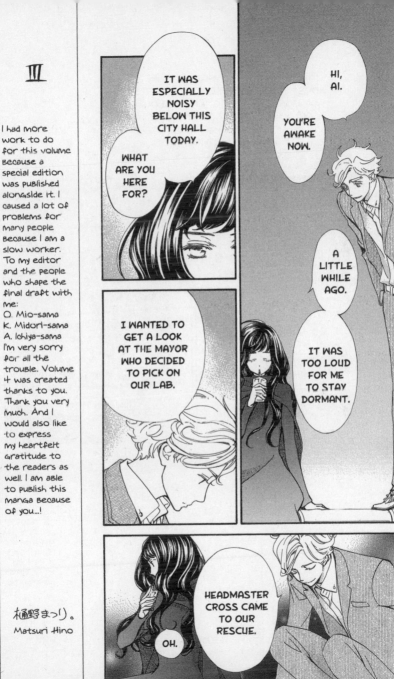

III

I had more work to do for this volume because a special edition was published alongside it. I caused a lot of problems for many people because I am a slow worker. To my editor and the people who shape the final draft with me:
O. Mio-sama
K. Midori-sama
A. Ichiya-sama
I'm very sorry for all the trouble. Volume 4 was created thanks to you. Thank you very much. And I would also like to express my heartfelt gratitude to the readers as well. I am able to publish this manga because of you...!

樋野まつり。
Matsuri Hino

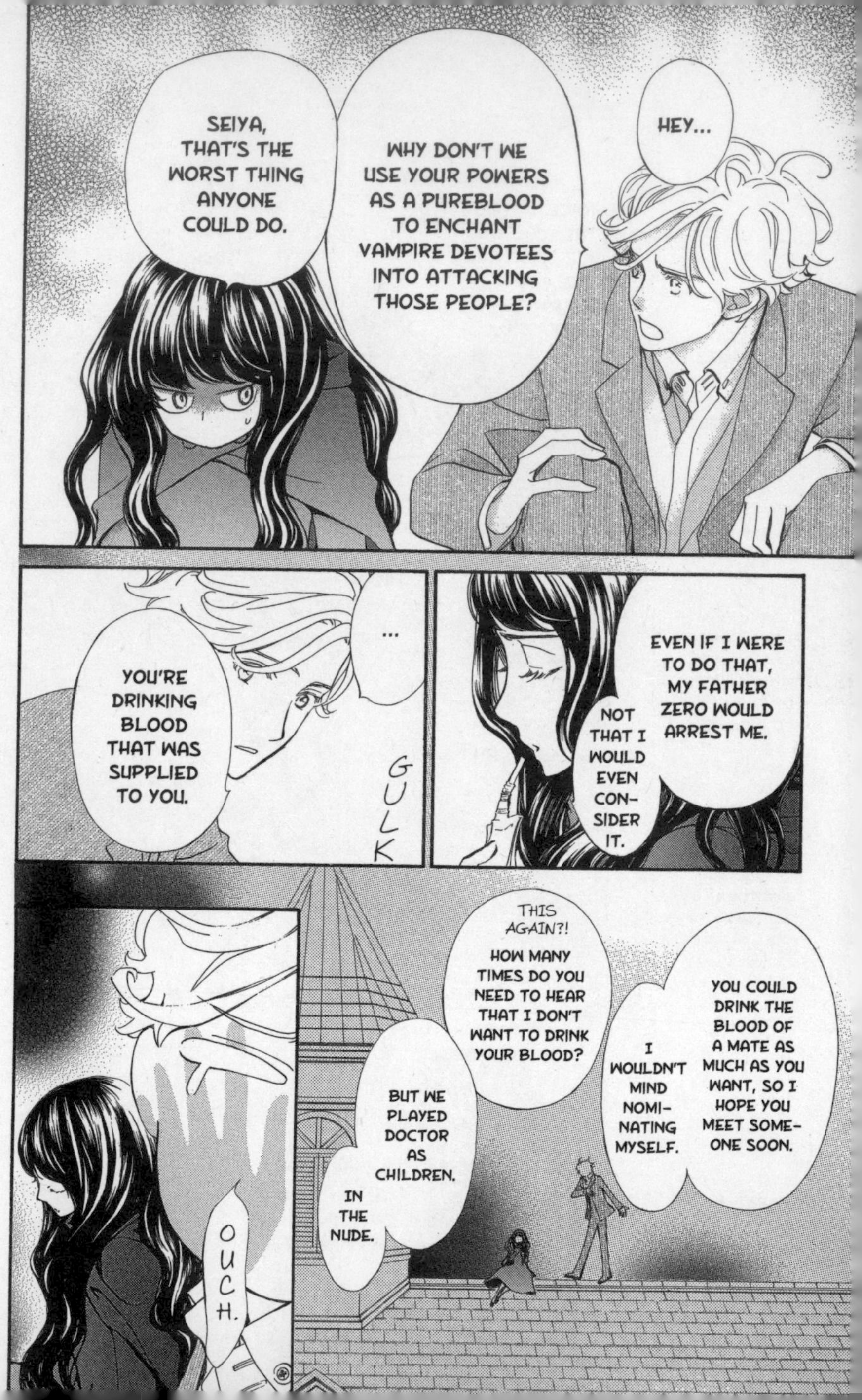
HEY...
WHY DON'T WE USE YOUR POWERS AS A PUREBLOOD TO ENCHANT VAMPIRE DEVOTEES INTO ATTACKING THOSE PEOPLE?
SEIYA, THAT'S THE WORST THING ANYONE COULD DO.
EVEN IF I WERE TO DO THAT, MY FATHER ZERO WOULD ARREST ME.
NOT THAT I WOULD EVEN CONSIDER IT.
...
YOU'RE DRINKING BLOOD THAT WAS SUPPLIED TO YOU.
GULK
YOU COULD DRINK THE BLOOD OF A MATE AS MUCH AS YOU WANT, SO I HOPE YOU MEET SOMEONE SOON.
I WOULDN'T MIND NOMINATING MYSELF.
THIS AGAIN?!
HOW MANY TIMES DO YOU NEED TO HEAR THAT I DON'T WANT TO DRINK YOUR BLOOD?
BUT WE PLAYED DOCTOR AS CHILDREN.
IN THE NUDE.
OUCH.

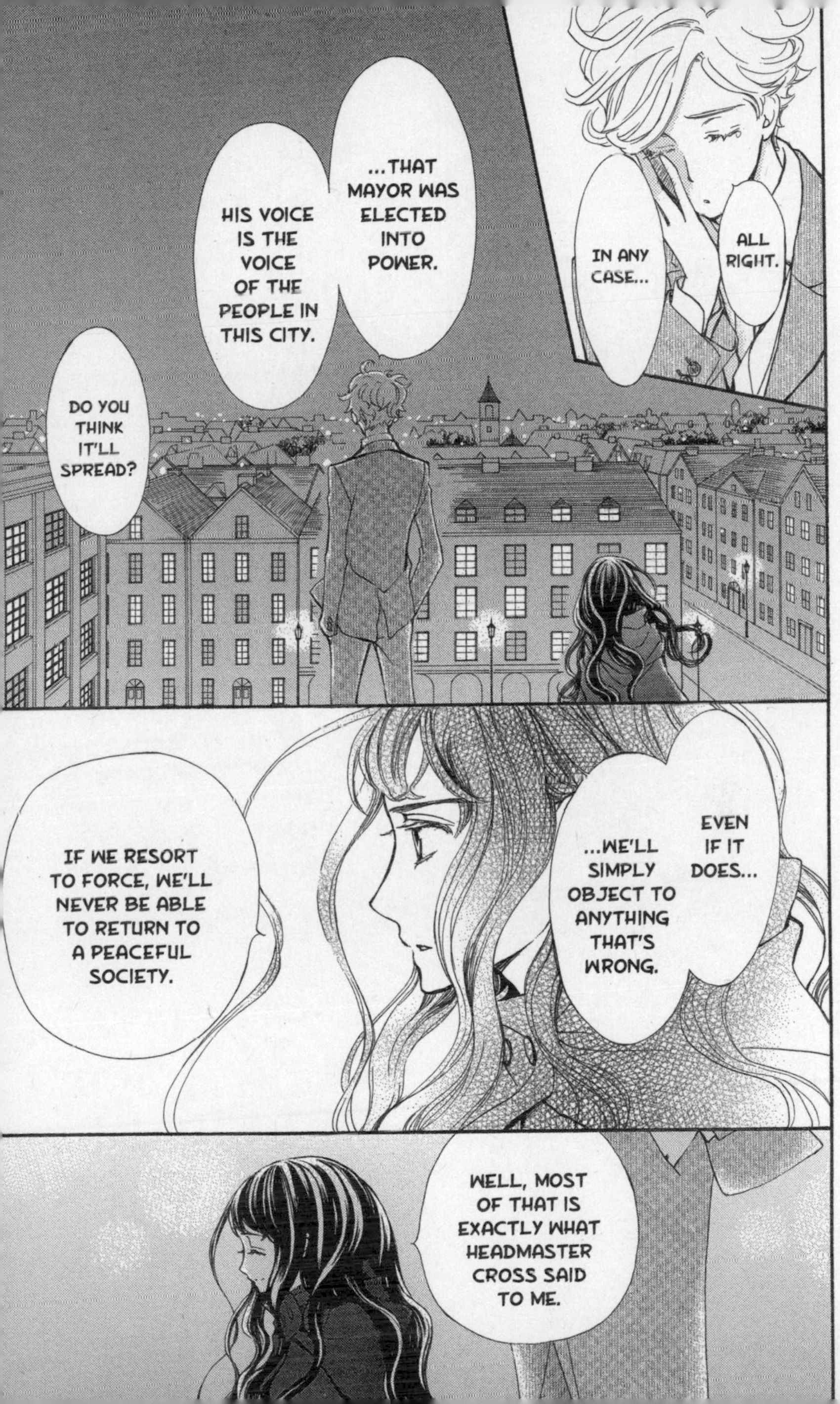
ALL RIGHT.
IN ANY CASE...
...THAT MAYOR WAS ELECTED INTO POWER.
HIS VOICE IS THE VOICE OF THE PEOPLE IN THIS CITY.
DO YOU THINK IT'LL SPREAD?
EVEN IF IT DOES...
...WE'LL SIMPLY OBJECT TO ANYTHING THAT'S WRONG.
IF WE RESORT TO FORCE, WE'LL NEVER BE ABLE TO RETURN TO A PEACEFUL SOCIETY.
WELL, MOST OF THAT IS EXACTLY WHAT HEADMASTER CROSS SAID TO ME.

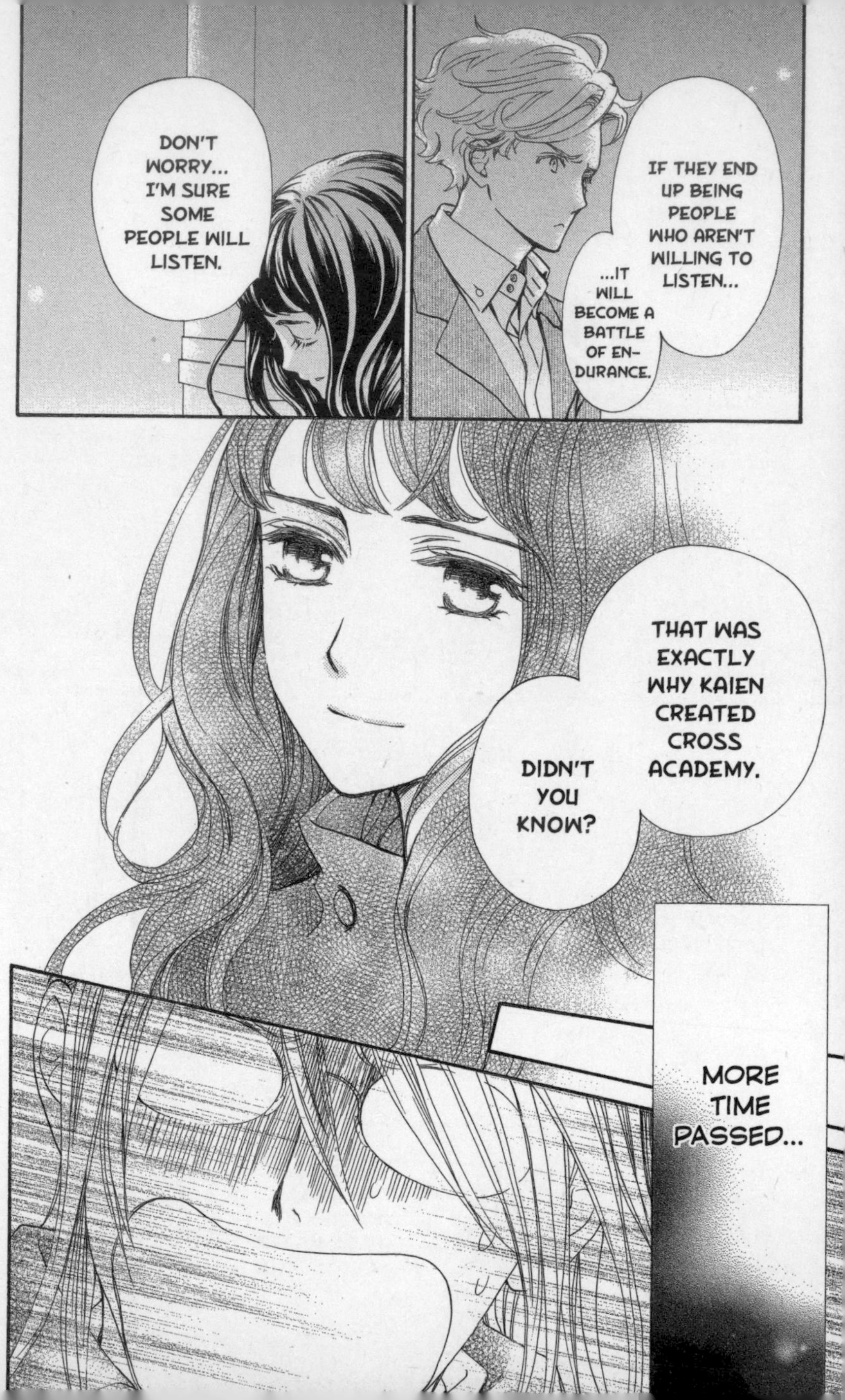
IF THEY END UP BEING PEOPLE WHO AREN'T WILLING TO LISTEN...
...IT WILL BECOME A BATTLE OF EN-DURANCE.
DON'T WORRY... I'M SURE SOME PEOPLE WILL LISTEN.
THAT WAS EXACTLY WHY KAIEN CREATED CROSS ACADEMY.
DIDN'T YOU KNOW?
MORE TIME PASSED...

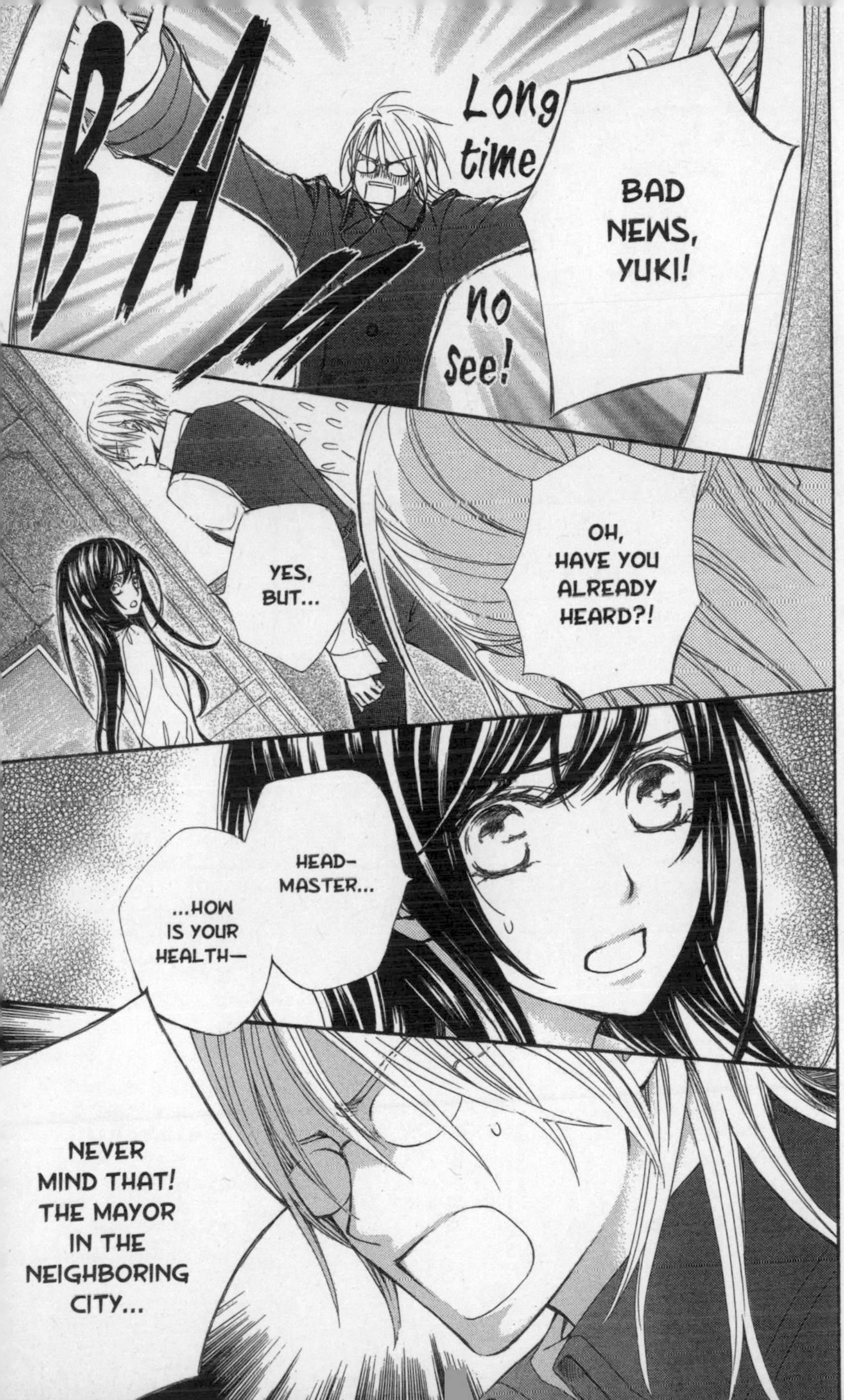
BAD NEWS, YUKI!
Long time no see!
BAM
OH, HAVE YOU ALREADY HEARD?!
YES, BUT...
HEAD-MASTER...
...HOW IS YOUR HEALTH—
NEVER MIND THAT! THE MAYOR IN THE NEIGHBORING CITY...

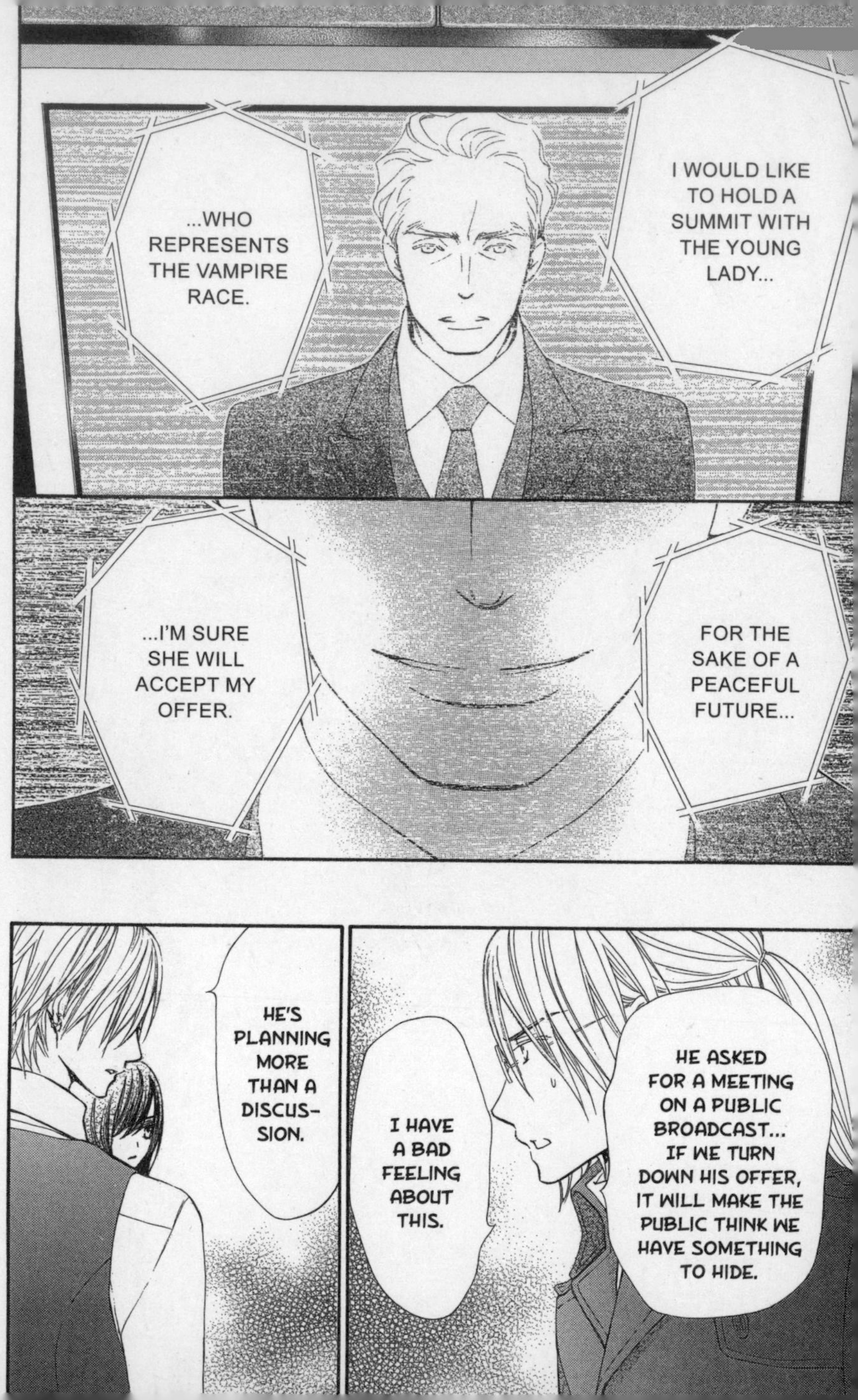
I WOULD LIKE TO HOLD A SUMMIT WITH THE YOUNG LADY...
...WHO REPRESENTS THE VAMPIRE RACE.
FOR THE SAKE OF A PEACEFUL FUTURE...
...I'M SURE SHE WILL ACCEPT MY OFFER.
HE ASKED FOR A MEETING ON A PUBLIC BROADCAST... IF WE TURN DOWN HIS OFFER, IT WILL MAKE THE PUBLIC THINK WE HAVE SOMETHING TO HIDE.
I HAVE A BAD FEELING ABOUT THIS.
HE'S PLANNING MORE THAN A DISCUSSION.

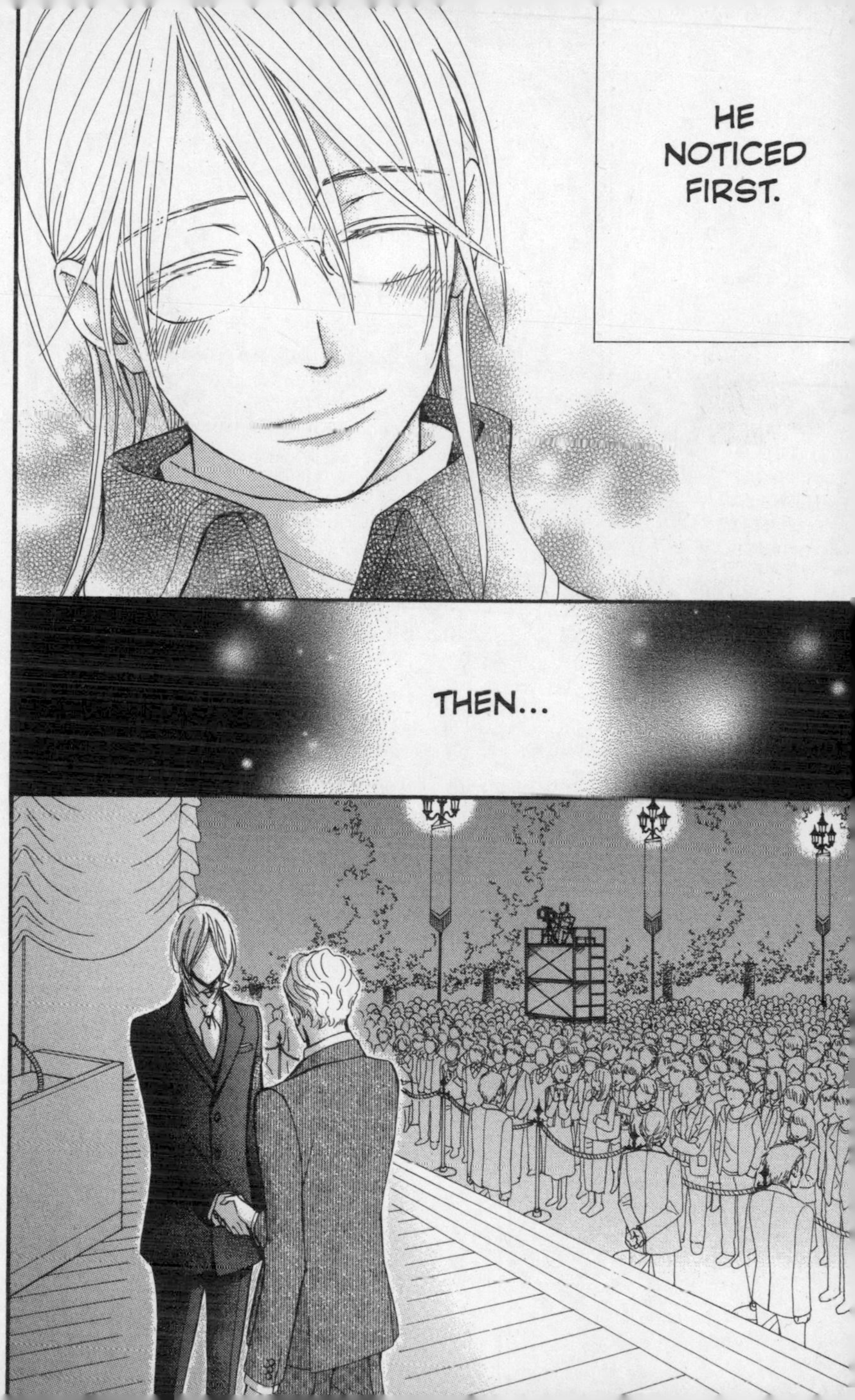
HE NOTICED FIRST.
THEN...

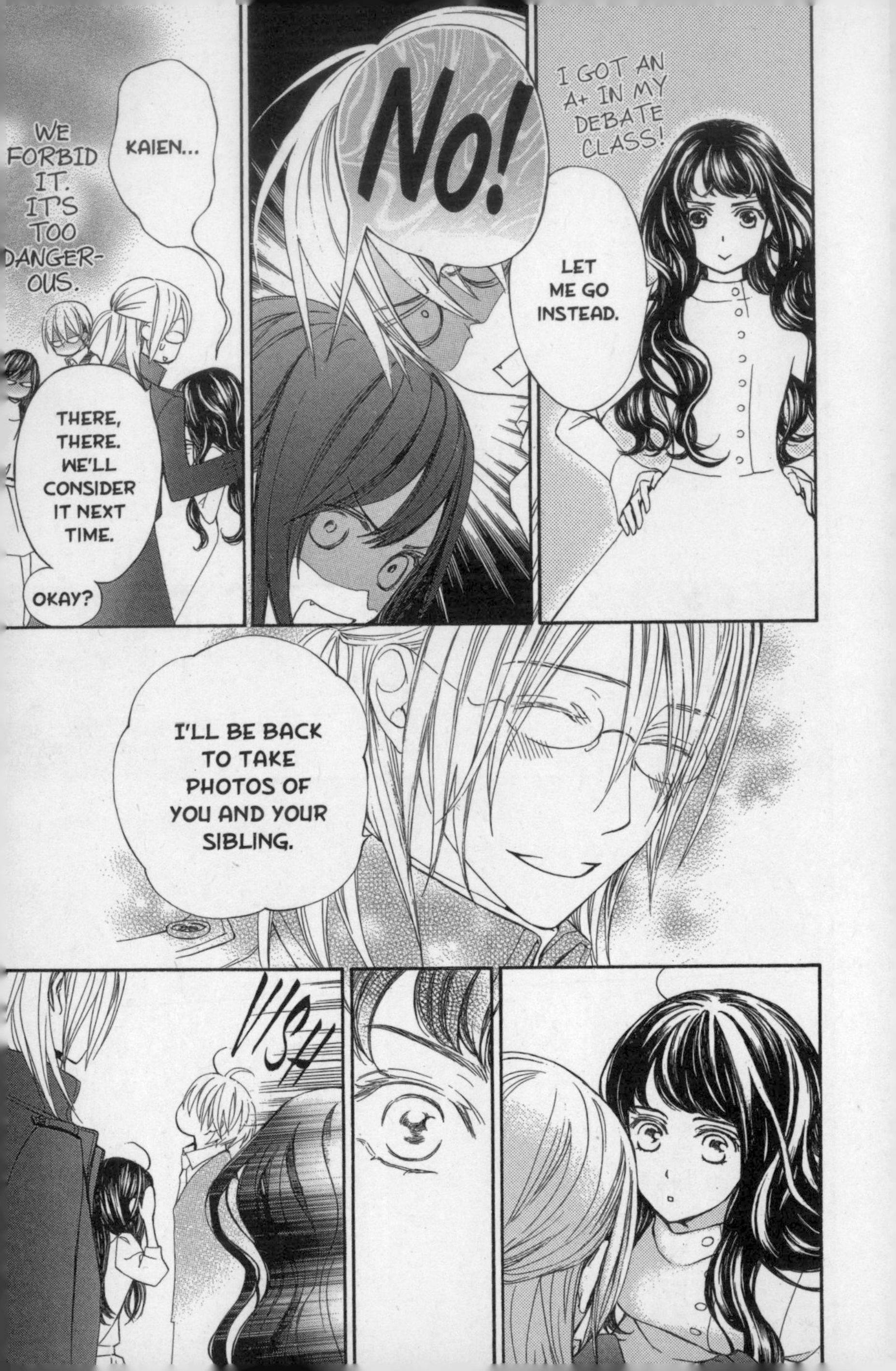
I GOT AN A+ IN MY DEBATE CLASS!
LET ME GO INSTEAD.
No!
KAIEN...
WE FORBID IT. IT'S TOO DANGER-OUS.
THERE, THERE. WE'LL CONSIDER IT NEXT TIME.
OKAY?
I'LL BE BACK TO TAKE PHOTOS OF YOU AND YOUR SIBLING.
WISH

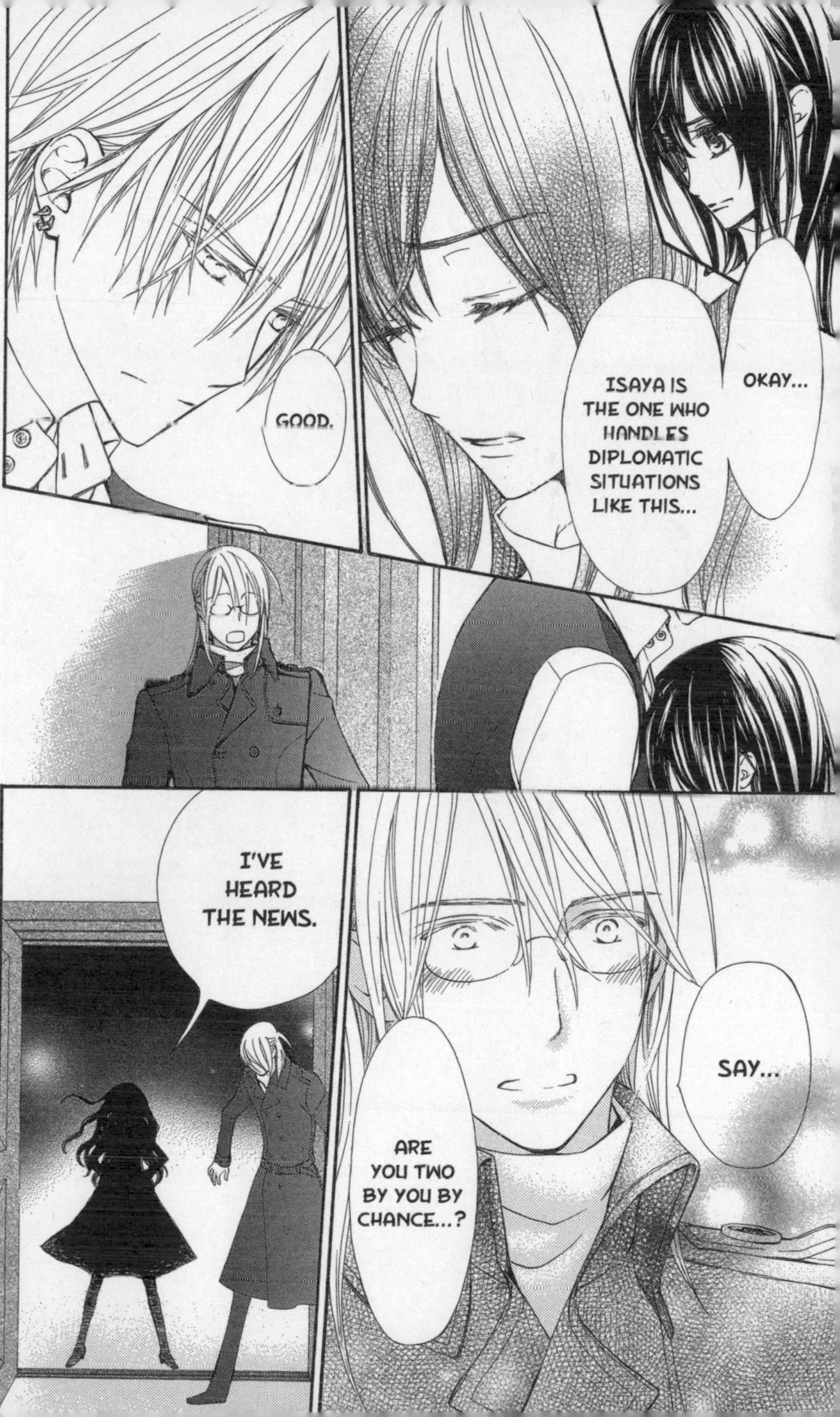
OKAY...
ISAYA IS THE ONE WHO HANDLES DIPLOMATIC SITUATIONS LIKE THIS...
GOOD.
SAY...
ARE YOU TWO BY YOU BY CHANCE...?
I'VE HEARD THE NEWS.

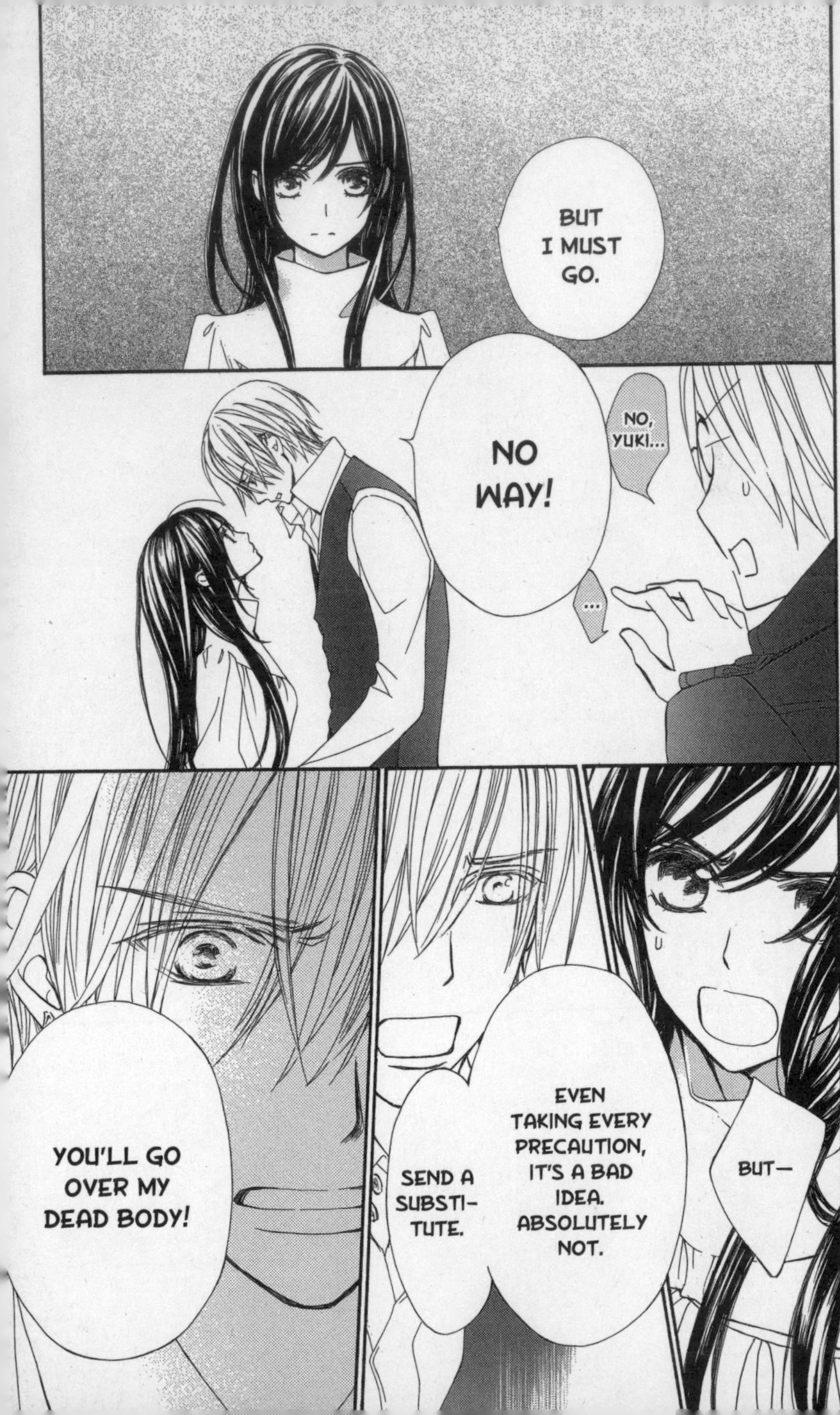
BUT I MUST GO.
NO, YUKI...
NO WAY!
...
BUT—
EVEN TAKING EVERY PRECAUTION, IT'S A BAD IDEA. ABSOLUTELY NOT.
SEND A SUBSTI-TUTE.
YOU'LL GO OVER MY DEAD BODY!

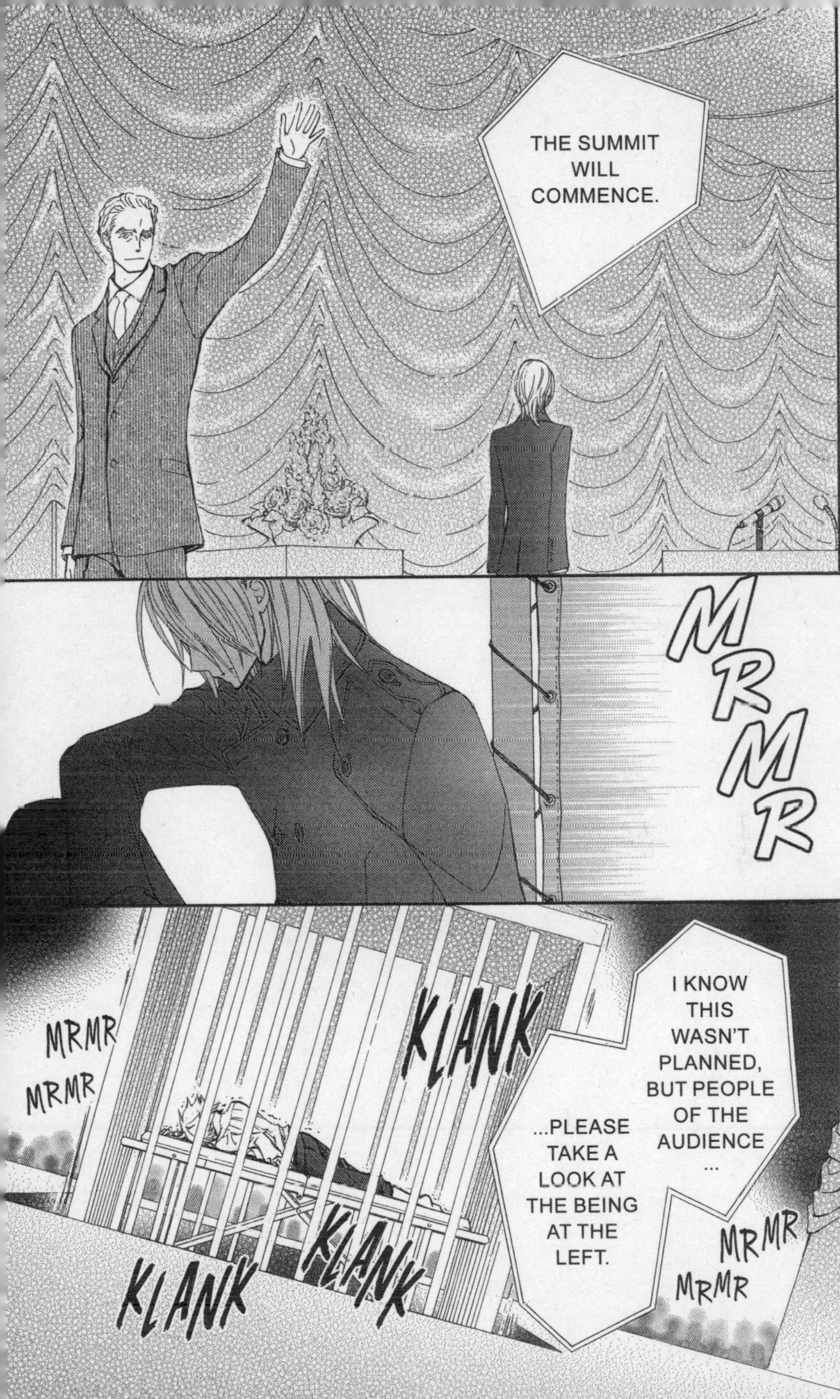
THE SUMMIT WILL COMMENCE.
MRMR
I KNOW THIS WASN'T PLANNED, BUT PEOPLE OF THE AUDIENCE ...
...PLEASE TAKE A LOOK AT THE BEING AT THE LEFT.
MRMR
MRMR
KLANK
KLANK
KLANK
MRMR
MRMR

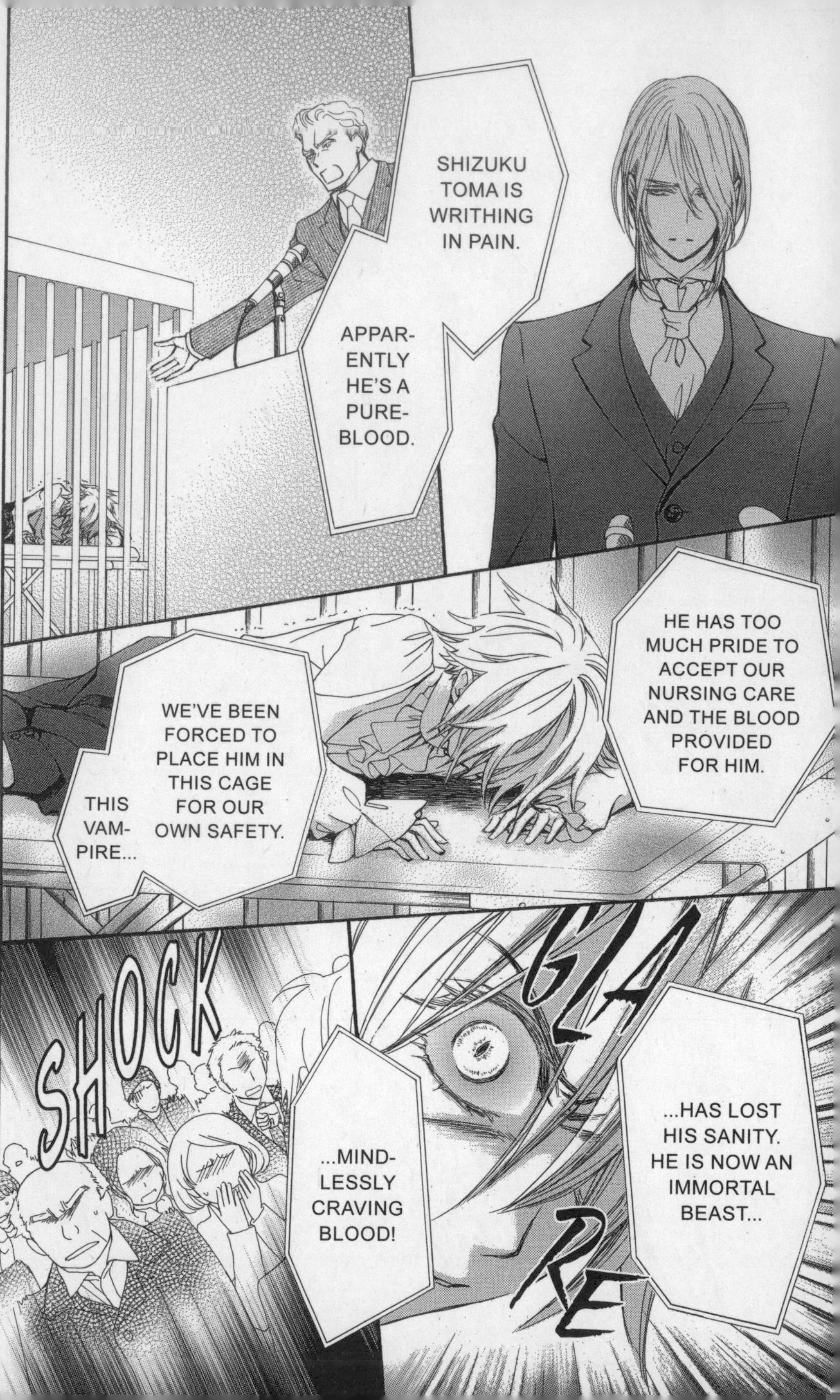
SHIZUKU TOMA IS WRITHING IN PAIN.
APPARENTLY HE'S A PUREBLOOD.
HE HAS TOO MUCH PRIDE TO ACCEPT OUR NURSING CARE AND THE BLOOD PROVIDED FOR HIM.
WE'VE BEEN FORCED TO PLACE HIM IN THIS CAGE FOR OUR OWN SAFETY.
THIS VAMPIRE...
GLARE
...HAS LOST HIS SANITY. HE IS NOW AN IMMORTAL BEAST...
...MINDLESSLY CRAVING BLOOD!
SHOCK

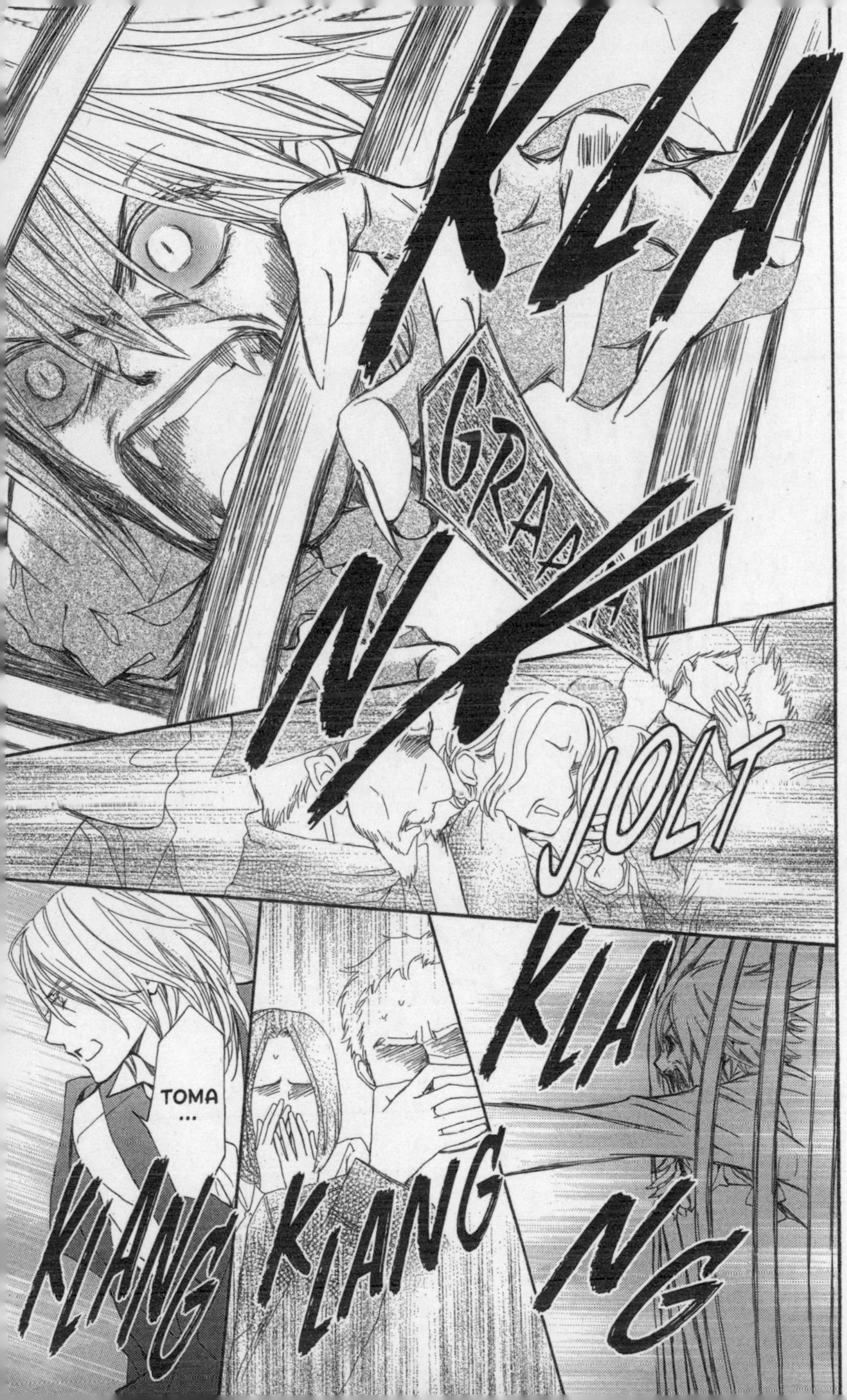

KLANK
GRA
JOLT
KLANG
TOMA ...
KLANG
KLANG

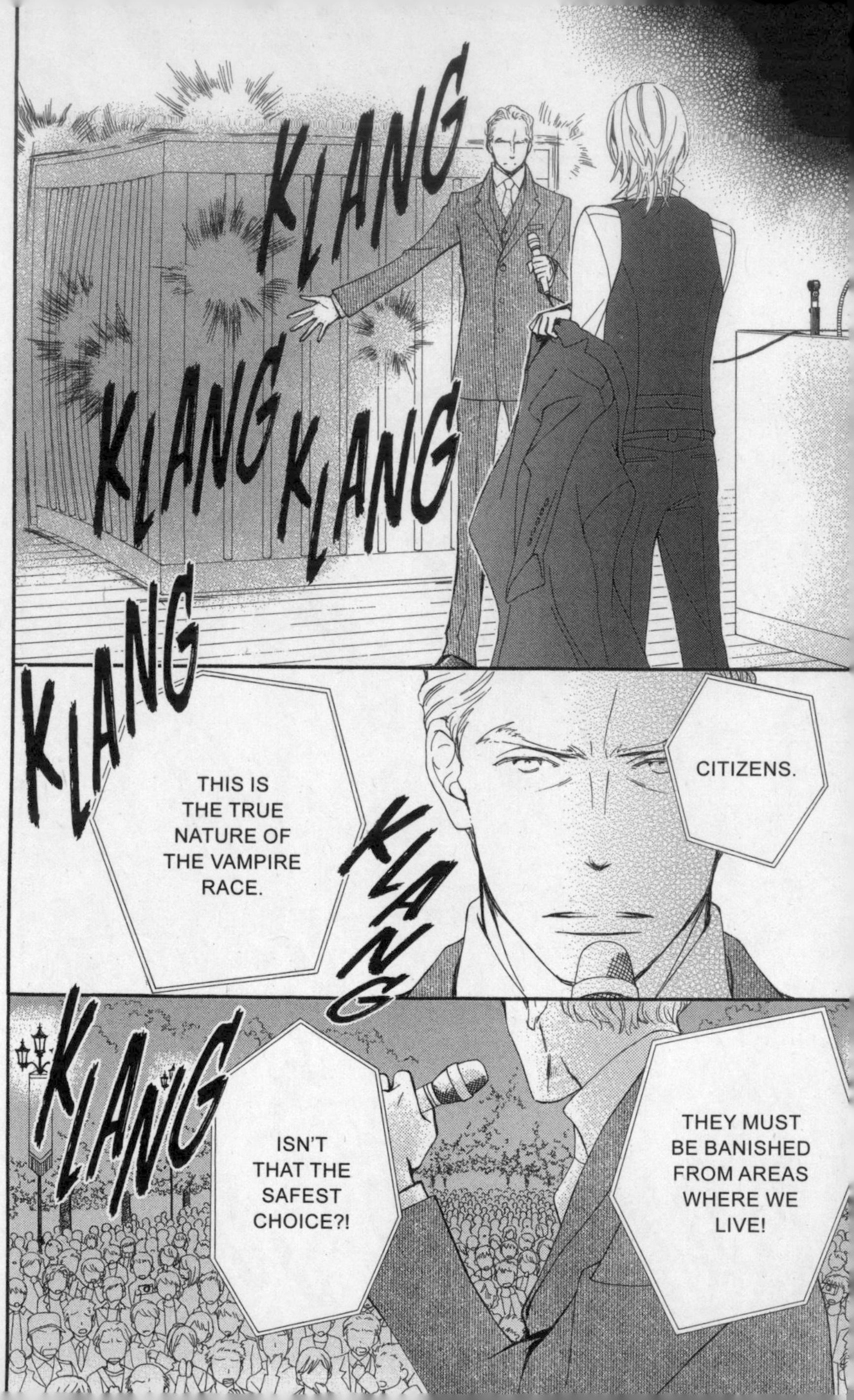
KLANG
KLANG
KLANG
KLANG
CITIZENS.
KLANG
THIS IS THE TRUE NATURE OF THE VAMPIRE RACE.
THEY MUST BE BANISHED FROM AREAS WHERE WE LIVE!
ISN'T THAT THE SAFEST CHOICE?!
KLANG

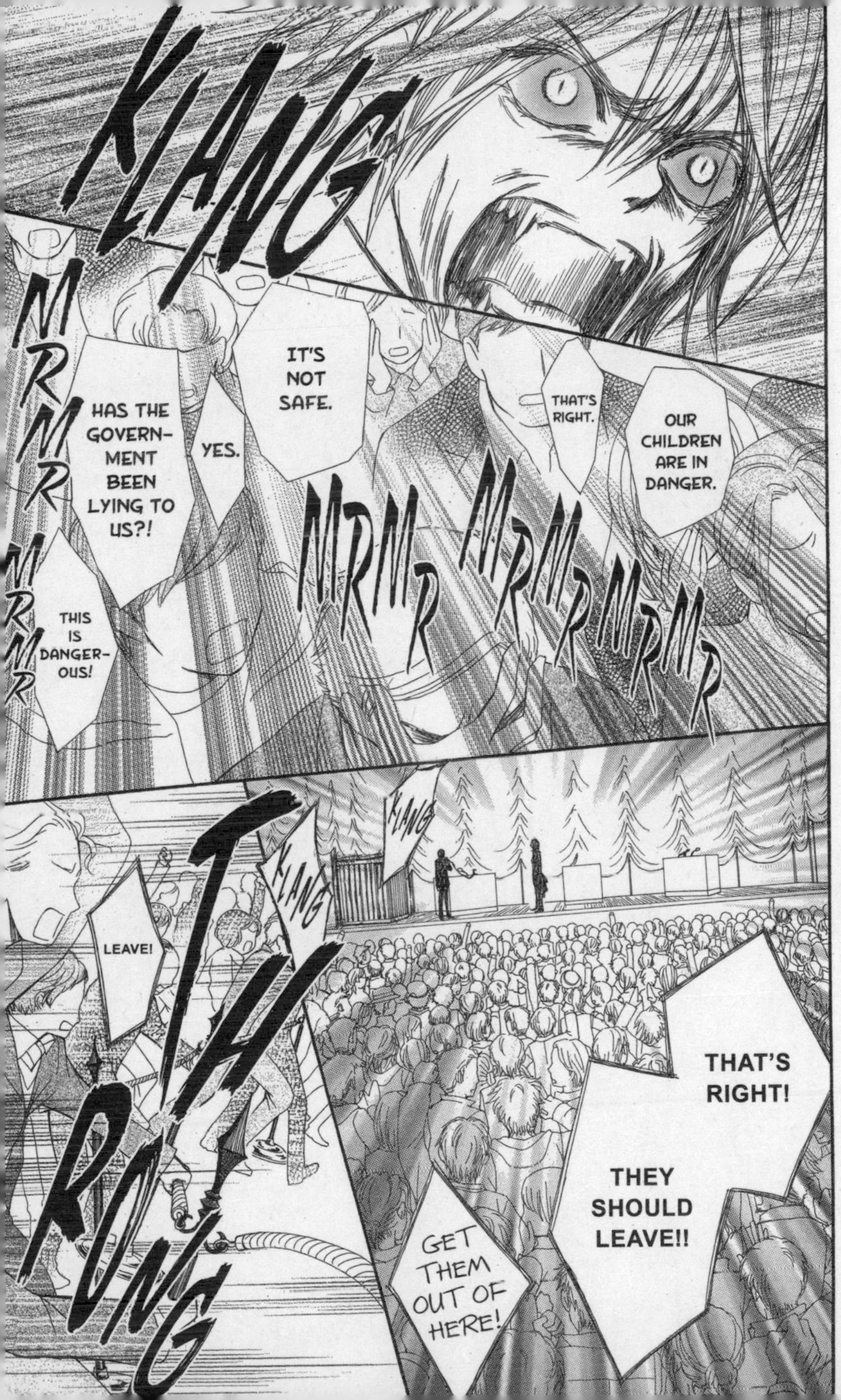
KLANG
MRMR MRMR
OUR CHILDREN ARE IN DANGER.
THAT'S RIGHT.
MRMR MRMR MRMR
IT'S NOT SAFE.
YES.
HAS THE GOVERNMENT BEEN LYING TO US?!
THIS IS DANGEROUS!
MRMR MRMR
THAT'S RIGHT!
THEY SHOULD LEAVE!!
GET THEM OUT OF HERE!
KLANG
KLANG
LEAVE!

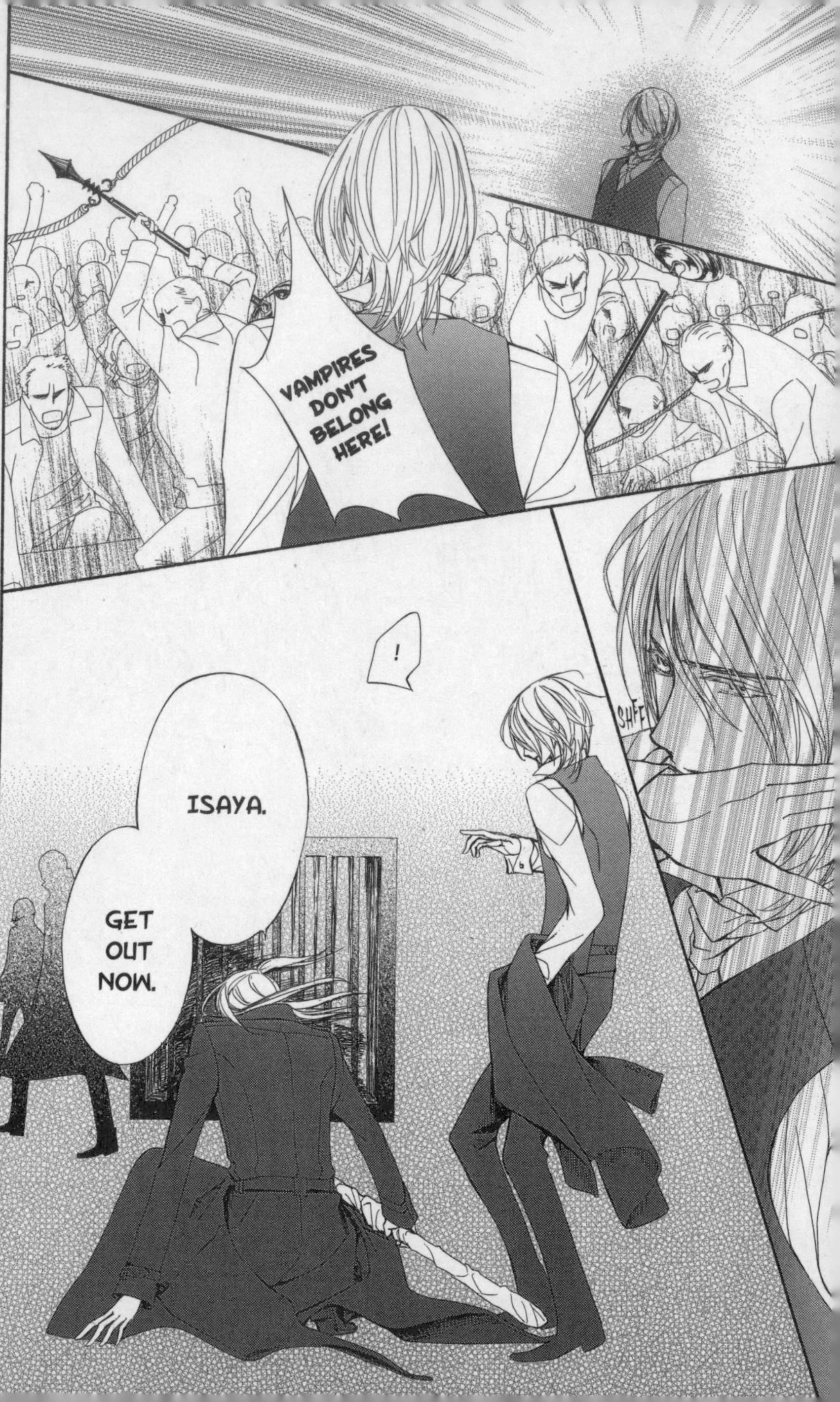
VAMPIRES DON'T BELONG HERE!
SHFF
!
ISAYA.
GET OUT NOW.

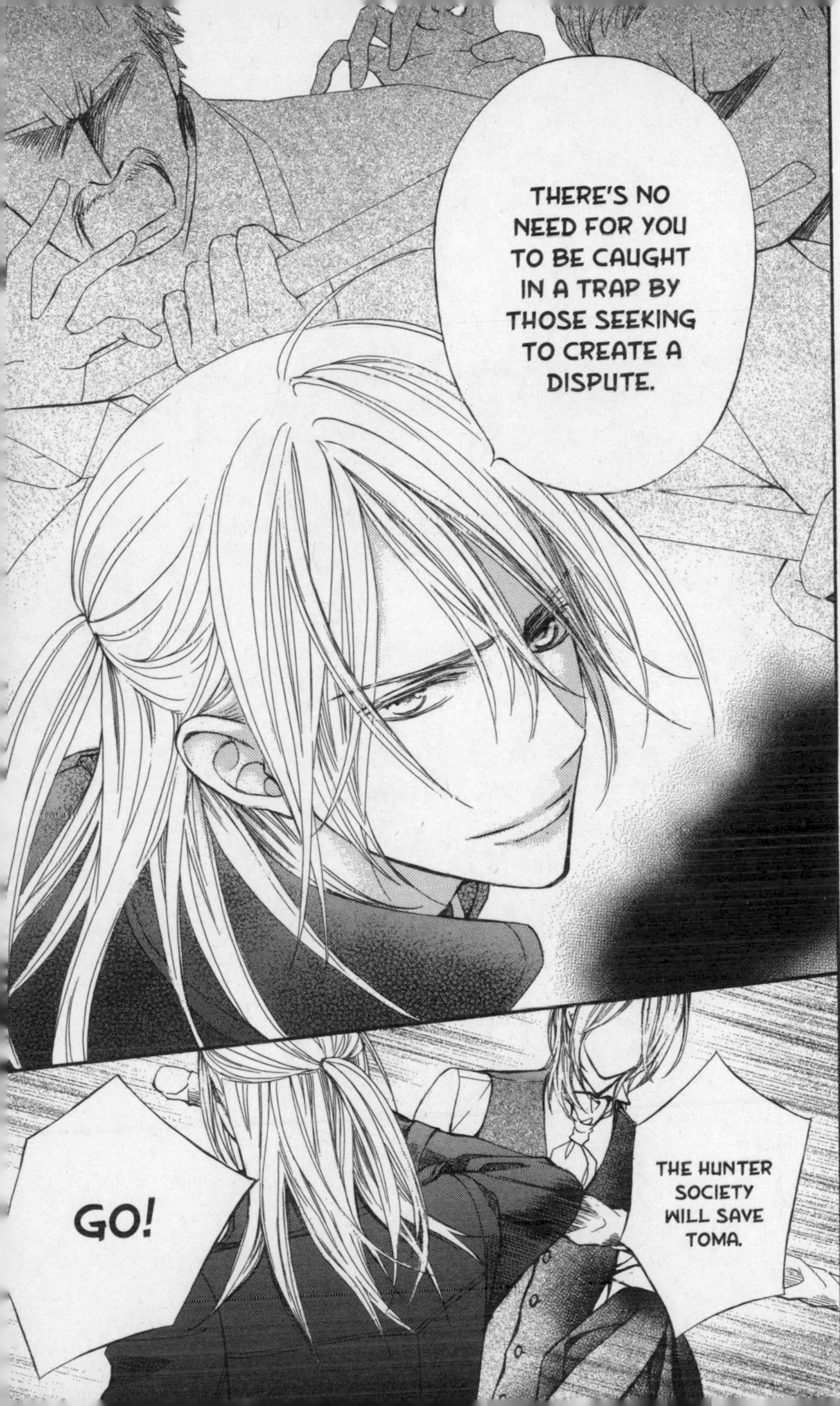
THERE'S NO NEED FOR YOU TO BE CAUGHT IN A TRAP BY THOSE SEEKING TO CREATE A DISPUTE.
THE HUNTER SOCIETY WILL SAVE TOMA.
GO!

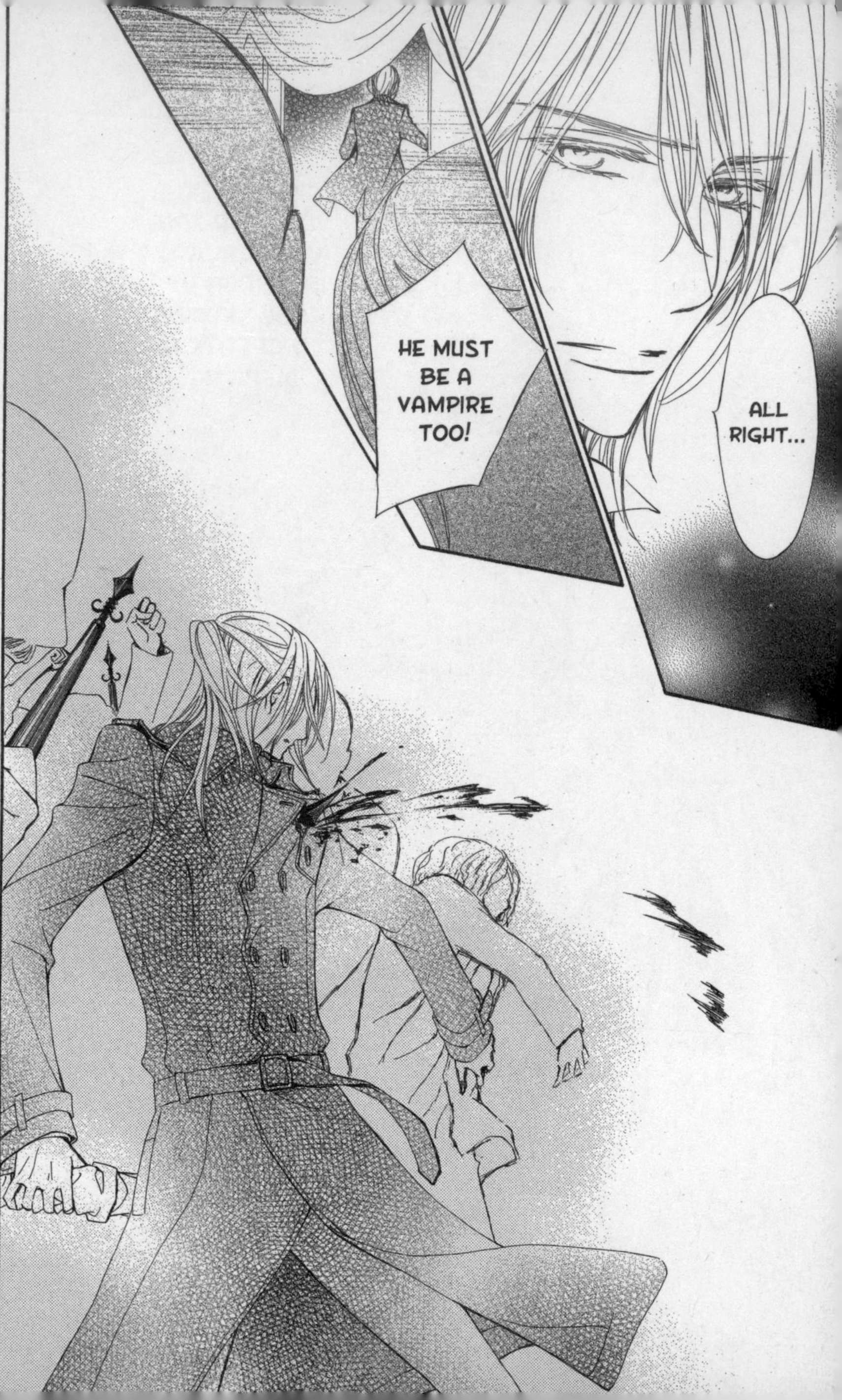
ALL RIGHT...
HE MUST BE A VAMPIRE TOO!

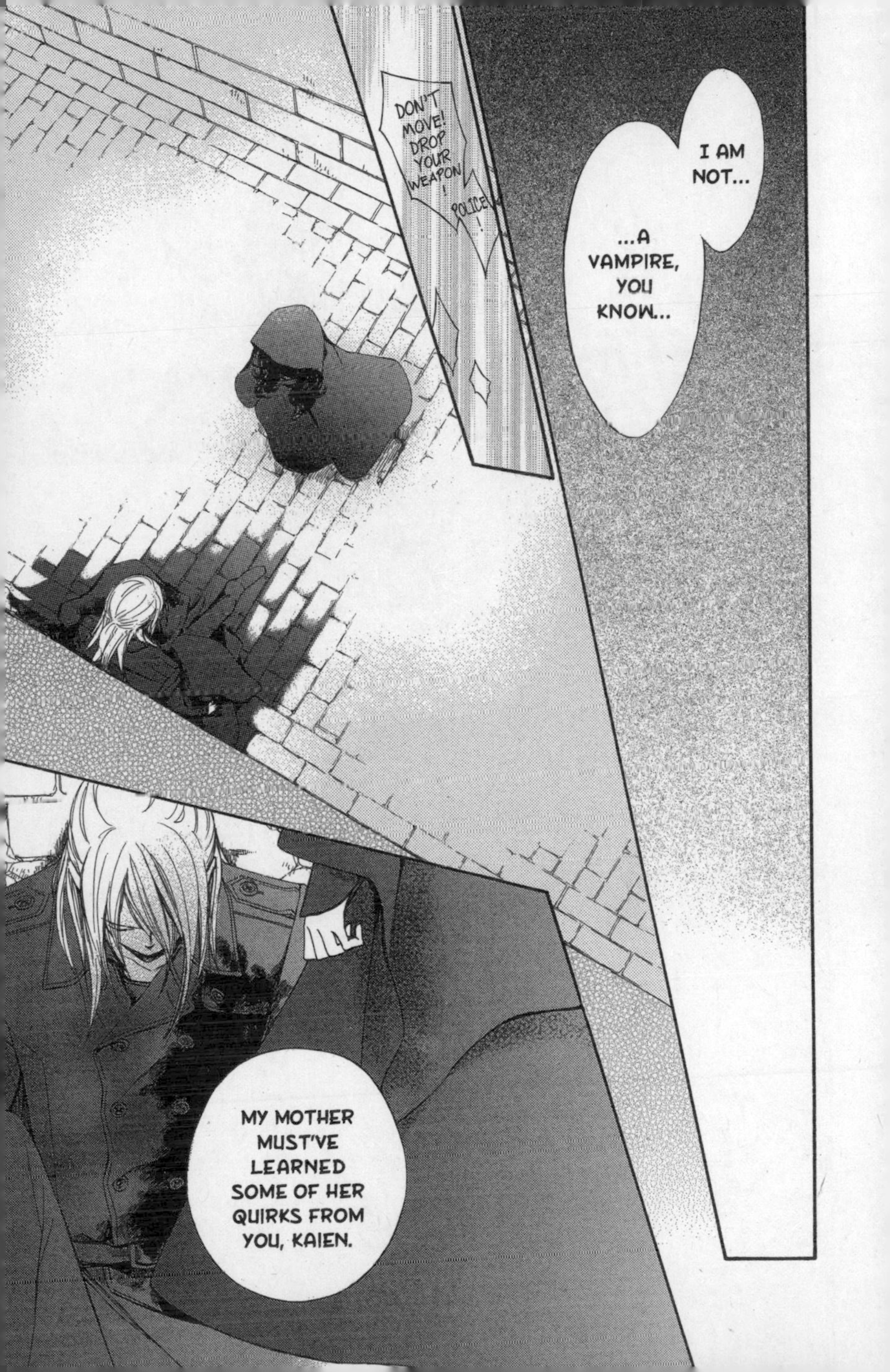
I AM NOT...
...A VAMPIRE, YOU KNOW...
DON'T MOVE! DROP YOUR WEAPON!
POLICE!
MY MOTHER MUST'VE LEARNED SOME OF HER QUIRKS FROM YOU, KAIEN.

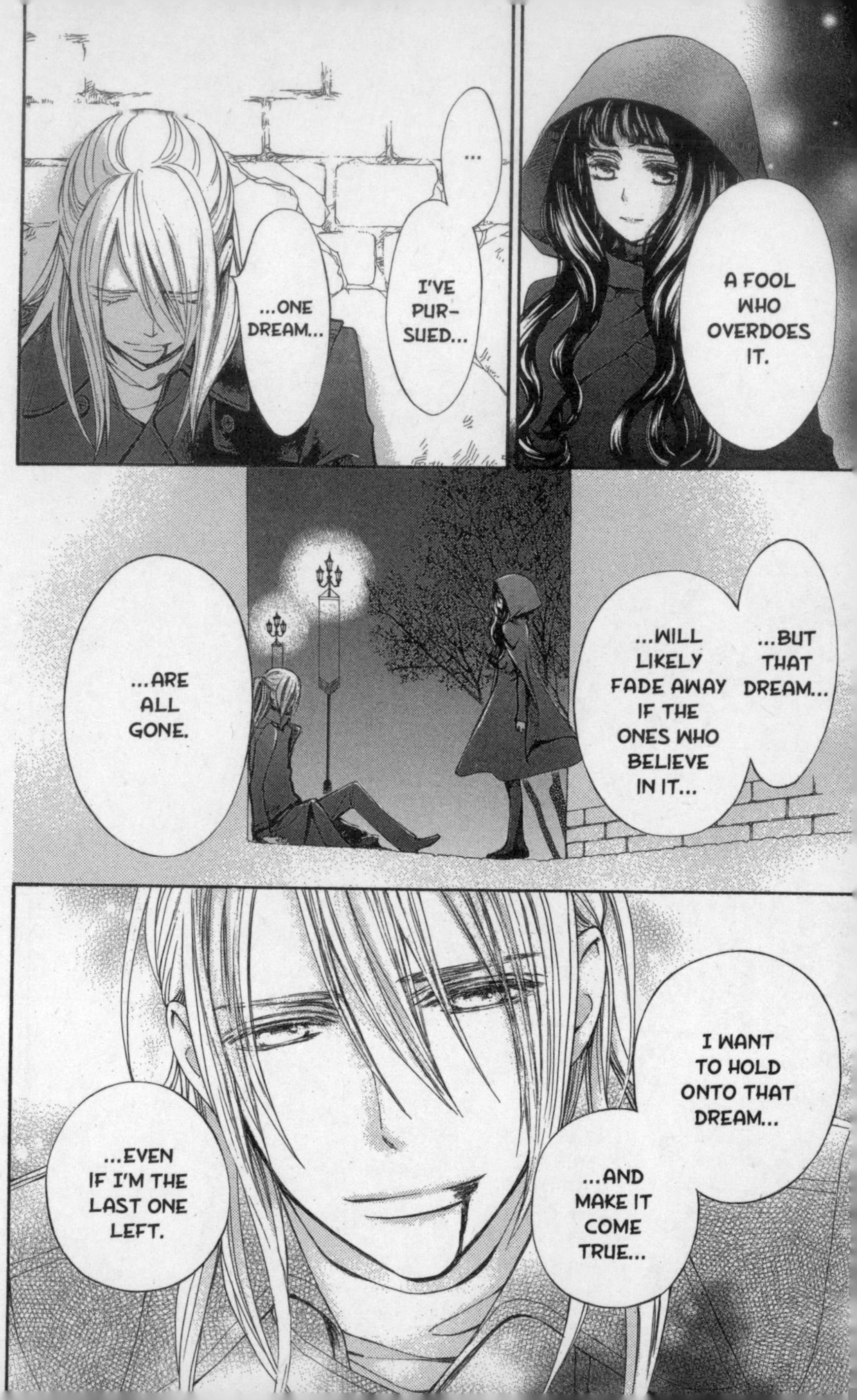
A FOOL WHO OVERDOES IT.
...
I'VE PUR-SUED...
...ONE DREAM...
...BUT THAT DREAM...
...WILL LIKELY FADE AWAY IF THE ONES WHO BELIEVE IN IT...
...ARE ALL GONE.
I WANT TO HOLD ONTO THAT DREAM...
...AND MAKE IT COME TRUE...
...EVEN IF I'M THE LAST ONE LEFT.

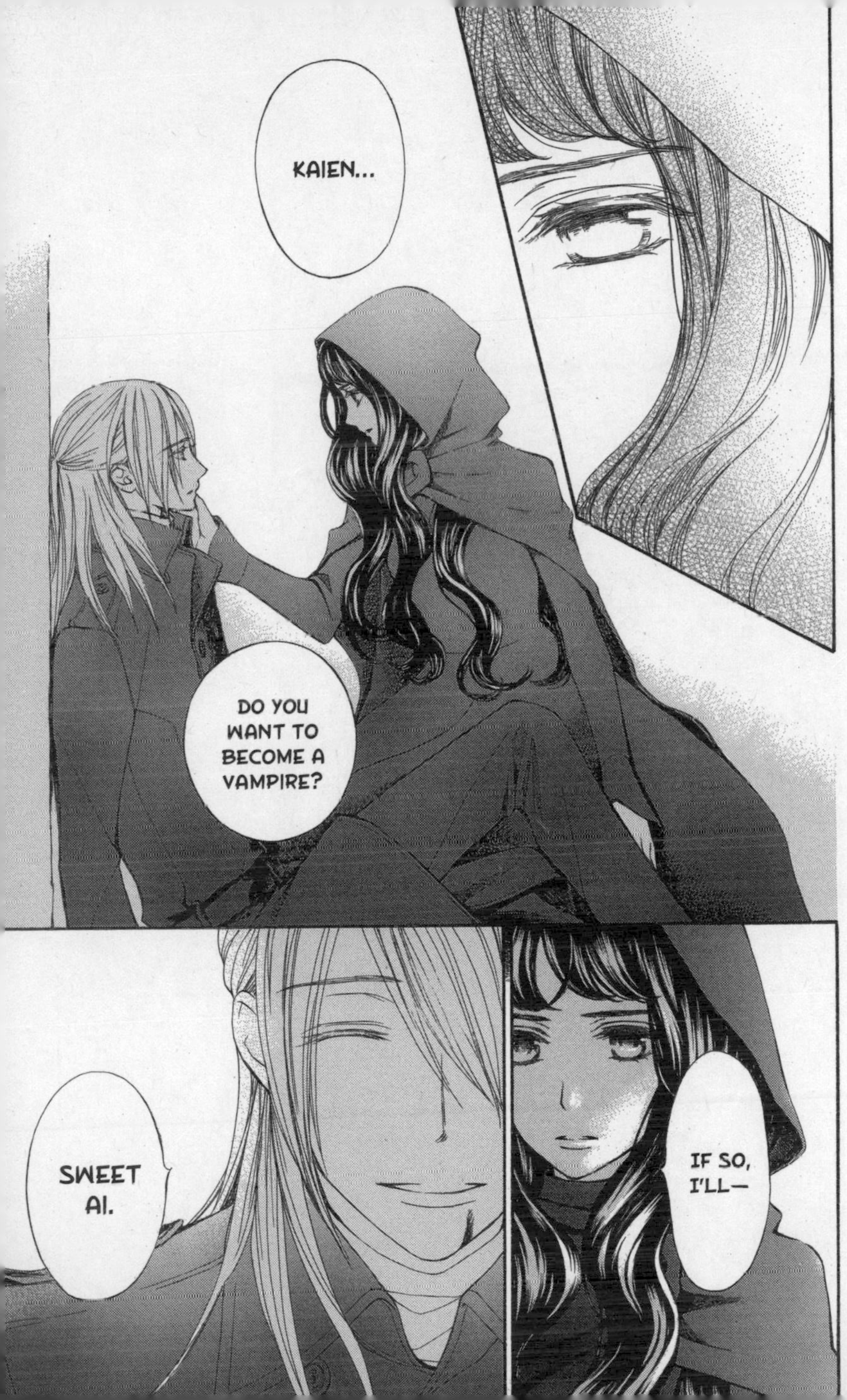
KAIEN...
DO YOU WANT TO BECOME A VAMPIRE?
IF SO, I'LL—
SWEET AI.

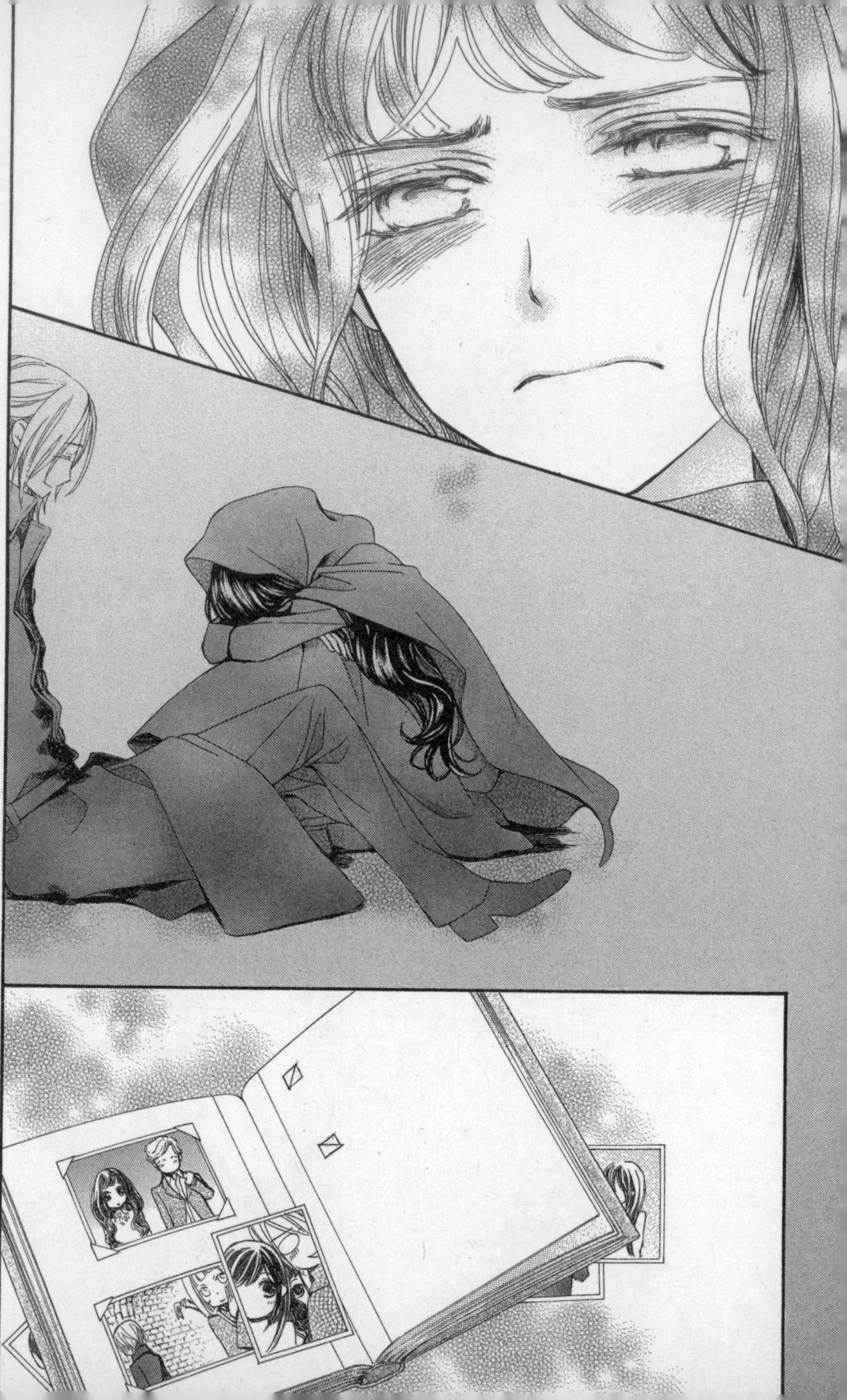

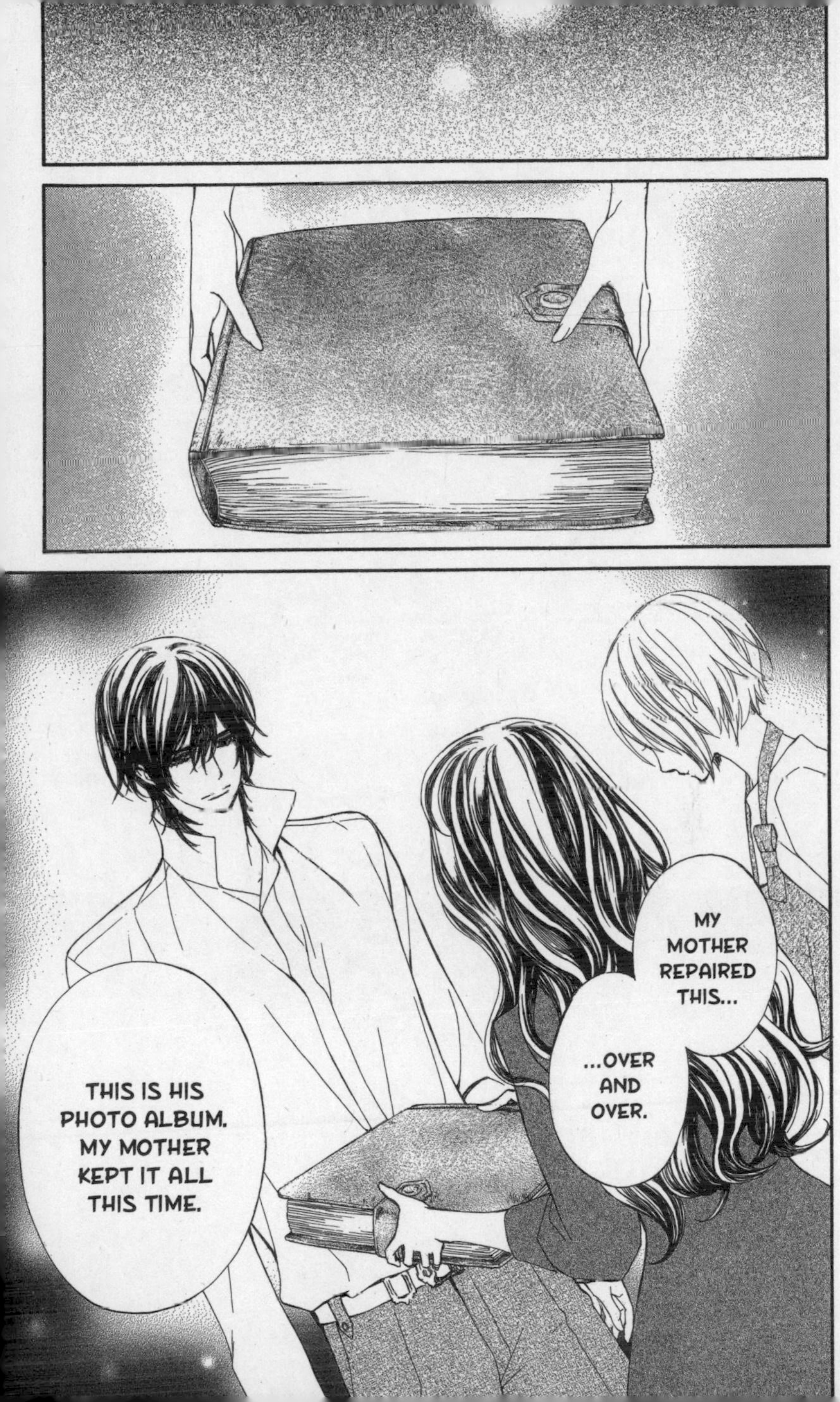
MY MOTHER REPAIRED THIS...
...OVER AND OVER.
THIS IS HIS PHOTO ALBUM. MY MOTHER KEPT IT ALL THIS TIME.

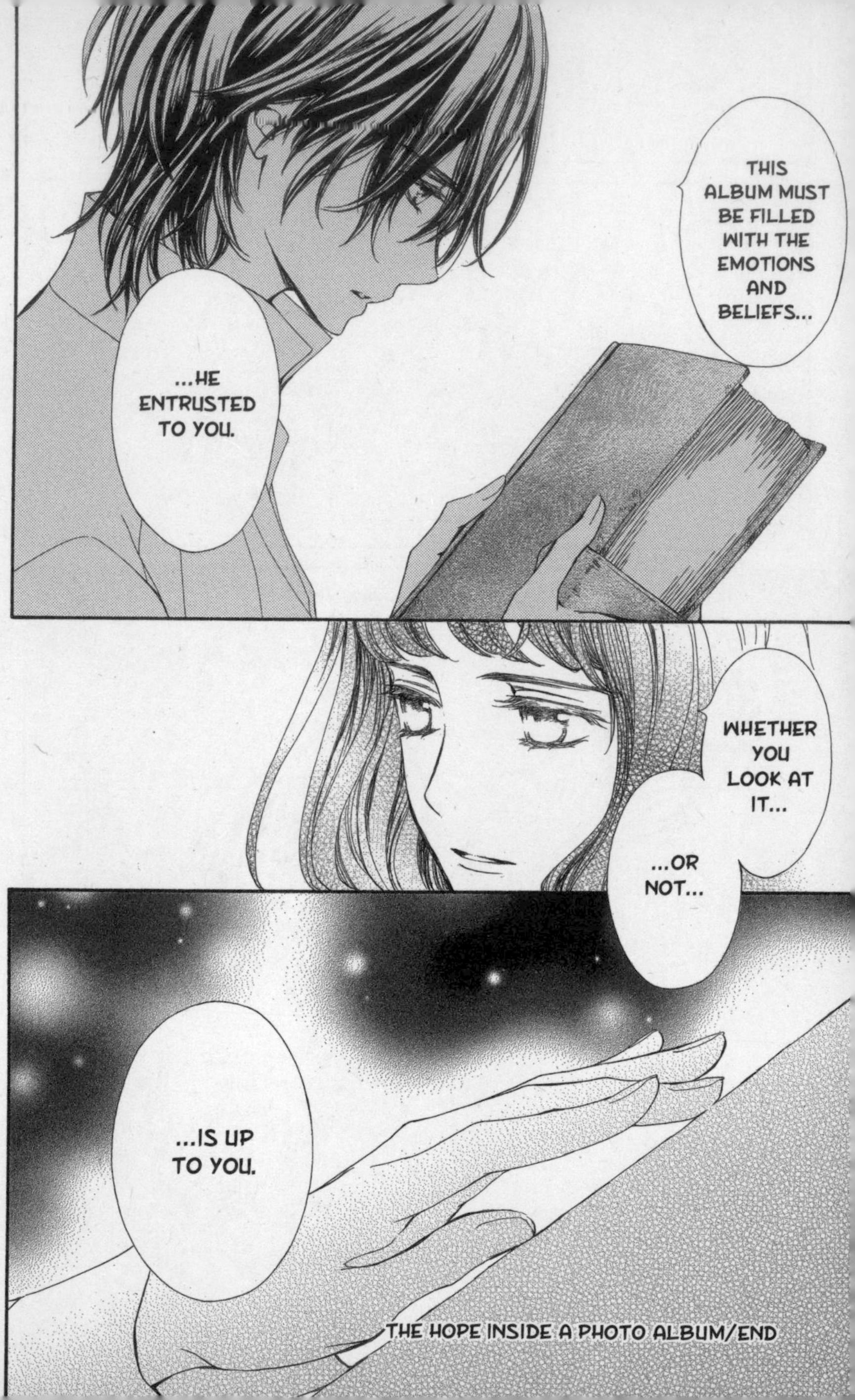
THIS ALBUM MUST BE FILLED WITH THE EMOTIONS AND BELIEFS...
...HE ENTRUSTED TO YOU.
WHETHER YOU LOOK AT IT...
...OR NOT...
...IS UP TO YOU.
THE HOPE INSIDE A PHOTO ALBUM/END

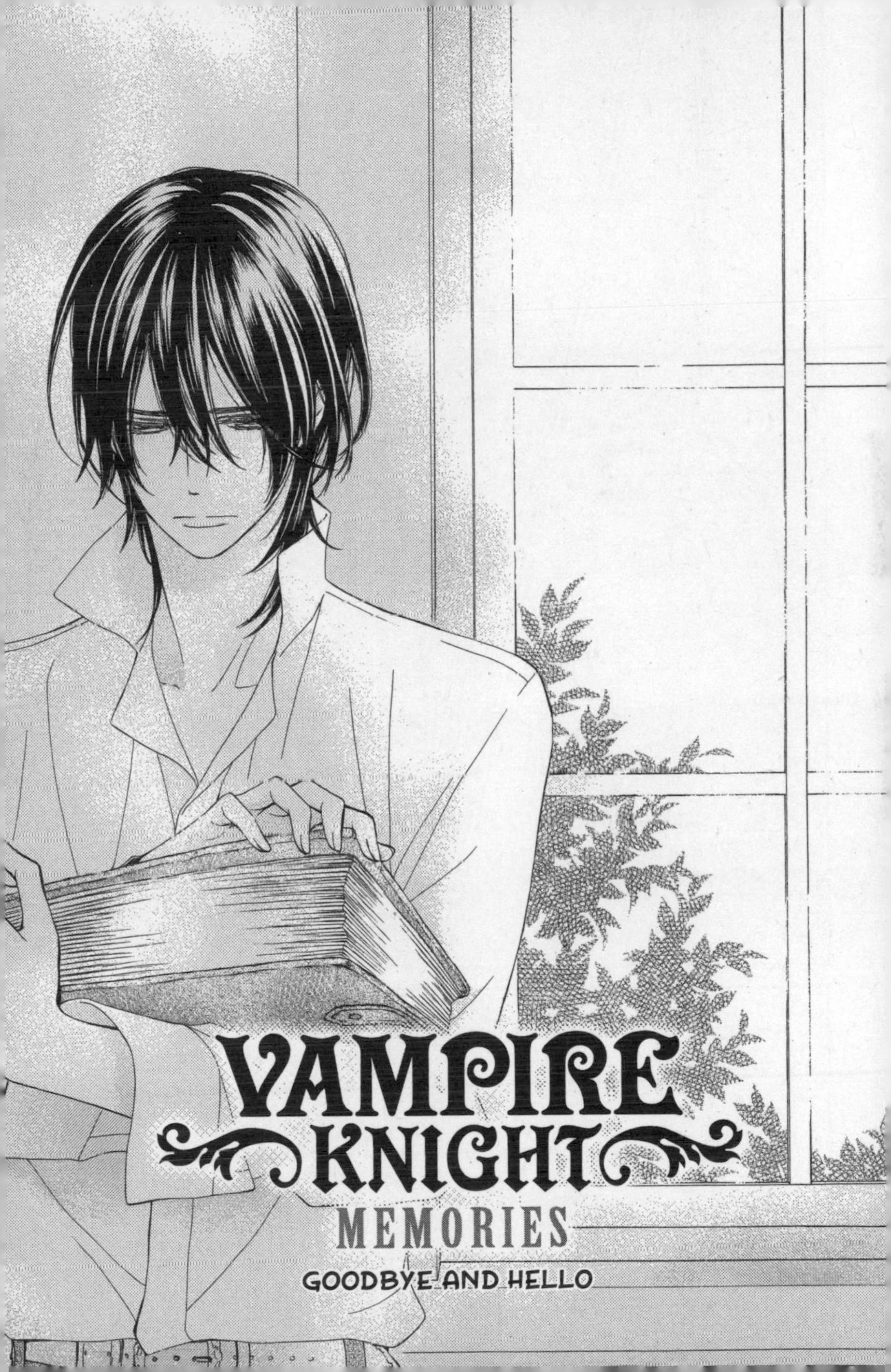
VAMPIRE KNIGHT
MEMORIES
GOODBYE AND HELLO

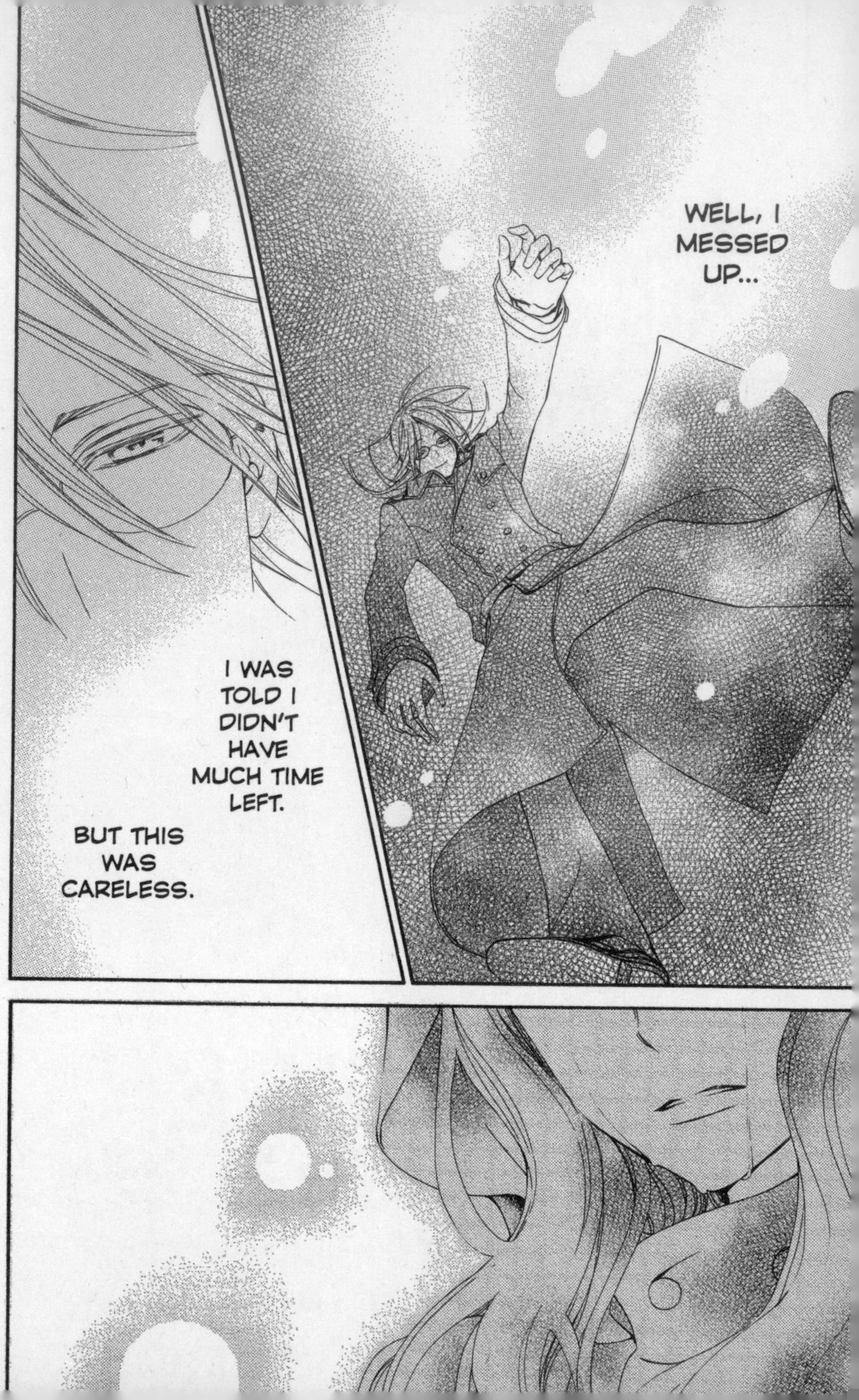
WELL, I MESSED UP...
I WAS TOLD I DIDN'T HAVE MUCH TIME LEFT.
BUT THIS WAS CARELESS.

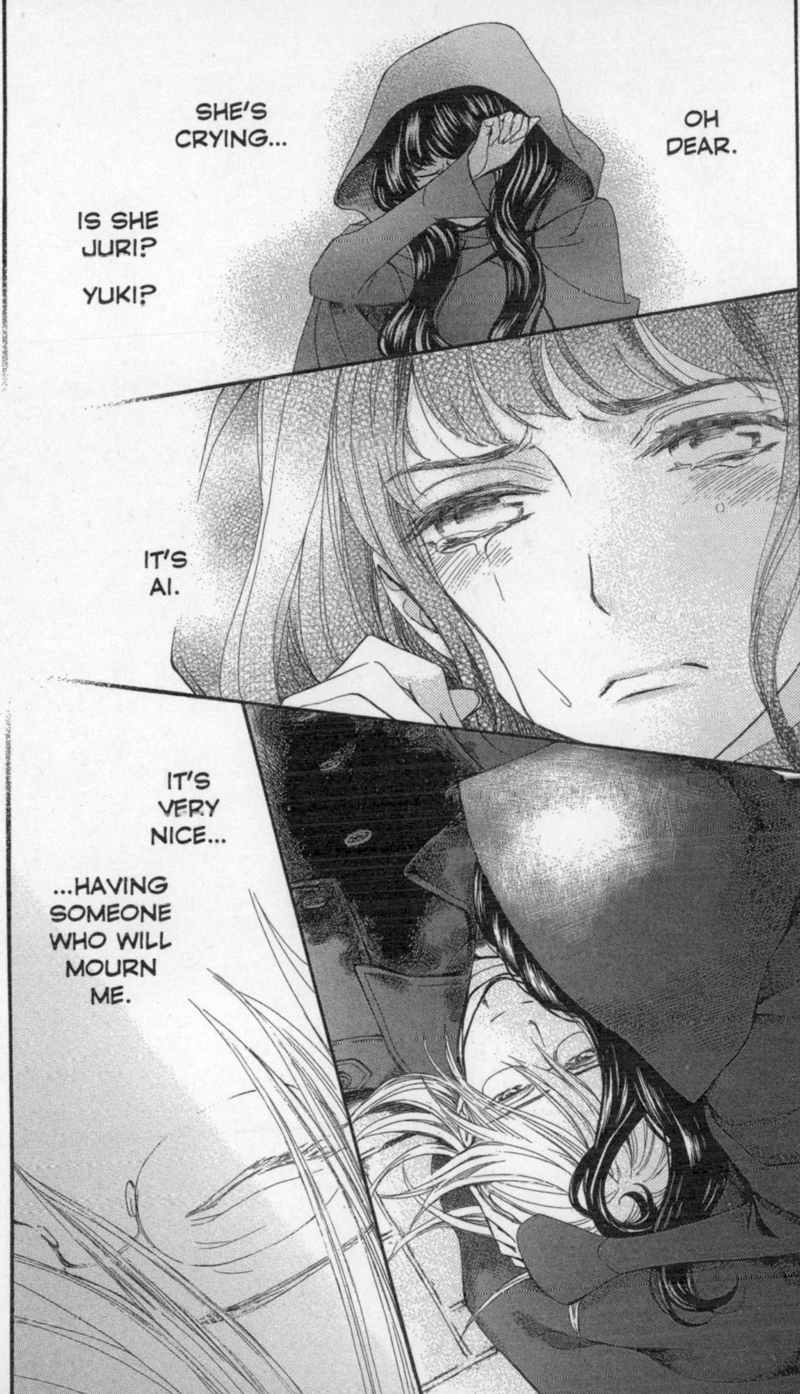
OH DEAR.
SHE'S CRYING...
IS SHE JURI?
YUKI?
IT'S AI.
IT'S VERY NICE...
...HAVING SOMEONE WHO WILL MOURN ME.

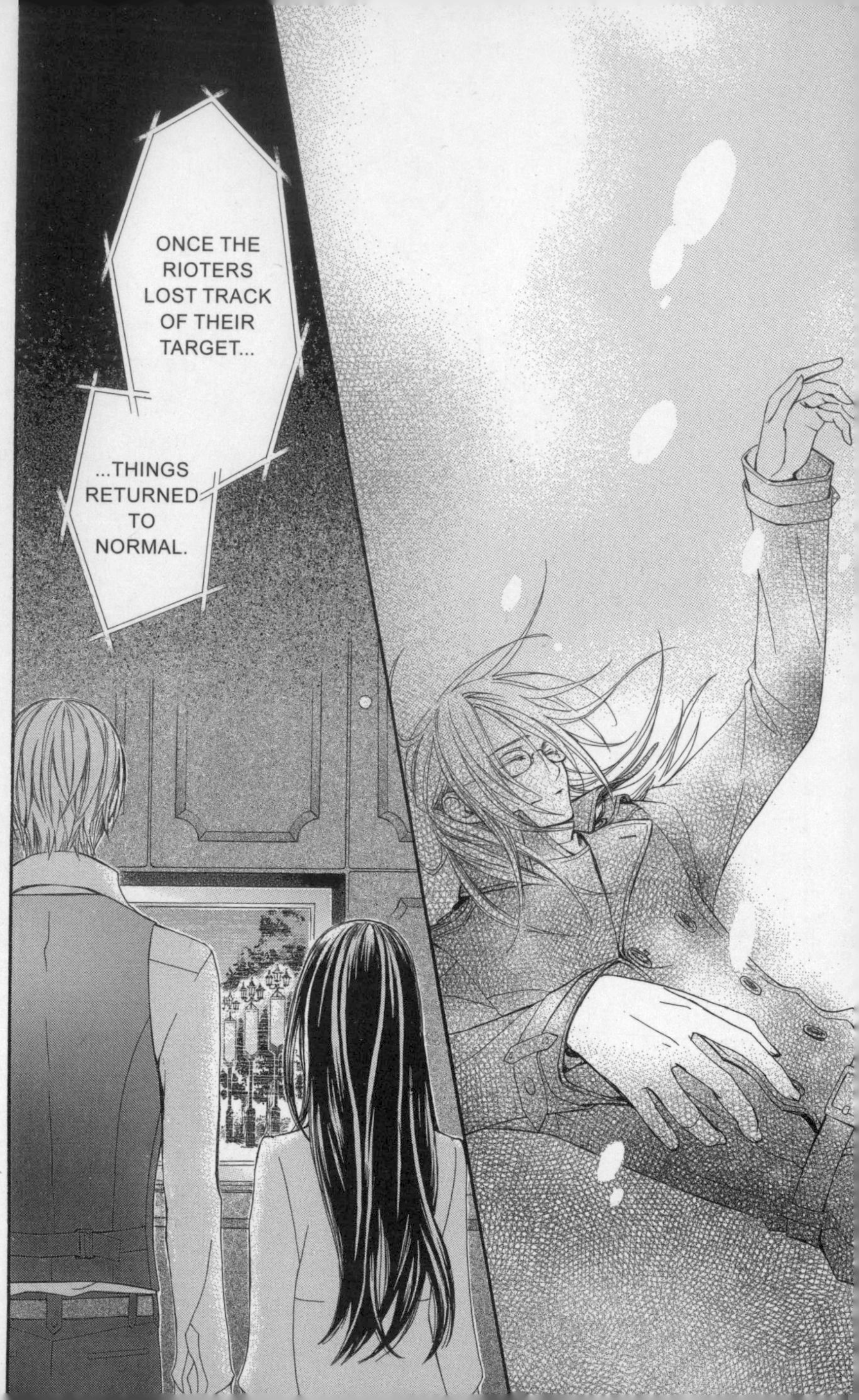
ONCE THE RIOTERS LOST TRACK OF THEIR TARGET...
...THINGS RETURNED TO NORMAL.

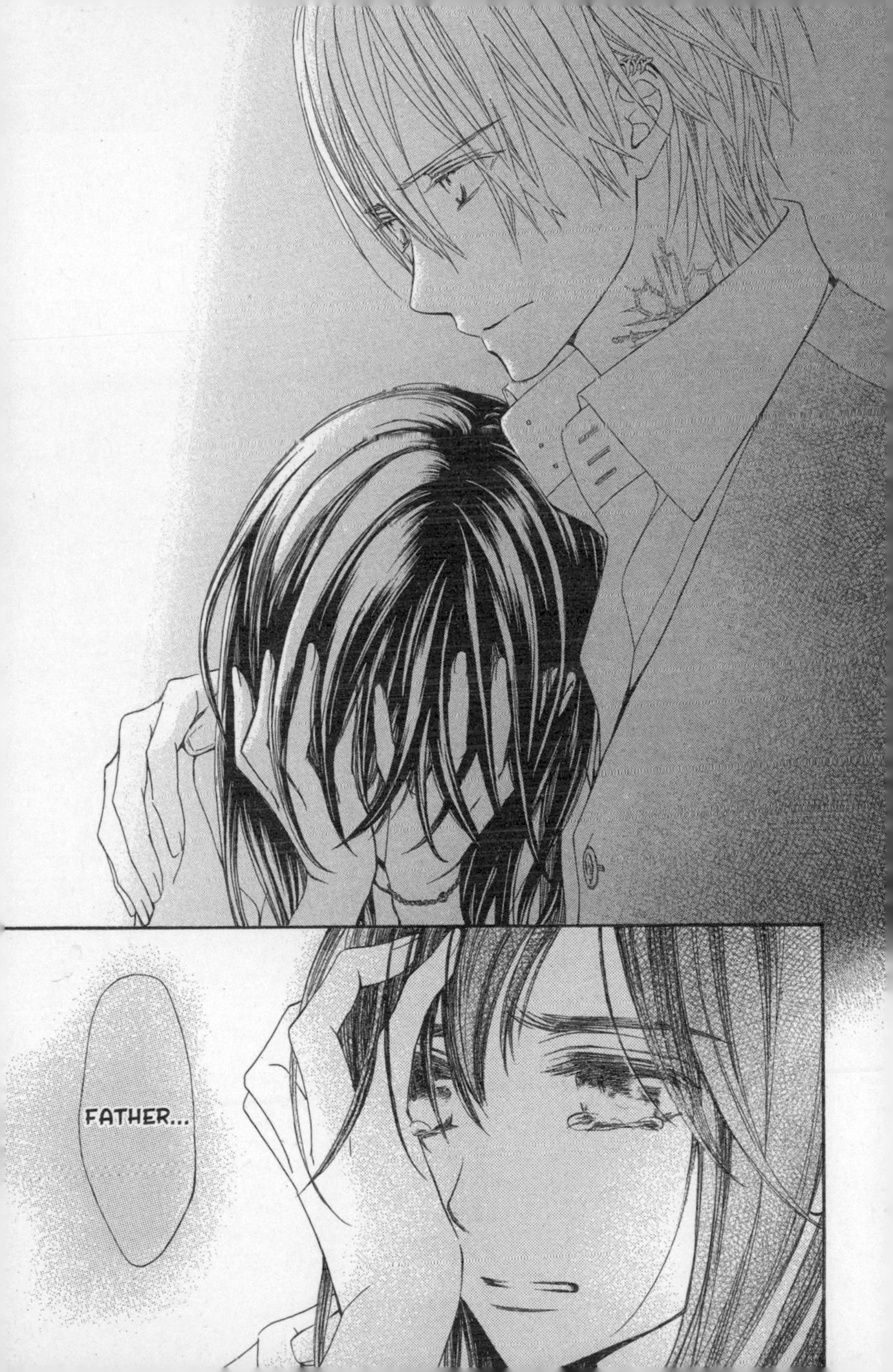
FATHER...

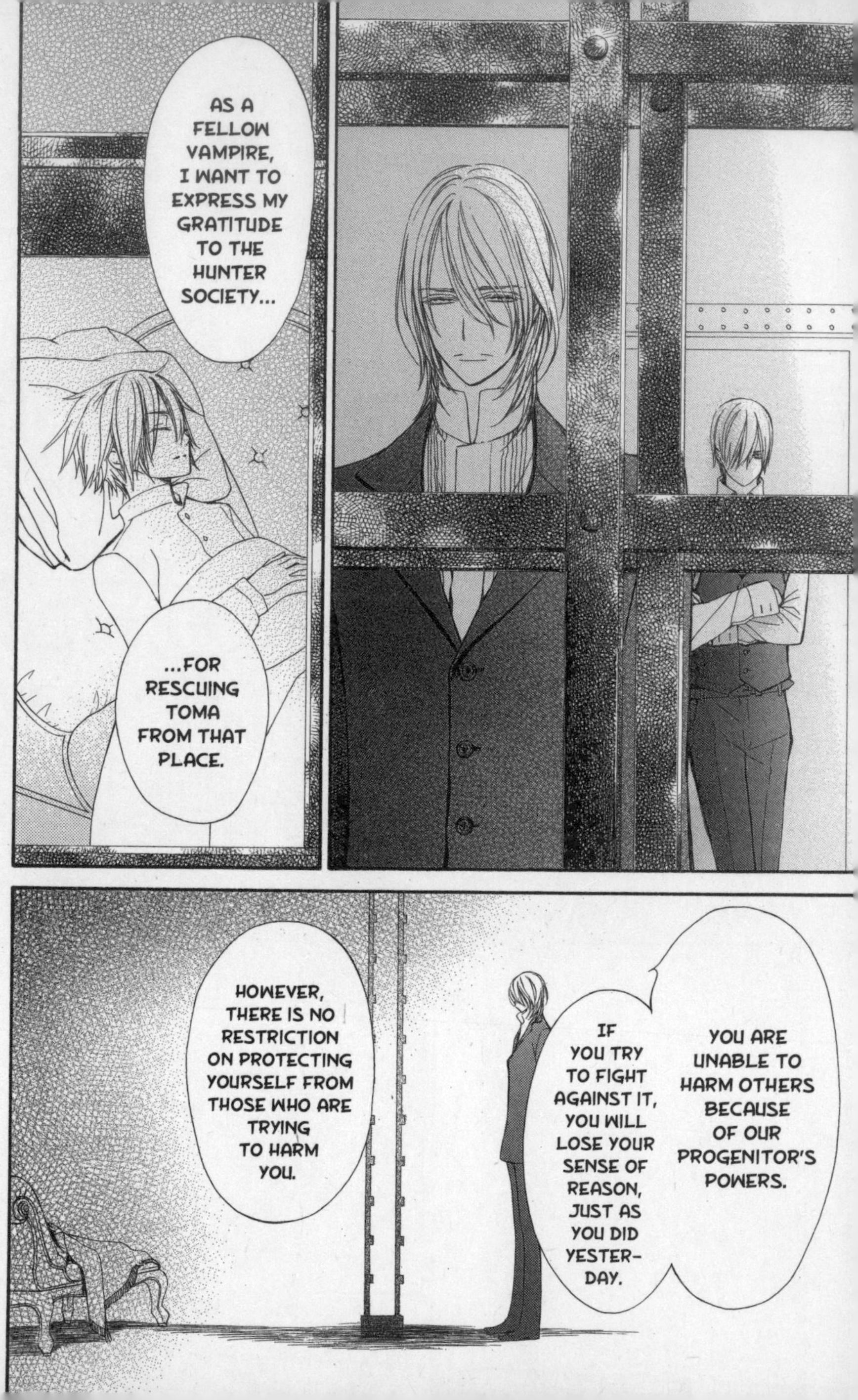
AS A FELLOW VAMPIRE, I WANT TO EXPRESS MY GRATITUDE TO THE HUNTER SOCIETY...
...FOR RESCUING TOMA FROM THAT PLACE.
YOU ARE UNABLE TO HARM OTHERS BECAUSE OF OUR PROGENITOR'S POWERS.
IF YOU TRY TO FIGHT AGAINST IT, YOU WILL LOSE YOUR SENSE OF REASON, JUST AS YOU DID YESTER-DAY.
HOWEVER, THERE IS NO RESTRICTION ON PROTECTING YOURSELF FROM THOSE WHO ARE TRYING TO HARM YOU.

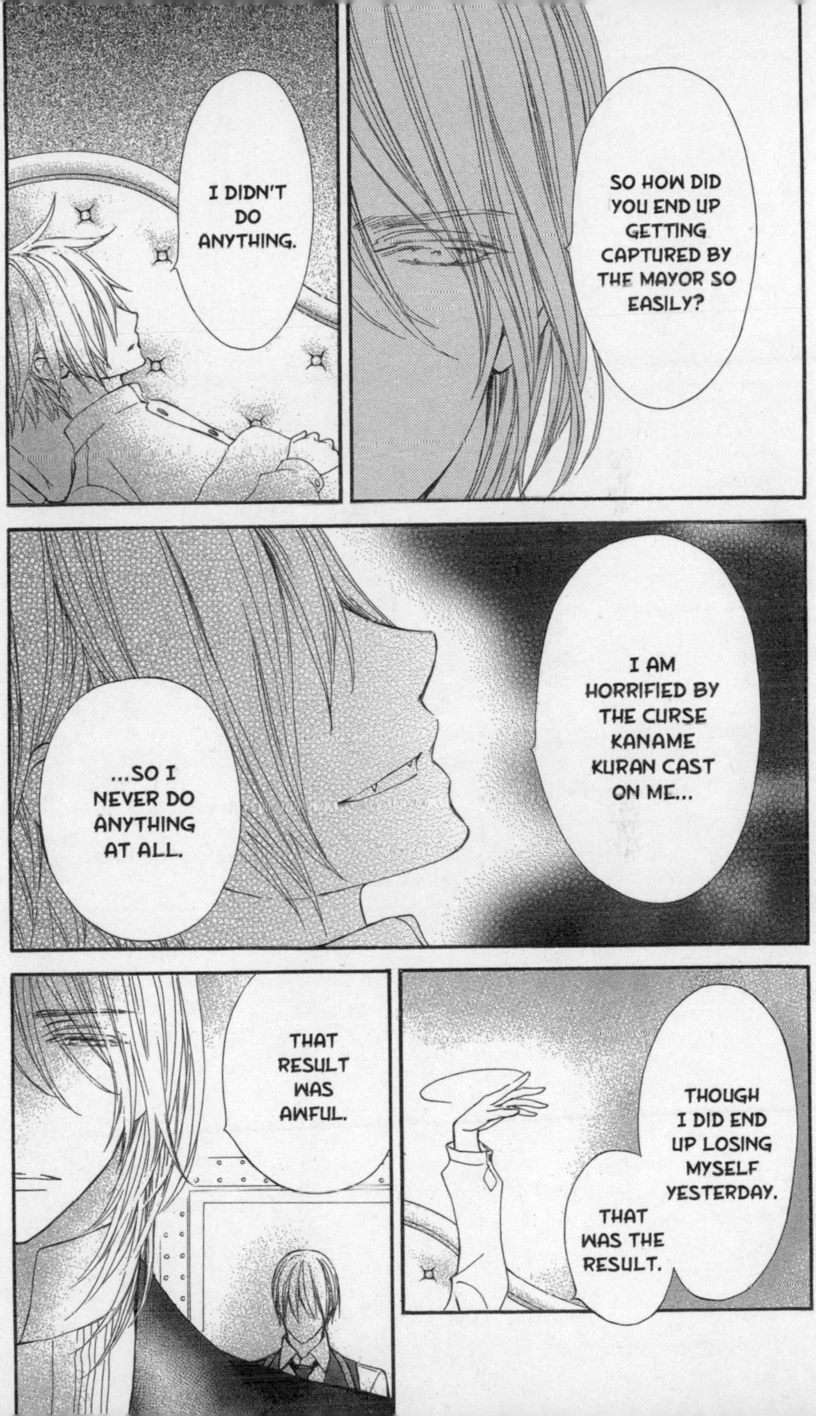
SO HOW DID YOU END UP GETTING CAPTURED BY THE MAYOR SO EASILY?
I DIDN'T DO ANYTHING.
I AM HORRIFIED BY THE CURSE KANAME KURAN CAST ON ME...
...SO I NEVER DO ANYTHING AT ALL.
THOUGH I DID END UP LOSING MYSELF YESTERDAY.
THAT WAS THE RESULT.
THAT RESULT WAS AWFUL.

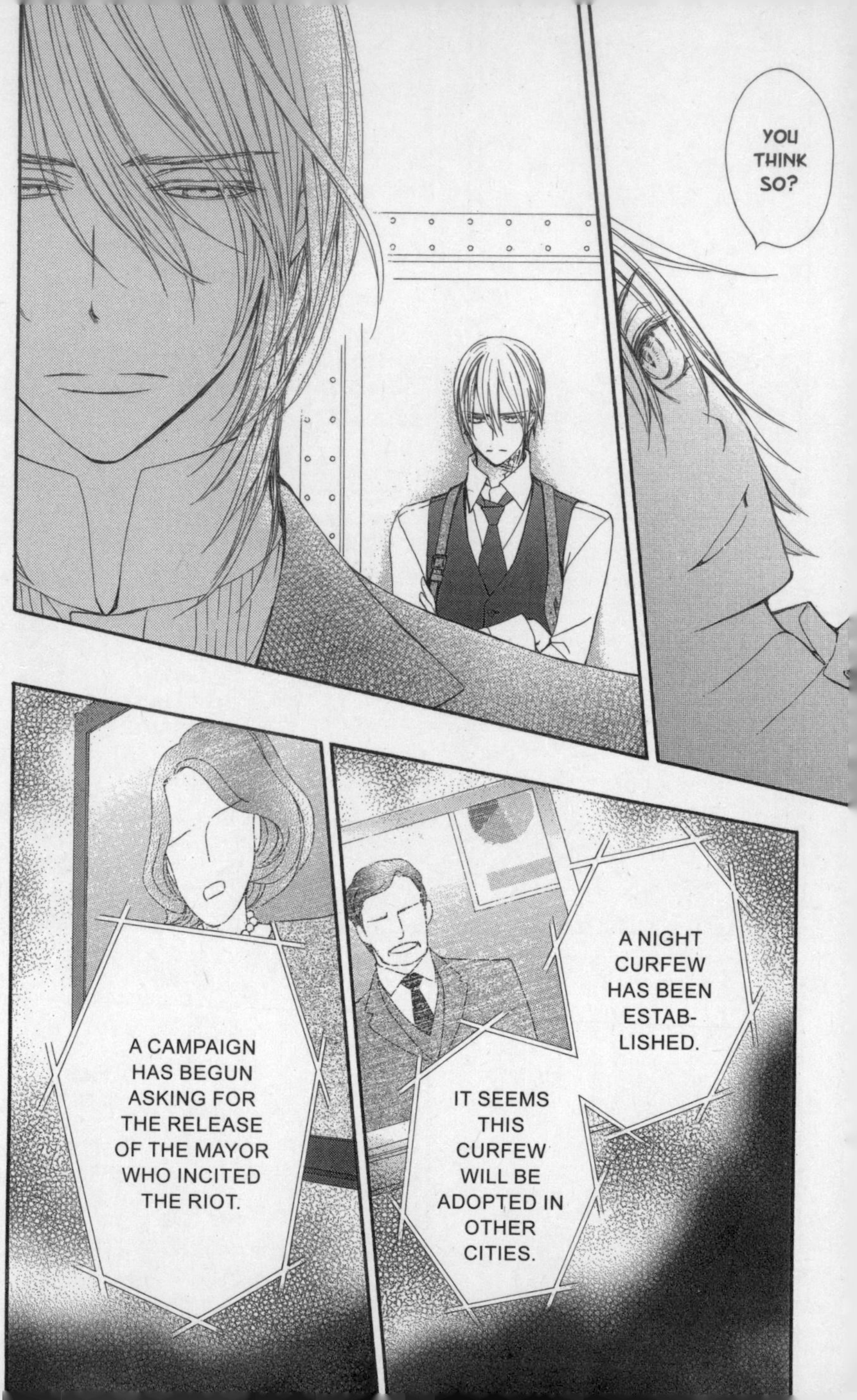
YOU THINK SO?
A NIGHT CURFEW HAS BEEN ESTAB-LISHED.
IT SEEMS THIS CURFEW WILL BE ADOPTED IN OTHER CITIES.
A CAMPAIGN HAS BEGUN ASKING FOR THE RELEASE OF THE MAYOR WHO INCITED THE RIOT.

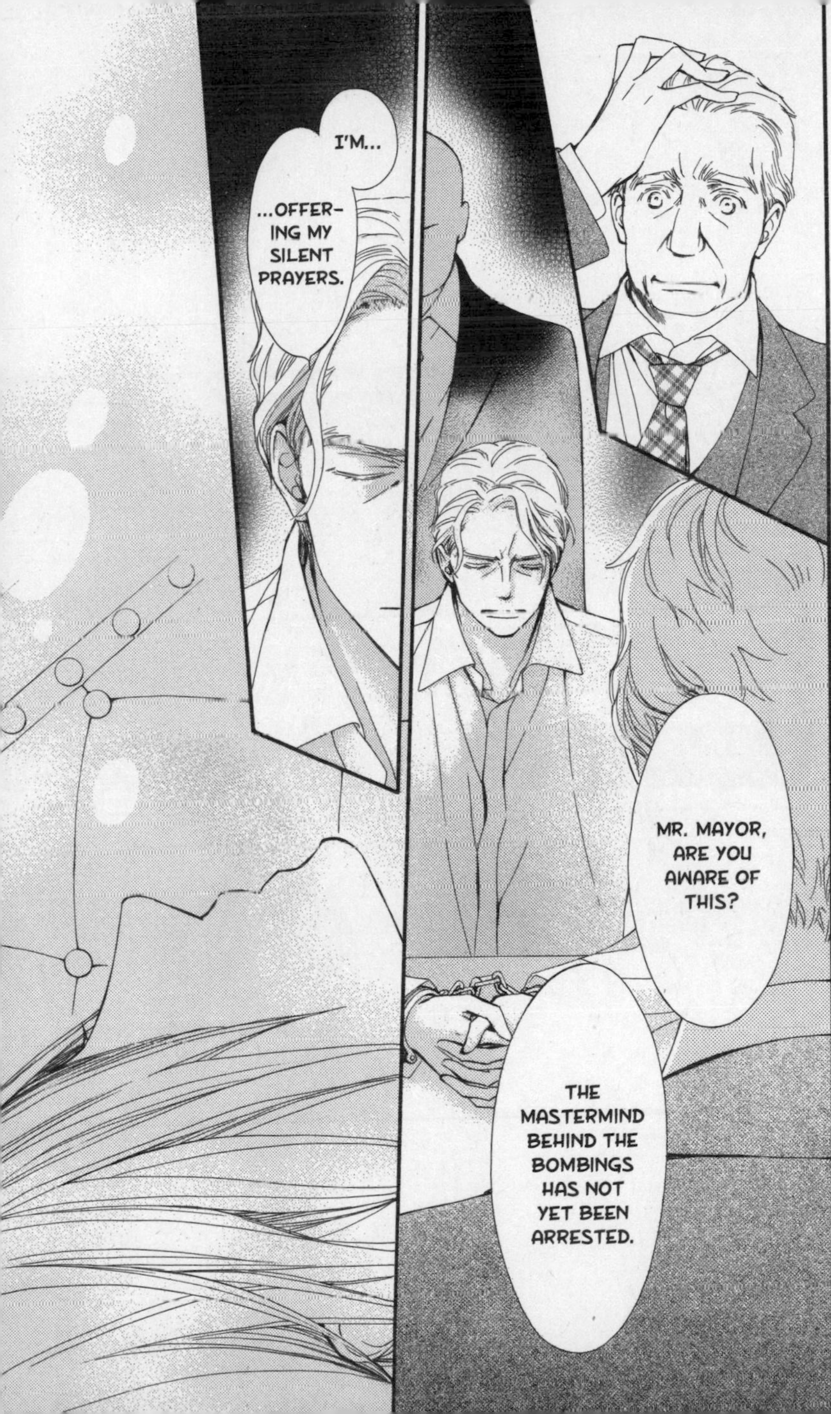
MR. MAYOR, ARE YOU AWARE OF THIS?
THE MASTERMIND BEHIND THE BOMBINGS HAS NOT YET BEEN ARRESTED.
I'M...
...OFFERING MY SILENT PRAYERS.

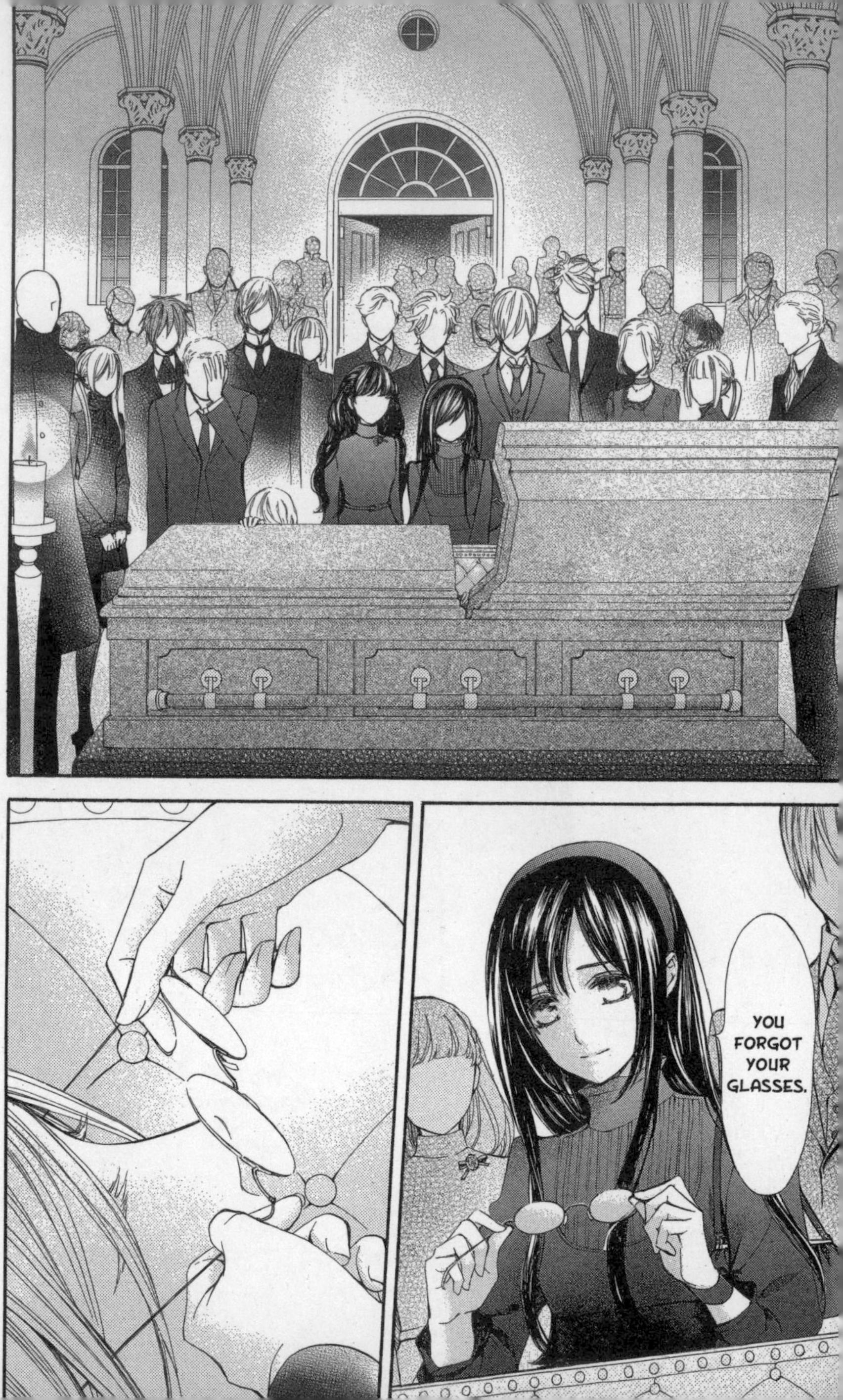
YOU FORGOT YOUR GLASSES.

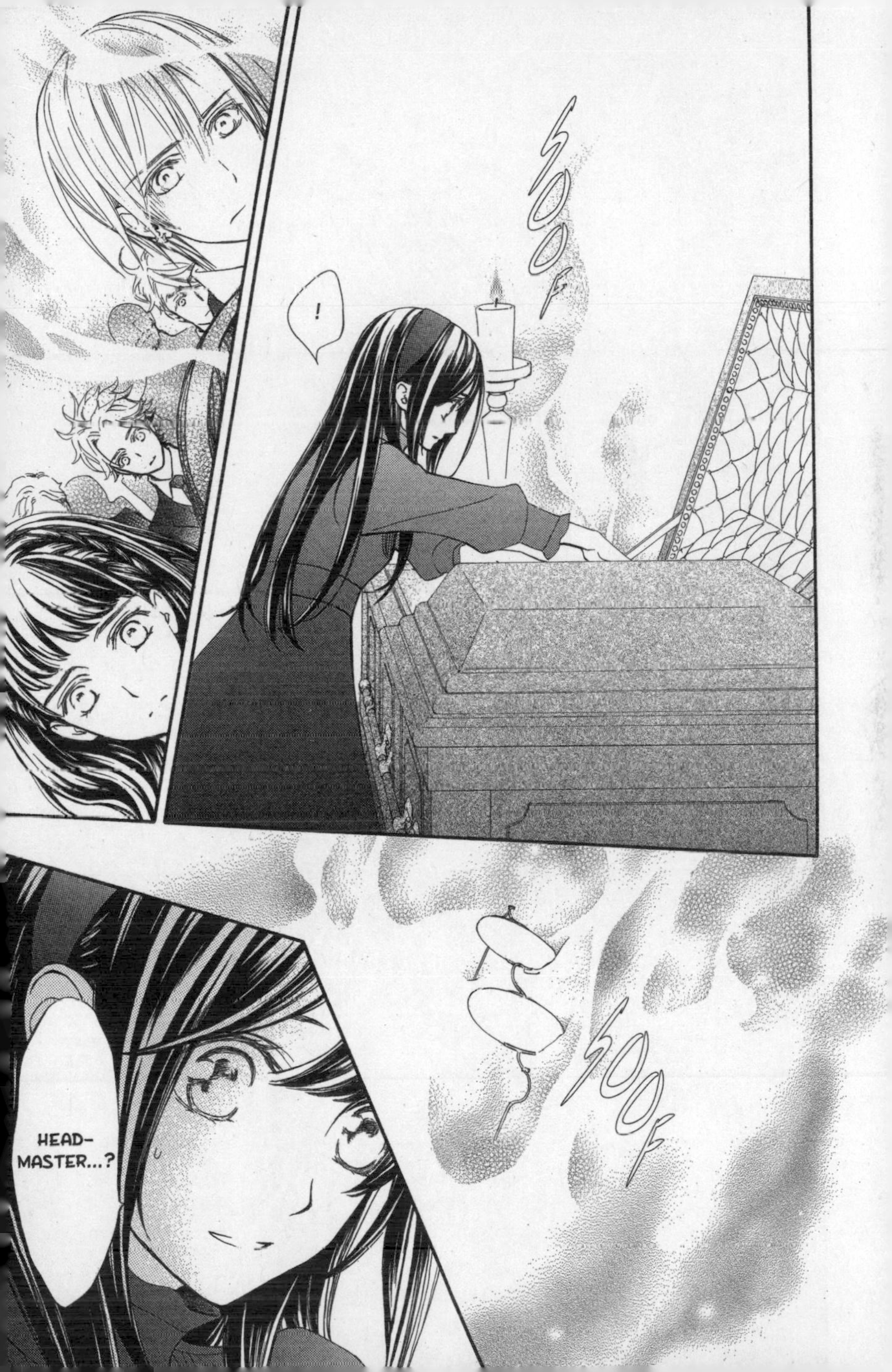
SHOOF
!
SHOOF
HEAD-MASTER...?

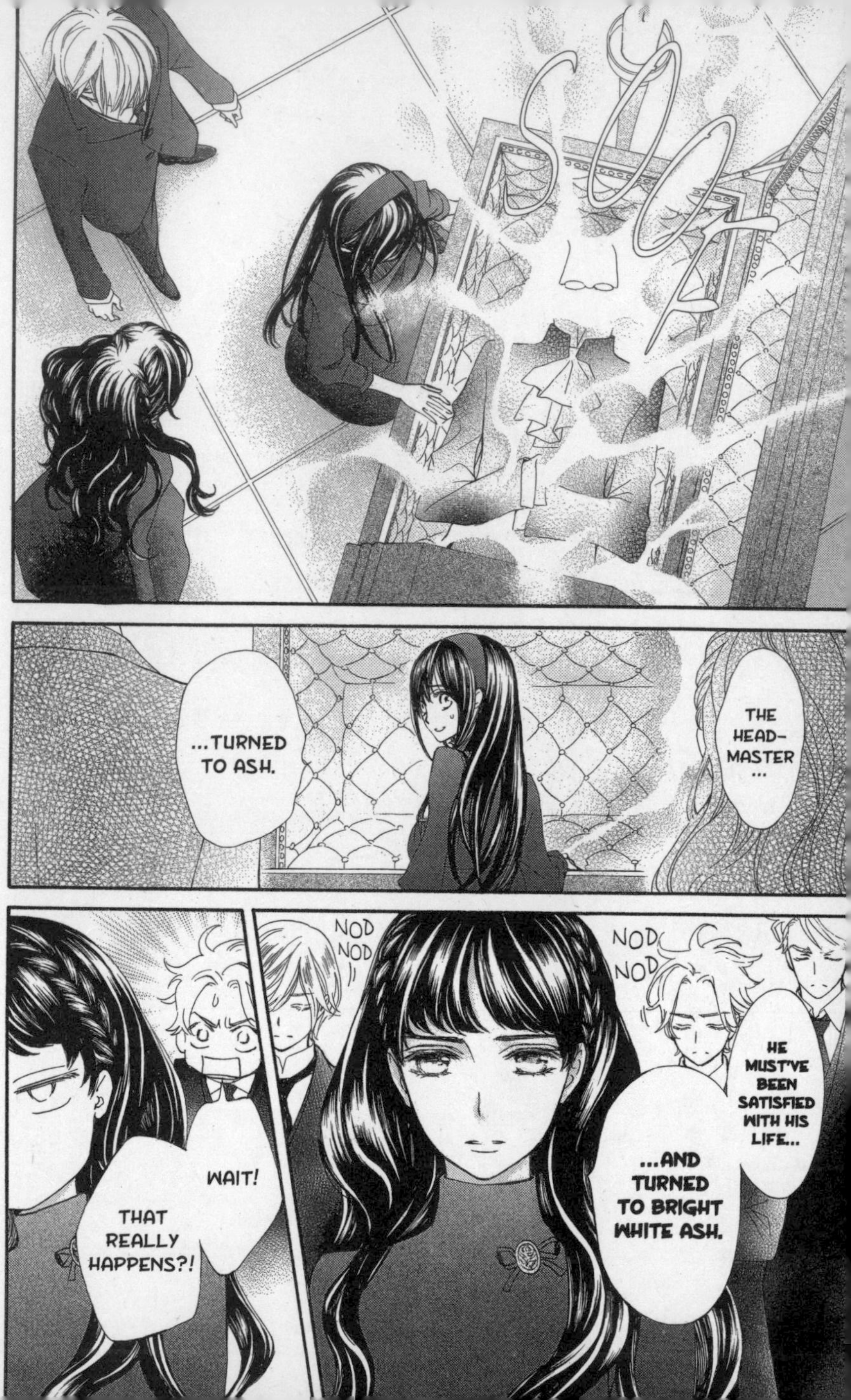
SOOT
THE HEAD-MASTER...
...TURNED TO ASH.
NOD NOD
HE MUST'VE BEEN SATISFIED WITH HIS LIFE...
...AND TURNED TO BRIGHT WHITE ASH.
NOD NOD
WAIT!
THAT REALLY HAPPENS?!

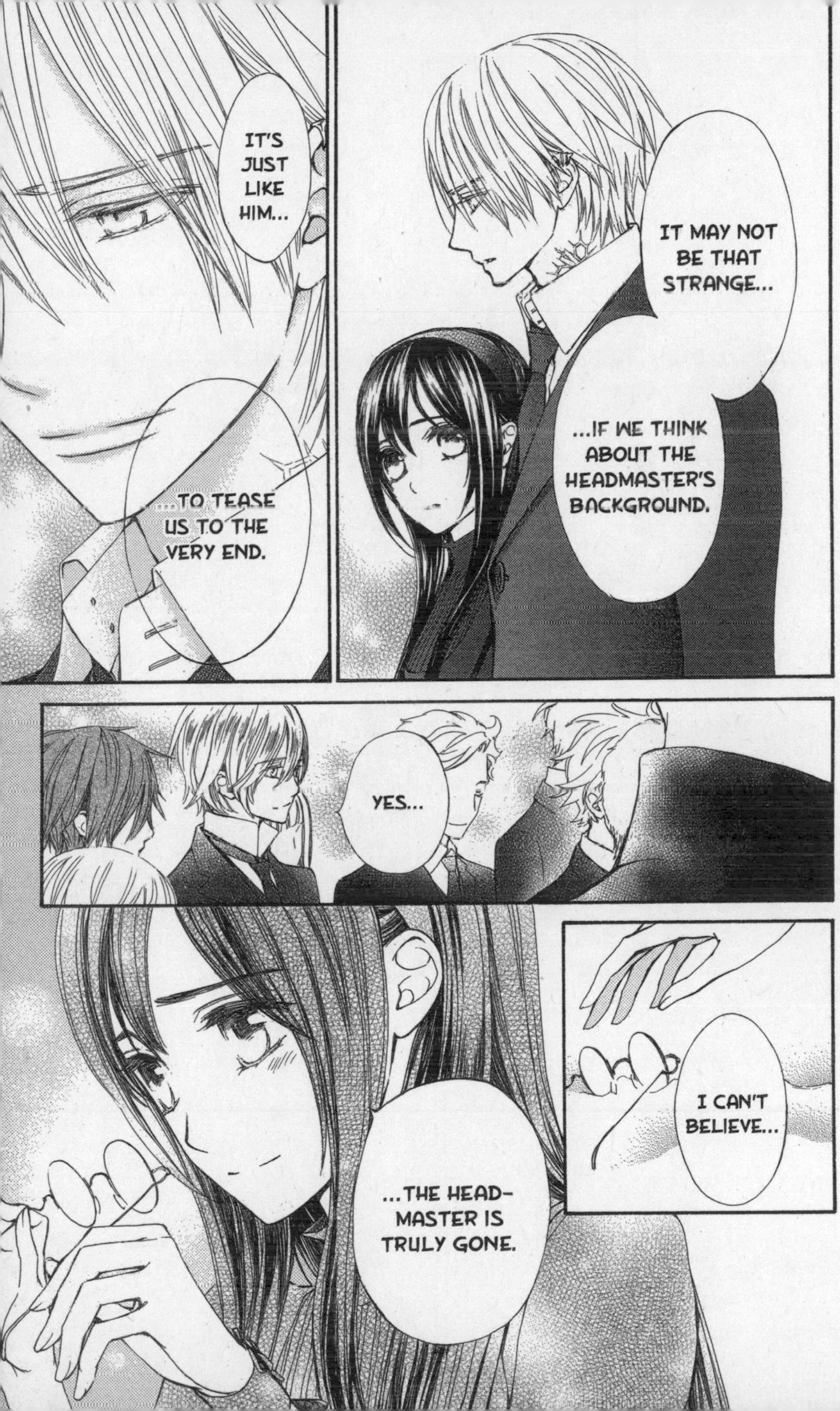
IT MAY NOT BE THAT STRANGE...
...IF WE THINK ABOUT THE HEADMASTER'S BACKGROUND.
IT'S JUST LIKE HIM...
...TO TEASE US TO THE VERY END.
YES...
I CAN'T BELIEVE...
...THE HEAD-MASTER IS TRULY GONE.

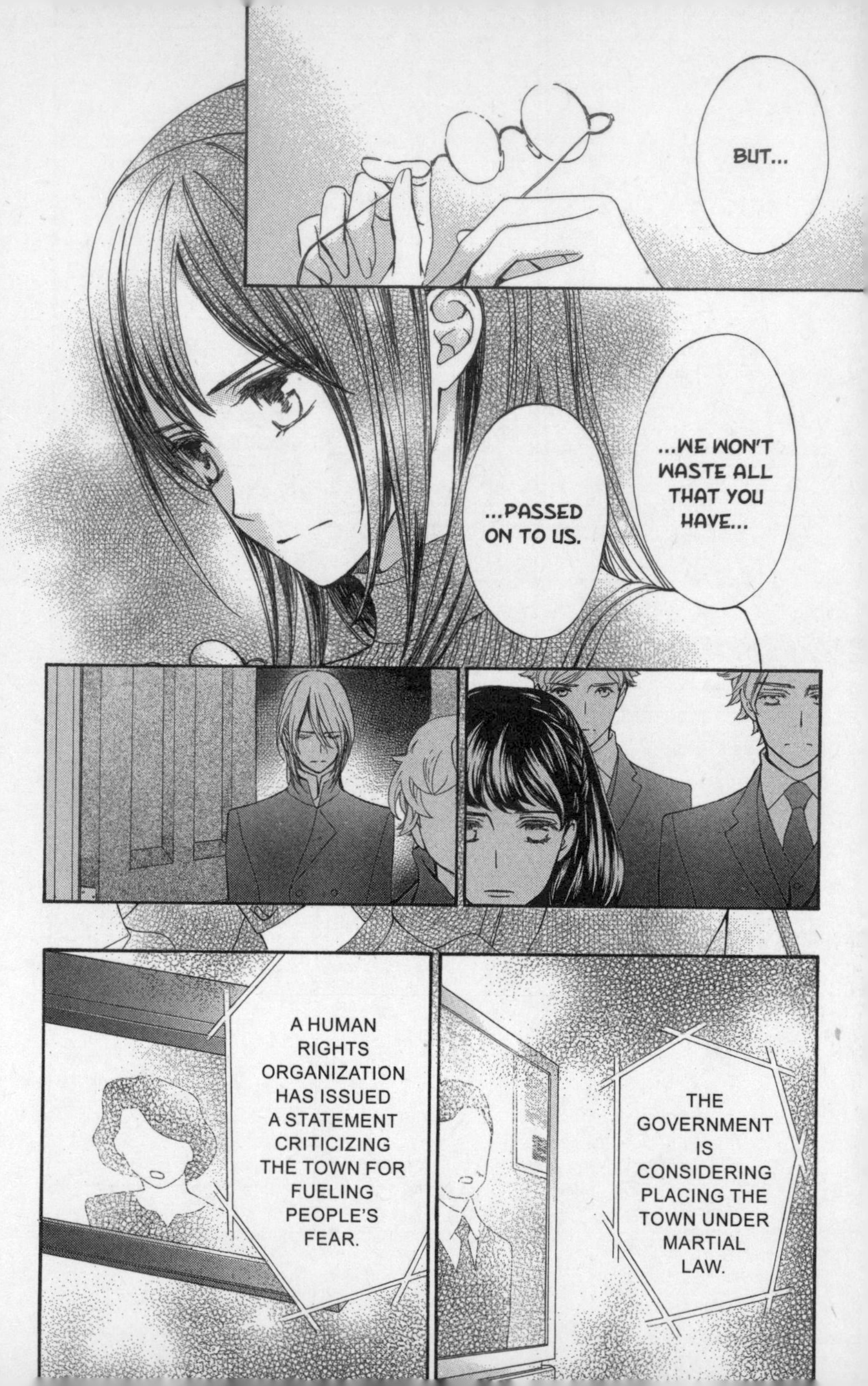
BUT...
...WE WON'T WASTE ALL THAT YOU HAVE...
...PASSED ON TO US.
THE GOVERNMENT IS CONSIDERING PLACING THE TOWN UNDER MARTIAL LAW.
A HUMAN RIGHTS ORGANIZATION HAS ISSUED A STATEMENT CRITICIZING THE TOWN FOR FUELING PEOPLE'S FEAR.

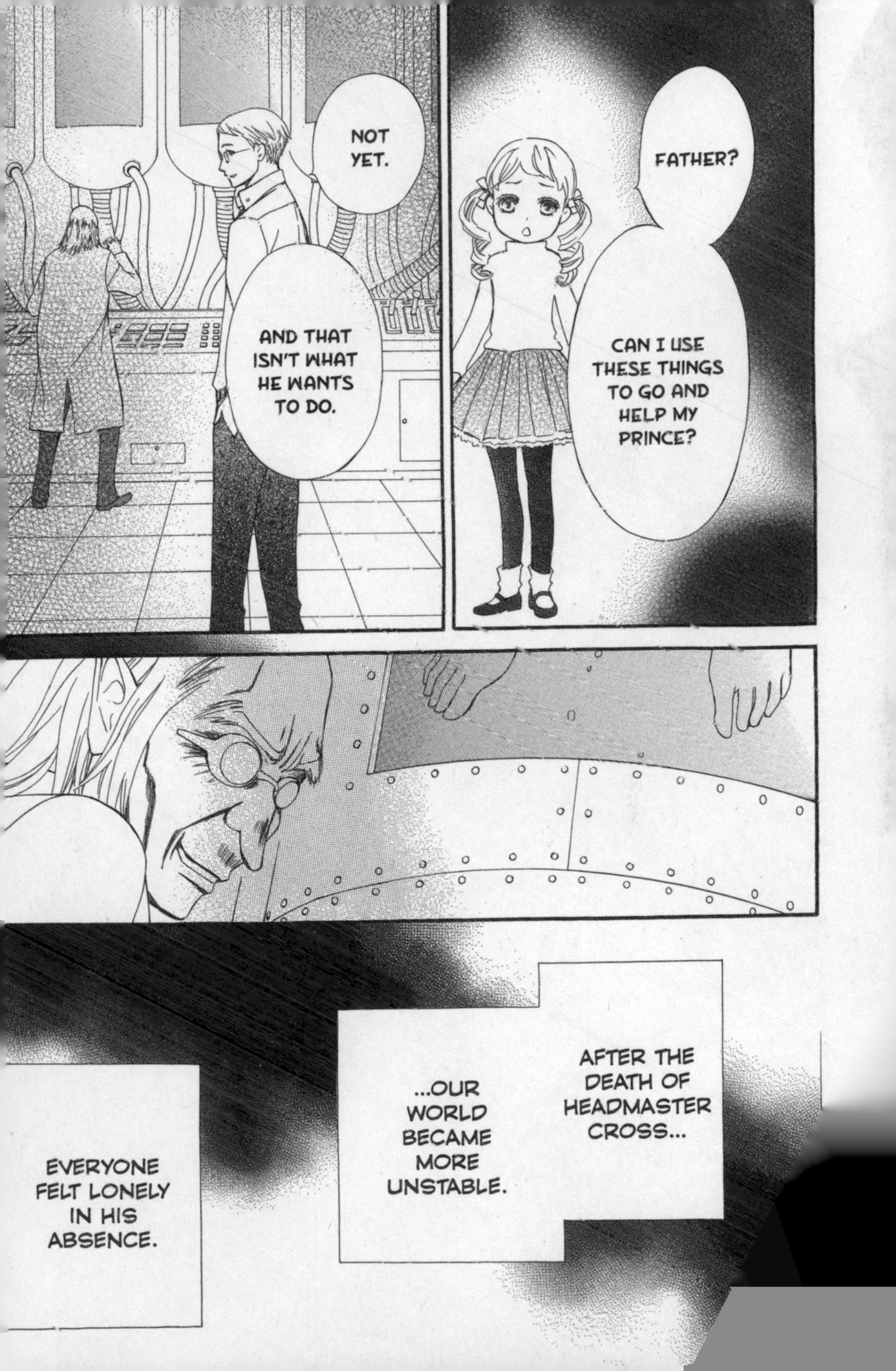
FATHER?
CAN I USE THESE THINGS TO GO AND HELP MY PRINCE?
NOT YET.
AND THAT ISN'T WHAT HE WANTS TO DO.
AFTER THE DEATH OF HEADMASTER CROSS...
...OUR WORLD BECAME MORE UNSTABLE.
EVERYONE FELT LONELY IN HIS ABSENCE.

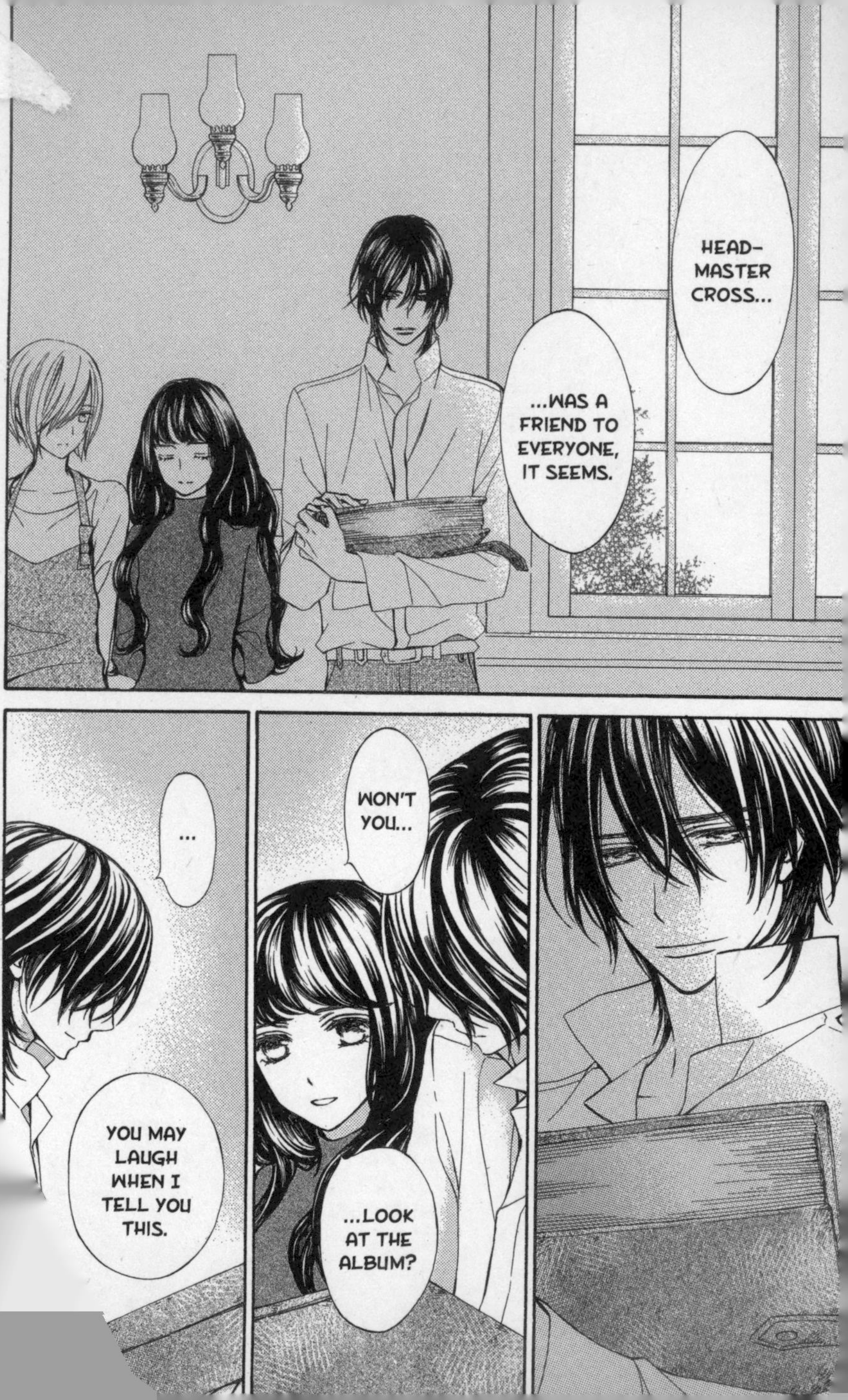
HEAD-MASTER CROSS...
...WAS A FRIEND TO EVERYONE, IT SEEMS.
WON'T YOU...
...LOOK AT THE ALBUM?
...
YOU MAY LAUGH WHEN I TELL YOU THIS.

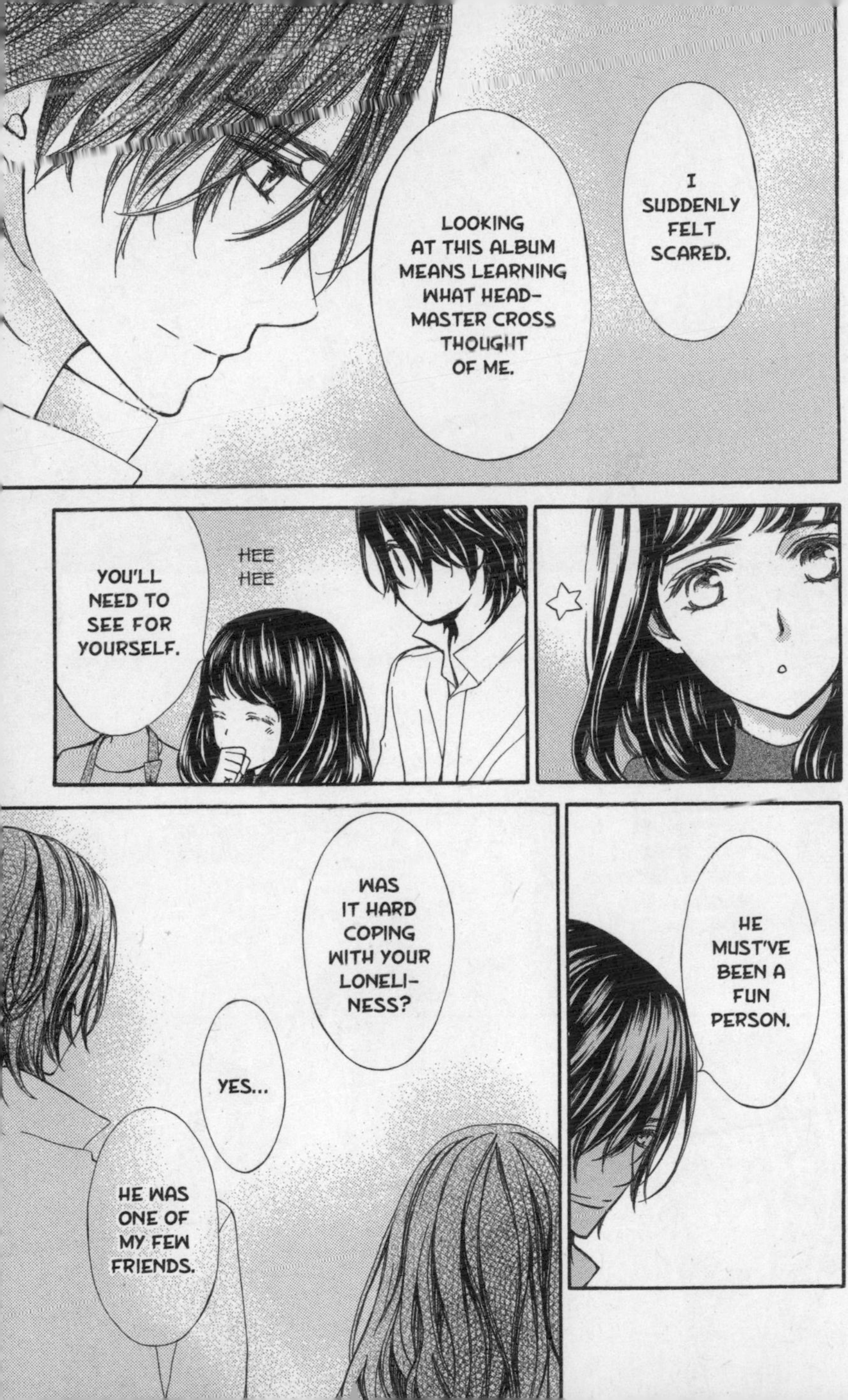
I SUDDENLY FELT SCARED.
LOOKING AT THIS ALBUM MEANS LEARNING WHAT HEAD-MASTER CROSS THOUGHT OF ME.
HEE HEE
YOU'LL NEED TO SEE FOR YOURSELF.
HE MUST'VE BEEN A FUN PERSON.
WAS IT HARD COPING WITH YOUR LONELI-NESS?
YES...
HE WAS ONE OF MY FEW FRIENDS.

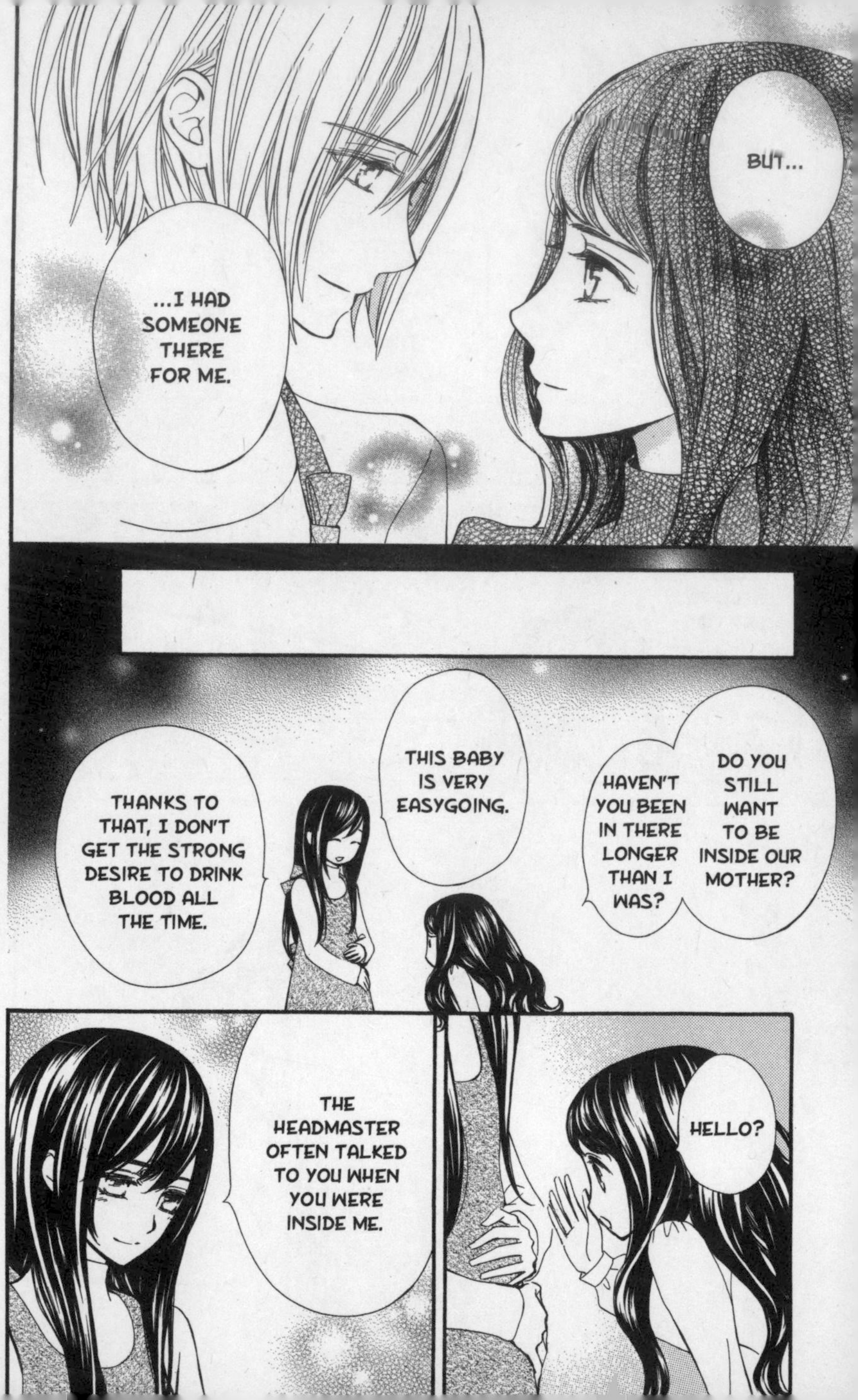
BUT...
...I HAD SOMEONE THERE FOR ME.
DO YOU STILL WANT TO BE INSIDE OUR MOTHER?
HAVEN'T YOU BEEN IN THERE LONGER THAN I WAS?
THIS BABY IS VERY EASYGOING.
THANKS TO THAT, I DON'T GET THE STRONG DESIRE TO DRINK BLOOD ALL THE TIME.
HELLO?
THE HEADMASTER OFTEN TALKED TO YOU WHEN YOU WERE INSIDE ME.

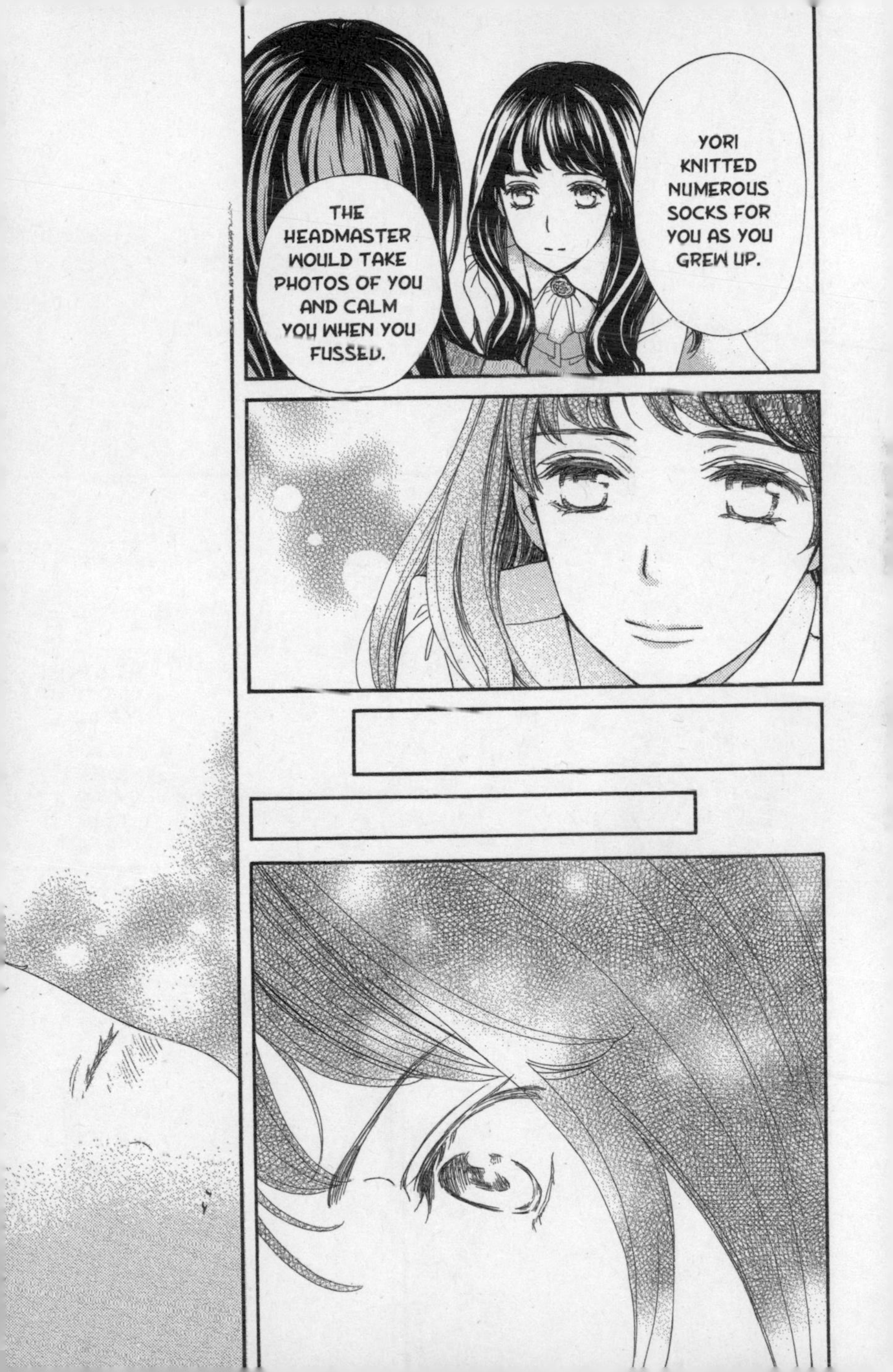
YORI KNITTED NUMEROUS SOCKS FOR YOU AS YOU GREW UP.
THE HEADMASTER WOULD TAKE PHOTOS OF YOU AND CALM YOU WHEN YOU FUSSED.

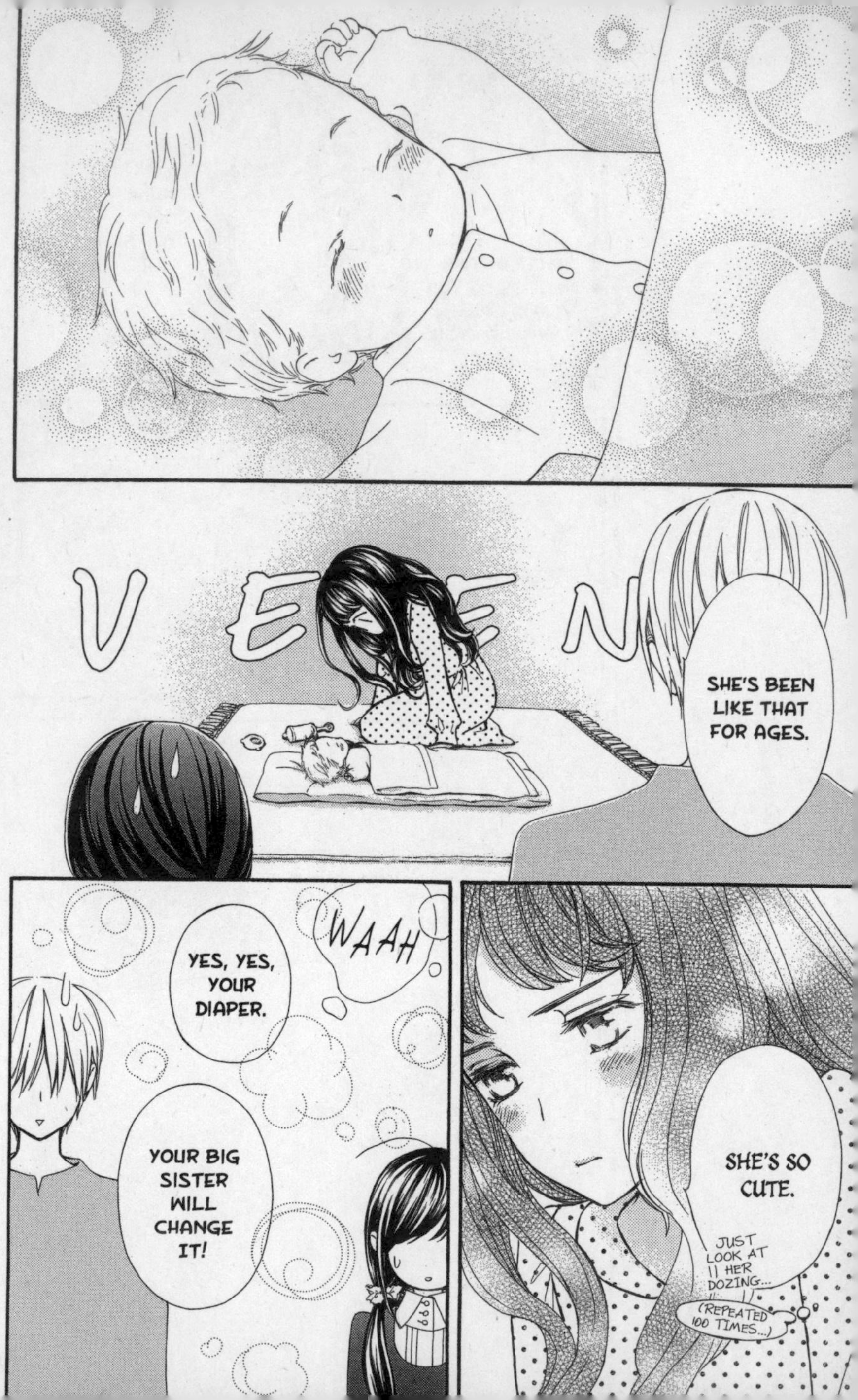

SHE'S BEEN LIKE THAT FOR AGES.
VEEN
SHE'S SO CUTE.
JUST LOOK AT HER DOZING...
(REPEATED 100 TIMES...)
WAAH
YES, YES, YOUR DIAPER.
YOUR BIG SISTER WILL CHANGE IT!

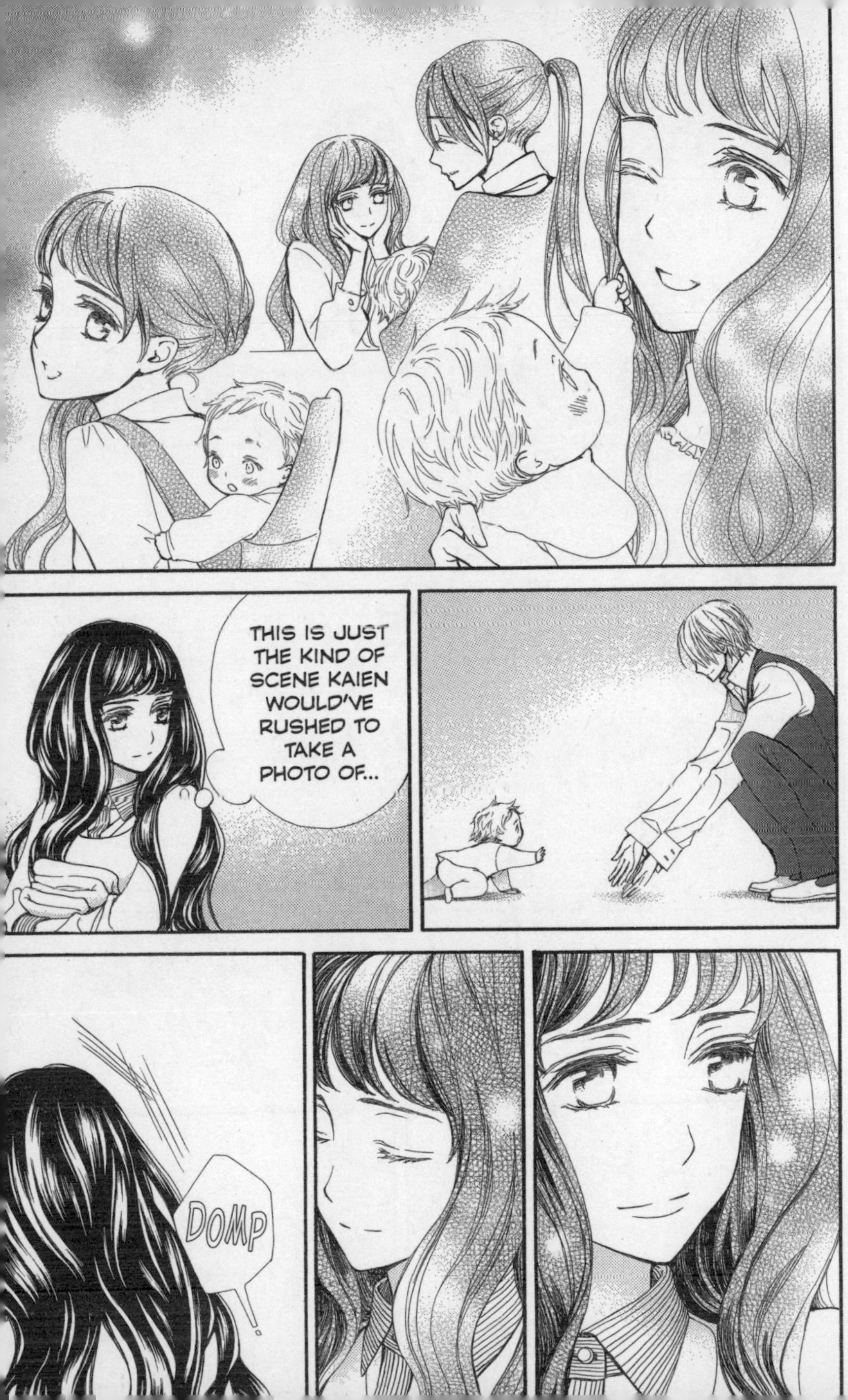
THIS IS JUST THE KIND OF SCENE KAIEN WOULD'VE RUSHED TO TAKE A PHOTO OF...
DOMP
!

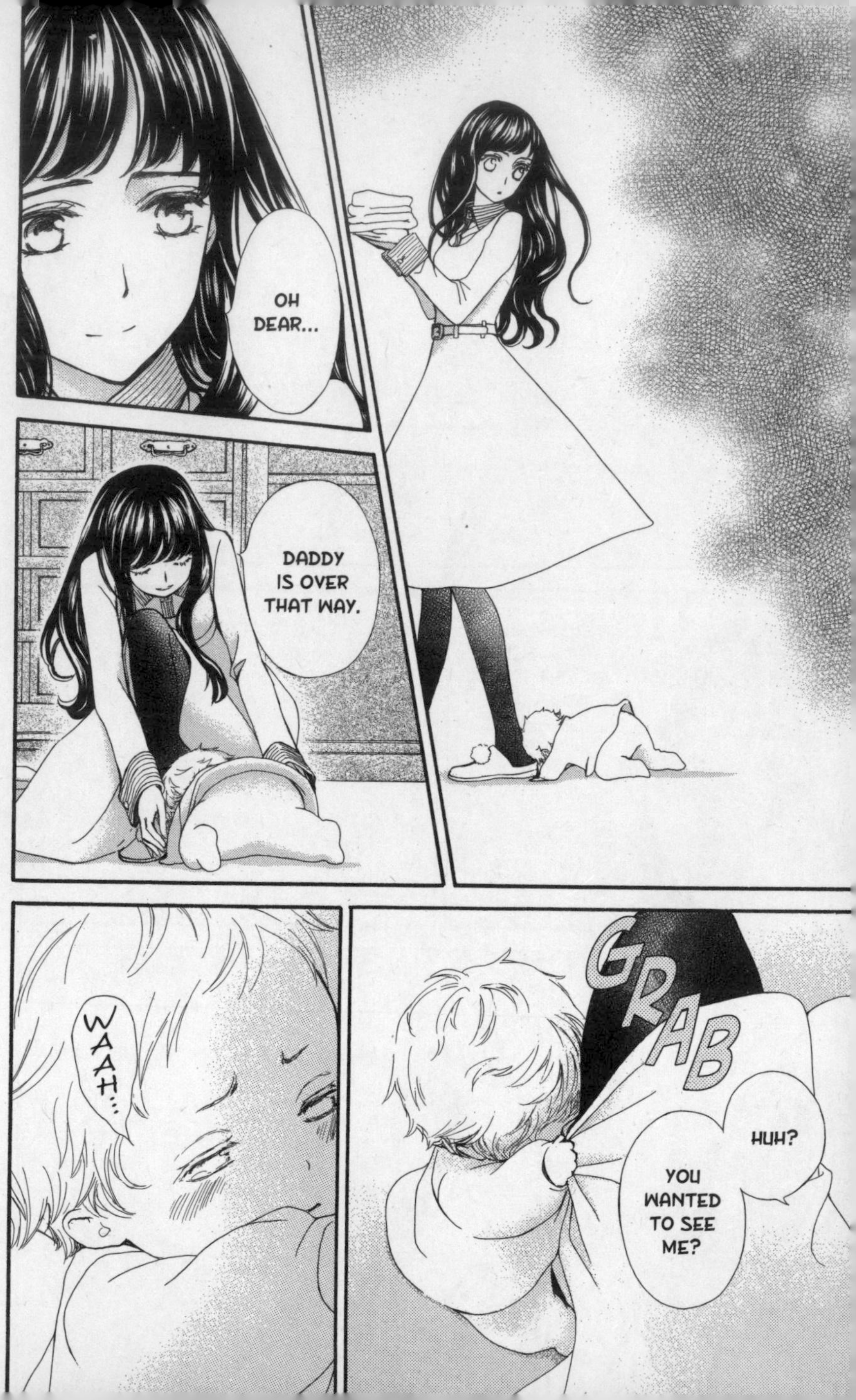
OH DEAR...
DADDY IS OVER THAT WAY.
GRAB
HUH?
YOU WANTED TO SEE ME?
WAAH...

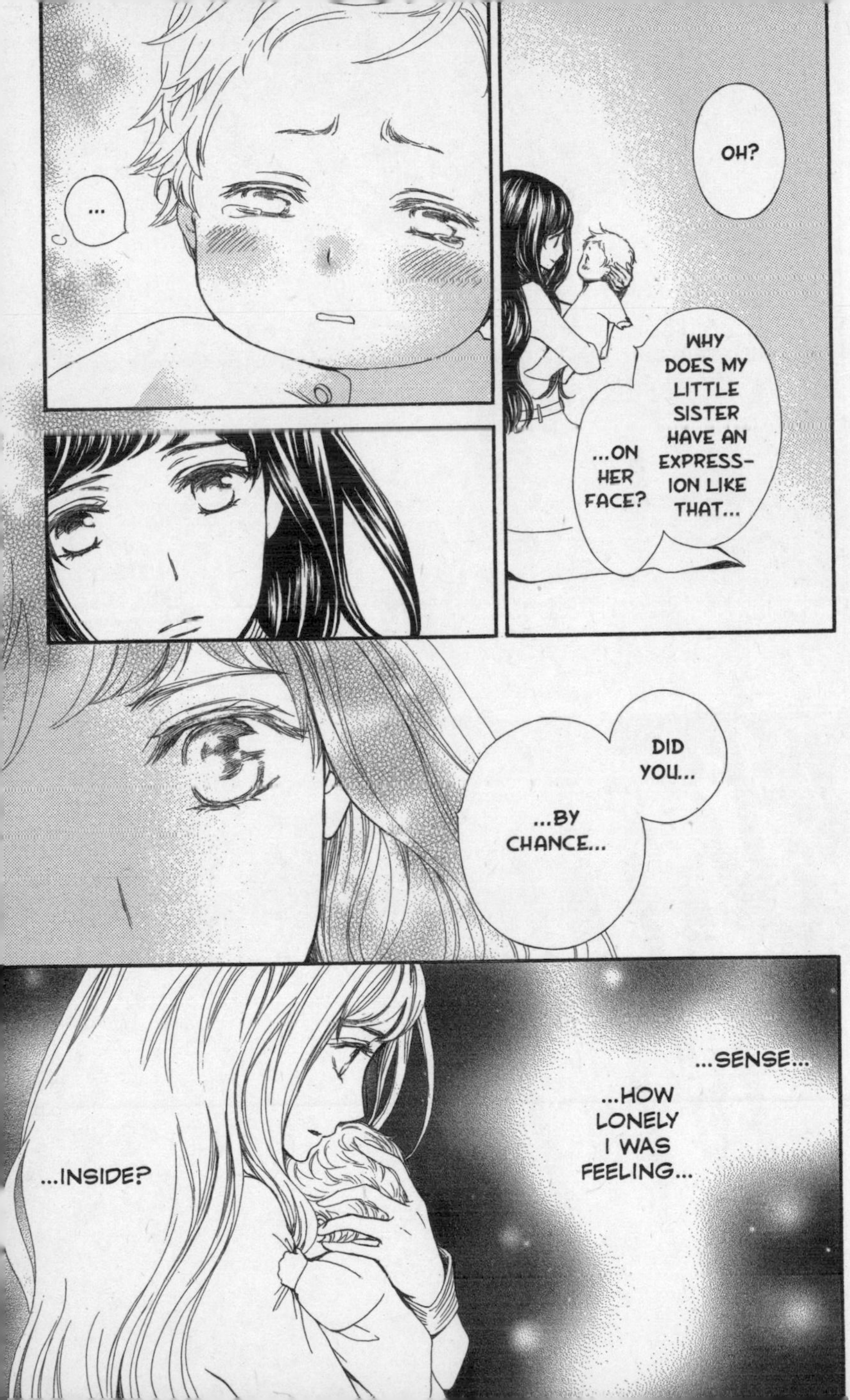
OH?
WHY DOES MY LITTLE SISTER HAVE AN EXPRESSION LIKE THAT...
...ON HER FACE?
...
DID YOU...
...BY CHANCE...
...SENSE...
...HOW LONELY I WAS FEELING...
...INSIDE?

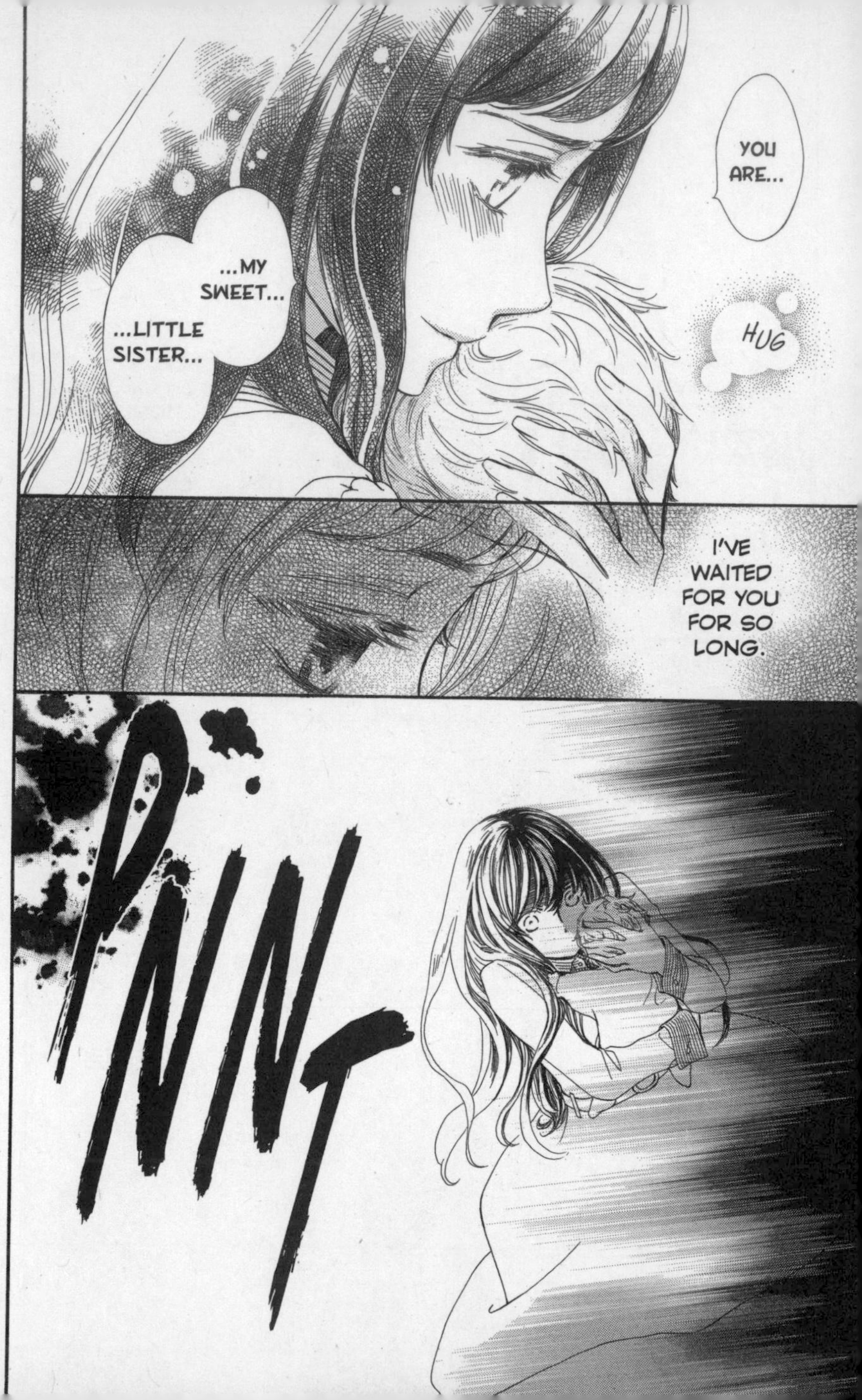
YOU ARE...
HUG
...MY SWEET...
...LITTLE SISTER...
I'VE WAITED FOR YOU FOR SO LONG.

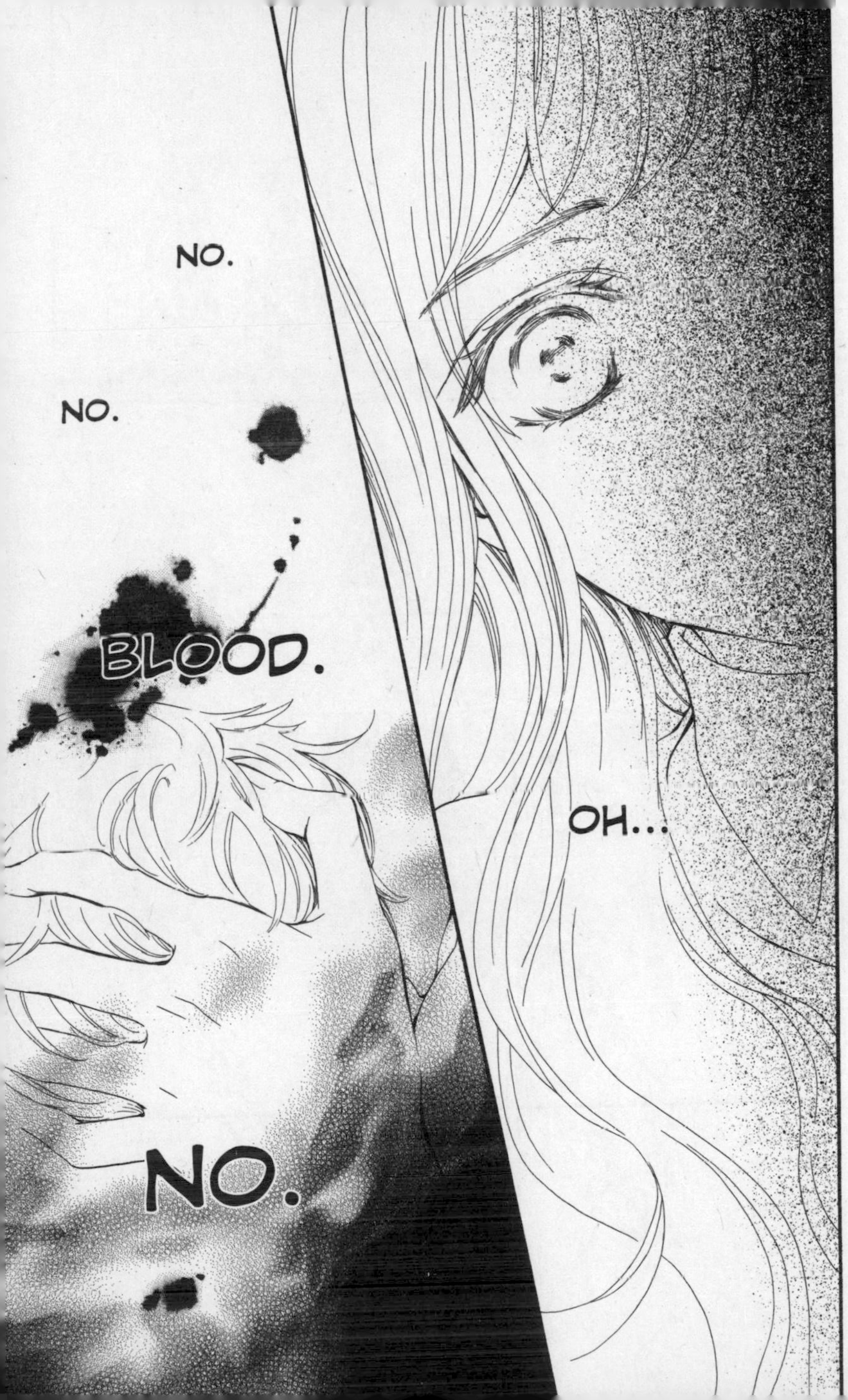
OH...
NO.
NO.
BLOOD.
NO.

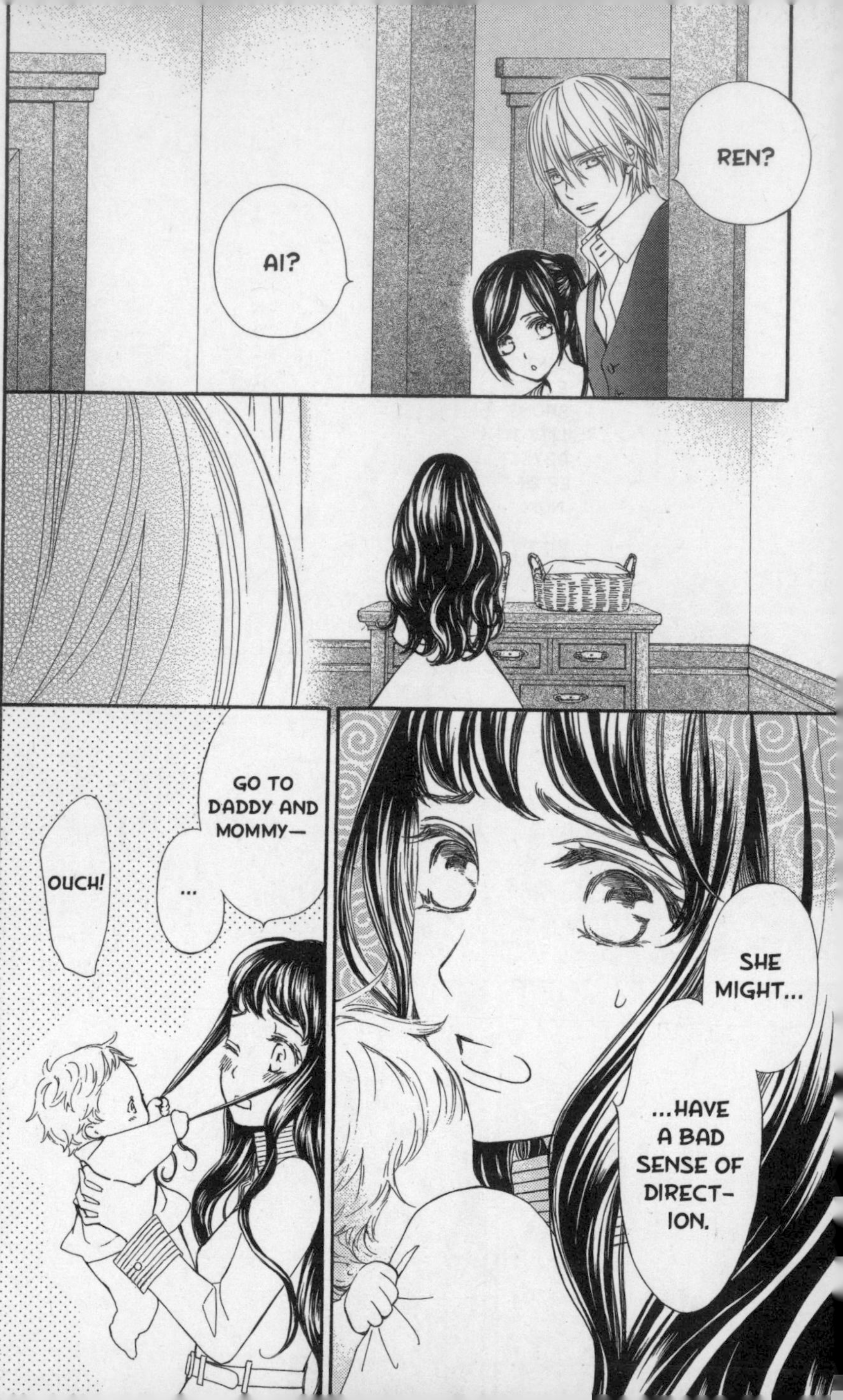
REN?
AI?
SHE MIGHT...
...HAVE A BAD SENSE OF DIRECT-ION.
GO TO DADDY AND MOMMY—
...
OUCH!

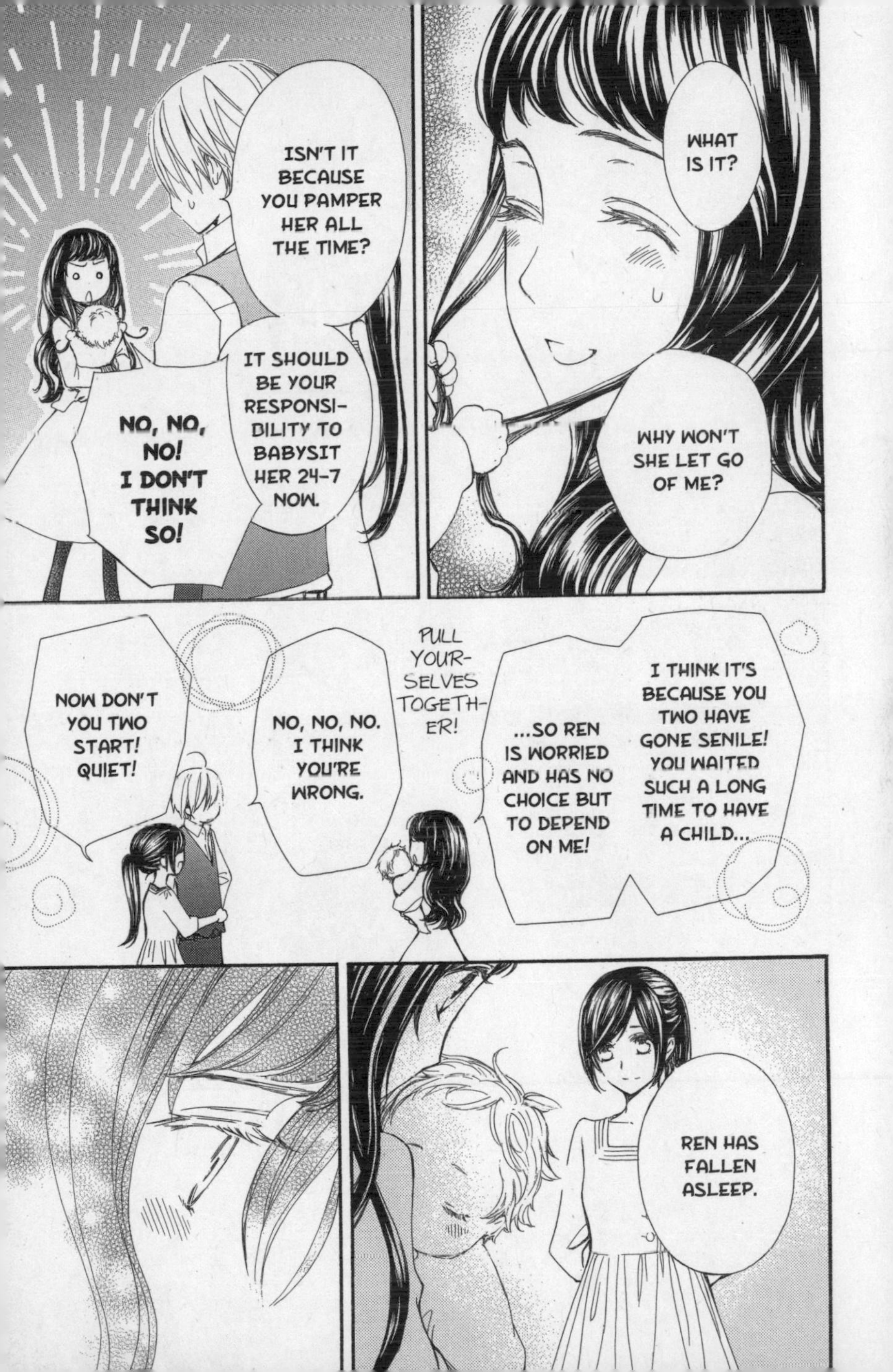
WHAT IS IT?
WHY WON'T SHE LET GO OF ME?
ISN'T IT BECAUSE YOU PAMPER HER ALL THE TIME?
IT SHOULD BE YOUR RESPONSI-BILITY TO BABYSIT HER 24-7 NOW.
NO, NO, NO! I DON'T THINK SO!
I THINK IT'S BECAUSE YOU TWO HAVE GONE SENILE! YOU WAITED SUCH A LONG TIME TO HAVE A CHILD...
...SO REN IS WORRIED AND HAS NO CHOICE BUT TO DEPEND ON ME!
PULL YOUR-SELVES TOGETH-ER!
NO, NO, NO. I THINK YOU'RE WRONG.
NOW DON'T YOU TWO START! QUIET!
REN HAS FALLEN ASLEEP.

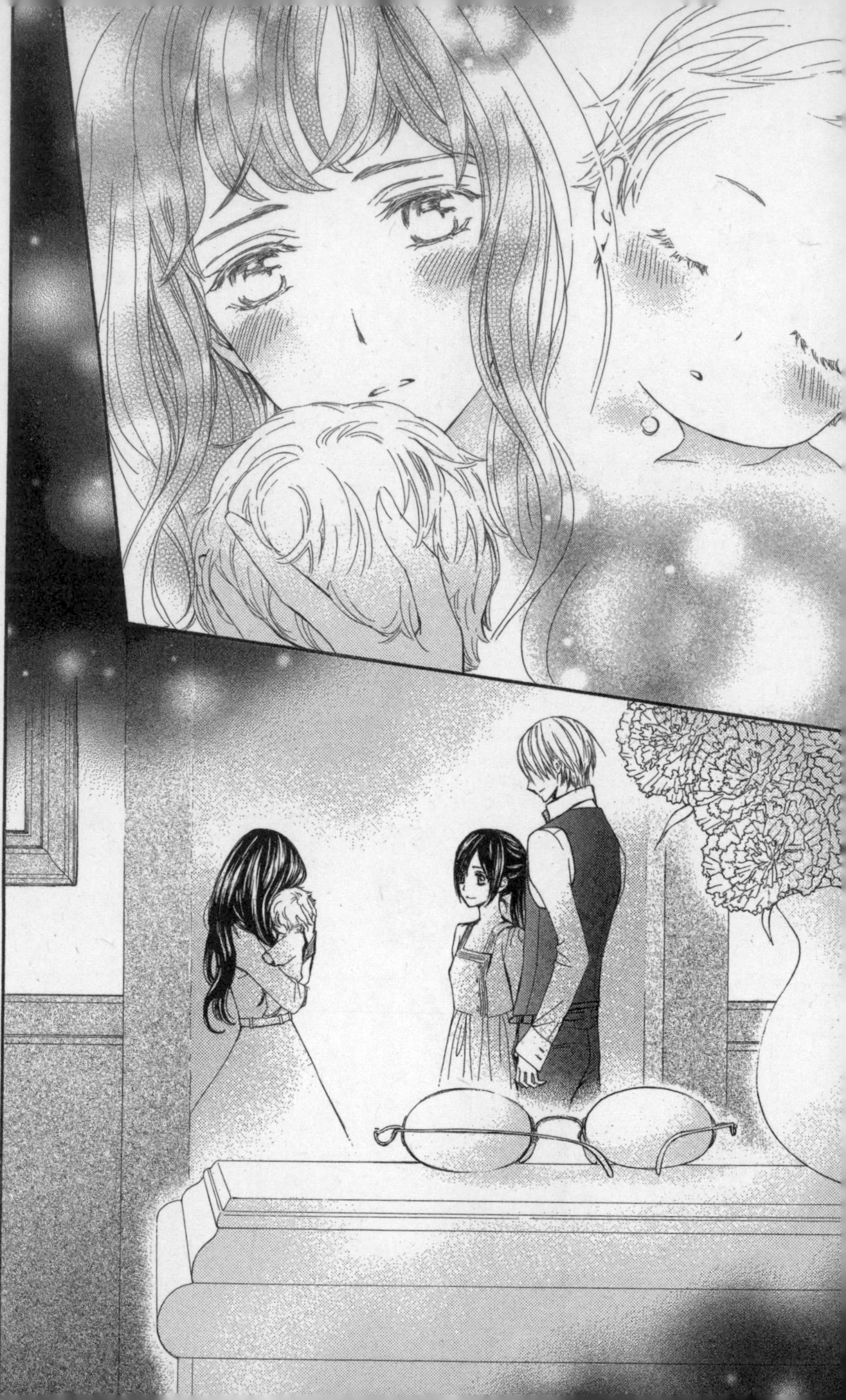

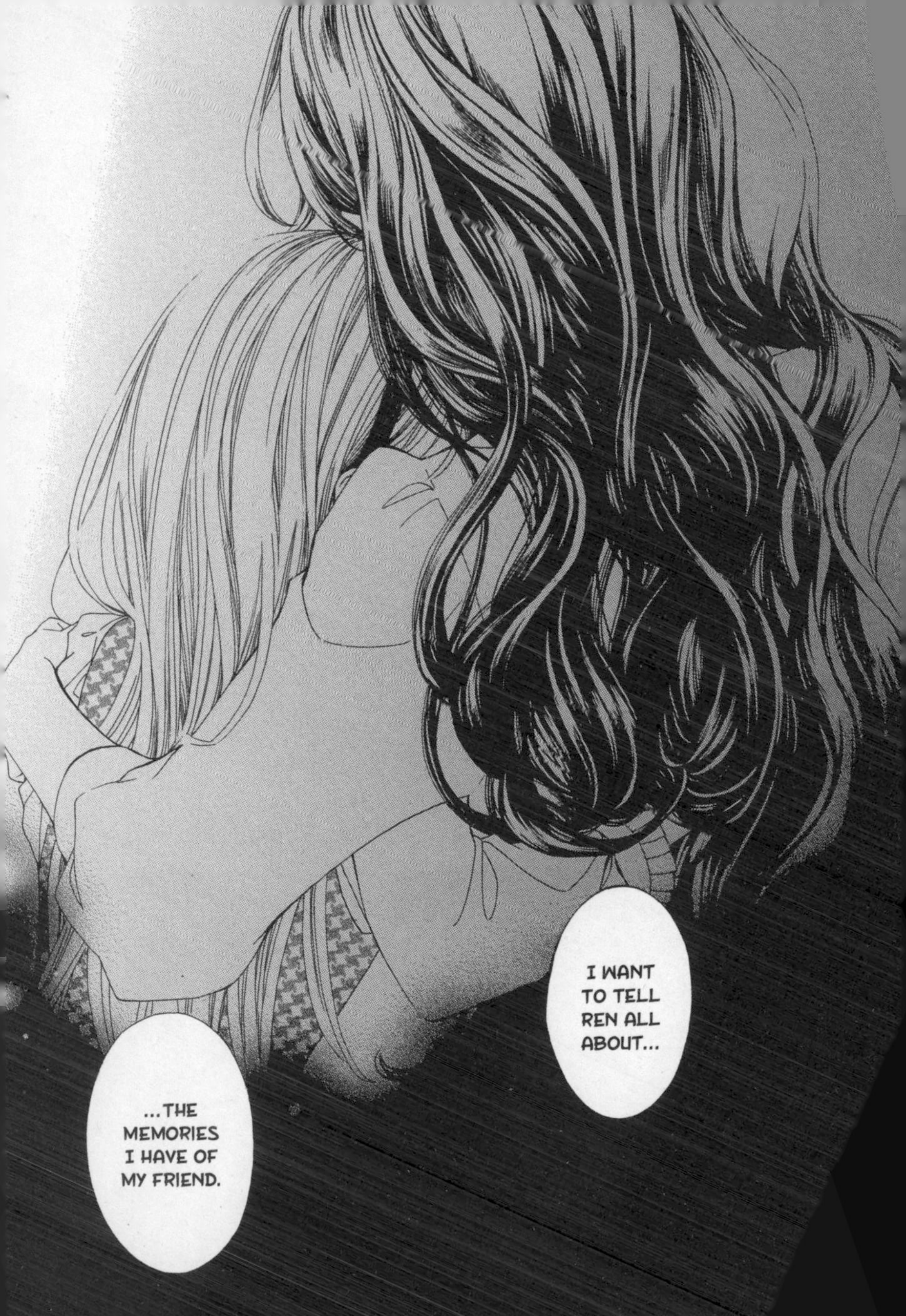
I WANT TO TELL REN ALL ABOUT...
...THE MEMORIES I HAVE OF MY FRIEND.

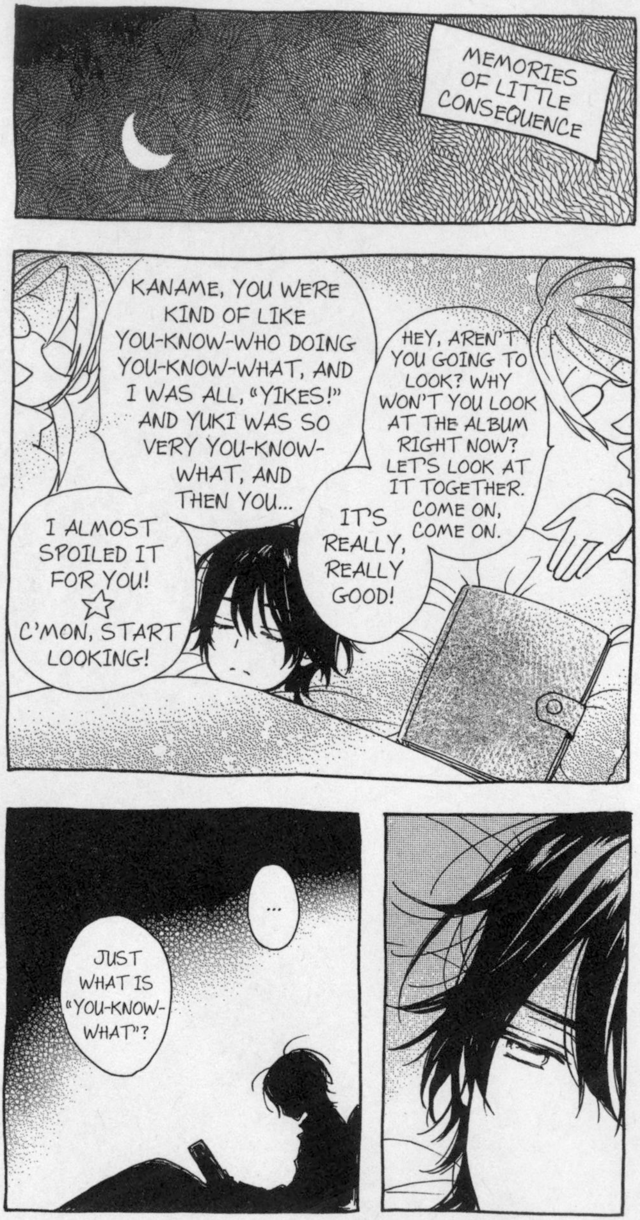
MEMORIES OF LITTLE CONSEQUENCE
HEY, AREN'T YOU GOING TO LOOK? WHY WON'T YOU LOOK AT THE ALBUM RIGHT NOW? LET'S LOOK AT IT TOGETHER. COME ON, COME ON.
KANAME, YOU WERE KIND OF LIKE YOU-KNOW-WHO DOING YOU-KNOW-WHAT, AND I WAS ALL, "YIKES!" AND YUKI WAS SO VERY YOU-KNOW-WHAT, AND THEN YOU...
IT'S REALLY, REALLY GOOD!
I ALMOST SPOILED IT FOR YOU! ☆ C'MON, START LOOKING!
...
JUST WHAT IS "YOU-KNOW-WHAT"?

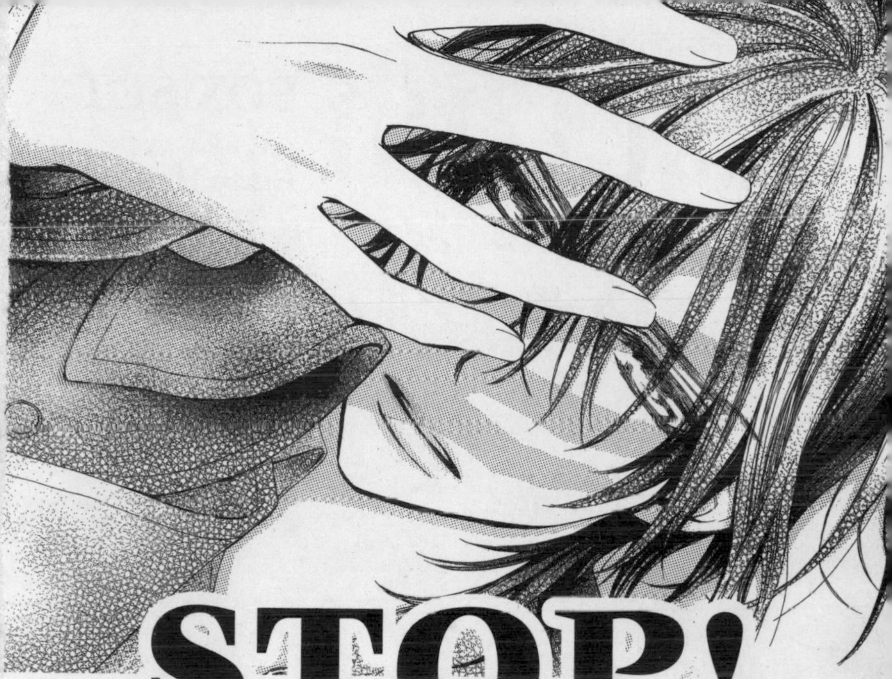

STOP!

You may be reading the wrong way!

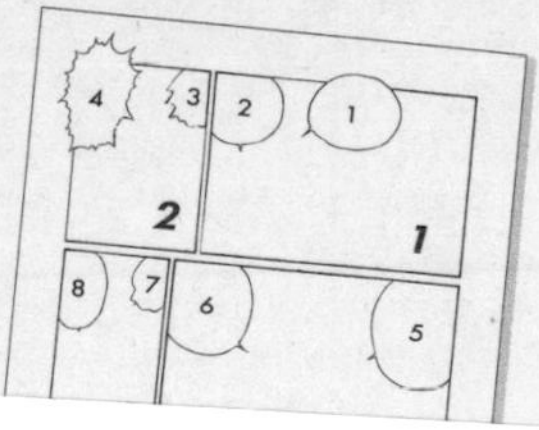
1
1
2
3
4
2
5
6
7
8

In keeping with the original Japanese comic format, this book reads from right to left—so word balloons, action and sound effects and are reversed to preserve the orientation of the original artwork.

Check out the diagram s
the hang of things, and t
other side of the book tc

Ouran High School

Host Club

BOX SET

Story and Art by
Bisco Hatori

Escape to the world of the young, rich and sexy

Ouran High School
Host Club
BOX SET (Vols. 1–18)
STORY & ART BY
BISCO HATORI

**All 18 volumes
in a collector's box
with an Ouran High
School stationery
notepad!**

In this screwball romantic
comedy, Haruhi, a poor girl at
a rich kids' school, is forced to
repay an $80,000 debt by working
for the school's swankiest, all-
male club—as a boy! There she
discovers just how wealthy the six
members are and how different
the rich are from everybody else...

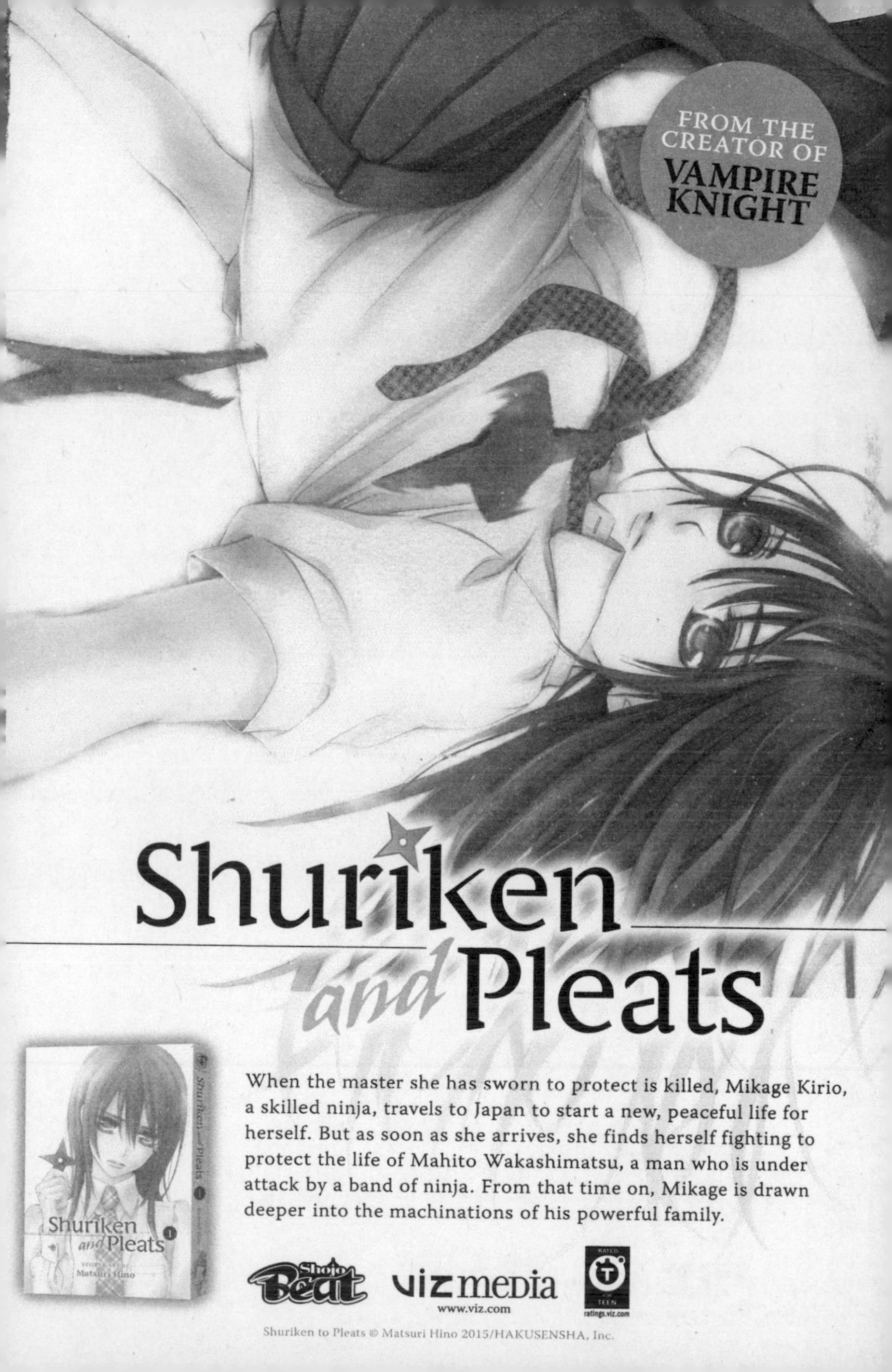
FROM THE CREATOR OF
VAMPIRE KNIGHT
Shuriken and Pleats
When the master she has sworn to protect is killed, Mikage Kirio, a skilled ninja, travels to Japan to start a new, peaceful life for herself. But as soon as she arrives, she finds herself fighting to protect the life of Mahito Wakashimatsu, a man who is under attack by a band of ninja. From that time on, Mikage is drawn deeper into the machinations of his powerful family.
Shuriken and Pleats
Matsuri Hino
Shojo Beat
VIZ MEDIA
www.viz.com
RATED T FOR TEEN
ratings.viz.com
Shuriken to Pleats © Matsuri Hino 2015/HAKUSENSHA, Inc.

VAMPIRE KNIGHT: MEMORIES
Vol. 4
Shojo Beat Manga Edition

STORY AND ART BY
MATSURI HINO

Adaptation/Nancy Thistlethwaite
Translation/Tetsuichiro Miyaki
Touch-Up Art & Lettering/Inori Fukuda Trant
Graphic Design/Alice Lewis
Editor/Nancy Thistlethwaite

Vampire Knight memories by Matsuri Hino © Matsuri Hino 2019
All rights reserved. First published in Japan in 2019 by HAKUSENSHA,
Inc., Tokyo. English language translation rights arranged with
HAKUSENSHA, Inc., Tokyo.

Printed in the U.S.A.

Published by VIZ Media, LLC
P.O. Box 77010
San Francisco, CA 94107

10 9 8 7 6 5 4 3 2 1
First printing, March 2020

viz.com

shojobeat.com

Matsuri Hino burst onto the manga scene with her title
Kono Yume ga Sametara (When This Dream Is Over), which
was published in *LaLa DX* magazine. Hino was a manga artist
a mere nine months after she decided to become one.

With the success of her popular series *Captive Hearts*,
MeruPuri and *Vampire Knight*, Hino is a major player in the
world of shojo manga.

Hino enjoys creative activities and has commented that
she would have been either an architect or an apprentice to
traditional Japanese craftsmasters if she had not become a
manga artist.

恋

Ren

Ren means "love." It is used in terms of a romantic love or crush.

藍堂星夜

Aido Seiya

Aido means "indigo temple." *Sei* means "star" and *ya* means "night": "starry night."

Terms

-sama: The suffix *-sama* is used in formal address for someone who ranks higher in the social hierarchy. The vampires call their leader "Kaname-sama" only when they are among their own kind.

Renai: The combination of Ren's and Ai's names (恋愛) means "romantic love."

Bright white ash: This is an *Ashita no Joe* reference. In this classic boxing manga, the main character talks about the satisfaction of "feeling burnt out like bright white ash."

縹木

Hanadagi

In this family name, *hanada* means "bright light blue" and *gi* means "tree."

影山霞

Kageyama Kasumi

In the Class Rep's family name, *kage* means "shadow" and *yama* means "mountain." His first name, *Kasumi*, means "haze" or "mist."

愛

Ai

Ai means "love." It is used in terms of unconditional, unending love and affection.

菖藤依砂也

Shoto Isaya

Sho means "Siberian iris" and *to* is "wisteria." The *I* in *Isaya* means "to rely on" while the *sa* means "sand." *Ya* is a suffix used for emphasis.

橙茉

Toma

In the family name *Toma*, *to* means "Seville orange" and *ma* means "jasmine flower."

藍堂永路

Aido Nagamichi

The name *Nagamichi* is a combination of *naga*, which means "long" or "eternal," and *michi*, which is the kanji for "road" or "path." *Aido* means "indigo temple."

玖蘭樹里

Kuran Juri

Kuran means "nine orchids." In her first name, *ju* means "tree" and a *ri* is a traditional Japanese unit of measure for distance. The kanji for *ri* is the same as in Senri's name.

玖蘭悠

Kuran Haruka

Kuran means "nine orchids." *Haruka* means "distant" or "remote."

鷹宮海斗

Takamiya Kaito

Taka means "hawk" and *miya* means "imperial palace" or "shrine." *Kai* is "sea" and *to* means "to measure" or "grid."

白蔀更

Shirabuki Sara

Shira is "white" and *buki* is "butterbur," a plant with white flowers. *Sara* means "to renew."

黒主灰閻

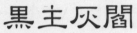

Cross Kaien

Cross, or *Kurosu*, means "black master." *Kaien* is a combination of *kai*, meaning "ashes," and *en*, meaning "village gate." The kanji for *en* is also used for Enma, the ruler of the underworld in Buddhist mythology.

玖蘭李土

Kuran Rido

Kuran means "nine orchids." In *Rido*, *ri* means "plum" and *do* means "earth."

錐生壱縷

Kiryu Ichiru

Ichi is the old-fashioned way of writing "one" and *ru* means "thread." In *Kiryu*, the *ki* means "auger" or "drill" and the *ryu* means "life."

緋桜閑, 狂咲姫

Hio Shizuka, Kuruizaki-hime

Shizuka means "calm and quiet." In Shizuka's family name, *hi* is "scarlet" and *ou* is "cherry blossoms." Shizuka Hio is also referred to as the "Kuruizaki-hime." *Kuruizaki* means "flowers blooming out of season" and *hime* means "princess."

藍堂月子

Aido Tsukiko

Aido means "indigo temple." *Tsukiko* means "moon child."

星煉

Seiren

Sei means "star" and ren means "to smelt" or "to refine." *Ren* is also the same kanji used in *rengoku*, or "purgatory." Her previous name, *Hoshino*, uses the same kanji for "star" (*hoshi*) and *no*, which can mean "from" and is often used at the end of traditional female names.

遠矢莉磨

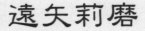

Toya Rima

Toya means a "far-reaching arrow." Rima's first name is a combination of *ri*, or "jasmine," and *ma*, which signifies enhancement by wearing away, such as by polishing or scouring.

紅まり亜

Kurenai Maria

Kurenai means "crimson." The kanji for the last *a* in Maria's first name is the same that is used in "Asia."

夜刈十牙

Yagari Toga

Yagari is a combination of *ya*, meaning "night," and *gari*, meaning "to harvest." *Toga* means "ten fangs."

一条麻遠, 一翁

Ichijo Asato, a.k.a. "Ichio"

Ichijo can mean a "ray" or "streak." Asato's first name is comprised of *asa*, meaning "hemp" or "flax," and *tou*, meaning "far-off." His nickname is *ichi*, or "one," combined with *ou*, which can be used as an honorific when referring to an older man.

若葉沙頼

Wakaba Sayori

Yori's full name is Sayori Wakaba. *Wakaba* means "young leaves." Her given name, *Sayori*, is a combination of *sa*, meaning "sand," and *yori*, meaning "trust."

早園瑠佳

Souen Ruka

In *Ruka*, the *ru* means "lapis lazuli" while the *ka* means "good-looking" or "beautiful." The *sou* in Ruka's surname, *Souen*, means "early," but this kanji also has an obscure meaning of "strong fragrance." The *en* means "garden."

一条拓麻

Ichijo Takuma

Ichijo can mean a "ray" or "streak." The kanji for *Takuma* is a combination of *taku*, meaning "to cultivate," and *ma*, which is the kanji for *asa*, meaning "hemp" or "flax," a plant with blue flowers.

支葵千里

Shiki Senri

Shiki's last name is a combination of *shi*, meaning "to support," and *ki*, meaning "mallow"—a flowering plant with pink or white blossoms. The *ri* in *Senri* is a traditional Japanese unit of measure for distance, and one *ri* is about 2.44 miles. *Senri* means "1,000 *ri*."

玖蘭枢

Kuran Kaname

Kaname means "hinge" or "door." The kanji for his last name is a combination of the old-fashioned way of writing *ku*, meaning "nine," and *ran*, meaning "orchid": "nine orchids."

藍堂英

Aido Hanabusa

Hanabusa means "petals of a flower." *Aido* means "indigo temple." In Japanese, the pronunciation of *Aido* is very close to the pronunciation of the English word *idol*.

架院暁

Kain Akatsuki

Akatsuki means "dawn" or "daybreak." In *Kain*, *ka* is a base or support, while *in* denotes a building that has high fences around it, such as a temple or school.

EDITOR'S NOTES

CHARACTERS

Matsuri Hino puts careful thought into the names of her characters in *Vampire Knight*. Below is the collection of characters throughout the manga. Each character's name is presented family name first, per the kanji reading.

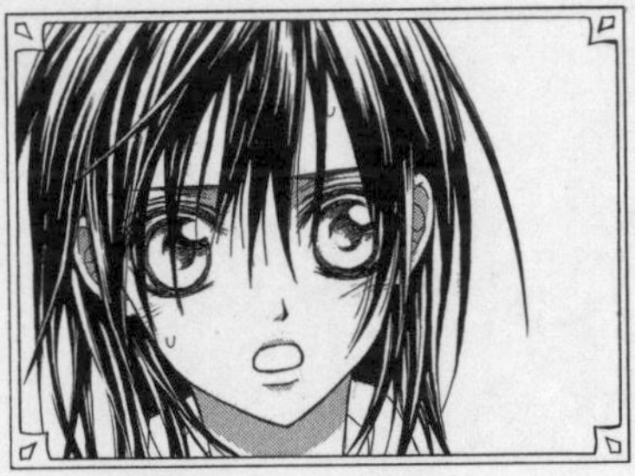

黒主優姫

Cross Yuki

Yuki's last name, *Kurosu*, is the Japanese pronunciation of the English word "cross." However, the kanji has a different meaning—*kuro* means "black" and *su* means "master." Her first name is a combination of *yuu*, meaning "tender" or "kind," and *ki*, meaning "princess."

錐生零

Kiryu Zero

Zero's first name is the kanji for *rei*, meaning "zero." In his last name, *Kiryu*, the *ki* means "auger" or "drill" and the *ryu* means "life."

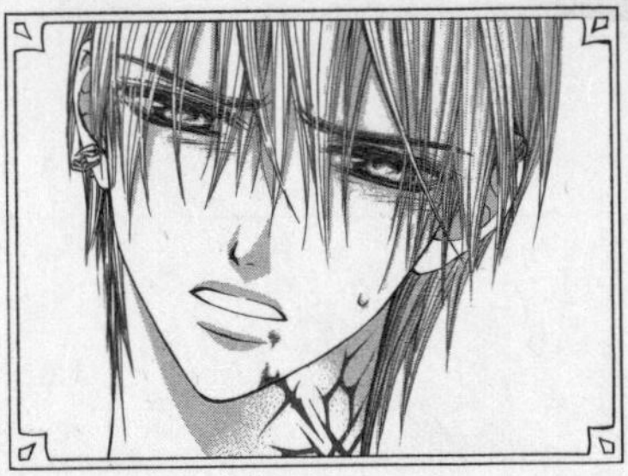